United States Department of Agriculture

PROCEEDINGS

Wildland Fire in the Appalachians: Discussions Among Managers and Scientists

Forest Service
Research & Development, Southern Research Station
General Technical Report SRS-199, September 2014

Cover: Fire researchers monitor fire behavior and weather during a stand replacement fire for Table Mountain pine, Chattahoochee National Forest, Chattooga Ranger District.

Disclaimers:

Sepember 2014
Southern Research Station
200 W.T. Weaver Blvd.
Asheville, NC 28804

www.srs.fs.usda.gov

PROCEEDINGS

Wildland Fire in the Appalachians: Discussions Among Managers and Scientists

Edited by

Thomas A. Waldrop

Roanoke, Virginia
October 8-10, 2013

Hosted by

Consortium of Appalachian Fire Managers and Scientists
Association for Fire Ecology

Sponsored by

Association for Fire Ecology
Consortium of Appalachian Fire Managers and Scientists
Joint Fire Science Program
The Nature Conservancy
Natural Lands Trust
USDA Forest Service, Southern Research Station
USDA Forest Service, Northern Research Station
USDA Forest Service, R-8 National Forest System
USDA Forest Service, Northeast Area State and Private Forestry

Published by

USDA Forest Service
Southern Research Station
Asheville, NC
September 2014

PREFACE

The Consortium of Appalachian Fire Managers and Scientists and the Association for Fire Ecology co-sponsored the conference on October 8-10, 2013 at the Hotel Roanoke and Conference Center in downtown Roanoke, Virginia.

Wildland Fire in the Appalachians: Discussions Among Managers and Scientists was designed for anyone with an interest in wildland fire in the Appalachian region and provided an unusual approach to sharing information. The objective of the conference was for fire managers and researchers to learn from each other so they could better understand and work together on problems specific to the highly diverse Appalachian Mountains. The conference design was unique: it was neither a research symposium nor a managers' meeting, but rather a synergy of both. Over 40 speakers were invited to discuss research updates, management experiences, and successful technology transfer. Research topics included plant and wildlife ecology, fire history, invasive plants, season of burning, and other topics. Managers shared experiences on how to apply fire to the landscape, how to work with media and the general public, and updates to fire management tools such as smoke prediction models, LANDFIRE, and IFT-DSS. A highlight was success stories from programs such as the Fire Learning Network, State Prescribed Fire Councils, and interagency cooperation. A field trip on the third day shared managers' experiences in applying research results on the ground.

The conference was also unique in that it occurred during a closure of the United States Government. Federal employees of all agencies had been furloughed and could not attend the conference. As a result, many invited speakers were not present. However, all invited speakers were requested to contribute a paper or extended abstract to these proceedings. These proceedings represent only a portion of the presentations planned for the conference.

Sponsors
CAFMS—The Consortium of Appalachian Fire Managers and Scientists (CAFMS) is a Joint Fire Science Program, Knowledge Exchange Consortium with a goal of promoting communication among fire managers and scientists in the Appalachian region. CAFMS is largely successful because of a strong relationship between the U.S. Forest Service, Southern Research Station and the Fire Learning Network of The Nature Conservancy. The organization promotes communication through workshops, Web-based seminars, summaries of important research publications, a Web site, face to face meetings with CAFMS members, and research syntheses. CAFMS members include fire managers along with government and university scientists throughout the Appalachian region, from Pennsylvania to Alabama.

AFE—The Association for Fire Ecology (AFE) is a nonprofit organization dedicated to improving the knowledge and use of fire in land management. Members include scientists, educators, students, managers, practitioners, policymakers, and interested citizens. Anyone who supports the AFE mission can become a member and through active involvement can help shape the emerging profession and growing field of fire ecology. The AFE vision is a membership of respected professionals from around the world who together play a key role in wildland fire and fire ecology research, education, management, and policy, to enhance our knowledge and management of fire as a fundamental ecological process.

Planning Committee
Many hours of work were required to plan a program with speakers that could engage both managers and scientists. Each person on the planning committee worked diligently to identify topics and potential speakers, and to invite speakers to attend. Many thanks are given to each member.

> Tom Waldrop, Chair, U.S. Forest Service, Southern Research Station
> Geoff Babb, Association for Fire Ecology
> Mike Brod, U.S. Forest Service, R-8 National Forest System
> Maureen Brooks, U.S. Forest Service, Northeastern Area State and Private Forestry
> Patrick Brose, U.S. Forest Service, Northern Research Station
> Beth Buchanan, U.S. Forest Service, R-8 National Forest System
> Steve Croy, U.S. Forest Service, R-8 National Forest System
> Tim Ingalsbee, Association for Fire Ecology
> Catia Juliana, Association for Fire Ecology
> Sam Lindblom, The Nature Conservancy
> Jim Thorne, Natural Lands Trust
> Dan Yaussy, U.S. Forest Service, Northern Research Station (retired)

Table of Contents

Tools for Fire Management

Manager/Scientist Success Stories

Ecology—
Plants and Plant Communities

OAK REGENERATION ECOLOGY AND DYNAMICS

Daniel C. Dey[1]

Abstract—The regeneration potential of oak following a disturbance or harvest that initiates stand regeneration is determined largely by the size structure of oak before the event. Collectively, regeneration from (1) seed, (2) advance reproduction, and (3) stump sprouts contribute to oak regeneration but vary in their competitive capacity. Oak regeneration potential is modified by site, competitor regeneration potential and management input. Prescribed fire is increasingly being used to promote oak regeneration with mixed results. Oak has many silvical traits that make it well adapted to fire. Fire can promote oak regeneration, but it also can reduce it, promote competing vegetation including invasive species, and retard oak recruitment into the overstory. Fire is a tool that can be used to sustain oak forests if it is applied judiciously with knowledge of oak forest ecology and stand dynamics, and with basic forest inventory information. Combining prescribed fire with thinning or harvesting can be effective in increasing oak regeneration potential and dominance in future stands.

INTRODUCTION

After 50 years of focused study on oak forests in eastern North America, managers still struggle to regenerate oak with certainty and scientists continue to research the oak regeneration problem (Fei and others 2011, Nowacki and Abrams 2008). We have made great advances in understanding oak biology and ecology, identifying drivers of oak regeneration problems, assessing silvicultural practices to promote oak, and modeling regeneration success. We know most about the commercially valuable oak species; more work is needed to discover basic information on the great diversity of oak species present throughout eastern North America. Valuable compilations and syntheses of what we know about oak ecology and silviculture have been published, e.g., Hicks (1998), Johnson and others (2009), and McShea and Healy (2002). This paper highlights our understanding of oak regeneration ecology and management with emphasis on the role that fire may play in sustaining oak forests through regeneration and recruitment into the overstory.

IMPORTANCE OF CURRENT FOREST COMPOSITION AND STRUCTURE

In eastern North American hardwood forests, initial floristics regulates future forest composition (Egler 1954, Johnson and others 2009, Loftis 2004); it is the current composition and size distribution of all trees from seedlings to mature trees that establishes the sources of regeneration and determines the competitiveness of individuals in a stand. In the East, oaks regenerate as newly germinated seedlings from acorns, advance reproduction, and stump sprouts. The abundance of mature dominant and codominant oak trees in the overstory defines seed production potential. The same holds true for many of oak's competitors, some of whom also may accumulate seed over the years in the forest floor, e.g., black cherry (*Prunus serotina* Ehrh.) and yellow-poplar (*Liriodendron tulipifera* L.). In general, total seed production for dominant/codominant oak trees increases with increasing diameter at breast height (dbh) to a threshold size beyond which it decreases, but this varies among the species (fig. 1) (Downs and McQuilken 1944). Consequently, the density of large (>10 inches dbh) oak trees in the upper crown classes is positively correlated with the abundance of oak advance reproduction in the understory (Fei and Steiner 2008, Johnson 1992), and density of large oak advance reproduction increases with decreasing overstory density (Johnson 1992, Larsen and others 1997). For advance reproduction, individual competitiveness following release by a regeneration harvest is directly related to the size of the seedling or sapling before harvest (fig. 2) (Dey 1991, Johnson and others 2009, Loftis 1990). The size and age of trees >2 inches dbh also determines the probability of stump sprout development after harvesting, which varies among oak species and their competitors (fig. 3) (Johnson and others 2009). Because initial floristics determines future forest composition, inventories of current forest overstory and understory tree populations can be used to predict the composition of future forests and aid in developing silvicultural prescriptions for oak regeneration (e.g., Brose and others 2008, Dey and others 1996, Vickers and others 2011).

SOURCES OF OAK REGENERATION

Johnson and others (2009) recognize three types of oak regeneration: seedlings, seedling sprouts, and stump sprouts. Any reproduction regardless of type that exists

---

[1]Daniel C. Dey, Research Forester, USDA Forest Service, Northern Research Station, Columbia, MO 65211

Citation for proceedings: Waldrop, Thomas A., ed. 2014. Proceedings, Wildland Fire in the Appalachians: Discussions among Managers and Scientists. Gen. Tech. Rep. SRS-199. Asheville, NC: U.S. Department of Agriculture Forest Service, Southern Research Station. 208 p.

before a regeneration harvest or disturbance is known as advance reproduction. In oak seedlings, shoot and taproot are the same age, as the shoot has not experienced dieback yet. A seedling sprout arises from the root system after death of throot;e original stem; hence, the shoot is younger than the taproot. Stump sprouts are vegetative reproduction that arise from the stump or base of stems (≥2 inches dbh) cut during harvest, removed by an herbivore, or killed by fire or drought.

Seedlings

Oak seedlings are ephemeral because they either die or experience shoot dieback and sprouting thus becoming seedling sprouts. Seedling populations are most abundant following good to heavy acorn crops. Initial seedling growth is fueled by acorn reserves in the cotyledons and survival may be high even on productive sites in the dark of a mature forest understory. But, after the first season, seedling survival and growth depend on photosynthesis. Seedling cohorts are nearly eliminated within a decade (Beck 1970, Loftis 1983, Crow 1992) due to inadequate light (<5 percent full sunlight), a common condition in the understory on high quality mesic and hydric sites (Gardiner and Yeiser 2006, Lorimer and others 1994, Lhotka and Loewenstein 2009, Motsinger and others 2010, Parker and Dey 2008). Today, it is only on xeric sites that understory light levels are high enough (e.g., 10 to 25 percent of full sunlight) to permit the accumulation and development of large oak advance reproduction in the absence of management, including periodic fire (Blizzard and others 2013, Johnson and others 2009, Sander 1979). Oak seedlings exhibit slow juvenile shoot growth because carbon is preferentially allocated to the developing root system (Johnson and others 2009). Thus, they are not competitive and are easily suppressed by other vegetation under most situations in regenerating stands.

Seedling Sprouts

Oak advance reproduction as seedling sprouts are able to persist and develop large roots and high root:shoot ratios provided there is sufficient light to support a positive growth balance. It is by the cycle of shoot dieback and sprouting over decades that oak advance reproduction increases its competitive capacity (Spetich and others 2002) by enlarging its root system, as evidenced by increasing root collar diameter and root:shoot ratios (Canadell and Rhoda 1991, Dey and Parker 1997). The probability that a stem of oak advance reproduction survives and assumes dominance in a regenerating stand increases exponentially with increasing initial basal stem diameter (fig. 2) (Dey 1991, Johnson and others 2009, Loftis 1990). However, a dense overstory and complex vertical stand structure including multiple canopy layers of shade-tolerant species reduce available light to levels insufficient for most oak species (Parker and Dey 2008, Rebbeck and others 2011). Historically, the accumulation

of large oak advance reproduction was promoted by factors that limited stand density and development of mid- and understory woody canopies such as cyclical drought, periodic fires, and site factors that limit tree growth. Available light levels over 20 percent of full sunlight promote growth of oak advance reproduction (Gardiner and Hodges 1998; Gottschalk 1985, 1987, 1994; Rebbeck and others 2011). Today, this may occur naturally in mature oak forests on low quality xeric sites located on south facing steep slopes and upper slope positions (Blizzard and others 2013), but elsewhere stand structure and density must be managed to increase available light in the understory. For example, in the Missouri Ozarks, Larsen and others (1997) found that the probability of having large oak advance reproduction increased with decreasing overstory density by timber harvesting, and they suggested that basal area be kept <65 ft²/ac to promote development of large oak advance reproduction in these oak ecosystems.

Stump Sprouts

Stump sprouts arise from cut stems that are >2 inches dbh by definition (Johnson and others 2009). They are the fastest growing source of oak reproduction and hence are the most competitive in regenerating stands. In fact, Beck and Hooper (1986), Gould and others (2003), Morrissey and others (2008), and Swaim (2013) reported that 45 to 75 percent of dominant oak reproduction in developing clearcuts were stump sprouts by the time stands reached stem exclusion (20 to 35 years old) in southern Indiana, Pennsylvania, and the southern Appalachians of North Carolina. In most of these studies, oak stocking had declined substantially from preharvest levels in the former oak-dominated forests, and it would have been relegated to minor associate status were it not for the stump sprouts. The probability of an oak stump producing a sprout varies by species, diameter, age, and site quality (fig. 3). In general, sprouting capacity increases with increasing stem diameter to a threshold (e.g., 4 to 5 inches) beyond which it declines (Dey and others 1996, Weigel and Peng 2002, Weigel and others 2011). Chestnut oak (*Quercus prinus* L.) and the red oaks [black oak (*Q. velutina* Lam.), scarlet oak (*Q. coccinea* Muenchh.), northern red oak (*Q. rubra* L.)] have higher sprouting capacity and are more competitive than white oak (*Q. alba* L.). Sprouting capacity in oaks declines with increasing tree ages older than 50 years, and trees that are 100 years old have low potential to produce sprouts, regardless of species. Initially, oak stump sprouting potential increases with increasing site quality, but over time site quality has a negative correlation with oak sprout dominance probabilities because the intensity of competition is higher on productive sites. It is unlikely that oak stump sprout reproduction alone can maintain initial stocking levels in mature oak forests when they are regenerated because not all oak stumps produce sprouts, and some produce sprouts of low vigor. Therefore, the mantra of oak silviculture has become that success in sustaining oak stocking is reliant upon having adequate numbers of large oak advance reproduction (Clark and Watt 1971, Johnson and others 2009). Oak stump sprouts are important contributors to future oak stocking, but advance reproduction must be competitive to sustain stocking. This in essence is the crux of the oak regeneration problem; oak advance reproduction either is absent or is small with low competitive capacity in most of our eastern forests on higher quality sites. The problem is magnified as we try to regenerate our aging oak forests that are experiencing a decline in their stump sprouting capacity with concurrent development of shade tolerant midstory and understory canopies.

FIRE IN THE LIFE CYCLE OF OAK

Fire has long been associated with the widespread dominance of oak over the millennia in the East (e.g., Delcourt and Delcourt 1998, Delcourt and others 1998), and oak has numerous traits (e.g., thick bark and high vegetative sprouting ability) and reproductive strategies (e.g., seed caching in soil by animals, root-centric growth, accumulation of large advance reproduction) that favor it when the disturbance regime includes frequent fire. But prescribed burning alone has not always promoted oak regeneration (Brose and others 2013). Arthur and others (2012) identified stages of stand development and conditions in which fire may promote oak regeneration and recruitment into the overstory in their life cycle analysis of an oak forest. Brose and others (2008, 2013) have developed silvicultural prescriptions for oak regeneration using prescribed burning. There are times in the life of an oak forest when prescribed fire may benefit oak regeneration, and certain stand conditions that normally inhibit oak establishment and development that can be corrected by burning.

Preparing for and Establishing Oak Advance Reproduction

Regenerating a mature oak forest is a common objective for managers in the East, and often there is little to no oak advance reproduction. Burning is recommended to prepare the site for the next good acorn crop. In the absence of fire, litter layers may have accumulated to depths that create a barrier to the oak germinant rooting itself in soil. Low-intensity dormant-season fires are effective for reducing litter and facilitating oak seedling establishment. Reductions in leaf litter may persist for several years, but litter accumulates rapidly to pre-burn levels (Stambaugh and others 2006), which may necessitate a second burn in the absence of a good acorn crop. Fire can also destroy seed of competing species that is stored in the forest floor, but it may also stimulate the germination of seed that has thermal- or chemical-

induced dormancy. However, new germinants and young seedlings of competing species arising after the initial fire are vulnerable to mortality in subsequent fires, and their growth will be suppressed under a fully stocked mature overstory. A final benefit of a low-intensity fire at this time is to increase understory light in advance of oak seedling establishment. Such a fire has little effect on overstory density but can reduce or eliminate the midstory canopy (if trees are predominantly <4 inches dbh) and increase understory light to about 10 to 15 percent of full sunlight (Dey and Hartman 2005, Green and others 2010, Lorimer and others 1994, Motsinger and others 2010, Waldrop and others 1992). The positive effect of midstory removal may last for several years (Parrott and others 2012), and maintaining an intact overstory canopy inhibits regrowth of competing tree and shrub sprouts (Dey and Hartman 2005). However, oak advance reproduction benefits from additional increases in light, and to achieve light levels >20 percent of full sunlight requires greater reductions in stand density. To affect this through prescribed burning requires more intense fires capable of killing larger trees, but this increases the risk of causing mortality of oak advance reproduction. Alternatively, chemical and mechanical thinning and harvesting can be used to more selectively remove trees, reduce mortality of oak advance reproduction, and in the case of chemical applications, limit sprouting of competitors. The need and timing of additional prescribed fires preceding a good acorn crop will be dictated by litter accumulation rates and regrowth of competing vegetation after the initial burn. But once acorns are on the ground, fire should be delayed or else most of the crop will be destroyed (Auchmoody and Smith 1993).

Promoting Oak Advance Reproduction

Another common condition in mature oak forests is for there to be thousands of small oak advance reproduction per acre. Burning these forests may be detrimental to oak regeneration because low intensity fires are capable of killing a high proportion of one-year-old oak seedlings (>50 percent) (Johnson 1974). In deciding to burn, consideration should be given to the number and size of oak advance reproduction. Size is an indication of the probability that a stem will survive a fire by sprouting, which increases exponentially with increasing basal diameter of oak seedlings. In general, oaks are better able to survive multiple fires than their competitors by sprouting and increasing root mass during fire-free periods under higher light regimes provided by midstory removal and random canopy gap formation (Brose and others 2013, Dey and Hartman 2005). But greater growth gains in oak advance reproduction are achieved when reproduction are growing in moderate to open light environments (i.e., >30 percent of full sunlight) (Gardiner and Hodges 1998; Gottschalk 1985, 1987, 1994). Benefits to oak advance reproduction when burning in mature oak forests are variable, and sometimes questionable according to studies conducted across eastern North America (Brose and others 2013). This is most likely due to the differences in initial size structure of advance reproduction for oak and its competitors, fire behavior, stand density, and presence of confounding factors such as deer (*Odocoileus virginianus* Zimmerman) browsing and competition from interference species such as hay-scented fern (*Dennstaedtia punctilobula* (Michx.) Moore). Fire effects can be more negative when oak seedlings are small (e.g., <0.25 inches basal diameter), fire intensity is moderate to high, and fires occur in a season when seedling physiological activity is on the rise. Low survival probabilities for small oak advance reproduction after burning may be offset by high densities, but it is less risky to use other means such as midstory removal by chemical or mechanical methods, or shelterwood harvesting to develop larger oak advance reproduction by increasing available light in the understory before burning.

Combining fire with thinning or harvesting is promising for developing larger oak advance reproduction. Hutchinson and others (2012) reported that multiple fires (three to five) beginning seven years before harvesting by the group selection method and ending in some cases a year or two after harvesting promoted the development of large white oak reproduction in southern Ohio. Brose and others (2013) recommended using the shelterwood method to increase light to oak advance reproduction and promote growth of small seedling sprouts before burning. Simply reducing stand density benefits oak advance reproduction for several years before the competition in the regeneration layer begins suppressing oak growth. During this time, oak advance reproduction seedlings are able to grow larger and increase their root mass (Brose 2008), thus increasing their probability of vigorously sprouting after a prescribed fire. If needed, prescribed fire may be used between the initial and final shelterwood harvest to release oak advance reproduction from encroaching competing vegetation that has also benefitted from improved light conditions. Alternatively, oak can be provided a second release by removal of the residual overstory. Several years after oak reproduction has been released by final overstory removal, fire can be used to favor oak development and dominance by periodically (e.g., every three to five years) setting back competing vegetation. This sequence may be repeated until the oak reproduction is capable of maintaining its dominance on its own.

Oak Recruitment into the Overstory

To sustain oak forests, the second most important process after regeneration is recruitment of oak saplings into the overstory (Dey 2014). Oaks eventually need a sufficiently long fire-free period to allow them to grow into the overstory by developing thick bark to resist topkill from any future fires. This may take 10 to 30 years to develop depending on source of oak regeneration, i.e., stump sprouts versus seedlings sprouts (Arthur and others 2012). Oaks that are in the dominant canopy position at the beginning of the stem exclusion stage have a high probability (>75 percent) of maintaining their dominance into maturity (Ward and Stephens 1994), but less dominant oaks have a high rate of attrition due to competition. Without release as saplings in the stem exclusion stage, oaks can be suppressed by yellow-poplar, red maple (*Acer rubrum* L.), black cherry and black birch (*Betual lenta* L.) (Brashears and others 2004, Groninger and Long 2008, Heiligmann and others 1985, Smith and Ashton 1993, Zenner and others 2012). Dominant oaks primarily remain at the end of stem exclusion; these are largely stump sprouts, especially on average and higher quality sites (Hilt 1985, Morrissey and others 2008, Zenner and others 2012). On xeric, lower quality sites, oaks are naturally more competitive and can rise to dominate stand basal area and volume at maturity. Crop tree release of codominant and lesser oak saplings early in the stem exclusion stage can significantly increase their persistence as dominants at maturity (Ward 2009, 2013). Fire is an ineffective tool for releasing oak saplings because it is indiscriminate in what trees are topkilled in the smaller diameter classes (<4 inches dbh); it may take out a smaller diameter oak as easily as a competitor. Fire's ability to topkill competing stems decreases as tree diameter increases, even for what are considered fire-sensitive trees. Hotter fires are needed to topkill larger trees of competing species and this increases the chances of removing oak saplings in the process. Prescribed burning affords little control over the spatial distribution of what trees are removed and hence the degree of release experienced by any individual oak. Fire may also scar residual trees, which has the potential to cause advanced decay in the butt log over decades if the wound does not heal rapidly (Marschall and others 2014). Alternative chemical and mechanical methods of crop tree release provide more control and certainty in releasing oak saplings and small poles.

CONCLUSION

Oak regeneration potential is a function of the collective contributions to future stand stocking from the main sources of oak regeneration, i.e., seed/seedlings, seedling sprouts (advance reproduction), and stump sprouts. The extent that oak regeneration potential contributes to stand regeneration potential determines if oak will dominate in the future after regeneration. Stump sprouts are no doubt the most competitive sources of oak regeneration and often comprise the majority of dominant oak in young stands following regeneration by even-aged methods. However, this in and of itself is an indictment of the failure of oak advance reproduction to contribute significantly to sustaining oak stocking in the future. Without contributions from oak advance reproduction, oak stocking will continue to decline through the generations. The focus of oak silviculture research has been the establishment and development of adequate densities of large, competitive oak advance reproduction. The shelterwood regeneration method has figured prominently in approaches to improve oak regeneration potential by increasing the role advance reproduction play in determining oak's future dominance. But midstory removal and the group selection method have also proven to enhance development of oak advance reproduction in conjunction with prescribed burning. Controlling competing vegetation before, during and after regeneration harvesting is an important, and sometimes overlooked, aspect of oak regeneration prescriptions. Prescribed fire is an effective tool to prepare the site for establishment of oak reproduction and to begin reducing competition and the regeneration potential of competing species. Care must be taken in determining the timing of prescribed burning to avoid destroying acorn crops or populations of small oak advance reproduction. After final overstory release, prescribed fire is effective in promoting oak dominance during stand initiation until the beginning of the stem exclusion stage. From this time until the next need for regeneration, the use of fire is problematic because it is a clumsy method for controlling stand density, composition, and spatial arrangement of trees, and because it can injure trees, which later leads to substantial loss of volume and value. Prescribed fire is another arrow in the quiver of the silviculturist who manages oak ecosystems.

LITERATURE CITED

Arthur, M.A.; Alexander, H.D.; Dey, D.C. [and others]. 2012. Refining the oak-fire hypothesis for management of oak-dominated forests of the eastern United States. Journal of Forestry. 110(5): 257-266.

Auchmoody, L.R.; Smith, H.C. 1993. Survival of acorns after fall burning. Res. Pap. NE-678. Radnor, PA: U.S. Department of Agriculture, Forest Service, Northeastern Forest Experiment Station. 5 p.

Beck, D.E. 1970. Effect of competition on survival and height growth of red oak seedlings. Res. Pap. SE-56. Asheville, NC: U.S. Department of Agriculture, Forest Service, Southeastern Forest Experiment Station. 7 p.

Beck, D.E.; Hooper, R.M. 1986. Development of a southern Appalachian hardwood stand after clearcutting. Southern Journal of Applied Forestry. 10: 168-172.

Blizzard, E.M.; Kabrick, J.M.; Dey, D.C. [and others]. 2013. Light, canopy closure and overstory retention in upland Ozark forests. Gen. Tech. Rep. SRS-175. Asheville, NC: U.S. Department of Agriculture, Forest Service, Southern Research Station: 73-79.

Brashears, M.B.; Fajvan, M.A.; Schuler, T.M. 2004. An assessment of canopy stratification and tree species diversity following clearcutting in central Appalachian hardwoods. Forest Science. 50: 54-64.

Brose, P.H. 2008. Root development of acorn-origin oak seedlings in shelterwood stands on the Appalachian Plateau of northern Pennsylvania: 4-year results. Forest Ecology and Management. 255: 3374-3381.

Brose, P.H.; Dey, D.C.; Phillips, R.J.; Waldrop, T.A. 2013. A meta-analysis of the fire-oak hypothesis: does prescribed burning promote oak reproduction in eastern North America? Forest Science. 59(3): 322-334.

Brose, P.H.; Gottschalk, K.W.; Horsley, S.B. [and others]. 2008. Prescribing regeneration treatments for mixed-oak forests in the Mid-Atlantic region. Gen. Tech. Rep. NRS-33. Newtown Square, PA: U.S. Department of Agriculture, Forest Service, Northern Research Station. 100 p.

Canadell, J.; Rhoda, F. 1991. Root biomass of *Quercus ilex* in a montane Mediterranean forest. Canadian Journal of Forest Research. 21: 1771-1778.

Clark, F.B.; Watt, R.F. 1971. Silvicultural methods for regenerating oaks. In: Oak Symp. Proc. Upper Darby, PA: U.S. Department of Agriculture, Forest Service, Northeastern Forest Experiment Station: 37-43.

Crow, T.R. 1992. Population dynamics and growth patterns for a cohort of northern red oak (*Quercus rubra*) seedlings. Oecologia. 91: 192-200.

Delcourt, P.A.; Delcourt, H.R. 1998. The influence of prehistoric human-set fires in oak-chestnut forests in the southern Appalachians. Castanea. 63(3): 337-345.

Delcourt, P.A.; Delcourt, H.R.; Ison, H.A. [and others]. 1998. Prehistoric human use of fire, the eastern agricultural complex, and Appalachian oak-chestnut forests: paleoecology of Cliff Palace Pond, Kentucky. American Antiquity. 63(2): 263-278.

Dey, D.C. 1991. A comprehensive Ozark regenerator. Columbia, MO: University of Missouri. 283 p. Ph.D. dissertation.

Dey, D.C. 2014. Sustaining oak forests in Eastern North America: regeneration and recruitment, the pillars of sustainability. Forest Science. 60(2). 17 p. doi: 10.5849/forsci.13-114.

Dey, D.C.; Hartman, G. 2005. Returning fire to Ozark Highland forest ecosystems: effects on advance regeneration. Forest Ecology and Management. 217: 37–53.

Dey, D.C.; Fan, Z. 2009. A review of fire and oak regeneration and overstory recruitment. In: Gen. Tech. Rep. NRS-P-46. Newtown Square, PA: U.S. Department of Agriculture, Forest Service, Northern Research Station: 2-20.

Dey, D.C.; Parker, W.C. 1997. Morphological indicators of stock quality and field performance of red oak (*Quercus rubra* L.) seedlings underplanted in a central Ontario shelterwood. New Forests. 14: 145-156.

Dey, D.C.; Johnson, P.S.; Garrett, H.E. 1996. Modeling the regeneration of oak stands in the Missouri Ozark Highlands. Canadian Journal of Forest Research. 26: 573-583.

Dey, D.C.; Ter-Mikaelian, M.; Johnson, P.S.; Shifley, S.R. 1996. Users guide to ACORn: a comprehensive Ozark regeneration simulator. Gen. Tech. Rep. NC-180. St. Paul, MN: U.S. Department of Agriculture, Forest Service, North Central Forest Experiment Station. 35 p.

Downs, A.A.; McQuilken, W.E. 1944. Seed production of southern Appalachian oaks. Journal of Forestry. 42: 913-920.

Egler, F.E. 1954. Vegetation science concepts I. Initial floristic composition: a factor in old-field vegetation management. Vegetatio. 4: 412-417.

Fei, S.; Steiner, K.C. 2008. Relationships between advance oak regeneration and biotic and abiotic factors. Tree Physiology. 28: 1111-1119.

Fei, S.; Kong, N.; Steiner, K.C.; Moser, W.K.; Steiner, E.B. 2011. Change in oak abundance in the eastern United States from 1980-2008. Forest Ecology and Management. 262: 1370-1377.

Gardiner, E.S.; Hodges, J.D. 1998. Growth and biomass distribution of cherrybark oak (*Quercus pagoda* Raf.) seedlings as influenced by light availability. Forest Ecology and Management. 108: 127-131.

Gardiner, E.S.; Yeiser, J.L. 2006. Underplanting cherrybark oak (*Quercus pagoda* Raf.) seedlings on a bottomland site in the southern United States. New Forests. 32: 105-119.

Gottschalk, K.W. 1985. Effects of shading on growth and development of northern red oak, black oak, black cherry, and red maple seedlings. I. height, diameter, and root/shoot ratio. In: Urbana, IL: Proceedings of 5th central hardwood forest conference: 189-195.

Gottschalk, K.W. 1987. Effects of shading on growth and development of northern red oak, black oak, black cherry, and red maple seedlings. II. Biomass partitioning and prediction. In: Knoxville, TN: Proceedings of 6th central hardwood forest conference: 99-110.

Gottschalk, K.W. 1994. Shade, leaf growth and crown development of *Quercus rubra*, *Quercus velutina*, *Prunus serotina* and *Acer rubrum* seedlings. Tree Physiology. 14: 735-749.

Gould, P.J.; Steiner, K.C.; Finley, J.C.; McDill, M.E. 2003. Regenerating mixed oak stands in Pennsylvania: a quarter-century perspective. In: Gen. Tech. Rep. NC-234. St. Paul, MN: U.S. Department of Agriculture, Forest Service, North Central Research Station: 254-258.

Green, S.R.; Arthur, M.A.; Blankenship, B.A. 2010. Oak and red maple seedling survival and growth following periodic prescribed fire on xeric ridgetops on the Cumberland Plateau. Forest Ecology and Management. 259: 2256-2266.

Groninger, J.W.; Long, M. 2008. Oak ecosystem management considerations for Central Hardwood stands arising from silvicultural clearcutting. Northern Journal of Applied Forestry. 25: 173-179.

Heiligmann, R.B.; Norland, E.R.; Hilt, D.E. 1985. 28-year-old reproduction on five cutting practices in upland oak. Northern Journal of Applied Forestry. 2: 17-22.

Hicks, Jr.; R.R. 1998. Ecology and management of Central Hardwood forests. New York, NY: John Wiley & Sons, Inc. 412 p.

Hilt, D.E. 1985. Species composition of young central hardwood stands that develop after clearcutting. In: Proceedings of 5th central hardwood forest conference. Champaign-Urbana, IL: University of Illinois: 11-14.

Hutchinson, T.F.; Long, R.P.; Rebbeck, J. [and others]. 2012. Repeated prescribed fires alter gap-phase regeneration in mixed-oak forests. Canadian Journal of Forest Research. 42: 303-314.

Johnson, P.S. 1974. Survival and growth of northern red oak seedlings following a prescribed burn. Res. Note NC-177. St. Paul, MN: U.S. Department of Agriculture, Forest Service, North Central Forest Experiment Station. 3 p.

Johnson, P.S. 1992. Oak overstory/reproduction relations in two xeric ecosystems in Michigan. Forest Ecology and Management. 48: 233-248.

Johnson, P.S.; Shifley, S.R.; Rogers, R. 2009. The ecology and silviculture of oaks, second ed. New York, NY: CABI Publishing. 580 p.

Kabrick, J.M.; Villwock, J.L.; Dey, D.C. [and others]. 2014. Modeling and mapping oak advance reproduction density using soil and site variables. Forest Science. 60(2). 11 p. doi: 10.5849/forsci.13-006.

Kabrick, J.M.; Zenner, E.K.; Dey, D.C. [and others]. 2008. Using ecological land types to examine landscape-scale oak regeneration dynamics. Forest Ecology and Management. 255: 3051-3062.

Larsen, D.R.; Metzger, M.A.; Johnson, P.S. 1997. Oak regeneration and overstory density in the Missouri Ozarks. Canadian Journal of Forest Research. 27: 869–875.

Lhotka, J.M.; Loewenstein, E.F. 2009. Effect of midstory removal on understory light availability and the 2-year response of underplanted cherrybark oak seedlings. Southern Journal of Applied Forestry. 33(4): 171-177.

Loftis, D.L. 1983. Regenerating red oak on productive sites in the southern Appalachians: a research approach. In: Gen. Tech. Rep. SE-24. Asheville, NC: U.S. Department of Agriculture Forest Service, Southeastern Forest Experiment Station: 144-150.

Loftis, D.L. 1990. Predicting post-harvest performance of advanced red oak reproduction in the southern Appalachians. Forest Science. 36(4): 908-916.

Loftis, D.L. 2004. Upland oak regeneration and management. In: Spetich, M.A., ed. Gen. Tech. Rep. SRS-73. Asheville, NC: U.S. Department of Agriculture Forest Service, Southern Research Station: 163-167.

Lorimer, C.G.; Chapman, J.W.; Lambert, W.D. 1994. Tall understory vegetation as a factor in the poor development of oak seedlings beneath mature stands. Journal of Ecology. 82(2): 227-237.

Marschall, J.M.; Guyette, R.P.; Stambaugh, M.C.; Stevenson, A.P. 2014. Fire damage effects on red oak timber product value. Forest Ecology and Management. 320: 182-189

McShea, W.J.; Healy, W.M. 2002. Oak forest ecosystems ecology and management for wildlife. The Johns Hopkins University Press. Baltimore, MD. 432 p.

Morrissey, R.C.; Jacobs, D.F.; Seifert, J.R. [and others]. 2008. Competitive success of natural oak regeneration in clearcuts during the stem exclusion stage. Canadian Journal of Forest Research. 38: 1419-1430.

Motsinger, J.R.; Kabrick, J.M.; Dey, D.C. [and others]. 2010. Effect of midstory and understory removal on the establishment and development of natural and artificial pin oak advance reproduction in bottomland forests. New Forests. 39: 195–213

Nowacki, G.J.; Abrams, M.D. 2008. The demise of fire and "mesophication" of forests in the Eastern United States. BioScience. 58(2): 123-138.

Parker, W.C.; Dey, D.C. 2008. Influence of overstory density on ecophysiology of red oak (*Quercus rubra*) and sugar maple (*Acer saccharum*) seedlings in central Ontario shelterwoods. Tree Physiology. 28: 797-804.

Parrott, D.L.; Lhotka, J.M.; Stringer, J.W.; Dillaway, D.N. 2012. Seven-year effects of midstory removal on natural and underplanted oak reproduction. Northern Journal Applied Forestry. 29(4): 182-190.

Rebbeck, J.; Gottschalk, K.; Scherzer, A. 2011. Do chestnut, northern red, and white oak germinant seedlings respond similarly to light treatments? Growth and biomass. Canadian Journal of Forest Research. 41: 2219-2230.

Sander, I.L. 1979. Regenerating oaks with the shelterwood system. In: Proceedings 1979 JS Wright Forestry Conference. West Lafayette, IN: Purdue University: 54-60.

Smith, D.M.; Ashton, P.M.S. 1993. Early dominance of pioneer hardwood after clearcutting and removal of advanced regeneration. Northern Journal of Applied Forestry. 10(1): 14-19.

Spetich, M.A.; Dey, D.C.; Johnson, P.S.; Graney, D.L. 2002. Competitive capacity of *Quercus rubra* L. planted in Arkansas' Boston Mountains. Forest Science. 48(3): 504-517.

Stambaugh, M.C.; Guyette, R.C.; Grabner, K.W.; Kolaks, J. 2006. Understanding Ozark forest litter variability through a synthesis of accumulation rates and fire events. In: Gen. Tech. Rep. RMRS-P-41. Fort Collins, CO: U.S. Department of Agriculture, Forest Service, Rocky Mountain Research Station: 321-332.

Swaim, J.T. 2013. Stand development and the competitive ability of oak (*Quercus* spp.) following silvicultural clearcutting on the Hoosier National Forest. West Lafayette, IN: Purdue University. M.S. thesis.

Vickers, L.A.; Fox, T.R.; Loftis, D.L.; Boucugnani, D.A.. 2011. Predicting forest regeneration in the Central Appalachians using the REGEN expert system. Journal of Sustainable Forestry. 30: 790-822.

Waldrop, T.A.; White, D.L.; Jones, S.M. 1992. Fire regimes for pine-grassland communities in the southeastern United States. Forest Ecology and Management. 47: 195-210.

Wang, Z.; Nyland, R.D. 1996. Changes in the condition and species composition of developing even-aged northern hardwood stands in central New York. Northern Journal of Applied Forestry. 13(4): 189-194.

Ward, J.S. 2009. Intensity of precommercial crop tree release increases diameter growth and survival of upland oaks. Canadian Journal of Forest Research. 39: 118-130.

Ward, J.S. 2013. Precommercial crop tree release increase upper canopy persistence and diameter growth of oak saplings. Northern Journal of Applied Forestry. 30(4): 156-163.

Ward, J.S.; Stephens, G.R. 1994. Crown class transition rates of maturing northern red oak (*Quercus rubra* L.). Forest Science. 40(2): 221-237.

Weigel, D.R.; Peng, C-Y.J. 2002. Predicting stump sprouting and competitive success of five oak species in southern Indiana. Canadian Journal of Forest Research. 32: 703-712.

Weigel, D.R.; Dey, D.C.; Peng, C-Y.J. 2011. Stump sprout dominance probabilities of five oak species in southern Indiana 20 years after clearcut harvesting. In: Gen. Tech. Rep. NRS-P-78. Newtown Square, PA: U.S. Department of Agriculture Forest Service, Southern Research Station: 10-22.

Zenner, E.K.; Heggenstaller, D.J.; Brose, P.H. [and others]. 2012. Reconstructing the competitive dynamics of mixed-oak neighborhoods. Canadian Journal of Forest Research. 42: 1714-1723.

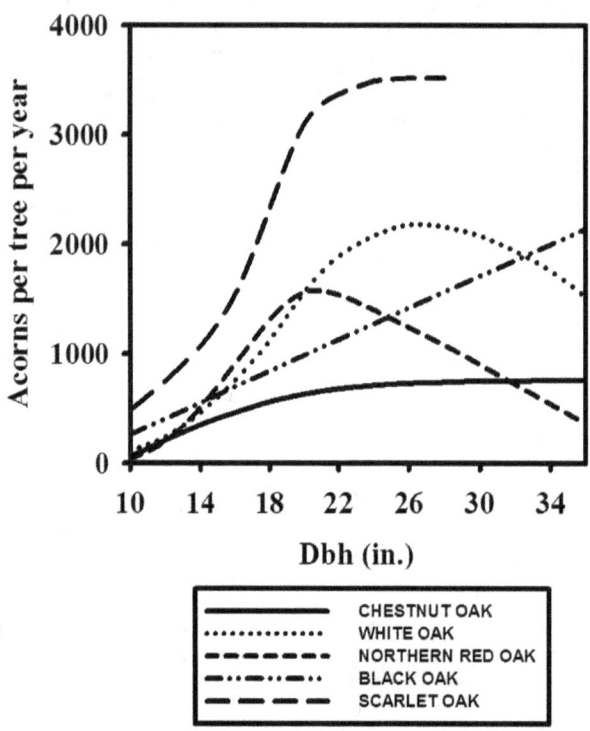

Figure 1—Average annual acorn production based on seven years of observations for five common oak species in eastern North America (adapted from Downs and McQuilken 1944).

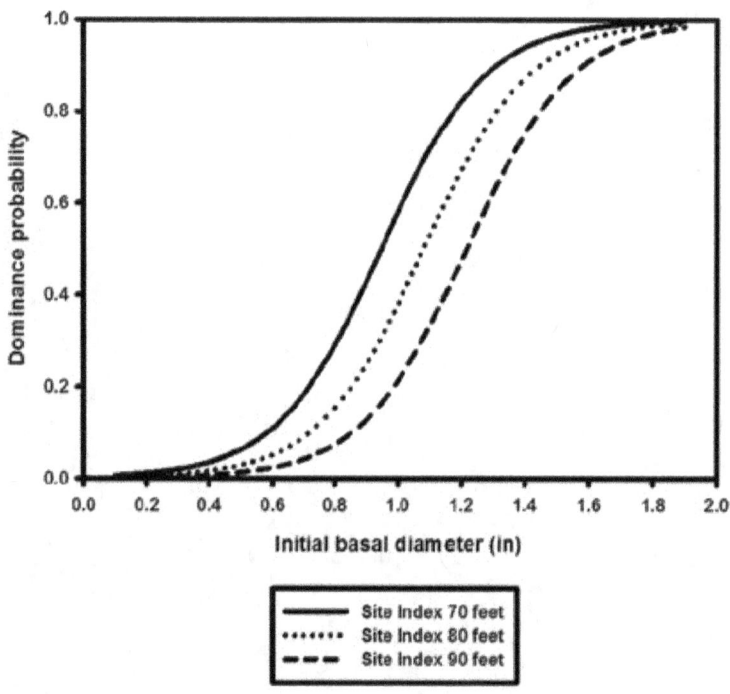

Figure 2—Probability of northern red oak advance reproduction becoming dominant/codominant stems eight years after clearcutting on various quality oak sites in the southern Appalachian Mountains (adapted from Loftis 1990).

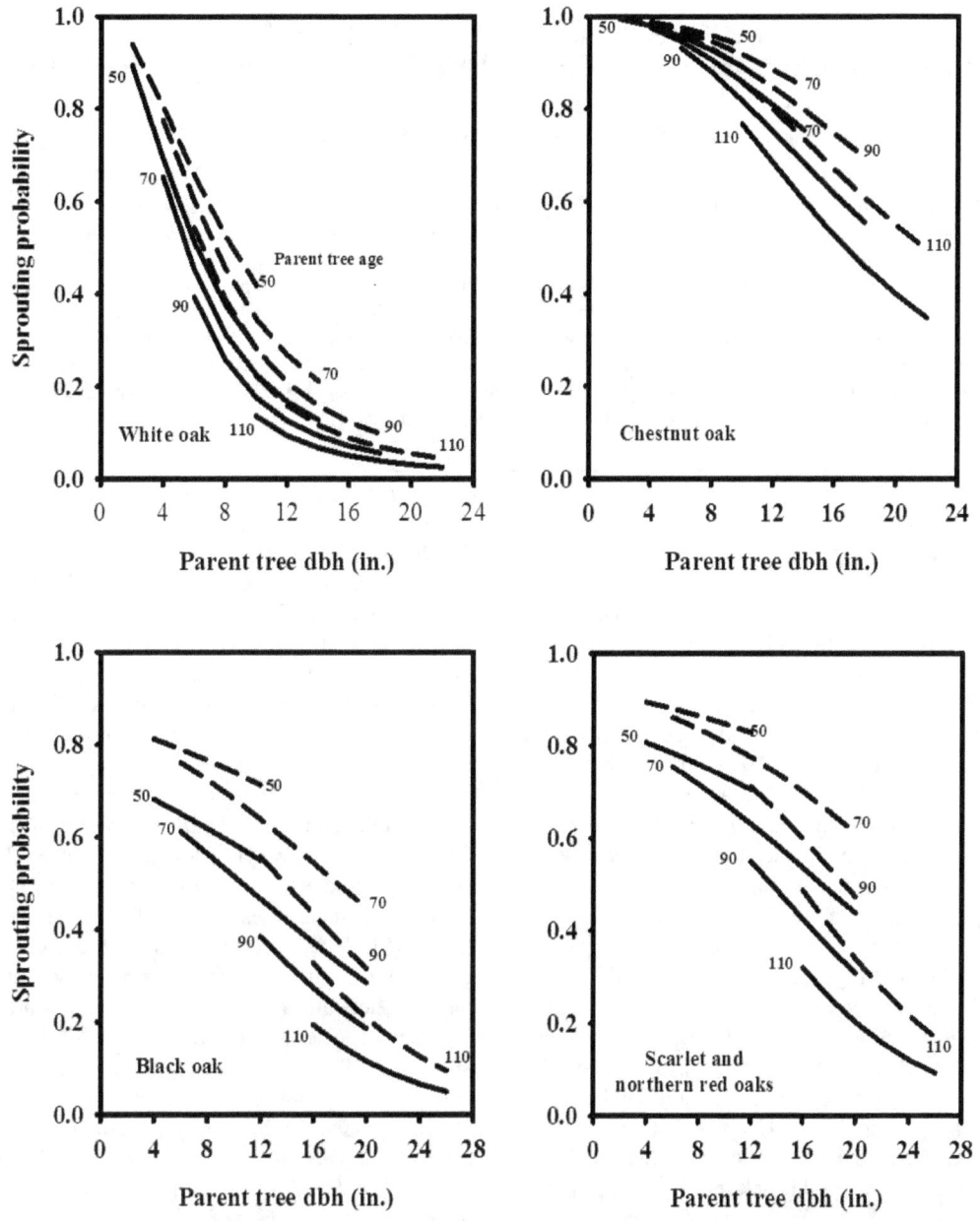

Figure 3—Probability that an oak will have at least one live sprout one year after harvest cutting in clearcuts of southern Indiana based on species, initial diameter breast height, tree age, and site quality (solid line = 59' oak site index, dashed line = 72' oak site index) (adapted from Weigel and Peng 2002).

MAKING SENSE OUT OF CONFUSION:
A REVIEW OF FIRE-OAK PAPERS PUBLISHED IN THE PAST 50 YEARS

Patrick H. Brose and Thomas A. Waldrop[1]

Abstract—The existing fire-oak literature is contradictory on whether fire helps or hinders the oak regeneration process. This confusion occurs because the fire-oak studies have been conducted under a wide variety of conditions. In this paper, we review the fire-oak literature by stand age class, season of burn, and number of burns to identify commonalities and trends. Overall, prescribed fire reduces the density of small diameter stems in the midstory, preferentially selects for oak reproduction and against mesophytic hardwood reproduction, equalizes the height growth rates between these two species groups, and promotes the establishment of new oak seedlings. Generally, prescribed burning provides the most benefit to oak reproduction when the fires occur during the growing season and several years after a substantial reduction in overstory density. Single fires conducted in closed-canopy stands have little impact in the short term, but multiple burns eventually do benefit oaks in the long term, especially when followed by a canopy disturbance.

INTRODUCTION

Throughout the Eastern United States, mixed-oak (*Quercus* spp.) forests on upland sites are highly valued for many ecological and economic reasons. Generally, these upland forests consist of one or more oak species [black (*Q. velutina* Lam.), chestnut (*Q. montana* Willd.), northern red (*Q. rubra* L.), scarlet (*Q. coccinea* Muenchh.), and white (*Q .alba* L.)] dominating the canopy with a mix of other hardwood species in the midstory and understory strata. Despite widespread abundance and dominance of mixed-oak forests, regenerating them is a chronic challenge for land managers throughout eastern North America, and they are slowly being replaced by mesophytic hardwoods such as black birch (*Betula lenta* L.), black cherry (*Prunus serotina* Ehrh.), red maple (*Acer rubrum* L.), sugar maple (*Acer saccharum* Marsh.) and yellow-poplar (*Liriodendron tulipifera* L.) (Abrams and Downs 1990, Aldrich and others 2005, Healy and others 1997, Schuler and Gillespie 2000, Woodall and others 2008). Many factors contribute to this oak regeneration problem including loss of seed sources; destruction of acorns and seedlings by insects, disease, weather, and wildlife; dense understory shade; competing vegetation; and lack of periodic fire (Crow 1988, Johnson and others 2009, Loftis and McGee 1993). The implication of the lack of periodic fire as a cause of the oak regeneration problem arises from the fact that many of these oak forests exist in part due to past fires. This relationship has led to the creation of the fire-oak hypothesis (Abrams 1992, Brose and others 2001, Lorimer 1993, Nowacki and Abrams 2008).

The fire-oak hypothesis consists of four parts: (1) periodic fire has been an integral disturbance in the mixed-oak forests of eastern North America for millennia; (2) oaks have several physical and physiological characteristics that allow them to survive at higher rates than their competitors in a periodic fire regime; (3) the lack of fire in the latter 20th century is a major reason for the chronic, widespread oak regeneration problem; and (4) reintroducing fire via prescribed burning will promote oak reproduction. The scientific literature supports the first three parts to varying degrees. For example, paleo-ecological studies and historical documents indicate that American Indian tribes used fire for numerous reasons (Day 1953, Patterson 2006, Ruffner 2006, Wilkins and others 1991). Many studies report the growth strategy and physiological differences between oaks and mesophytic hardwood species (Gottschalk 1985, 1987, 1994; Kolb and others 1990) and the concomitant decline of fire and increase in mesophytic hardwoods during the early 1900s is evident from fire history research (Aldrich and others 2010, Guyette and others 2006, Hutchinson and others 2008, Shumway and others 2001). It remains hard to verify the fourth part of the fire-oak hypothesis—that prescribed burning promotes oaks—as the results reported in the literature vary widely. Results range from positive (Brown 1960, Kruger and Reich 1997, Swan 1970, Ward and Stephens 1989), to neutral (Hutchinson and others 2005a, Merritt and Pope 1991, Teuke and Van Lear 1982), to negative (Collins and Carson 2003, Johnson 1974, Loftis 1990, Wendel and Smith 1986). This confusion among findings inhibits resource managers from making more and better use of prescribed fire to regenerate and restore eastern oak forests. A systematic

[1]Patrick Brose, Research Forester, USDA Forest Service, Northern Research Station, Irvine, PA 16329

Thomas Waldrop, Research Forester, USDA Forest Service, Southern Research Station, Clemson, SC 29634

Citation for proceedings: Waldrop, Thomas A., ed. 2014. Proceedings, Wildland Fire in the Appalachians: Discussions among Managers and Scientists. Gen. Tech. Rep. SRS-199. Asheville, NC: U.S. Department of Agriculture Forest Service, Southern Research Station. 208 p.

review of the fire-oak literature would cut through this confusion and shed light on the conditions under which prescribed fire helps or hinders the oak regeneration process.

METHODS

For this review, we obtained 59 fire-oak papers that have been published within the past 50 years in various conference proceedings and scientific journals (table 1). We sorted the papers by stand type (mature, young, or immature), season of burn (dormant or growing), and number of fires [single (1), dual (2), or multiple (>2)] based on the site descriptions and methods provided in the text. Mature stands were those in the understory re-initiation stage of development (Oliver and Larson 1990) and were characterized by an intact, closed-canopy, fully stocked overstory. These were stands that had been undisturbed for years or had only been recently disturbed by light, thin-from-below treatments. These stands were at the beginning of the oak regeneration process. They either lacked oak seedlings or the seedlings were quite small. Young stands were ones undergoing a shelterwood harvest sequence or had recently received a final harvest. In these stands, the oak and mesophytic hardwood reproduction was abundant and vigorous. They were near or at the end of the oak regeneration process. Immature stands are intermediate between young and mature stands. Their canopies had recently closed, but they were several decades from being mature. They were in the stem exclusion stage of stand development (Oliver and Larson 1990). Dormant-season fires occur between leaf abscission in autumn and leaf expansion the following spring. During this time, the hardwood reproduction is not photosynthesizing, although sap flow may be occurring, as early spring is included in the dormant season. Growing-season fires occur from leaf expansion in the spring to leaf abscission in autumn. The exact starting time of the growing season for prescribed burning purposes is highly variable, as it is governed by location, weather, and the physiological characteristics of the hardwood species.

After sorting the papers by stand type, season of burn, and number of prescribed fires, we examined the quantitative data provided in the results section of each paper to determine whether the fire treatment effects were positive, negative, or ambiguous for the oak reproduction. Positive results for the oak reproduction were absolute increases in oak seedling density via establishment of new germinants, relative increases to the oak portion of the regeneration pool via differential survival rates between oak and mesophytic hardwoods, and acceleration of oak seedling height growth postfire relative to that of other species. Negative fire effects to the oak reproduction were the opposite of the positive

results, such as decreases in the absolute or relative abundance of oak reproduction or loss of the relative oak seedling height growth. Ambiguous results were when there was no or little meaningful change in competitive relationships between oak and mesophytic hardwood reproduction from pre-burn to post-burn.

RESULTS

Mature Stands

As previously stated, these stands are in the understory re-initiation stage of development (Oliver and Larson 1990). The overstory is intact with stocking levels exceeding 80 percent. The midstory is ubiquitous and well developed. Dense shade covers the forest floor and strongly influences understory composition and growth. Generally, these stands have not experienced any substantial disturbance for decades. Of the 59 fire-oak papers, 39 (66 percent) took place in mature stands and 37 (95 percent) of those involved dormant-season fires (table 1). These were relatively evenly spread among the number of fires (11 single burns, 11 dual burns, and 17 multiple burns) and among effects on oak (11 ambiguous, 11 negative, 17 positive). However, when we combined these two groupings (number of fires and effects on oak), a pattern of improving benefit to oak as the number of fires increased was evident (table 2). The remainder of this section will review some of the noteworthy publications that are representative of the studies conducted in mature stands.

One fire—The effect of a single prescribed fire on existing oak seedlings was either negative or ambiguous (table 2). Of the 11 studies, 7 found that the number of oak seedlings decreased following the fire while the other 4 found no substantial change. Noteworthy negative studies include Johnson (1974), Huntley and McGee (1983), Loftis (1990), and Wendel and Smith (1986). Studies reporting ambiguous results include Albrecht and McCarthy (2006), Dolan and Parker (2004), Elliott and others (2004), and Teuke and Van Lear (1982). Of these, the Johnson (1974) study is fairly typical in terms of study design, implementation and outcome.

Johnson's (1974) study took place in southwestern Wisconsin and involved the Forest Service, U.S. Department of Agriculture (USFS) North Central Forest Experiment Station and the Wisconsin Department of Natural Resources. The study site was an 8-acre stand dominated by northern red oak. The stand was moderately thinned from below (basal area reduced from 120 to 80 cubic feet per acre) in fall 1969. At this same time, an acorn crop resulted in the establishment of 7,000 new red oak seedlings per acre in spring 1970. A year later, the stand was split in two and one section was burned with a low-intensity prescribed fire while the other served as an unburned control. Data collected that fall indicated that the burned seedlings had a 40 percent survival rate while the control seedlings had a 90 percent survival rate. The fire had killed approximately half of the northern red oak seedlings.

One of the criticisms of the Johnson (1974) study is that it reports results collected from one inventory conducted just a few months after the fire. A comparable study with a longer interval between treatment and inventory is Wendel and Smith (1986). That study occurred in east-central West Virginia and was a cooperative effort by the USFS Northeastern Forest Experiment Station, the Washington National Forest, and the West Virginia Department of Natural Resources. Like the Johnson study, this site was thinned to 90 cubic feet per acre basal area and burned a year later. Prior to the fire, desirable hardwood reproduction was 3,814 stems per acre and 5 years later the density was 3,500 stems per acre. However, within these numbers the amount of oak dropped by nearly 80 percent while the amount of red maple and black locust (*Robinia psuedoacacia* L.) increased by 17 and 120 percent, respectively. Clearly, the fire had a negative impact on the oak regeneration process.

Why did these prescribed fires produce such negative results for the oak reproduction? The main factor in both of these studies was that the oak seedlings were small and had been growing in dense understory shade for all of their lives. Consequently, they had small root systems with little root carbohydrate reserves and simply could not sprout postfire. Second, the prescribed fires were conducted in mid- to late-April so the small seedlings may have already begun expanding their leaves, further lowering their root carbohydrate reserves. Finally, neither study excluded white-tailed deer from the sites so excessive deer browsing may have subsequently eliminated many oaks that sprouted postfire. Regardless of why these studies had a negative impact on oak reproduction, it is evident that prescribed burning could impede the oak regeneration process under some circumstances.

Another potential negative impact of prescribed fires on the oak regeneration process is their effect on recently fallen acorns. This facet of fire and the oak regeneration process was the earliest one reported in the scientific literature (Korstian 1927). He found that fires exceeding 400 °F readily killed acorns, but there was a mortality gradient among species with acorns of the red oak group surviving fire at a higher rate than those of the white oak group. Korstian surmised that this gradient was caused by the differences in germination timing (fall for white oaks, spring for red oaks) between the two groups.

Subsequent research has confirmed that acorns are easily killed by fires (Auchmoody and Smith 1993, Dey and Fan 2009, Greenberg and others 2012).

Two fires—The studies utilizing two prescribed fires showed varying responses (tables 1 and 2). Four papers reported ambiguous effects (Franklin and others 2003, McGee and others 1995, Merritt and Pope 1991) on oak reproduction with five showing positive outcomes (Barnes and Van Lear 1998, Schuler and others 2013) and two showing negative outcomes (Arthur and others 1998, Luken and Shea 2000). Illustrative of this confusion are the two oak sites that were part of the National Fire and Fire Surrogate Project as they report differing outcomes between sites as well as among topographic positions (Iverson and others 2008, Waldrop and others 2008).

The oak sites of the National Fire and Fire Surrogates Project located in western North Carolina and southern Ohio examined the responses of hardwood reproduction and many other variables to prescribed fire and mechanical fuel reduction treatments. Dormant-season strip-heading fires were conducted twice at both sites with and without a mechanical treatment. In North Carolina, the mechanical treatment was chainsaw felling of shrubs, while midstory and overstory thinning was the mechanical treatment used in Ohio. Oak regeneration varied by treatment at both the sites. In North Carolina, the oaks showed little response to any treatment during the first year after treatment but increased significantly in number between years 1 and 3 in the burn-only and mechanical + burn plots. A decrease was observed in year 5 after the second burn but the difference was not significant. The mechanical-only treatment had little initial impact on oak regeneration in North Carolina but a significant increase was observed between years 3 and 5. Oak reproduction decreased at Ohio in all treatment units during the first year after treatment, although the difference was not significant in the mechanical-only treatment unit. No changes occurred between years 1 and 4.

Competitors of oak tended to follow the same patterns at North Carolina and Ohio. Red maple showed little response to treatment during the first year in North Carolina, but in Ohio there were significant decreases in number of red maple seedlings in all treatments, including the control. Burning, with and without mechanical treatment, significantly increased red maple numbers at years 3 (North Carolina) or 4 (Ohio) but the second burn in North Carolina reduced numbers to pretreatment levels. Yellow-poplar increased over time in the mechanical-only plots in Ohio. However, this response was small in comparison to the large increase in numbers of yellow-poplar seedlings observed the first year after burning at both sites. These numbers decreased by the third measurement at both sites and even more after the second burn in North Carolina. This result agrees with the results of Brose and Van Lear (1998) who emphasized the need for prescribed burning after yellow-poplar seedlings become established. Oaks were four to six times more numerous after the second burn in North Carolina than were seedlings of yellow-poplar. The burn-only treatment changed stand structure by reducing the sapling/shrub layer but it did little to thin the overstory.

Iverson and others (2008) used the same study area in Ohio reported by Waldrop and others (2008) to compare treatment impacts as they varied across different positions of the landscape. Study plots in Ohio were larger than those in North Carolina (50 acres vs. 20 acres) thus allowing a comparison of treatment impacts across dry and mesic sites. The drier landscape positions generally had more intense fires, more canopy openness, and more oak and hickory advance regeneration; several other tree species also exhibited marked landscape variation in regeneration after treatments. Though advance regeneration of several competing species became abundant after the initial treatments, the second fires reduced the high densities of the two major competitors, red maple and yellow-poplar. The authors suggested that on dry or intermediate sites with at least 2,000 oak and hickory seedlings per acre, opening the canopy to 8.5–19 percent followed by at least two fires should promote oak and hickory to be "competitive" over about 50 percent of the area. However, no appreciable oak and hickory regeneration developed on mesic sites.

The study by Iverson and others (2008) on relatively large (>50 acres) treatment units showed some promise and also showed some of the problems that managers face. Though thinning and burning increased the density of oak advance regeneration, there also was ample competition from species that had different strategies in dealing with the new conditions brought about by the thinning and burning. There was a large spatial variation in oak regeneration across the large sites because topography, fire intensity, and canopy openness were also highly variable.

More than two fires—Even though prescribed burning in hardwoods has been discussed for several decades, it was not used on an operational scale until the 1980s (Van Lear and Waldrop 1991). Consequently, long-term studies involving multiple fires in hardwood forests are rare, but a number of new publications are available describing results after three or four periodic fires. Generally, these studies describe positive effects of multiple prescribed fires on oak reproduction, but a few report negative effects (tables 1 and 2).

One of the longest running fire studies in eastern hardwood forests is located in south-central Tennessee (Stratton 2007). Since 1962, an oak barren has been burned in late winter annually or every 5 years. During that time, oak has come to dominate the understory as mesophyitc hardwood reproduction gradually died out. An interesting finding is that none of the oak reproduction has ever successfully grown into the canopy in any of the fire treatments. Apparently, a 5-year fire return interval is too short for oak reproduction to grow large enough to withstand a surface fire without being topkilled and forced to sprout again.

Blankenship and Arthur (2006) used a study site on the Cumberland Plateau in eastern Kentucky to examine stand structure after prescribed burning two or three times. The same study site was used by Green and others (2010) after another set of burns (three and four burns) to examine oak and red maple seedling survival. Burning was conducted by backing fire down the ridge and by point source or strip heading fires if a higher intensity was desired. The first two fires were in the dormant season; later burns were in the growing season. Burning altered stand structure by reducing overstory stem density by 30 percent and midstory stem density by 91 percent (Blankenship and Arthur 2006). Midstory oak and red maple stem densities were reduced by 94 and 85 percent, respectively. Damaged or dead overstory and midstory stems sprouted to greatly increase the number of trees in the ground layer, with oak, red maple, and dogwood being most common after three burns. Green and others (2010) tagged chestnut oak, scarlet oak, and red maple seedlings to follow survival and growth through three and four prescribed fires. Burning reduced the numbers of seedlings of all three species, but scarlet oak had significantly higher survival than chestnut oak and red maple. Scarlet oaks burned four times were significantly taller than chestnut oak and red maple burned either three or four times. Overall, scarlet oaks had better survival and growth than red maples, but red maples were not eliminated as some continued to resprout. Both papers (Blankenship and Arthur 2006, Green and others 2010) emphasized that after several burns, oak regeneration was in a better competitive position than was red maple, but goals of producing predominately oak regeneration had not been reached. Additional trials with other burning regimes and/or silvicultural tools would be necessary to reach that goal.

Alexander and others (2008), also working in Kentucky, had similar results to Blankenship and Arthur (2006) and Green and others (2010). Numbers of mid-story trees were reduced by burning one or three times, but sprouting caused large increases in the numbers of trees in the smaller size classes. Both single and repeated prescribed burns increased understory light and reduced red maple survival. However, neither burning regime placed oaks in an improved competitive position. The authors suggest that successful oak regeneration is difficult to predict because it is controlled by three highly variable and interdependent factors: life history traits of oaks compared to competitors, pre-burn stature of oak seedlings, and variability of fire temperature and how it affects light. Although not suggested by these authors, other factors that also control oak regeneration are site quality and position on the landscape (aspect and position on the slope).

Hutchinson and others (2005a, b) studied regeneration after two and four dormant-season prescribed burns on xeric, intermediate, and mesic sites in southern Ohio. Burning, conducted by strip heading fires, had little impact on overstory trees over 10-inch diameter at breast height (dbh). Smaller trees (4 to 10 inch dbh) were reduced in density by 31 percent by burning twice and by 19 percent by burning four times. The two-burn treatment had higher fire intensity, resulting in greater mortality of small trees. Burning also reduced sapling density by 86 percent. Regeneration after burning was abundant and largely of the same species as were killed by burning. In this trial, results were similar among xeric, intermediate, and mesic sites. The largest change was brought about by the higher fire intensities associated with the two-burn scenario because they better opened the canopy to a greater degree. In addition, burning at longer intervals may allow greater buildup of fuels, as stems and branches of trees killed by one fire fall over and become fuel for the next fire. Waldrop and others (2010) found that after burning, fine woody fuels increase in abundance over time until the next prescribed fire. A factor often overlooked is delayed mortality, which can occur for several years after a single fire. Yaussy and Waldrop (2010) showed that the likelihood of mortality was related to prior tree health, size class, species, and first-order fire effects. Hutchinson and others (2012) concluded that periodic fire, coupled with natural gap dynamics, may be a feasible management strategy for perpetuating oak forests where harvesting is not an option.

Growing-season fire—In our survey of the fire and oak literature, we found only three studies reporting results of a single growing-season fire (foliage of mesophytic hardwood reproduction was more than 50 percent expanded) in a mature stand. The Barnes and Van Lear (1998) study occurred on the Clemson University Forest in South Carolina, while the Brose and others (2007) and Gottschalk and others (2013) studies took place in Pennsylvania on the Clear Creek and Moshannon State Forests, respectively.

Barnes and Van Lear (1998) compared a single growing-season fire in 1992 to three dormant-season fires conducted in 1900, 1992, and 1993. All burns began with backing fires and were completed with strip heading fires. Oak density was not significantly different between the two burning treatments. However, the single growing season burn was as effective at promoting open growing conditions, as were the three dormant-season burns. Burning in the growing season was also more effective at reducing competition from yellow-poplar. This study suggests that even though burning in the growing season is more difficult than in the dormant season because of increased humidity and shading, it can be more effective and, ultimately, less expensive.

In the two Pennsylvania studies, postfire sprouting of oak seedlings was 65 percent *less* than that of mesophytic hardwood reproduction. This large difference between the two species groups was likely due to the oak seedlings having much smaller root systems relative to the larger non-oak reproduction.

Two or more growing-season fires—None of the prescribed fire studies conducted in mature hardwood stands fell into this group. However, a long-term fire study conducted in pine-dominated stands on the Santee Experimental Forest of South Carolina does provide some insight into this type of fire regime (Langdon 1981, Lewis and Harshbarger 1976, Lotti and others 1960, McKee 1982). The study was established in 1946 with annual and periodic (3 to 5 years) burning conducted in summer and winter until Hurricane Hugo severely damaged the study in September 1989. Waldrop and others (1992) reported on changes to vegetation through 43 years of treatment. When plots were burned every 3 to 5 years, in either summer or winter, trees over 5 inches dbh were largely unaffected as they were too tall and their bark was too thick to be impacted by low-intensity burning. Hardwoods between 1 and 5 inches dbh were topkilled gradually over time. These stems then sprouted, resulting in a large increase in stems less than 1 inch dbh. Annual winter burning produced similar results but had the largest number of sprouts. With each of these treatments, vegetation had at least one growing season to recover from burning. It was only in the annual summer burn treatment that hardwoods were nearly eliminated from the forest floor, and that required many burns. The most resilient species were the oaks, which persisted through 18 to 20 annual summer fires (Langdon 1981). This result has been cited by many authors as an indication of the competitive advantage of oaks over other hardwoods in a regime of frequent burning. However, density of oak competitors increased in all fire regimes except annual summer burning, which is impractical for almost all land managers.

Young Stands

These stands received a complete or heavy partial harvest (≥50 percent basal area reduction) or comparable disturbance within the past 10 years. They are at the end of the understory re-initiation stage (overstory still somewhat intact, but it no longer controls understory development) or in the stand initiation stage (Oliver and Larson 1990). Examples of young stands include those that have recently received a final harvest, stands undergoing a two-cut shelterwood sequence, and stands heavily damaged by insects, weather, or wildfire. The key characteristics of these stands are that the event released the hardwood reproduction from dense understory shading and there has been sufficient time (≥3 growing seasons) for that reproduction to respond to the release.

We found 16 fire-oak papers involving young stands (tables 1 and 3). Unlike the papers reporting results of burning in mature stands, only six of these involved dormant-season fires, while eight used growing-season burns (note that three papers provided data on both seasons of burn). Similarly, the fire studies in young stands were not evenly distributed by number of burns and effects on oak reproduction like those conducted in mature stands. Rather, they were concentrated in the single fire and positive effects categories.

Dormant-season fires—Just six papers reported results of single fires conducted during the dormant season and all of these originated from three studies. Huntley and McGee (1981) burned 3-year-old hardwood clearcuts in northern Alabama. They found that the dormant-season fire reduced the density of yellow-poplar reproduction, but had virtually no impact on that of red maple. Density of oak reproduction was also unaffected. In central Virginia, Brose and Van Lear (1998) investigated the impact of a single dormant-season burn on hardwood reproduction in oak shelterwood stands. Like the Alabama study, they found decreases in the density of yellow-poplar reproduction, but little reduction of red maple density, except where the fires were intense. A follow-up study (Brose 2010) showed that these initial findings persisted, especially on the more intensely burned plots, and were leading towards eventual oak domination.

Growing-season fires—Research into the effects of growing-season fires (foliage of mesophytic hardwood reproduction was more than 50 percent expanded) is limited. We found eight papers that had growing-season prescribed fires as one of the treatments. In central Virginia, Keyser and others (1996) found that summer fires in oak shelterwood stands reduced the density of red maple and yellow-poplar seedlings by 82 percent and 97 percent, respectively, relative to the unburned controls.

Oak reproduction decreased by only 11 percent following summer burning. Post-fire height growth among the species groups was equal. This small study spawned a more comprehensive research project, also conducted in central Virginia, that examined late spring and summer prescribed fires as treatments in oak shelterwood stands (Brose and Van Lear 1998, Brose and others 1999). The previous summer-burn results were verified. Densities of red maple and yellow-poplar reproduction declined by 46 percent and 72 percent, respectively, while oak seedling density dropped by only 5 percent. Additionally, late spring burning (foliage of mesophytic hardwood reproduction was more than 50 percent expanded) resulted in a 45 percent decline in stem density for the two non-oak species. The importance of fire intensity was evident in that the largest reductions in stem densities of maples and yellow-poplars occurred where the fires burned the hottest. These outcomes were still present 11 years later, especially the relationship between fire intensity and oak dominance (Brose 2010).

Besides burning in oak shelterwoods, growing-season fires after the final harvest have been studied to a limited extent. In Connecticut, Ward and Brose (2004) found that mortality of black birch ranged from 66 to 86 percent following late spring burning (foliage of mesophytic hardwood reproduction was more than 50 percent expanded) in a recently-regenerated, mixed hardwood stand. Mortality of red maple averaged 15 percent, but exhibited wide variability, 0 to 100 percent, depending on fire intensity and size of the red maple reproduction prior to the fires. Oak mortality averaged just 9 percent with low variability. In Pennsylvania, Brose (2013) investigated the effects of early-May prescribed fires on hardwood reproduction in former oak stands that had recently received the final harvest of a three-cut shelterwood sequence. Like in Connecticut, black birch exhibited large decreases in stem densities (~90 percent) while stem density of red maple declined approximately 50 percent. Density of oak reproduction was unchanged by the burning; virtually all oak stems sprouted after the fires. Likewise, densities of black cherry, cucumbertree (*Magnolia acuminata* L.), and serviceberry (*Amelanchier arborea* Michx.f.) Fern.) seedlings were the same after the fires as before. Besides reducing the stem densities of black birch and red maple, the growing-season fire equalized the height growth among the various species.

Immature Stands

Only four publications address fire effects during the stem exclusion stage (table 1). All are reviewed here.

In southern West Virginia, Carvell and Maxey (1969) studied a sapling stand partly burned by an autumn wildfire 5 years earlier. In the unburned portion, yellow-poplar was the dominant species in terms of density and size. However in the burned section, oak and hickory (*Carya* spp. Nutt.) dominated. They noted that 40 to 70 percent of the saplings that survived the fire had large basal scars and concluded that fire was a poor means to manipulate species composition in sapling stands given the loss of future timber value.

In southern Pennsylvania, Abrams and Johnson (2013) reported that an intense fall wildfire in a 15-year-old mixed oak stand resulted in a 43 percent reduction in stem density, including fewer oaks and black cherry and an increase in low-value trees like black locust. Additionally, the surviving oaks suffered major damage to their boles that will persist for decades and decrease the ultimate future value of the stand.

Maslen (1989) reported on a single high-intensity dormant-season strip-heading fire in a mixed hardwood pole stand in the Piedmont of North Carolina. This study looked at understory characteristics 7 years after burning, giving a slightly longer-term view of fire impacts. By then, there were no significant differences in the numbers of oaks and competitors less than 2 feet tall, as seedlings and sprouts had grown into the next larger size class. In the 2- to 12-foot height class, oaks, yellow-poplar, and all other species were significantly higher in number than prior to burning. Oaks over 12 feet tall at the time of the fire were essentially unaffected by burning; they survived the fire. The results of this study indicated that a single prescribed fire did little to the stand other than to remove small regeneration and allow sprouts to grow back over time.

In Connecticut, Ward and Stephens (1989) report the long-term (55-year) effects of a summer wildfire that burned through part of a 30-year-old mixed hardwood stand in 1932. Prior to the wildfire, the stand contained approximately 1,050 stems >1.0 inch dbh per acre and 74.0 square feet per acre of basal area. Oak and hickory comprised 21.3 and 6.4 percent of the stems, respectively, with the balance consisting of birch, maple, and other hardwoods. In the years just after the 1932 fire, stem densities and basal area in the burned area dropped by 84 and 38 percent, respectively, with few differences among species. In the subsequent decades in the burned area, stem densities quickly recovered due to sprouting of the fire-killed stems before declining due to natural stand thinning. At the same time, basal area gradually increased. By 1987, stem densities and basal areas were similar in the burned and unburned areas, but the burned area contained considerably more oak than the unburned area; 160 stems per acre versus 65 stems per acre. The negative effects of the 1932 fire were the widespread bole damage of the trees that survived the fire and the poor stem form of many of the sprouts that developed postfire.

DISCUSSION

From tables 1, 2, and 3, and the observations, insights, and interpretations provided in the reviewed fire-oak papers, several findings and trends emerge that are useful to managers of oak-dominated ecosystems. They are:

Many factors influence the outcome of a prescribed fire. Among these, the important biological ones are the developmental stage of the oak stand and the degree of root development by the oak reproduction. Important fire factors are season of burn, fire intensity, and their interaction. Finally, critical site factors include topography and the disturbance history of the stand, both of which influence fire behavior, fire size, and the species composition of the reproduction.

In mature stands (understory re-initiation stage), as the number of fires increases, so does the benefit to oak. Single fires and the initial burn of a multi-fire sequence will provide little, if any, benefit to the oak reproduction and may actually be detrimental in the short term. Conversely, multiple burns spread over a decade or more will generally benefit the oak component of the regeneration pool via an improved seedbed for oak seedling establishment and enhanced understory light conditions for the subsequent growth of the new seedlings and any existing oak reproduction.

In young stands (initiation stage), single fires can rapidly benefit the oak reproduction. This is likely due to differences in root development between the oaks and the competing mesophytic hardwoods that give the oaks a higher postfire sprouting probability.

In immature stands (stem exclusion stage), prescribed fire can increase the relative proportion of oak, but there will be large economic losses due to bole damage to the trees that survive the fire and stem defect (crook and sweep) of the new sprouts.

Among the various eastern species, post-fire sprouting ability of the reproduction varies widely. Some are non-sprouters (eastern hemlock (*Tsuga Canadensis* (L.) Carr.) and eastern white pine (*Pinus strobus* L.), some are poor sprouters (sweet birch and yellow-poplar), some are moderate sprouters (blackgum and red maple), and some are excellent sprouters (oak and hickory). A species' sprouting ability is a function of its capability to form dormant basal buds coupled with its germination strategy (epigeal or hypogeal), its juvenile growth strategy (root-centric or stem-centric), and its shade tolerance, i.e., the optimal light regime for juvenile growth. Sprouting ability is also influenced by season of burn, fire intensity, and their interaction.

Growing-season fires will have more impact, i.e., kill more stems, than dormant-season fires because the vegetation is physiologically active. Similarly, multiple fires kill more stems than single fires due to accumulated damage on midstory and overstory trees. Across the range of prescribed fire regimes, a single dormant-season fire will have the least impact on forest structure while multiple growing-season fires will have the most impact. Multiple dormant-season fires and single growing-season fires will have an intermediate impact. Within any of these, fire intensity will also play a role, as hotter fires have more impact than cooler fires.

Immediate mortality from a single fire is mostly confined to the regeneration layer and small saplings (<3 inch dbh). Midstory trees, large saplings (3 to 6 inch dbh) and pole-size trees (6 to 10 inch dbh), are periodically killed and some may succumb to delayed mortality. Overstory trees (>11 inch dbh) are generally unscathed unless there is an accumulation of fuel at or near their bases.

Long-term fire studies in young stands are needed. We found only 10 fire studies done in oak shelterwoods or recently regenerated oaks stands, and just one of them reported results more than 10 years postfire. While the vast majority of these studies reported positive results for the oak reproduction, more research is needed to understand the other ramifications of this approach.

In some situations, prescribed burning can make the oak regeneration process more difficult. If conducted shortly after a good masting event, fire will kill many of the acorns on the ground. Small oak seedlings with undeveloped root systems are virtually defenseless against a fire, especially a growing season burn. Prescribed fires can also cause a large influx of new non-oak seedlings from seed stored in the forest floor, exacerbate invasive species problems, and incite excessive browsing by white-tailed deer.

ACKNOWLEDGMENTS

This paper is the product of many conversations with many scientists over the years. We are especially indebted to David Van Lear — the "father" of prescribed burning for sustaining oaks and our advisor when we were graduate students at Clemson University many years ago. Other contributors via conversations include Mary Arthur, Ed Buckner, Daniel Dey, David Loftis, Gary Miller, Charles Ruffner, Thomas Schuler, Jeffrey Ward, and Daniel Yaussy. Todd Hutchinson and Aaron Stottlemyer graciously reviewed an earlier version of this manuscript and provided many suggestions that helped with brevity and clarity.

LITERATURE CITED

Abrams, M.D. 1992. Fire and the development of oak forests. BioScience. 42: 346-353.

Abrams, M.D.; Downs, J.A. 1990. Successional replacement of old-growth white oak by mixed mesophytic hardwoods in southwestern Pennsylvania. Canadian Journal of Forest Research. 20: 1864-1870.

Abrams, M.D.; Johnson, S.E. 2013. Wildfire damage assessment of a young oak forest in Pennsylvania. Journal of Applied Fire Science. 23: 91-104.

Albrecht, M.A.; McCarthy, B.C. 2006. Effects of prescribed fire and thinning on tree recruitment patterns in central hardwood forests. Forest Ecology and Management. 226: 88-103.

Aldrich, S.R.; Lafon, C.W.; Grissino-Mayer, H.D.; DeWeese, G.G.; Hoss, J.A. 2010. Three centuries of fire in montane pine-oak stands on a temperate forest landscape. Applied Vegetation Science. 13: 36-46.

Aldrich, P.R.; Parker, G.R.; Severson, J.R.; Michler, C.H. 2005. Confirmation of oak recruitment failure in Indiana old-growth forest: 75 years of data. Forest Science. 51(5): 406-416.

Alexander, H.D.; Arthur, M.A.; Loftis, D.L.; Green, S.R. 2008. Survival and growth of upland oak and co-occurring competitor seedlings following single and repeated prescribed fires. Forest Ecology and Management. 256: 1021-1030.

Arthur, M.A.; Paratley, R.D.; Blankenship, B.A. 1998. Single and repeated fires affect survival and regeneration of woody and herbaceous species in an oak-pine forest. Journal of the Torrey Botanical Society. 125: 225-236.

Auchmoody, L.R.; Smith, H.C. 1993. Survival of acorns after fall burning. Res. Pap. NE-678. Radnor, PA: U.S. Department of Agriculture Forest Service, Northeastern Forest Experiment Station. 5 p.

Barnes, T.A.; Van Lear, D.H. 1998. Prescribed fire effects on advanced regeneration in mixed hardwood stands. Southern Journal of Applied Forestry. 22: 138-142.

Blankenship, B.A.; Arthur, M.A. 2006. Stand structure over 9 years in burned and fire-excluded oak stands on the Cumberland Plateau, Kentucky. Forest Ecology and Management. 225: 134-145.

Brose, P.H. 2010. Long-term effects of single prescribed fires on hardwood regeneration in oak shelterwood stands. Forest Ecology and Management. 260: 1516-1524.

Brose, P.H. 2013. Post-harvest prescribed burning of oak stands: An alternative to the shelterwood-burn technique? In: Miller, G.W.; Schuler, T.M.; Gottschalk, K.W. [and others], eds. Proceedings of the 18th central hardwoods forest conference. Gen. Tech. Rep. NRS-P-117. Newtown Square, PA: U.S. Department of Agriculture Forest Service, Northern Research Station: 352-364.

Brose, P.H.; Miller, G.W.; Gottschalk, K.W. 2007. Reintroducing fire to the oak forests of Pennsylvania: response of striped maple. In: Powers, R.F., ed. Restoring fire-adapted ecosystems: Proceedings of the 2005 national silviculture workshop. Gen. Tech. Rep. PSW-203. Albany, CA: U.S. Department of Agriculture Forest Service, Pacific Southwest Research Station: 67-77.

Brose, P.H.; Schuler, T.M; Van Lear, D.H.; Berst, J. 2001. Bringing fire back: the changing regimes of the Appalachian mixed-oak forests. Journal of Forestry. 99(11): 30-35.

Brose, P.H.; Van Lear, D.H. 1998. Responses of hardwood advance regeneration to seasonal prescribed fires in oak dominated shelterwood stands. Canadian Journal of Forest Research. 28: 331-339.

Brose, P.H.; Van Lear, D.H.; Cooper, R. 1999. Using shelterwood harvests and prescribed fire to regenerate oak stands on productive upland sites. Forest Ecology and Management. 113(2): 125-141.

Brown, J.H. 1960. The role of fire in altering the species composition of forests in Rhode Island. Ecology. 41(2): 310-316.

Carvell, K.L.; Maxey, W.R. 1969. Wildfire destroys! Bulletin 2. Morgantown, WV: West Virginia Agriculture Experiment Station: 4-5, 12.

Collins, R.J.; Carson, W.P. 2003. The fire and oak hypothesis: Incorporating the influence of deer browsing and canopy gaps. In: Van Sambeek, J.W.; Dawson, J.O.; Ponder, F. [and others], eds. Proceedings of the 13th central hardwoods forest conference. Gen. Tech. Rep. NC-234. St Paul, MN: U.S. Department of Agriculture Forest Service, North Central Research Station: 44-60.

Crow, T.R. 1988. Reproductive mode and mechanisms for self-replacement of northern red oak (*Quercus rubra*) – a review. Forest Science. 34(1):19-40.

Day, G.M. 1953. The Indian as an ecological factor in the northeastern forest. Ecology. 34: 329-346.

DeSelm, H.R.; Clebsch, E.E.C.; Rennie, J.C. 1991. Effects of 27 years of prescribed fire on an oak forest and its soils in middle Tennessee. In: Coleman, S.S.; Neary, D.G., eds. Proceedings of the 6th biennial southern silviculture research conference. Gen. Tech. Rep. SE-70. Asheville, NC: U.S. Department of Agriculture Forest Service, Southeastern Forest Experiment Station: 409-417.

Dey, D.C.; Fan, Z. 2009. A review of fire and oak regeneration and overstory recruitment. In: Proceedings of the 3rd fire in eastern oak forests conference. Gen. Tech. Rep. NRS-P-46. Newtown Square, PA: U.S. Department of Agriculture Forest Service, Northern Research Station: 2-20.

Dey, D.C., Hartman, G. 2005. Returning fire to Ozark Highland forest ecosystems: Effects on advance regeneration. Forest Ecology and Management. 217: 37-53.

Dolan, B.J., and G.R. Parker. 2004. Understory response to disturbance: an investigation of prescribed burning and understory removal treatments. In: Spetich, M.A., ed. Upland oak ecology symposium: history, current conditions, and sustainability. Gen. Tech. Rep. SRS-73. Asheville, NC: U.S. Department of Agriculture Forest Service, Southern Research Station: 285-291.

Elliott, K.J.; Vose, J.M.; Clinton, B.D.; Knoepp, J.D. 2004. Effects of understory burning in a mesic mixed-oak forest of the Southern Appalachians. In: Engstrom, R.T.; Galley, K.E.M.; de Groot, W.J., eds. Proceedings of the 22nd Tall Timbers fire ecology conference. Tall Timbers Research Station, Tallahassee, FL: 272-283.

Fan, Z.; Ma, Z.; Dey, D.C.; Roberts, S.D. 2012. Response of advance reproduction of oaks and associated species to repeated prescribed fires in upland oak-hickory forests, Missouri. Forest Ecology and Management. 266: 160-169.

Franklin, S.B.; Robertson, P.A.; Fralish, J.S. 2003. Prescribed burning effects on upland *Quercus* forest structure and function. Forest Ecology and Management. 184: 315-335.

Geisinger, D.R.; Waldrop, T.A.; Haymond, J.L.; Van Lear, D.H. 1989. Sprout growth following winter and spring felling with and without summer broadcast burning. In: Waldrop, T.A., ed. Proceedings of pine-hardwood mixtures symposium. Gen. Tech. Rep. SE-58. Asheville, NC: U.S. Department of Agriculture Forest Service, Southeastern Forest Experiment Station: 91-94.

Gilbert, N.L.; Johnson, S.L.; Gleeson, S.K. [and others]. 2003. Effects of prescribed fire on physiology and growth of *Acer rubrum* and *Quercus* spp. seedlings in an oak-pine forest on the Cumberland Plateau, KY. Journal of Torrey Botanical Society. 130: 253-264.

Gottschalk, K.W. 1985. Effects of shading on growth and development of northern red oak, black oak, black cherry, and red maple seedlings I: height, diameter, and root/shoot ratio. In: Dawson, J.O.; Majerus, K.A., eds. Proceedings of the 5th central hardwoods forest conference. Urbana-Champaign, IL: Univ. Illinois Press: 189-195.

Gottschalk, K.W. 1987. Effects of shading on growth and development of northern red oak, black oak, black cherry, and red maple seedlings. II. Biomass partitioning and prediction. In: Hay, R.L.; Woods, F.W.; DeSelm, H., eds. Proceedings of the 6th central hardwood forest conference. Knoxville, TN: University of Tennessee, Department of Forestry, Wildlife, and Fisheries: 99-110.

Gottschalk, K.W. 1994. Shade, leaf growth and crown development of *Quercus rubra*, *Quercus velutina*, *Prunus serotina* and *Acer rubrum* seedlings. Tree Physiology. 14: 735-749.

Gottschalk, K.W.; Miller, G.W.; Brose, P.H. 2013. Advanced oak seedling development as influenced by shelterwood treatments, fern control, deer fencing, and prescribed fire. In: Miller, G.W.; Schuler, T.M.; Gottschalk, K.W. [and others], eds. Proceedings of the 18th central hardwoods forest conference. Gen. Tech. Rep. NRS-P-117. Newtown Square, PA: U.S. Department of Agriculture Forest Service, Northern Research Station: 466.

Green, S.R.; Arthur, M.A; Blankenship, B.A. 2010. Oak and red maple seedling survival and growth following periodic prescribed fire on xeric ridgetops on the Cumberland Plateau. Forest Ecology and Management. 259: 2256-2266.

Greenberg, C.H.; Keyser, T.L.; Zarnoch, S.J. [and others]. 2012. Acorn viability following prescribed fire in upland hardwood forests. Forest Ecology and Management. 275: 79-86.

Guyette, R.P.; Dey, D.C.; Stambaugh, M.C.; Muzika, R.M. 2006. Fire scars reveal variability and dynamics of eastern fire regimes. In: Dickinson, M.B., ed. Fire in eastern oak forests: delivering science to land managers. Gen. Tech. Rep. NRS-P-1. Newtown Square, PA: U.S. Department of Agriculture Forest Service, Northern Research Station: 20-39.

Healy, W.M.; Gottschalk, K.W.; Long, R.P.; Wargo, P.M. 1997. Changes in eastern forests: chestnuts are gone, are the oaks far behind? In: McClure, C.M.; Wadsworth, K.L., eds. Transactions of the 62nd North American wildlife and natural resources conference. Washington, DC: Wildlife Management Institute: 249-263.

Huddle, J.A.; Pallardy, S.G. 1996. Effects of long-term annual and periodic burning on tree survival and growth in a Missouri Ozark oak-hickory forest. Forest Ecology and Management. 82: 1-9.

Huntley, J.C.; McGee, C.E. 1981. Timber and wildlife implications of fire in young upland hardwoods. In: Barnett, J.P., ed. Proceedings of the 1st biennial southern silviculture research conference. Gen. Tech. Rep. SO-34. New Orleans, LA: U.S. Department of Agriculture Forest Service, Southern Forest Experiment Station: 56-66.

Huntley, J.C.; McGee, C.E. 1983. Impact of fire on regeneration and wildlife habitat in upland hardwoods. In: Proceedings of the 1982 Society of American Foresters National Convention: 158-162.

Hutchinson, T.F.; Boerner, R.E.J.; Sutherland, S.; Sutherland, E.K.; Ortt, M.; Iverson, L.R. 2005b. Prescribed fire effects on the herbaceous layer of mixed-oak forests. Canadian Journal of Forest Research 35: 877-890.

Hutchinson, T.F.; Long, R.P.; Ford, R.D.; Sutherland, E.K. 2008. Fire history and the establishment of oaks and maples in second-growth forests. Canadian Journal of Forest Research. 38: 1184-1198.

Hutchinson, T.F.; Long, R.P.; Rebbeck, J. [and others]. 2012. Repeated prescribed fires alter gap-phase regeneration in mixed-oak forests. Canadian Journal of Forest Research. 42: 303-314.

Hutchinson, T.F.; Sutherland, E.K.; Yaussy, D.A. 2005a. Effects of repeated prescribed fires on the structure, composition, and regeneration of mixed-oak forests in Ohio. Forest Ecology and Management. 260: 1516-1524.

Iverson, L.R.; Hutchinson, T.F.; Prasad, A.M.; Peters, M.P. 2008. Thinning, fire, and oak regeneration across a heterogeneous landscape in the Eastern U.S.: 7-year results. Forest Ecology and Management. 255: 3135-3050.

Johnson, P.S. 1974. Survival and growth of red oak seedlings following a prescribed burn. Res. Note NC-177. St Paul, MN: U.S. Department of Agriculture Forest Service, North Central Research Station. 6 p.

Johnson, P.S.; Shifley, S.R.; Rogers, R. 2009. The ecology and silviculture of oaks (2nd ed.). New York: CABI Publishing. 580 p.

Keyser, P.K.; Brose, P.H.; Van Lear, D.H.; Burtner, K.M. 1996. Enhancing oak regeneration with fire in shelterwood stands: Preliminary trials. In: McClure, C.M.; Wadsworth, K.L., eds. Transactions of the 61st North American wildlife and natural resources conference. Washington, DC: Wildlife Management Institute: 215-219.

Kolb, T.E.; Steiner, K.C.; McCormick, L.H.; Bowersox, T.W. 1990. Growth and biomass partitioning of northern red oak and yellow-poplar seedlings to light, soil moisture and nutrients in relation to ecological strategy. Forest Ecology and Management. 38: 65-78.

Korstian, C.F. 1927. Factors controlling germination and early survival of oaks. Forestry Bulletin 19. New Haven, CT: Yale University. 115 p.

Kruger, E.L.; Reich, P.B. 1997. Responses of hardwood regeneration to fire in mesic forest openings I: Post-fire community dynamics. Canadian Journal of Forest Research. 27: 1822-1831.

Langdon, O.G. 1981. Some effects of prescribed fire on understory vegetation in loblolly pine stands. In: Wood, G.W., ed. Prescribed fire and wildlife in southern forests conference. Georgetown, SC: Clemson University, Belle W. Baruch Institute: 143-153.

Lewis, C.E.; Harshbarger, T.J. 1976. Shrub and herbaceous vegetation after 20 years of prescribed burning in the South Carolina Coastal Plain. Journal of Range Management. 29: 13-18.

Loftis, D.L. 1990. A shelterwood method for regenerating red oak in the Southern Appalachians. Forest Science. 36(4): 917-929.

Loftis, D.L.; McGee, C.E., eds. 1993. Oak regeneration: serious problems, practical recommendations. Gen. Tech. Rep. SE-84. Asheville, NC: U.S. Department of Agriculture Forest Service, Southeastern Forest Experiment Station. 319 p.

Lorimer, C.G. 1993. Causes of the oak regeneration problem. In: Loftis, D.L.; McGee, C.E., eds. Oak regeneration: serious problems, practical recommendations. Gen. Tech. Rep. SE-84. Asheville, NC: U.S. Department of Agriculture Forest Service, Southeastern Forest Experiment Station: 14-39.

Lotti, T.; Klawitter, R.A.; LeGrande, W.P. 1960. Prescribed burning for understory control in loblolly pine stands of the Coastal Plain. Stat. Pap. 116. Asheville, NC: U.S. Department of Agriculture Forest Service, Southeastern Forest Experiment Station. 19 p.

Luken, J.O.; Shea, M. 2000. Repeated prescribed burning at Dinsmore Woods State Nature Preserve (Kentucky, USA): responses of the understory community. Natural Areas Journal. 20: 150-158.

Maslen, P. 1989. Response of immature oaks to prescribed fire in the North Carolina Piedmont. In: Miller, J.H., ed. Proceedings of the 5th biennial southern silviculture research conference. Gen. Tech. Rep. SE-34. Asheville, NC: U.S. Department of Agriculture Forest Service, Southeastern Forest Experiment Station: 259-266.

McGee, C.E. 1979. Fire and other factors related to oak regeneration. In: Fischer, B.C.; Holt, H.A., eds. Proceedings of the John S. Wright forestry conference. West Lafayette, IN: Purdue University, Department of Forestry and Natural Resources: 75-80.

McGee, C.E. 1980. The effect of fire on species dominance in young upland hardwood stands. In: Shropshire, F.; Sims, D., eds. Proceedings of the mid-south upland hardwood symposium. Technical Paper SA-TP-12. Atlanta, GA: U.S. Department of Agriculture Forest Service, Southeastern Area State and Private Forestry: 97-104.

McGee, G.G.; Leopold, D.J.; Nyland, R.D. 1995. Understory response to springtime prescribed fire in two New York transition oak forests. Forest Ecology and Management. 76: 149-168.

McKee, W.H. 1982. Changes in soil fertility following prescribed burning on Coastal Plains pine sites. Res. Pap. SE-234. U.S. Department of Agriculture Forest Service, Southeastern Forest Experiment Station.

Merritt, C.; Pope, P.E. 1991. The effect of environmental factors, including wildfire and prescribed burning, on the regeneration of oaks in Indiana. Bulletin 612. West Lafayette, IN: Purdue University Agricultural Experiment Station. 45 p.

Nowacki, G.J.; Abrams, M.D. 2008. The demise of fire and the mesophication of forests in the Eastern United States. BioScience. 58(2): 123-138.

Oliver, C.D.; Larson, B.C. 1990. Forest stand dynamics. New York City, NY: McGraw Hill. 520 p.

Patterson, W.P. 2006. The paleoecology of fire and oaks in eastern forests. In: Dickinson, M.B., ed. Fire in eastern oak forests: delivering science to land managers. Gen. Tech. Rep. NRS-P-1. Newtown Square, PA: U.S. Department of Agriculture Forest Service, Northern Research Station: 2-19.

Paulsell, L.K. 1957. Effects of burning on Ozark hardwood timberlands. Bulletin 640. Columbia, MO: University of Missouri Agricultural Experiment Station. 24 p.

Reich, P.B.; Abrams, M.D.; Ellsworth, D.S. [and others]. 1990. Fire affects ecophysiology and community dynamics of central Wisconsin oak forest regeneration. Ecology. 71: 2179-2190.

Ruffner, C.M. 2006. Understanding the evidence for historical fire across eastern forests. In: Dickinson, M.B., ed. Fire in eastern oak forests: delivering science to land managers. Gen. Tech. Rep. NRS-P-1. Newtown Square, PA: U.S. Department of Agriculture Forest Service, Northern Research Station: 40-48.

Sasseen, A.N.; Muzika, R.M. 2004. Timber harvesting, prescribed fire, and vegetation dynamics in the Missouri Ozarks. In: Yaussy, D.A.; Hix, D.M.; Long, R.P.; Goebel, P.C., eds. Proceedings of the 14th central hardwood forest conference. Gen. Tech. Rep. NE-316. Newtown Square, PA: Northeastern Forest Experiment Station: 179-192.

Schuler, T.M.; Gillespie, A.R. 2000. Temporal patterns of woody species diversity in a central Appalachian forest from 1856 to 1997. Journal of the Torrey Botanical Society. 127(2): 149-161.

Schuler, T.M.; Thomas-Van Gundy, M.; Adams, M.B.; Ford, W.M. 2013. Analysis of two pre-shelterwood prescribed fires in a mesic mixed-oak forest in West Virginia. In: Miller, G.W.; Schuler, T.M.; Gottschalk, K.W. [and others], eds. Proceedings of the 18th central hardwoods forest conference. Gen. Tech. Rep. NRS-P-117. Newtown Square, PA: U.S. Department of Agriculture Forest Service, Northern Research Station: 430-446.

Shumway, D.L.; Abrams, M.D.; Ruffner, C.M. 2001. A 400-year history of fire and oak recruitment in an old-growth oak forest in western Maryland. Canadian Journal of Forest Research. 31: 1437-1443.

Signell, S.A.; Abrams, M.D.; Hovis, J.C.; Henry, S.W. 2005. Impact of multiple fires on stand structure and tree regeneration in central Appalachian oak forests. Forest Ecology and Management. 218: 146-158.

Stottlemyer, A.D. 2011. Ecosystem responses to fuel reduction treatments in stands killed by southern pine beetle. Clemson, SC: Clemson University. 184 p. Ph.D. dissertation.

Stratton, R.L. 2007. Effects of long-term late winter prescribed fire on forest stand dynamics, small mammal populations, and habitat demographics in a Tennessee oak barrens. Knoxville, TN: University of Tennessee. 89 p. M.S. thesis.

Swan, F.R. 1970. Post-fire response of four plant communities in south-central New York State. Journal of Ecology. 51(6): 1074-1082.

Teuke, M.J.; Van Lear, D.H. 1982. Prescribed burning and oak advance regeneration in the southern Appalachians. Res. Pap. 30. Atlanta, GA: Georgia Forestry Commission. 24 p.

Thor, E.; Nichols, G.M. 1973. Some effects of fires on litter, soil, and hardwood regeneration. In: Proceedings of the 13th Tall Timbers fire ecology conference. Tallahasee, FL: Tall Timbers Research, Inc.: 317-329.

Van Lear, D.H.; Waldrop, T.A. 1991. Prescribed burning for regeneration. In: Duryea, M.L.; Dougherty, P.M., eds. Forest regeneration manual. Kluwer Academic Publishers: 235-250.

Waldrop, T.A.; Phillips, R.J.; Simon, D.A. 2010. Fuels and fire behavior in the southern Appalachian Mountains after fire and fire surrogate treatments. Forest Science. 56: 32-45.

Waldrop, T.A.; White, D.L.; Jones, S.M. 1992. Fire regimes for pine-grassland communities in the southeastern United States. Forest Ecology and Management. 47: 195-210.

Waldrop, T.A.; Yaussy, D.A.; Phillips, R.J. [and others]. 2008. Fuel reduction treatments affect stand structure of hardwood forests in western North Carolina and southern Ohio, USA. Forest Ecology and Management. 255: 3117-3129.

Wang, G.G.; Van Lear, D.H.; Bauerle, W.L. 2005. Effects of prescribed fires on first-year establishment of white oak (Quercus alba L.) seedlings in the upper Piedmont of South Carolina, USA. Forest Ecology and Management. 213: 328-337.

Ward, J.S.; Brose, P.H. 2004. Mortality, survival, and growth of individual stems after prescribed burning in recent hardwood clearcuts. In: Yaussy, D.A.; Hix, D.M.; Long, R.P.; Goebel, P.C., eds. Proceedings of the 14th central hardwoods forest conference. Gen. Tech. Rep. NE-316. Newtown Square, PA: U.S. Department of Agriculture Forest Service, Northeastern Forest Experiment Station: 193-199.

Ward, J.S.; Stephens, G.R. 1989. Long-term effects of a 1932 surface fire on stand structure in a Connecticut mixed hardwood forest. In: Rink, G.; Budelsky, C.A., eds. Proceedings of the 7th central hardwoods forest conference. Gen. Tech. Rep. NC-132. St Paul, MN: U.S. Department of Agriculture Forest Service, North Central Forest Experiment Station: 267-273.

Wendel, G.W.; Smith, H.C. 1986. Effects of a prescribed fire in a central Appalachian oak-hickory stand. Res. Pap. NE-594. Broomall, PA: U.S. Department of Agriculture Forest Service, Northeastern Forest Experiment Station. 8 p.

Wilkins, G.R.; Delcourt, P.A.; Delcourt, H.R. [and others]. 1991. Paleoecology of Kentucky since the last glacial maximum. Quaternary Research. 36: 224-239.

Will-Wolf, S. 1991. Role of fire in maintaining oaks in mesic oak maple forests. In: Proceedings of the oak resource of the upper midwest conference. Minneapolis, MN: University of Minnesota Extension Service: 27-33.

Woodall, C.W.; Morin, R.S.; Steinman, J.R.; Perry, C.H. 2008. Status of oak seedlings and saplings in the northern United States: implications for sustainability of oak forests. In: Jacobs, D.F.; Michler, C.H., eds. Proceedings of the 16th central hardwoods forest conference. Gen. Tech. Rep NRS-P-24. Newtown Square, PA: U.S. Department of Agriculture Forest Service, Northern Research Station: 535-542.

Yaussy, D.A.; Waldrop, T.A. 2010. Delayed mortality of eastern hardwoods after prescribed fire. In: Stanturf, J.A., ed. Proceedings of the 14th biennial southern silviculture research conference. Gen. Tech. Rep. SRS-121. Asheville, NC: U.S. Department of Agriculture Forest Service, Southern Research Station: 609-612.

Table 1—Prescribed fire papers reviewed for assessing fire effects on hardwood reproduction

Publication	State	Type of stand	Season-of-burn	Number of burns	Effect on oak
brecht & McCarthy 2006	OH	M	D	1	A
Co ns & Carson 2003	WV	M	D	1	N
Do an & Parker 2004	KY	M	D	1	A
E ott & others 2004	NC	M	D	1	A
Hunt ey & McGee 1983	AL	M	D	1	N
Johnson 1974	WI	M	D	1	N
Loft s 1990	GA	M	D	1	N
Teuke & Van Lear 1982	SC	M	D	1	A
Wende & Sm th 1986	WV	M	D	1	N
Arthur & others 1998	KY	M	D	2	N
Barnes & Van Lear 1998	SC	M	D, G	2	P
Frank n & others 2003	KY	M	D	2	A
Iverson & others 2008	OH	M	D	2	P
McGee & others 1995	NY	M	D	2	A
Merr tt & Pope 1991	IN	M	D	2	A
Schu er & others 2013	WV	M	D	2	P
Wa drop & others 2008	NC	M	D	2	P
Wa drop & others 2008	OH	M	D	2	N
Wang & others 2005	SC	M	D	2	P
W -Wo f 1991	WI	M	D	2	A
A exander & others 2008	KY	M	D	3	N
B ankensh p & Arthur 2006	KY	M	D	3	A
DeSe m & others 1991	TN	M	D	10+	P
Dey & Hartman 2005	MO	M	D	4	P
Fan & others 2012	MO	M	D	4	P
G bert & others 2003	KY	M	D	3	A
Green & others 2010	KY	M	D	3	A
Hudd e & Pa ardy 1996	MO	M	D	10+	P
Hutch nson and others 2005a, b	OH	M	D	4	P
Hutch nson & others 2012	OH	M	D	4	P
Luken & Shea 2000	KY	M	D	3	N
Pau se 1957	MO	M	D	10+	P
Sassen & Muz ka 2004	MO	M	D	4	P
S gne & others 2005	PA	M	D	4	P
Stratton 2007	TN	M	D	10+	P
Thor & N cho s 1973	TN	M	D	10+	P
Brose & others 2007	PA	M	G	1	N
Gottscha k & others[a]	PA	M	G	1	N
Hunt ey & McGee 1981, 1983	AL	Y	D	1	N
McGee 1979, 1980	AL	Y	D	1	N
Re ch & others 1990	WI	Y	D	1	A
Brose 2010	VA	Y	D, G	1	P
Brose 2013	PA	Y	G	1	P
Brose & others 1999	VA	Y	D, G	1	P
Brose & Van Lear 1998, 2004	VA	Y	D, G	1	P
Ge s nger & others 1989	SC	Y	G	1	A
Keyser & others 1996	VA	Y	G	1	P
Stott emyer 2011	SC	Y	G	1	P
Ward & Brose 2004	CT	Y	G	1	P
Brose[a]	PA	Y	G	2	P
Kruger & Re ch 1997	WI	Y	G	2	P
Abrams & Johnson 2013	PA	I	D	1	N
Carve & Maxey 1969	WV	I	D	1	P
Mas en 1989	NC	I	D	1	A
Ward & Stevens 1989	CT	I	G	1	P

[a] Unpublished data on file at the Forestry Sciences Lab in Irvine, PA or Morgantown, WV.

Studies are organized by stand type (M=Mature, Y=Young, I=Immature), season-of-burn (D=Dormant, G=Growing), and number of fires (1, 2, or >2).

Effect on oak abbreviations are A=Ambiguous, N=Negative, P=Positive.

Table 2—Distribution of fire-oak publications by the number of burns and the effect on oak regeneration process for studies conducted in mature stands

Effect on Oak	1	2	>2	Total
	|--------------- Number of Fires ---------------|		
Positive	0	5	12	17
Ambiguous	4	4	3	11
Negative	7	2	2	11
Total	11	11	17	39

Note the trend ine ustrat ng the ncreas ng y pos t ve effects on oak as the number of fires ncrease from one to more than two.

INTRODUCTION

Table 3—Distribution of fire-oak publications by the number of burns and the effect on oak regeneration process for studies conducted in young stand

Effect on Oak	1	2	>2	Total
	|--------------- Number of Fires ---------------|		
Positive	8	2	0	10
Ambiguous	2	0	0	2
Negative	4	0	0	4
Total	14	2	0	16

Note the c uster ng of stud es report ng pos t ve effects on oak after just one or two burns.

REPEATED FIRES, CANOPY GAPS, AND TREE REGENERATION IN APPALACHIAN MIXED OAK FORESTS

Todd F. Hutchinson, Robert P. Long, Joanne Rebbeck,
Elaine Kennedy Sutherland, and Daniel A. Yaussy[1]

Abstract—We studied the response of tree regeneration to a sequence of several low-intensity prescribed fires followed by canopy gap formation in southern Ohio. Advance reproduction was recorded in 52 gaps (average size = four dead canopy trees) that formed following a white oak decline event, 13 years after fires began and 5 years after the gaps had formed. Of the 52 gaps, 28 were in three burned stands and 24 were in three unburned stands. Unburned gaps were being filled by shade-tolerant saplings and poles. In contrast, shade-tolerant saplings had been greatly reduced in the burned stands and larger oak advance reproduction (>2 feet tall) was much more abundant in burned gaps, as was sassafras. Advance reproduction of shade-tolerant species was equally abundant in burned and unburned gaps. Results indicate that the regeneration potential of oaks can be improved with multiple prescribed fires followed by the creation of canopy gaps.

Recent analyses of data from the U.S. Forest Service's Forest Inventory and Analysis Program (FIA) indicate shifts in forest composition within the central hardwoods region, with oaks (*Quercus*) declining in some areas and other species such as red maple (*Acer rubrum*) increasing (Fei and Steiner 2007, Hanberry 2013). FIA data show that in Ohio oaks continue to dominate the overstory in many stands, but shade-tolerant species typically dominate the midstory and understory (Widmann and others 2009). In these stands, overstory oaks that die or are removed through harvesting will often be replaced by other species unless effective management strategies to favor oak regeneration are implemented.

In the past 20 years, there has been a growing interest in using prescribed fire to sustain oak forests (Arthur and others 2012, Brose and others 2008). Under certain circumstances, prescribed fire can improve the competitive status of oak regeneration relative to their competitors when a greater proportion of oaks survive and sprout after fire (Brose 2010, Brose and Van Lear 1998). The ability of oak seedlings to sprout from the root collar after topkill is a function of resources devoted to root development rather than height growth (Johnson and others 2009). Additionally for oak seedlings, the relatively deep location of root collar in the soil provides greater protection from fire damage (Brose and Van Lear 2004).

However, studies of prescribed fire effects on oak regeneration have had mixed results. Recently, Brose and others (2013) conducted a meta-analysis of 32 studies that reported the effects of prescribed fire in oak forests. They found that prescribed fire had the greatest positive impact on oak regeneration when burning was conducted during the growing season several years after a partial timber harvest, and they found that prescribed fires in closed canopy forests generally did not have a positive impact on oak regeneration in the short term, particularly when only a single fire was applied.

In 1995, we began a long-term study in southern Ohio mixed-oak forests to determine the effects of repeated prescribed fires on forest structure, tree regeneration, and other ecosystem properties (Sutherland and Hutchinson 2003). By 2002, repeated low-intensity dormant-season fires (2X or 4X) had greatly reduced the density of shade-tolerant saplings, thinned the midstory to a lesser degree, and had very little effect on the density of overstory trees (Hutchinson and others 2005). Oak seedlings generally remained small (<1 foot tall) as canopy cover continued to be >90 percent. We concluded that fire alone had not improved the competitive position of oak regeneration. In 2003, a white oak (*Quercus alba*) decline event became apparent at the Vinton Furnace State Experimental Forest (VFSEF), where two of the study sites were located. The death of overstory white oaks created small canopy gaps.

[1]Todd F. Hutchinson, Research Ecologist, USDA Forest Service, Northern Research Station, Delaware, OH 43015

Robert P. Long, Research Plant Pathologist, USDA Forest Service, Northern Research Station, Irvine, PA 16329

Joanne Rebbeck, Research Plant Physiologist, USDA Forest Service, Northern Research Station, Delaware, OH 43015

Elaine Kennedy Sutherland, Supervisory Research Biologist, USDA Forest Service, Rocky Mountain Research Station, Missoula, MT 59801

Daniel A. Yaussy, Research Forester Emeritus, USDA Forest Service, Northern Research Station, Delaware, OH 43015

Citation for proceedings: Waldrop, Thomas A., ed. 2014. Proceedings, Wildland Fire in the Appalachians: Discussions among Managers and Scientists. Gen. Tech. Rep. SRS-199. Asheville, NC: U.S. Department of Agriculture Forest Service, Southern Research Station. 208 p.

Several years after the gaps had formed, we observed the presence of larger oak advance reproduction, stems 2 to 4 feet tall, in several of the gaps that were located within stands that had been burned in the prescribed fire study. These canopy gaps provided an opportunity to study the response of advance reproduction to a series of repeated fires followed by the creation of small canopy openings. The sequence and type of disturbance events—repeated fires followed by small-scale gap formation—to the best of our knowledge had not been studied previously in oak forests.

The main objective was to determine whether the competitive position of oak regeneration, based on its size and abundance relative to competitors, was different in burned gaps than in unburned gaps. We also compared other characteristics of the burned and unburned gaps, such as soil moisture, gap size, sapling and pole density, and understory light levels. This paper summarizes the major findings of a recently published journal article (Hutchinson and others 2012a).

METHODS

Study Area

The study was located in the Vinton Furnace State Experimental Forest (VFSEF), Vinton County, OH. The VFSEF is owned by the Ohio Department of Natural Resources, Division of Forestry. The unglaciated landscape consists of narrow ridges and steep slopes. Bedrocks are primarily sandstones and siltstones. Soils are mostly sandy loams and silt loams that are moderately deep (20 to 40 inches to bedrock), acidic, and have low water-holding capacity (Lemaster and Gilmore 2004). Site quality is highly variable across the landscape. Black oak (*Quercus velutina*) site indices range from 55 feet on the driest ridges and upper south facing slopes to 80 feet on lower north facing slopes and stream terraces (Carmean 1965, Iverson and others 1997).

The entire landscape of the VFSEF was clearcut in the middle to late 1800s to provide charcoal to fuel iron production at the Vinton and Eagle Furnaces. Fires occurred frequently from 1880 to 1930 when forest stands were redeveloping after clearcutting (Hutchinson and others 2008, Sutherland 1997). However, fire suppression eliminated nearly all wildfires after 1935. Today's mature forests are dominated by oaks, primarily white oak, chestnut oak (*Quercus prinus*), and black oak, and hickories (*Carya* spp.). Yellow-poplar (*Liriodendron tulipifera*) and northern red oak (*Quercus rubra*) are common on higher quality sites. In the midstory (trees 4 to 10 inches diameter at breast height [dbh]), red maple is often prominent, and sugar maple (*Acer saccharum*)

is also common on mesic sites. In the understory (trees <4 inches dbh), one or more shade-tolerant species are typically abundant, including red maple, sugar maple, blackgum, (*Nyssa sylvatica*), American beech (*Fagus grandifolia*), sourwood (*Oxydendrum arboreum*), and musclewood (*Carpinus caroliniana*).

The white oak decline event was characterized by the death of overstory white oaks, usually in patches of several trees and located on middle and lower slope positions. A combination of several factors, including insect defoliations, drought, excessive rainfall, and the exotic root rotting fungi *Phytophthora cinnamomi*, were implicated in the decline (Balci and others 2009, Nagle and others 2010). The white oak decline created small canopy gaps located throughout the forest.

Study Design

In 1995, a long-term study of prescribed fire was installed at two sites on the VFSEF and two additional sites located in Lawrence County, OH (Hutchinson and others 2005). From that larger study, we selected three burned stands and two unburned stands at VFSEF, where the oak decline even had occurred, for the present study of tree regeneration in canopy gaps. To increase sample size within the unburned treatment, we added a third unburned stand within VFSEF that was being used as an untreated control in another study (see Waldrop and others 2008). Pretreatment plot data show that oaks and hickories dominated the overstory, shade-tolerant species dominated the sapling layer, and oak plus hickory seedling densities averaged more than 2,000 per acre (table 1).

Among the three burned stands, two were burned five times and one was burned three times, all from 1996 through 2005 (table 2). In each burned stand, one of the fires occurred after gaps were formed. All but one fire was conducted in the spring dormant season, late March to mid-April, prior to substantial understory greening; the single fall fire occurred in early November. Fires were generally low-intensity, with flame lengths of 1 to 2 feet, and caused little mortality of overstory trees (Hutchinson and others, 2012b).

For this study, we selected 28 gaps in the three burned stands and 24 gaps in the three unburned stands. When choosing gaps to include in the study, we generally avoided single tree gaps. Gaps were on a variety of aspects, but nearly all were on midslope and lower slope positions. By chance, none of the gaps occurred within the 9 or 10 permanent vegetation plots located in each stand. To characterize soil moisture for each gap, based on its GPS-located landscape position, we used the Integrated Moisture Index (IMI) of Iverson and others (1997).

Field Data Collection

All data were collected in summer 2008. First, we established an approximate center point in each gap and flagged the perimeter of the gap. We then measured the length and width of the gap to estimate its area. All data were collected in metric units, but are reported here in English units. Within the perimeter of each gap, we recorded the species and diameter of standing dead trees ≥3.9 inches dbh, and also counted, by species, the number of saplings plus poles (stems 1.2 to 7.9 inches dbh). From the gap center point, we established four subplots, each 16.4 by 6.6 feet, to record advance reproduction. Each subplot was located halfway between the gap center and perimeter, along the length and width axes. In the subplots, we counted the number of stems of advance reproduction by species, in three size classes: 1.0 to 2.0 feet tall, 2.0 to 4.6 feet tall, and 4.6 feet tall to 1.1 inches dbh. Within each gap, we also measured light as a percentage of full sunlight, with a Decagon AccuPAR LP 80 ceptometer. For further details on field data collection, see Hutchinson and others (2012a).

Data Analysis

To test for significant differences between gaps in burned and unburned stands, we used generalized linear mixed models. Stand was the experimental unit and gaps within stands were the sampling units. Stand was treated as a random effect nested within the fixed effect of fire. We tested whether unburned and burned gaps were significantly different (p <0.05) in several characteristics: soil moisture (IMI), size (area in acres), the number and size (dbh) of dead trees, sapling and pole density, and percentage of full sunlight. We also tested for significant differences in the density of several major species and species groups (oaks, hickories, sassafras, shade-tolerant species, other species), between burned and unburned gaps. A more comprehensive description of data analyses can be found in Hutchinson and others (2012a).

RESULTS

Characteristics of Gaps

Gaps in burned stands were similar (p > 0.05) to those in unburned stands, with respect to soil moisture (IMI), gap size, number of dead trees per gap, and dbh of dead trees (fig. 1). Overall, the mean IMI was 46.2, indicating intermediate soil moisture levels (Iverson and Prasad 2003). Gaps were small, averaging 0.06 acres (range = 0.03 to 0.12 acres). The mean number of dead white oak trees per gap was 4.0 (range = 1 to 10) and these trees averaged 16.6 inches dbh (range = 6.8 to 31.0).

Though similar in size and soil moisture, burned gaps had significantly fewer saplings and poles (p = 0.002), compared to unburned gaps (fig. 1). In unburned gaps, sapling and pole density averaged 404 stems per acre (range = 205 to 644); the most abundant species were American beech, red maple, sugar maple and blackgum. In burned gaps, sapling and pole density averaged 63 stems per acre and all but one burned gap had less than 200 stems per acre. Understory light levels were also significantly greater (p = 0.033) in burned gaps than in unburned gaps (fig. 1). Approximately 5 years after the gaps had formed, burned gaps averaged 18.7 percent of full sunlight compared to 7.3 percent in unburned gaps.

Advance Reproduction

In burned gaps, the density of advance reproduction (stems 12 inches tall to 1.1 inches dbh) for all species combined was more than twice that found in unburned gaps. Stem densities averaged 8,738 and 3,653 per acre in burned and unburned gaps, respectively. Among the major species and species groups, the density of oaks (p = 0.036) and sassafras (*Sassafras albidum*, p = 0.002) were significantly greater in burned gaps than in unburned gaps, while the density of shade-tolerant species was not different (p = 0.810) between burned and unburned gaps (fig. 2). Across the burned and unburned gaps, eight species comprised 96 percent of stems in the shade-tolerant group. These species were, in descending order of average density: red maple, white ash (*Fraxinus americana*), musclewood, blackgum, flowering dogwood (*Cornus florida*), American beech, sourwood, and downy serviceberry (*Amelanchier arborea*). For hickories, the average density in burned gaps was 2.2 times greater than in unburned gaps; however, that difference approached but did not meet statistical significance (p = 0.086).

The average density of oaks was 3.6 times greater in burned gaps (3,670 stems per acre) than in unburned gaps (1,021 stems per acre). Among the oaks in the burned gaps, white oak was the most abundant species, making up, on average, 67 percent of all oak stems, followed by black oak (17 percent), chestnut oak (7 percent), scarlet oak (*Quercus coccinea*, 6 percent), and northern red oak (3 percent). White oak was also the most abundant oak in the unburned gaps, making up 57 percent of oak stems.

In burned gaps, the greater densities of oak and hickory (combined) advance reproduction resulted from greater numbers of larger stems. While smaller oak and hickory stems (1 to 2 feet height) were equally abundant in burned and unburned gaps (p = 0.537), larger oak and hickory (2 feet height to 1.1 inches dbh) were significantly more abundant in burned gaps (p = 0.018, fig. 3). Burned gaps had an average density of 2,643 larger oak and hickory stems per acre, while unburned gaps averaged 318 larger stems per acre.

Among individual gaps in the burned stands, densities of larger oak and hickory were consistently high: 20 of 28 burned gaps had more than 2,000 larger stems per acre (fig. 4). Similarly, in unburned stands, densities of larger oak plus hickory were consistently low; nearly all (22 of 24) unburned gaps had fewer than 2,000 stems per acre. Larger sassafras occurred at very high densities in several burned gaps, but its abundance was more variable than oak and hickory; larger sassafras were absent from more than one third of burned gaps (fig. 4). In addition, the density of larger oak plus hickory stems was more than twice that of shade-tolerant species in over half of the burned gaps.

For the largest size class of advance reproduction, stems 4.6 feet tall to 1.1 inches dbh, oaks and hickories averaged 806 stems per acre in burned gaps compared to 55 per acre in unburned gaps. Oaks and hickories in this size class were present in 82 percent of the burned gaps but occurred in only 20 percent of unburned gaps. In burned gaps, the density of oaks and hickories >4.6 feet tall was 2.5 times greater than that of shade-tolerant species. By contrast, in unburned gaps, shade-tolerant stems were 5.3 times more abundant than oaks and hickories.

DISCUSSION

In this study we found that a series of low-intensity fires, conducted over about a decade, coupled with small canopy openings formed 7 to 8 years after fires began, resulted in high densities of larger (>2 feet tall) oak advance reproduction. Gaps in the burned stands had 84 percent fewer shade-tolerant saplings and poles and more sunlight was reaching the understory even 5 years after gap formation. The larger oak advance reproduction that developed consistently in the burned gaps will have a higher probability of being competitive after a stand-level disturbance compared to the smaller oak reproduction in the unburned stands (Loftis 1990, Sander 1971). The single fire that occurred after gap formation in each of the burned stands may also have been important in the development of larger oak reproduction (Brose and Van Lear 1998). However, because we did not follow individual seedlings through the sequence of repeated fires, gap formation, and the single fire after gap formation, the relative importance of the pre-gap fires vs. the post-gap fire is unclear.

In our study sites, oak and hickory seedlings were present at moderate densities (>2,000 per acre) before the prescribed fire treatments began, which was likely important for the ultimate development of larger oaks after the sequence of fires and gap formation (Johnson and others 2009). However, in a more mesic oak forest in West Virginia, with fewer and smaller oak seedlings,

Schuler and others (2013) also found that repeated preharvest prescribed fires favored the development of larger oak reproduction. In their study, two dormant-season fires greatly reduced the dense layer of shade-tolerant saplings that had been present. Soon after the fires, a bumper crop of northern red oak acorns resulted in large numbers of new seedlings. Those new red oak seedlings grew larger in the burned areas where the sapling layer had been topkilled than in adjacent unburned areas. After the mast event, further fires were withheld to allow the new oak seedlings to develop. Their study highlights the importance of timing prescribed fires with acorn crops, particularly in mesic forests where oak seedlings fail to accumulate over time.

In addition to the oaks, sassafras advance reproduction was more abundant in burned gaps than in unburned gaps. Advance reproduction of sassafras often exhibits clonal growth (Burns and Honkala 1990). When fire topkills sassafras stems, densities typically increase as multiple new root sprouts are initiated (Alexander and others 2008). In our study, we hypothesize that the higher densities of sassafras in burned gaps resulted from clonal expansion and root sprouting after fires. Through the course of the prescribed burn study, newly germinated sassafras seedlings were seldom observed after fires (T. Hutchinson, personal observation). Although sassafras is abundant in a number of the burned gaps, it is unclear whether it would be a long-term competitor of the oaks if a stand-level disturbance were to occur. In the study region, advance reproduction of sassafras is common, particularly on drier sites, but sassafras is uncommon in the overstory of mature stands.

Management Considerations

In management areas where timber harvesting is not desired or permitted, our findings show that periodic prescribed fires can help create conditions favorable for the development of larger oak reproduction in relatively small canopy openings. However, the eventual recruitment of oak into the overstory may require larger gaps than those formed in our study (Loftis 2004). In stands where timber harvesting is planned, repeated fires conducted prior to the harvest could favor dominance by oaks after the harvest by reducing competition from shade-tolerant saplings. This will be most effective when oak seedlings are present at moderate densities initially and are also large enough to resprout after fires. In addition to prescribed fire, herbicide application may be necessary to kill larger saplings and poles (>6 inches dbh), those that are resistant to topkill by fire. However, after repeated fires have greatly reduced sapling densities, much less effort and cost are required to find and apply herbicide to the remaining stems not topkilled by fire.

ACKNOWLEDGMENTS

We thank Tom Waldrop and the conference committee for inviting us to present our research at the Wildland Fire in the Appalachians Conference. We thank William Borovicka, Levi Miller, Richard Craig, Timothy Fox, Matthew Peters, Zachary Moor, and Jonathan Schaeffer for assistance in the field. We thank Joan Jolliff for data entry. We thank John Stanovick for statistical consultation and Stacy Clark and Melissa Thomas Van Gundy for technical reviews. We thank our land management partner, the Ohio Division of Forestry.

LITERATURE CITED

Alexander, H.D.; Arthur, M.A.; Loftis, D.L.; Green, S.R. 2008. Survival and growth of upland oak and co-occurring competitor seedlings following single and repeated prescribed fires. Forest Ecology and Management. 256: 1021-1030.

Arthur, M.A.; Alexander, H.D.; Dey, D.C. [and others]. 2012. Refining the oak-fire hypothesis for management of oak-dominated forests in the Eastern United States. Journal of Forestry. 10: 257-266.

Balci, Y.; Long, R.P.; Balser, D.; MacDonald, W.L. 2009. Involvement of *Phytophthora* species in white oak (*Q. alba*) decline in southern Ohio. Forest Pathology. 40: 430-442.

Brose, P.H. 2010. Long-term effects of single prescribed fires on hardwood regeneration in oak shelterwood stands. Forest Ecology and Management. 260:1516-1524.

Brose, P.H.; Dey, D.C.; Phillips, R.J.; Waldrop, T.A. 2013. A meta-analysis of the fire-oak hypothesis: does prescribed burning promote oak reproduction in eastern North America? Forest Science. 59: 322-334.

Brose, P.H.; Gottschalk, K.W.; Horsley, S.B. [and others]. 2008. Prescribing regeneration treatments for mixed oak forests in the mid-Atlantic region. Gen. Tech. Rep. NRS-33. Newtown Square, PA: U.S. Department of Agriculture Forest Service, Northern Research Station. 90 p.

Brose, P.H.; Van Lear, D.H. 1998. Responses of hardwood advance regeneration to seasonal prescribed fires in oak dominated shelterwood stands. Canadian Journal of Forest Research. 28: 331-339.

Brose, P.H.; Van Lear, D.H. 2004. Survival of hardwood regeneration during prescribed fires: the importance of root development and root collar location. In: Spetich, M.A., ed. Upland oak ecology symposium: history, current conditions, and sustainability. Gen. Tech. Rep. SRS-73. Asheville, NC: U.S. Department of Agriculture Forest Service, Sothern Research Station: 123-127.

Burns, R.M.; Honkala, B.H., tech. coords. 1990. Silvics of North America volume 2, Hardwoods. Agric. Handb. 654. Washington, DC: U.S. Department of Agriculture Forest Service. 877 p.

Carmean, W.H. 1965. Black oak site quality in relation to soil and topography in southeastern Ohio. Soil Science Society of America Proceedings. 29: 308-312.

Fei, S.; Steiner, K. 2007. Evidence for increasing red maple abundance in the Eastern United States. Forest Science. 53: 473-477.

Hanberry, B.B. 2013. Changing eastern broadleaf, southern mixed, and northern mixed forest ecosystems of the eastern United States. Forest Ecology and Management. 306: 171-178.

Hutchinson, T.F.; Long, R.P.; Ford, R.D.; Sutherland, E.K. 2008. Fire history and the establishment of oaks and maples in second growth forests. Canadian Journal of Forest Research. 38: 391-403.

Hutchinson, T.F.; Long, R.P.; Rebbeck, J. [and others]. 2012a. Repeated prescribed fires alter gap phase regeneration in mixed oak forests. Canadian Journal of Forest Research. 42: 303-314.

Hutchinson, T.F.; Sutherland, E.K.; Yaussy, D.A. 2005. Effects of repeated fires on the structure, composition, and regeneration of mixed oak forests in Ohio. Forest Ecology and Management. 218: 210-228.

Hutchinson, T.F.; Yaussy, D.A.; Long, R.P. [and others]. 2012b. Long-term (13-year) effects of repeated prescribed fires on stand structure and tree regeneration in mixed-oak forests. Forest Ecology and Management. 286: 87-100.

Iverson, L.R.; Dale, M.E.; Scott, C.T.; Prasad, A. 1997. A GIS-derived integrated moisture index to predict forest composition and productivity of Ohio forests (U.S.A.). Landscape Ecology. 12: 331-348.

Iverson, L.R.; Prasad A. 2003. A GIS-derived integrated moisture index. In: Sutherland, E.K.; Hutchinson, T.F., eds. Characteristics of mixed oak forest ecosystems in southern Ohio prior to the reintroduction of fire. Gen. Tech. Rep. NE-299. Newtown Square, PA: U.S. Department of Agriculture Forest Service, Northeastern Research Station: 29-41.

Johnson, P.S.; Shifley, S.R.; Rogers, R. 2009. The ecology and silviculture of oaks, 2nd edition. New York, NY: CABI International. 580 p.

Lemaster, D.D.; Gilmore, G.M. 2004. Soil survey of Vinton County, Ohio. U.S. Department of Agriculture Natural Resources Conservation Service and Forest Service. 358 p.

Loftis, D.L. 1990. Predicting post-harvest performance of advance red oak reproduction in the southern Appalachians. Forest Science. 36: 908-916.

Loftis, D.L. 2004. Upland oak regeneration and management. In: Spetich, M.A., ed. Upland oak ecology symposium: history, current conditions, and sustainability. Gen. Tech. Rep. SRS-73. Asheville, NC: U.S. Department of Agriculture Forest Service, Southern Research Station: 163-167.

Nagle, A.M.; Long, R.P.; Maden, L.V.; Bonello, P. 2010. Association of *Phytophthora cinnamomi* with white oak decline in southern Ohio. Plant Disease. 94: 1026-1034.

Sander, I.L. 1971. Height growth of new oak sprouts depends on size of advance regeneration. Journal of Forestry. 69: 809-811.

Schuler, T.M.; Thomas-Van Gundy, M.; Adams, M.B.; Ford, W.M. 2013. Analysis of two pre-shelterwood prescribed fires in a mesic mixed-oak forest in West Virginia. In: Miller, G.W.; Schuler, T.M.; Gottschalk, K.W. [and others], eds. Proceedings of the 18th central hardwoods forest conference. Gen. Tech. Rep. NRS-P-117. Newtown Square, PA: U.S. Department of Agriculture Forest Service, Northern Research Station: 430-446.

Sutherland, E.K. 1997. The history of fire in a southern Ohio second growth mixed oak forest. In: Pallardy, S.G.; Cecich, R.A.; Garrett, H.E.; Johnson, P.S., eds. Proceedings, 11th Central Hardwoods Forest Conference. Gen. Tech. Rep. NC-188. St. Paul, MN: U.S. Department of Agriculture Forest Service, North Central Forest Experiment Station: 172-183.

Sutherland, E.K.; Hutchinson, T.F. 2003. Characteristics of mixed oak forest ecosystems in southern Ohio prior to the reintroduction of fire. Gen. Tech. Rep. NE-299. Newtown Square, PA: U.S. Department of Agriculture Forest Service, Northeastern Research Station. 159 p.

Waldrop, T.A.; Yaussy, D.A.; Phillips, R.J. [and others]. 2008. Fuel reduction treatments affect stand structure of hardwood forests in western North Carolina and southern Ohio, USA. Forest Ecology and Management. 255: 3117-3129.

Widmann, R.H.; Balser, D.; Barnett, C. [and others]. 2009. Ohio Forests 2006. Resour. Bull. NRS-36. Newtown Square, PA: United States Department of Agriculture Forest Service, Northern Research Station. 119 p.

Table 1—Characteristics of the six stands before prescribed fire treatments were applied

Stand	Area (acres)	Overstory[a] Basal area (ft^2/ac)	Basal area (% oak hickory)	Saplings[b] Density (stems/ac)	Density (% tolerant)	Seedlings[c] Oak hickory (stems/ac)
Arch Rock unburned	59	113	83	812	87	5578
Watch Rock unburned	49	113	82	675	96	2159
REMA unburned	57	120	82	837	97	4049
Arch Rock 3X	59	119	91	766	96	4228
Arch Rock 5X	79	124	77	866	94	2834
Watch Rock 5X	77	102	82	724	78	3959

Note: Vegetat on data were co ected n 1995 from n ne 0.3 acre p ots n a stands other than REMA unburned, where data were co ected n 2000 from ten 0.25 acre p ots.

[a]Trees >3.9 nches d.b.h.

[b]Trees 4.6 feet he ght to 3.9 nches d.b.h.

[c]A stems <4.6 feet he ght.

Table 2—Dates of the 13 prescribed fires in relation to canopy gap formation

Stand	Before gap formation 1996	1997	1998	1999	After gap formation 2004	2005
Arch Rock 3X	April 18	–	–	March 26	–	April 15
Arch Rock 5X	April 19	April 2	April 6	March 26	April 17	–
Watch Rock 5X	April 21	April 3	April 6	March 27	November 9	–

– Dashes represent no fire occured n that ocat on dur ng that year.

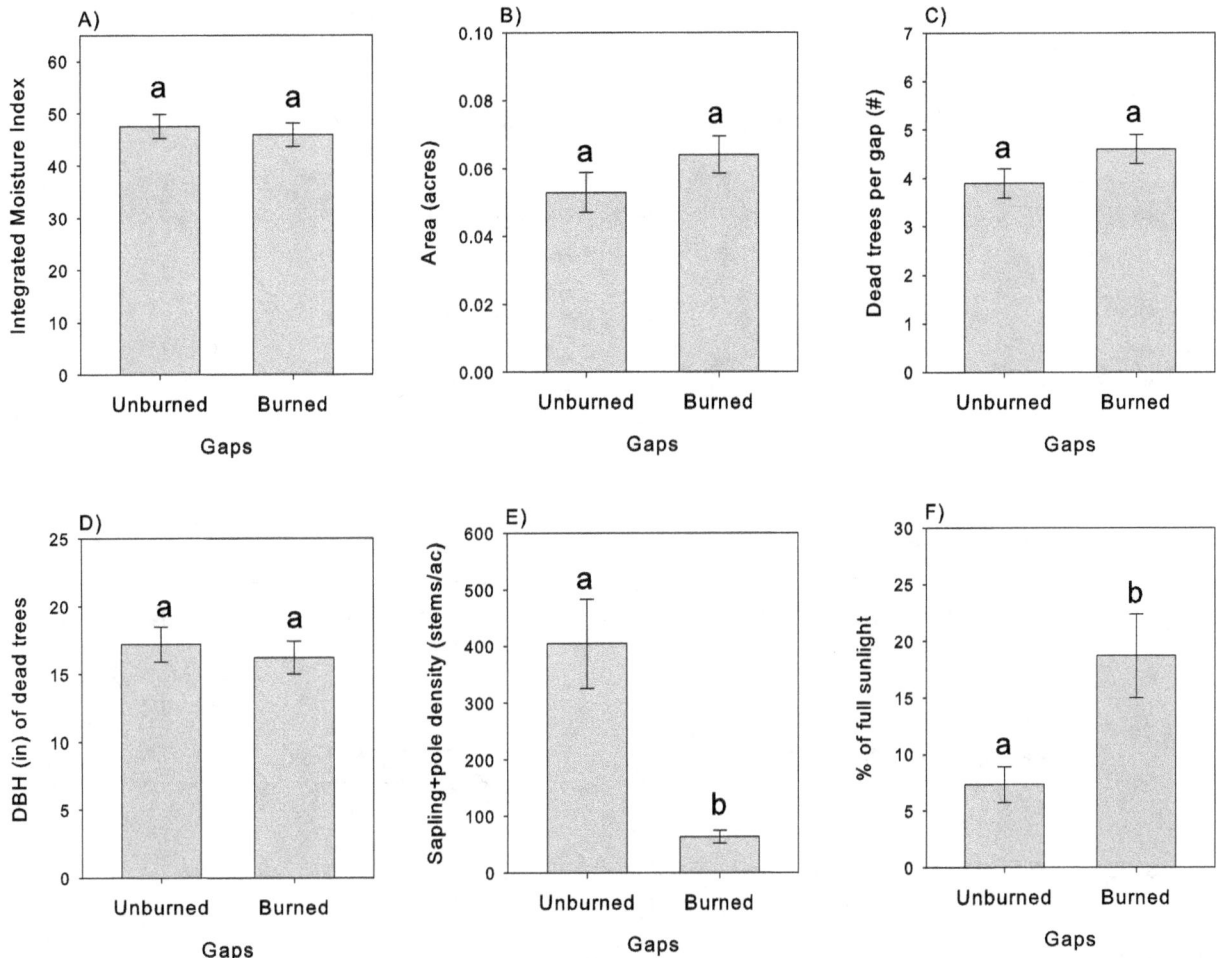

Figure 1—Mean values (±1 standard error) in unburned and burned gaps for A) Integrated Moisture Index (0 to 100 scale), B) area, C) number of dead trees per gap, D) dbh of dead trees, E) density of saplings and poles (stems 1.2 to 7.9 inches dbh), F) percentage of full sunlight. In each graph, different lower case letters above the two bars indicate a significant difference ($p < 0.05$) between unburned and burned gaps.

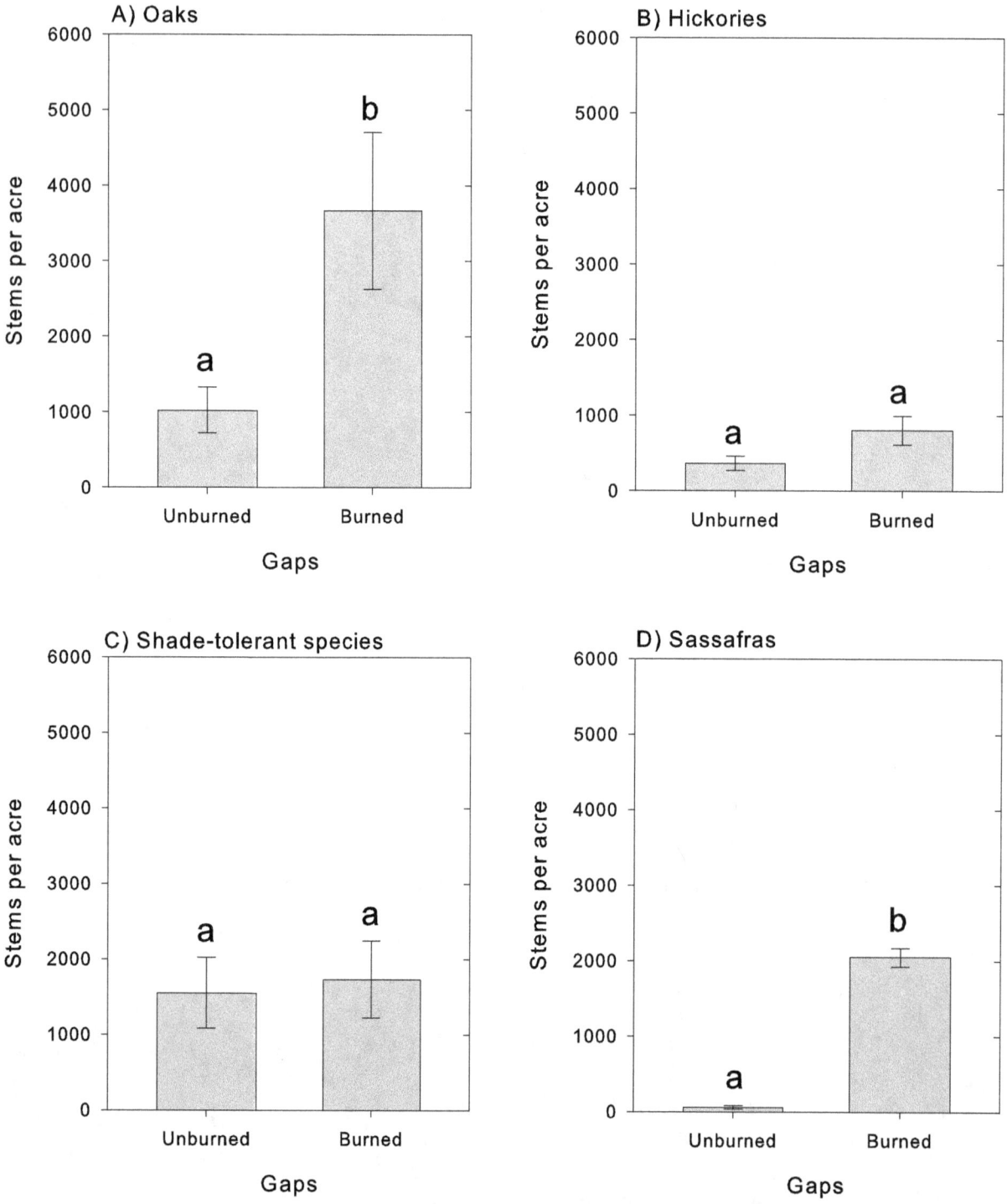

Figure 2—Mean values (±1 standard error) in unburned and burned gaps for the density of advance reproduction (stems 1 foot tall to 1.1 inches dbh) for four major species or species groups: A) oaks, B) hickories, C) shade-tolerant species, and D) sassafras. In each graph, different lower case letters above the two bars indicate a significant difference (p < 0.05) between unburned and burned gaps.

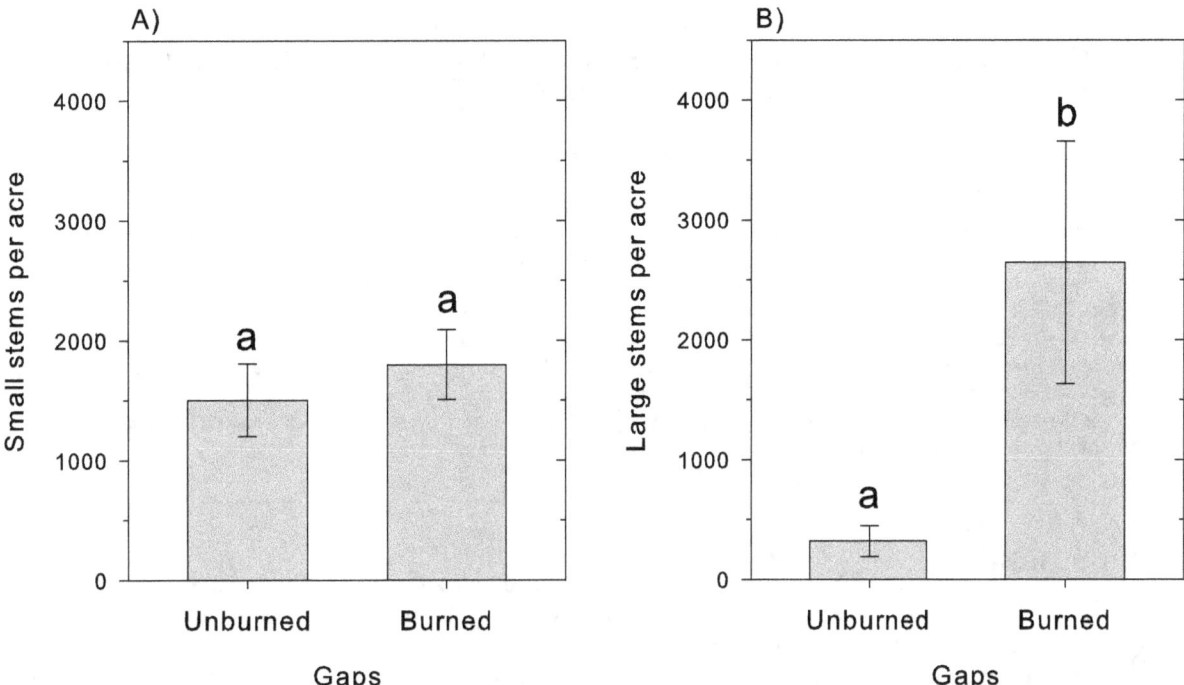

Figure 3—Mean values (±1 standard error) in unburned and burned gaps for the density of oak hickory advance reproduction for A) smaller stems (1 to 2 feet tall) and B) larger stems (2 feet tall to 1.1 inches dbh). In each graph, different lower case letters above the two bars indicate a significant difference (p < 0.05) between unburned and burned gaps.

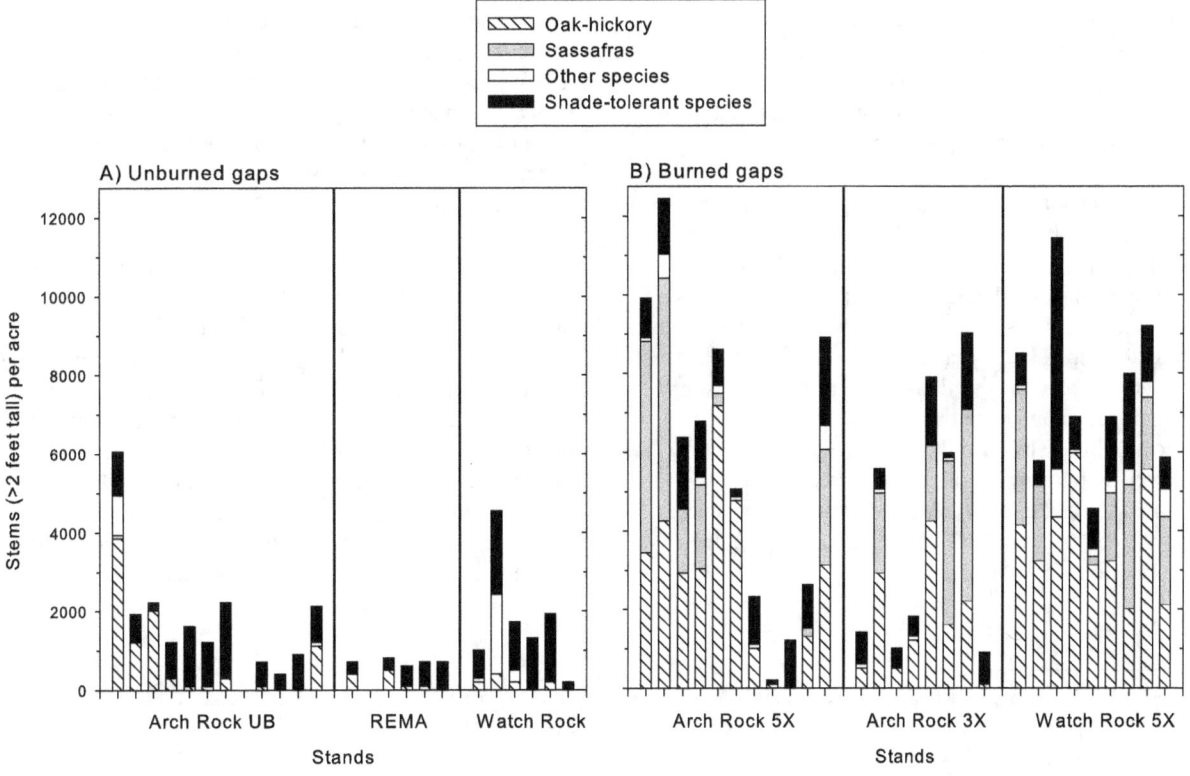

Figure 4—The density of larger advance reproduction (stems 2 feet tall to 1.1 inches dbh) in each gap for four major species groups in A) unburned gaps and B) burned gaps.

THE NATIONAL FIRE AND FIRE SURROGATE STUDY: VEGETATION CHANGES OVER 11 YEARS OF FUEL REDUCTION TREATMENTS IN THE SOUTHERN APPALACHIAN MOUNTAINS

Thomas A. Waldrop, Helen H. Mohr, Ross J. Phillips, and Dean M. Simon[1]

Abstract—At the Appalachian site of the National Fire and Fire Surrogate Study, prescribed burning was repeated three times and chainsaw felling of shrubs was done twice between 2002 and 2012. Goals were to reduce fuel loading and to promote restoration of an open woodland community. Chainsaw felling created a vertical fuel break, but the effect was temporary, and no restoration goals for other vegetation were achieved. Prescribed burning opened the canopy only slightly and supported graminoids and oak regeneration for a short time after each burn. The combination of mechanical and burning treatments provided open canopies and removed the shrub layer. Graminoid cover increased and oak regeneration was abundant the year after treatment, but both decreased as sprouts of competing shrubs and trees overtopped them. The burn-only and mechanical-plus-burn treatments show promise for eventually creating an open woodland community. However, treatments may need to be repeated numerous times to reach that goal.

INTRODUCTION

Management of forests in the southern Appalachian Mountains is as difficult as the region is complex. The region is one of the most biologically significant in the United States. Covering over 80 million acres, the Appalachian Plateau, Ridge and Valley Province, and the Blue Ridge Mountains include portions of NC, SC, TN, GA, AL, VA, and KY. The region has high ecosystem diversity because of its wide variety of land types, soils, precipitation levels, and disturbance histories. Some areas have the fastest growing wildland-urban interfaces in the United States; ecosystems are changing and losing key ecological functions because of fire exclusion, and managers have only recently begun to establish guidelines for ecosystem restoration using fire.

The Appalachian region has the largest cluster of public lands east of the Rocky Mountains—and the greatest need for fire management. Prescribed fire is used to restore the historical woodland character of pine-oak and oak-hickory forests. Appalachian hardwood ecosystems were developed by a broad array of natural disturbances, but the role played by natural and anthropogenic fire has not been appreciated until recent years (Brose and others 2001, Waldrop and others 2007). In some areas, prescribed burning is not possible, such as along the wildland/urban interface. Mechanical treatments may prove to be an acceptable surrogate for fire, but little information is available.

In 2000, a team of Federal, State, university, and private scientists and land managers designed the Fire and Fire Surrogate (FFS) study, an integrated national network to address the need for many types of information. The national network included 12 sites on Federal and State lands extending from Washington to Florida. At each site, impacts of fuel reduction treatments were studied on a broad array of variables, including flora, fauna, fuels, soils, forest health, and economics (see Youngblood and others 2005 for a description of the national study). Treatments were designed to restore ecosystems by re-establishing an ecosystem process (fire), stand structure (mechanical fuel reduction), or both. Changes in stand structure can alter ecosystem components such as vegetative diversity (Hutchinson 2006), fire behavior and return interval (Phillips and others 2006), and soil processes (Boerner and others 2008).

Most FFS sites were abandoned after reporting impacts that occurred within 1 year after treatment. However, managers at the FFS site in the southern Appalachian Mountains have been able to continue the prescribed burning treatment on a 3- to 5-year rotation. The primary management objective is to reduce wildfire severity by reducing live and dead fuels. Secondary objectives are to increase oak regeneration and to improve wildlife habitat by increasing cover of grasses and forbs. It may be possible to obtain each of these goals by restoring this community to the open woodland habitats once common

[1]Thomas A. Waldrop, Supervisory Research Forester, USDA Forest Service, Southern Research Station, Clemson, SC 29634

Helen H. Mohr, Forester, USDA Forest Service, Southern Research Station, Clemson, SC 29634

Ross J. Phillips, Ecologist, USDA Forest Service, Southern Research Station, Clemson, SC 29634

Dean M. Simon, Wildlife Forester, North Carolina Wildlife Resources Commission, Morganton, NC 28655

Citation for proceedings: Waldrop, Thomas A., ed. 2014. Proceedings, Wildland Fire in the Appalachians: Discussions among Managers and Scientists. Gen. Tech. Rep. SRS-199. Asheville, NC: U.S. Department of Agriculture Forest Service, Southern Research Station. 208 p.

in these regions (described in syntheses by Stanturf and others 2002 and Van Lear and Waldrop 1989). Fire and mechanical treatments at the southern Appalachian FFS site were designed to restore stand structure to an open woodland condition.

At the southern Appalachian FFS site, two fires and one mechanical treatment over a 6-year period achieved few management objectives, and the need for repeated treatment was evident. Mechanical treatment altered stand structure by eliminating vertical fuels within the shrub layer, but without prescribed burning, this treatment added litter and fine woody fuels that increased several measures of simulated fire behavior (Waldrop and others 2010). Prescribed burning promoted abundant regeneration of hardwood and shrub sprouts (Waldrop and others 2008), but there was no increase in understory species richness or grass cover (Phillips and others 2007). The combined mechanical and burning treatments had hot prescribed fires during the first burn that killed some overstory trees, resulting in increased amounts of woody fuels on the forest floor. However, the impact of those fuels was short-lived because this treatment was the most effective at reducing all measures of fire behavior and advancing restoration objectives (Waldrop and others 2010). Understory diversity and grass cover increased for 1 year after each burn but did not persist, as mountain laurel sprouts became competitive (Phillips and others 2007).

The numerous variables measured in the first years of the study strongly indicated that repeated entries of fire and/or mechanical treatments were necessary to reach fire protection, restoration, and wildlife management objectives. This paper examines the impacts of a third fire and a second mechanical treatment to vegetation and forest structure.

METHODS

The Southern Appalachian Mountains site of the FFS study is located in Polk County, NC, on the Green River Game Land, which is managed for wildlife habitat, timber, and other resources by the North Carolina Wildlife Resources Commission. Elevations range from 1100 to 2500 feet. Forests of the study area were 80 to 120 years old, and showed no indication of past agriculture or recent fire. Forest composition is mixed-oak with pitch pine (*Pinus rigida*) and Table Mountain pine (*P. pungens*) on xeric ridges and eastern white pine (*P. strobus*) in moist coves. A dense layer of ericaceous shrubs—mostly mountain laurel (*Kalmia latifolia*) and rhododendron (*Rhododendron maximum*)—is found throughout. Soils are primarily Evard series (file loamy, oxidic, mesic Typic Hapludults). These are moderately deep, well-drained, mountain upland soils (Keenan 1998).

The experiment was designed as a randomized complete block with three replicate blocks composed of four factorial treatment units. Individual treatment units were 25 to 30 acres in size. All treatment units were surrounded by buffer zones of approximately 10 to 25 acres, and both the treatment unit and its corresponding buffer received the experimental treatment. These treatment units were designed to include all prevailing combinations of elevation, aspect, and slope. However, these conditions varied within experimental units (treatment areas) and could not be separated for analysis. A 164- by 164-foot grid was established in each treatment unit to measure fuels. Grid points were permanently marked and georeferenced. Ten sample plots of 0.25 acres each were established at randomly selected grid points within each treatment unit to measure vegetation.

Treatments were selected to alter stand structure in a manner to reduce fuels, improve density of oak regeneration, and improve habitat for some wildlife species by reducing shrub cover and increasing herbaceous density. Factorial treatments were randomly allocated among treatment units within a site, and all treatment units were sampled through the pretreatment year (2001). Treatments consisted of prescribed burning (B), mechanical fuel reduction (M), a combination of mechanical treatment and prescribed burning (MB), and an untreated control (C). M involved creating a vertical fuel break by chainsaw-felling all tree stems >6 feet tall and <4 inches diameter at breast height (dbh) as well as all stems of ericaceous shrubs, regardless of size. This treatment was accomplished between December 2001 and February 2002. Prescribed fires were applied in B and MB units during March 2003 and again in March 2006. B and MB plots were burned for the third time in winter 2011. Chainsaw felling of small trees and shrubs was completed in early 2012 (January to February) in M units only. The objectives of prescribed burning were to remove vertical fuels and create a few snags. All fires were burned with a spot-fire technique.

Vegetation and fuels data were collected before treatment (2001) and at various years after treatment, depending on the date the treatment was completed. B plots were measured in 2003 (1 year after burning), 2005 (3 years after burning), 2006 (1 year after the second burn), 2011 (1 year before the third burn) and 2012 (1 year after the third burn). M plots were measured in 2002 (1 year after felling), 2004 (3 years after felling), 2006 (5 years after felling), 2011 (1 year before the second felling), and 2012 (1 year after the second felling). MB plots were measured in 2002 (1 year after felling), 2003 (1 year after burning), 2005 (3 years after burning), 2006 (1 year after the second burn), 2011 (1 year before the third burn and second felling), and 2012 (1 year after the third burn and second felling). C plots were measured every year from 2001 through 2006 and again in 2011 and 2012.

Vegetation data were collected on the 0.25-acre sample plots. Each plot was 164 by 66 feet in size and divided into 10 subplots, each 33 by 33 feet in size. All trees 4 inches dbh or larger were measured in five subplots at each sample date. For each tree, the tree number, species, dbh, and status (i.e., standing live or dead) were recorded. Shrubs >3.3 feet tall were measured on five 33- by 33-foot subplots using ocular estimates of the percentage of area covered by the crowns of each shrub species. Herbaceous cover was estimated for each species in 20 subplots, 3.3 by 3.3 feet in size, within each 0.25-acre plot.

Litter and duff depth and mass were determined by destructively sampling the forest floor at each of the 36 grid points and in the center of each 0.25-acre plot. A square wooden frame with sides 3.3 feet long was used along with a cutter to collect each sample by layer (L and F/H), and each layer was bagged separately. After careful removal of the frame, each layer was measured on each side of the sampled area. Each sample was then washed to remove soil and rocks and dried to a constant weight in an oven set at 185 °F. Litter and duff samples were then weighed in the laboratory.

The down dead-woody fuels were measured before and after treatment using the planar intercept method described by Brown (1974). Three 50-foot transects were established approximately 6 feet from each grid point in a randomly selected direction. This method produced a total of over 70,000 feet of fuel transects.

Analysis of treatment effects on vegetation and fuels was conducted using repeated-measures analysis of variance, with treatment and year modeled as fixed effects and block as a random effect. To account for differences among years, we interpreted significant treatment and (or) treatment-by-year interactions ($\alpha = 0.05$) as evidence of treatment effects, and we made post hoc comparisons using linear contrasts. Because much of the data did not meet the assumption of normality, it was necessary to use data transformations to normalize the distributions. Logarithmic and square root transformations were used in these analyses.

RESULTS

Through 11 years of post-treatment measurement, basal area in C and M treatment areas is gradually increasing as trees grow; there have been no significant differences in basal area between these two treatment areas at any time (fig. 1). The B treatment resulted in the death of a few trees in 2003, and more trees died each year after, especially after the second burn. Basal area (BA) was

significantly lower in B units than in C and M units every year. However, basal area in B units was high throughout the measurement period, remaining near 120 square feet per acre or more. Overstory BA was most affected by the MB treatment. The initial burn was very hot, with flame heights of 10 to 15 feet, because of heavy residual fuels from the mechanical treatment. Some trees died in MB plots during every year after the initial burn. Basal area in these treatment areas was significantly lower than in all other treatment areas during every year. Over time, BA reduced from 119 to 82 square feet per acre in MB plots and may continue to decline with delayed mortality after each burn (Yaussy and Waldrop 2010).

Canopy openness was significantly greater in both B and MB treatment areas than in C areas each year (fig. 2). The MB treatment created the most open canopy by far, and openness there did not change after the initial treatment, remaining at about 29 percent. Even though surviving trees were likely filling open space, delayed mortality was sufficient to prevent canopy closure. In the B areas, openness was greater than in M areas the first year after treatment, but there were no significant differences in any later year, possibly because trees in B areas grew faster from a fertilizing effect of fire and less competition. Openness did not differ significantly between M and C areas at any time. Both M and C areas had increased openness over time, which was attributed to ice storms that occurred in 2005 and 2009 and to mortality of individual trees from unknown sources.

All active treatments reduced shrub cover the first year after treatment, and it remained significantly lower than in C plots throughout the study period (fig. 3). With time, however, shrub cover increased in the M (from 1 to 9 percent) and MB (from 0 to 7 percent) treatments as stump sprouts grew into the minimum size class for measurement. Shrub cover remained at about 4 percent in B plots until the third fire. In the 11th year after initial treatment, the third burn and second mechanical treatment reduced shrub cover to approximately 1 percent in M, B, and MB treatment areas.

Ground cover was reduced by the B and MB treatments the first year after burning, but was not affected by the M treatment without fire (fig. 4). Over time, ground cover in the B and M treatment areas was low and at about the same amount as measured in C plots. Ground cover in MB areas remained significantly higher than in C areas beyond the first year after the initial treatment. Burning and mechanical treatments during the 11th year significantly reduced ground cover in all active treatment areas. At that time, ground cover was significantly higher (40 percent) in MB areas than in all other areas. Ground cover reduced to 24, 23, and 19 percent in C, B, and M areas, respectively; these differences were not significant.

The goal of increasing cover of graminoids was not successful in any of the treatment areas. Although the MB treatment areas had significantly more cover than in other treatment areas, the total was never more than 2 ½ percent (fig. 5). In MB areas, graminoid cover decreased between the second and third burns; the 6 years between these burns was sufficient for shrubs, tree sprouts, smilax, and other plants to grow tall enough to shade out grasses and sedges.

Numbers of oak seedlings and sprouts were stimulated by burning but not by chainsaw felling. Numbers in M areas never differed from those in C areas (fig. 6). However oak regeneration significantly increased after the first burn in B and MB areas and remained significantly higher than in M and C areas throughout the study. A decline in oak numbers that occurred during the 6-year period between the second and third burns suggests the need for more frequent burning. That suggestion is supported by the large increase in oak numbers that occurred immediately after the third fire in B and MB areas.

DISCUSSION AND CONCLUSIONS

Each fuel reduction treatment changed stand structure differently, resulting in different degrees of success in achieving restoration goals. After three burns and two mechanical treatments, none of the treatment areas exhibited all of the characteristics of the target open woodland community.

Chainsaw felling of small trees and shrubs (M) left a dense canopy with little change in canopy openness. The treatment did reduce the shrub layer cover for 7 years; most sprouts did not grow back into the shrub layer (>3 feet) during that time. However, shrub cover increased greatly through year 11. A second treatment in the 11th year reduced the shrub cover to almost zero percent. None of the target variables showed a positive response to this change in structure with the possible exception of fire behavior. Without a shrub layer there was a vertical fuel break, especially after 8 to 10 years, as felled decomposed stems were flat on the ground. Even though there was a reduction in the cover of shrubs, there was not a positive response in forest floor vegetation, graminoid cover, or oak regeneration. This treatment left an intact overstory and forest floor. The best practical use of mechanical shrub felling may be for reducing fuels where prescribed burning is difficult or impossible. Even frequent use of this treatment is unlikely to produce our restoration goals.

Prescribed burning alone produced a two-storied stand structure, similar to that of the mechanical only treatment. The first burn essentially removed the shrub layer, and subsequent burns were frequent enough to keep it low. The canopy layer was thinned somewhat, but basal area remained high and openness was low. Ground cover, graminoid cover, and oak regeneration increased for a short period after each of the first two fires but declined by the time of the next burn. The structure of the burn-only plots was closer to that of open woodlands than it was before burning, but the restoration objective was not met. An initial burn of high intensity followed by more frequent prescribed burning may be necessary to open the overstory and to maintain gains in graminoid cover and oak regeneration.

The combination of mechanical and burn treatments produced immediate and large reductions to basal area, shrub cover, and ground cover. Stand structure in these areas was closest to the desired open woodland condition, with a 40 percent reduction in basal area and 30 percent canopy openness. However, understory shrubs, tree sprouts, and herbaceous plants quickly claimed the open forest floor and prevented successful growth of graminoids and oaks. These results agree with the substantial body of literature stating restoration will require numerous fires occurring more frequently than every 3 years.

Even though the stand structures produced in this study largely did not support desired objectives for most variables, progress was observed after prescribed burning, particularly when burning was done in combination with chainsaw felling of the shrub layer. With frequent burning, the MB areas may eventually support an open woodland community. These areas have an open canopy and improved wildlife habitat. Frequent burning will be needed for fuel reduction and spread of graminoids and oaks.

The Appalachian site of the National Fire and Fire Surrogate continues to be an important source of information about fire effects in this region, where prescribed fire is relatively new and little research is available. The study remains active with current efforts to continue treatments and follow their impacts on vegetation, fuels, soils, herpetofauna, and avifauna.

LITERATURE CITED

Boerner, R.E.J.; Coates, T.A.; Yaussy, D.A.; Waldrop, T.A. 2008. Assessing ecosystem restoration alternatives in eastern deciduous forests: the view from belowground. Restoration Ecology. 16(3): 425-434.

Brose, P.H.; Schuler, T.M.; Van Lear, D.H.; Berst, J. 2001. Bringing fire back: the changing regimes of the Appalachian mixed oak forest. Journal of Forestry. 99: 30-35.

Brown, J.K. 1974. Handbook for inventorying downed woody material. Gen. Tech. Rep. INT-16. Ogden, UT: U.S. Department of Agriculture Forest Service, Intermountain Forest & Range Experiment Station. 24 p.

Hutchinson, T.F. 2006. Fire and the herbaceous layer of eastern oak forests. In: Dickinson, M.B., ed. Fire in eastern oak forests: delivering science to land managers, proceedings of a conference. Gen. Tech. Rep. NRS-P-1. Newtown Square, PA: U.S. Department of Agriculture Forest Service, Northern Research Station: 136-151.

Keenan, S.C. 1998. Soil survey of Polk County, NC. Washington, DC: U.S. Department of Agriculture, Natural Resources Conservation Service. 218 p.

Phillips, R.J.; Waldrop, T.A.; Simon, D.M. 2006. Assessment of the FARSITE model for predicting fire behavior in the Southern Appalachian Mountains. In: Konnor, K.S., ed. Proceedings of the 13th biennial Southern Silvicultural Research Conference. Gen. Tech. Rep. SRS-92. Asheville, NC: U.S. Department of Agriculture Forest Service, Southern Research Station: 521-525.

Phillips, R.J.; Hutchinson, T.F.; Brudnak, L.; Waldrop, T.A. 2007. Fire and fire surrogate treatments in mixed-oak forests: effects on herbaceous layer vegetation. In: Butler, B.W.; Cook, W., comps. The fire environment innovations, management, and policy; conference proceedings. Proceedings RMRS-P-46. Fort Collins, CO: U.S. Department of Agriculture Forest Service, Rocky Mountain Research Station: 475-485.

Stanturf, J.A.; Wade, D.D.; Waldrop, T.A. [and others]. 2002. Fire in southern forest landscapes. In: Wear, D.M, Greis, J.G., eds. Southern Forest Resource Assessment. Gen. Tech. Rep. SRS-53. Asheville, NC: U.S. Department of Agriculture Forest Service, Southern Research Station: 607-630.

Van Lear, D.H.; Waldrop, T.A. 1989. History, use, and effects of fire in the Southern Appalachians. Gen. Tech. Rep. SE-54. Asheville, NC: U.S. Department of Agriculture Forest Service, Southeastern Forest Experiment Station. 20 p.

Waldrop, T.A.; Brudnak, L.; Rideout-Hanzak, S. 2007. Fuels on disturbed and undisturbed sites in the southern Appalachian Mountains, USA. Canadian Journal of Forest Research. 37: 1134-1141.

Waldrop, T.A.; Phillips, R.J.; Simon, D.M. 2010. Fuels and predicted fire behavior in the southern Appalachian Mountains after fire and fire surrogate treatments. Forest Science. 56(1): 32-45.

Waldrop, T.A., Yaussy, D.A., Phillips, R.J. [and others]. 2008. Fuel reduction treatments affect stand structure of hardwood forests in western North Carolina and southern Ohio, USA. Forest Ecology and Management. 255: 3117-3129.

Yaussy, D.A.; Waldrop, T.A. 2010. Delayed mortality of eastern hardwoods after prescribed fire. In: Stanturf, J.A., ed. Proceedings of the 14th biennial southern silvicultural research conference. Gen. Tech. Rep. SRS-121. Asheville, NC: U.S. Department of Agriculture Forest Service, Southern Research Station: 609-611.

Youngblood, A.; Metlen, K.L.; Knapp, E.E.; Outcalt, K.W.; Stephens, S.L.; Waldrop, T.A.; Yaussy, D. 2005. Implementation of the fire and fire surrogate study—a national research effort to evaluate the consequences of fuel reduction treatment. In: Peterson, C.E., Maguire, D.A., eds. Balancing Ecosystem Values: Innovative Experiments for Sustainable Forestry. Portland, OR: U.S. Department of Agriculture Forest Service, Pacific Northwest Station: 315-321.

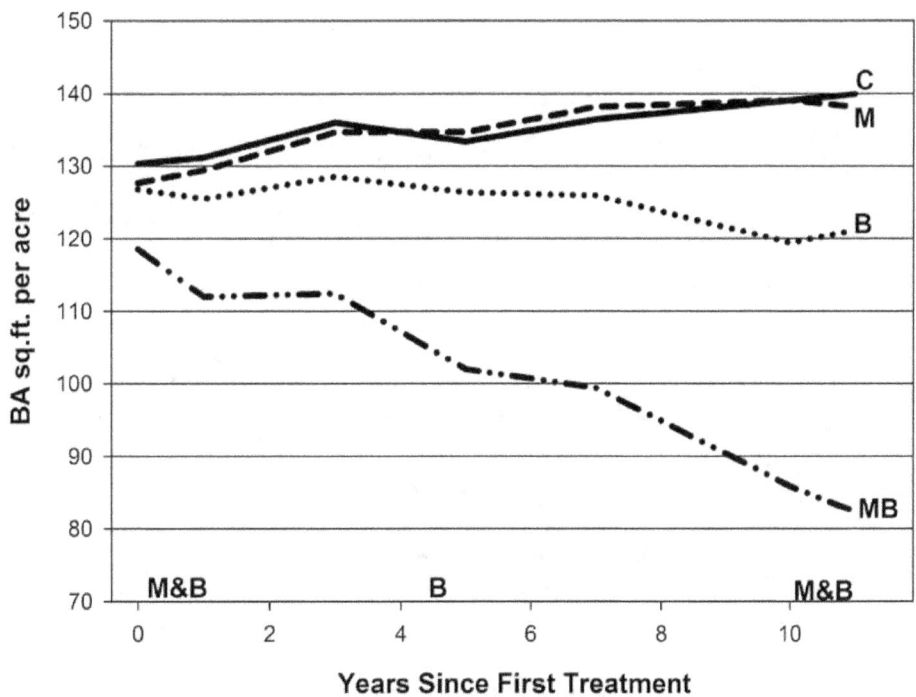

Figure 1—Change in basal area over the number of years since the first treatment. Letters by each line represent the treatment (C=untreated control, B=burn only, M=mechanical only, MB=combined mechanical and burn treatments). Letters along the X axis show the timing of each treatment.

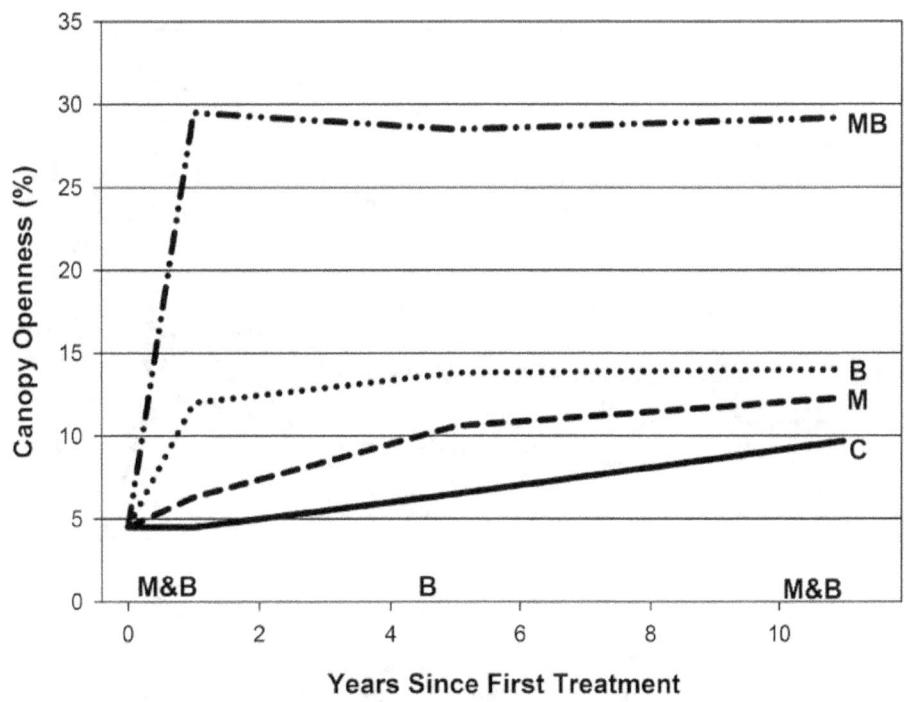

Figure 2—Change in canopy openness over the number of years since the first treatment. Letters by each line represent the treatment (C=untreated control, B=burn only, M=mechanical only, MB=combined mechanical and burn treatments). Letters along the X axis show the timing of each treatment.

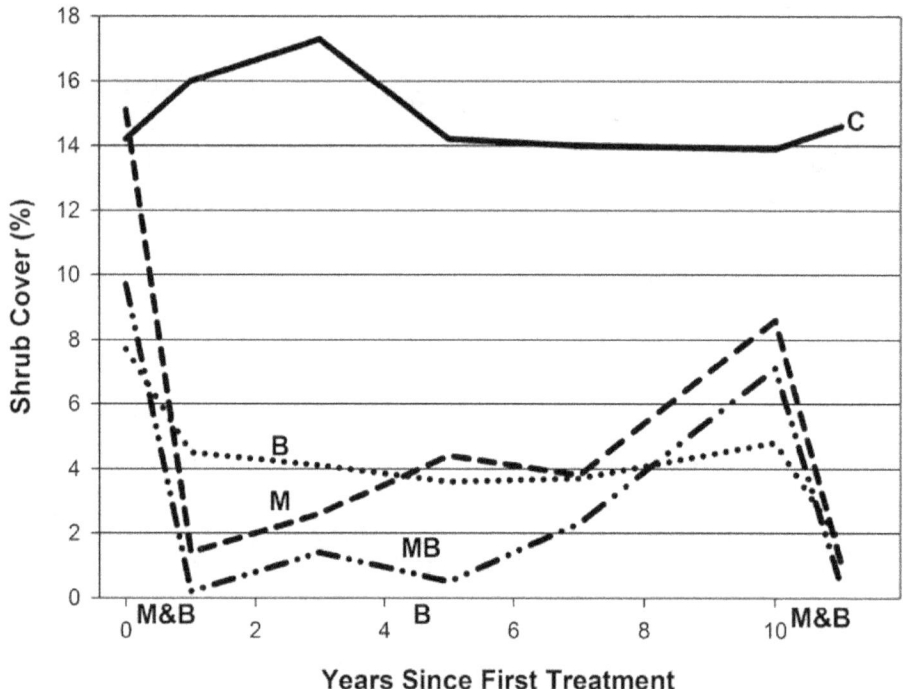

Figure 3—Change in shrub cover over the number of years since the first treatment. Letters by each line represent the treatment (C=untreated control, B=burn only, M=mechanical only, MB=combined mechanical and burn treatments). Letters along the X axis show the timing of each treatment.

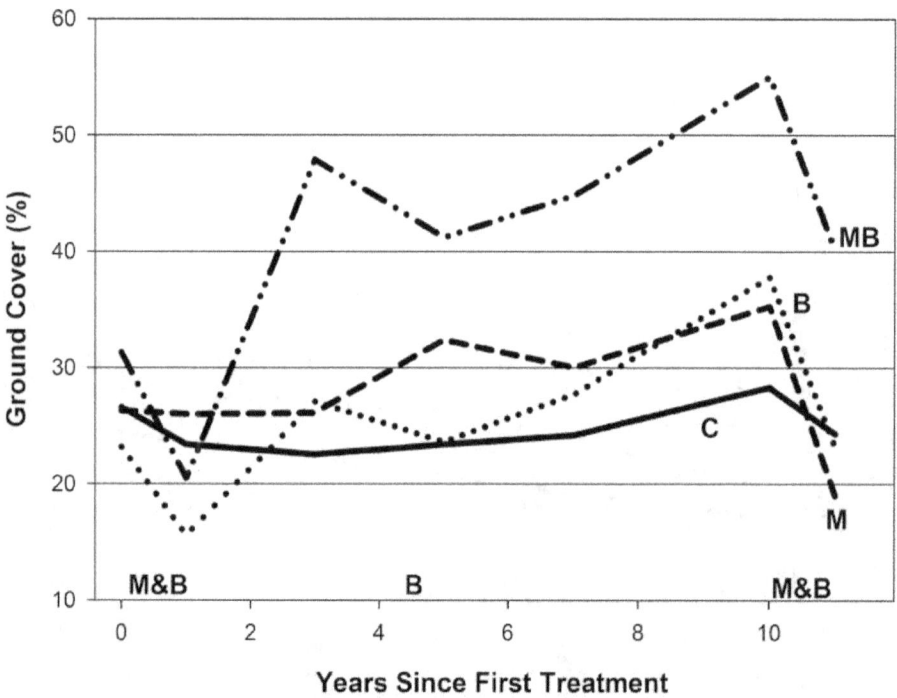

Figure 4—Change in ground cover over the number of years since the first treatment. Letters by each line represent the treatment (C=untreated control, B=burn only, M=mechanical only, MB=combined mechanical and burn treatments). Letters along the X axis show the timing of each treatment.

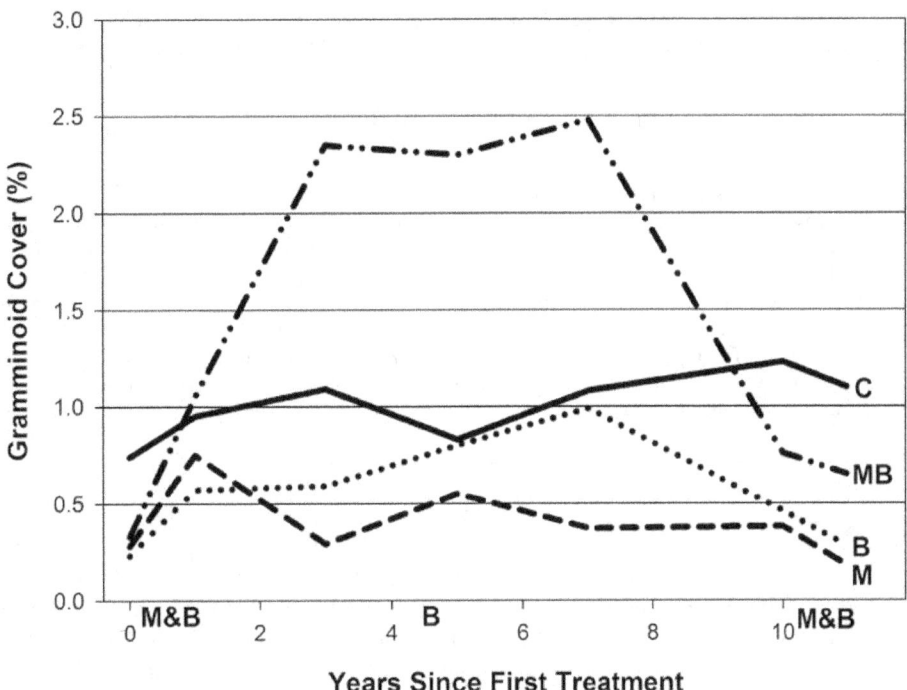

Figure 5—Change in Graminoid cover over the number of years since the first treatment. Letters by each line represent the treatment (C=untreated control, B=burn only, M=mechanical only, MB=combined mechanical and burn treatments). Letters along the X axis show the timing of each treatment.

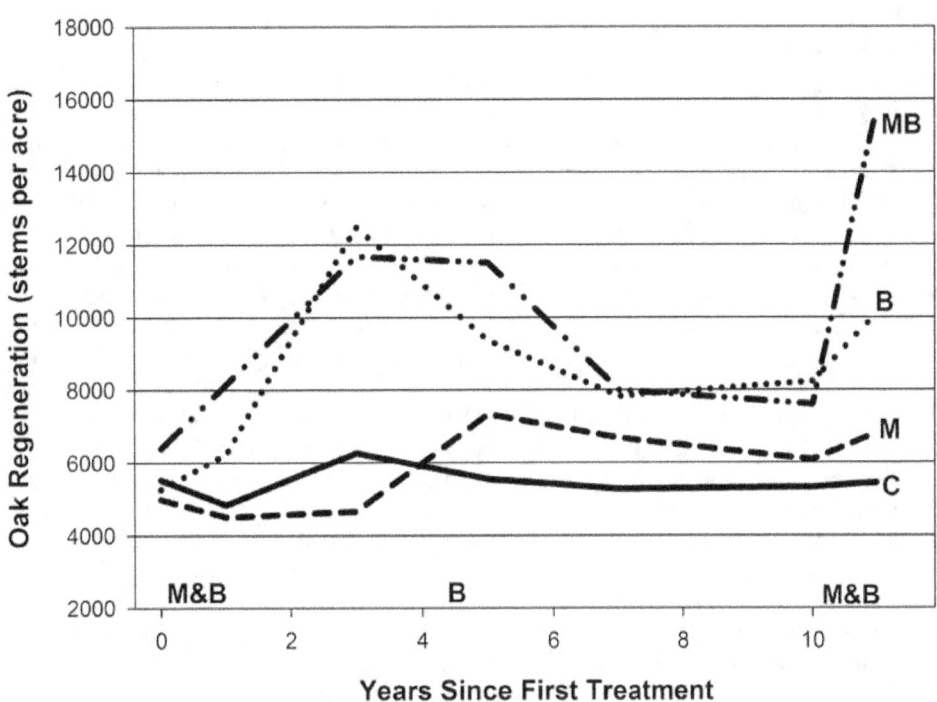

Figure 6—Change in density of oak regeneration over the number of years since the first treatment. Letters by each line represent the treatment (C=untreated control, B=burn only, M=mechanical only, MB=combined mechanical and burn treatments). Letters along the X axis show the timing of each treatment.

SPROUTING CAPABILITY AND GROWTH OF ONE-YEAR-OLD SHORTLEAF PINE SEEDLINGS AFTER DIFFERENT TIMES OF BURNING AND CLIPPING

David C. Clabo and Wayne K. Clatterbuck[1]

Abstract—Shortleaf pine (*Pinus echinata* Mill.) is capable of sprouting after the stem is killed. The sprouting ability of shortleaf pine could be used to favor the species silviculturally for specific management objectives. Information is limited on burning effects at different periods of the growing season on shortleaf pine survival and growth. This study was located on the Cumberland Plateau region of east Tennessee and was conducted on one-year-old seedlings. Replicated treatments analyzed as a randomized block design included: clipping in March, burning in April, burning in July, burning in November, and an untreated control. Results indicate that after one full growing season after the treatment year, survival and growth of shortleaf pine sprouts did not differ among the three burning times (treatments) although differences were observed between burning and clipping and burning and control (unburned) treatments. Sprout number was statistically different among treatments with maximum burn temperatures as a covariate.

INTRODUCTION

The wide range of soil and moisture conditions on which shortleaf pine (*Pinus echinata* Mill.) can flourish makes it a ubiquitous species across the southeastern and eastern United States. Shortleaf pine is found in 22 States covering over 440,000 square miles (Lawson 1990). The species can form almost pure stands on shallow, well-drained upland soils in areas such as the Ouachita Mountains of Arkansas. Shortleaf pine typically becomes a more minor tree species component with increasing site productivity. The species' rooting habit, low demand for soil nutrients, and sprouting capability enable it to flourish on a wide variety of sites (Fowells 1965, Guldin 1986). Initial seedling height growth is typically slow due to the formation of a large taproot, but the taproot gives shortleaf pine a distinct advantage on poor sites over other species. Sprouting maintains the species on sites with frequent disturbances where other species unable to sprout may decline over time (Lawson 1990). These characteristics perpetuate shortleaf pine on poorer sites and make it a transitional successional species on more productive sites.

Shortleaf pine has the ability to sprout during the seedling or sapling developmental stages, and stems approaching 6 to 8 inches diameter at breast height (dbh) (Fowells 1965, Lawson 1990, Little and Somes 1956). The species' sprouting ability decreases with increasing age and size, similar to other tree species that can sprout. Sprouts initiate from axillary dormant buds located at or just above a unique physiological feature known as the basal crook. The basal crook typically develops within two to three months following germination. When shoot growth begins, the stem grows horizontally for a time and then turns vertically at a point slightly above the cotyledons just before it reaches the soil surface, forming a horizontal crook (Stone and Stone 1954). Seedlings growing in full sun typically grow more developed basal crooks than those growing in full or partial shade (Guldin 1986, Lilly and others 2010, Little and Mergen 1966). Detrimental agents such as fire, herbivory, or injury cause a sprouting response in vigorous, young trees. As many as sixty sprouts may initiate on a damaged seedling, but typically only one to three sprouts will reach maturity if no further disturbances occur (Mattoon 1915).

Landscape-wide factors such as urbanization, fire suppression, cessation of free-roaming livestock grazing, Southern pine beetle outbreaks, paucity of young shortleaf pine age classes, and loblolly pine (*P. taeda* L.) preponderance have all combined in the last few decades to diminish shortleaf pine populations (Birch and others 1986, Coffey 2012, Moser and others 2007). The shortleaf pine resource declined by 52 percent across its range from the early 1980s to 2010 (Oswalt 2012). Restoration efforts of shortleaf pine ecosystems were initiated by the U.S. Forest Service in the Ouachita Mountains in the early 1990s, but other national forests, government agencies, and private landowners have shown interest in restoring shortleaf pine ecosystems in recent years (Atkinson 2010, Bukenhofer and others 1994). Knowledge of shortleaf pine sprouting capability and propensity provides insight to the management methods associated with restoration activities, especially prescribed burning. Ecosystem restoration frequently involves disturbances such as burning intended to favor shortleaf pine over other species and reintroduce fire dependent species into those systems.

[1]David C. Clabo, Graduate Research Assistant, The University of Tennessee, Department of Forestry, Wildlife & Fisheries, Knoxville, TN 37996-4563

Wayne K. Clatterbuck, Professor, The University of Tennessee, Knoxville, TN 37996

Citation for proceedings: Waldrop, Thomas A., ed. 2014. Proceedings, Wildland Fire in the Appalachians: Discussions among Managers and Scientists. Gen. Tech. Rep. SRS-199. Asheville, NC: U.S. Department of Agriculture Forest Service, Southern Research Station. 208 p.

Few studies (e.g. Campbell 1985, Cain and Shelton 2000, Lilly and others 2012, Shelton and Cain 2002), especially in the eastern portion of the species' range outside of Arkansas, have examined when disturbances such as stem clipping and burning can be applied to young seedlings during the growing season to produce the largest and greatest number of sprouts.

The objectives of this study were to determine the optimum timing for shortleaf pine survival and the sprouting response among four treatments: clipping during the early growing season or burning at three separate periods of the growing season. We compared seedling survival, height of the dominant sprout, and the number of sprouts produced among treatments one full growing season after the year treatments were applied.

METHODS

The study was conducted on the Cumberland Forest, a unit of the University of Tennessee's Forest Resources Research and Education Center (FRREC). The Cumberland Forest is located on the Walden Ridge subregion of the Cumberland Plateau (Smalley 1982). The study site was a previously maintained field with soils consisting of fine-loamy, siliceous, semi-active, mesic Typic Hapludults on 5-12 percent slopes from the Lonewood series. Shortleaf pine has a site index of 70 feet at base age 50 years for these soils (U.S. Department of Agriculture Natural Resources Conservation Service 2012). Shortleaf pine seedlings (1-0 stock) were purchased from the Tennessee Division of Forestry Nursery at Delano, TN, which used Tennessee seed sources. Seedlings were planted on February 25, 2011 and averaged 11 inches tall at planting.

The study was established on a 5,796 square foot section (69 feet by 84 feet) of the field. Three blocks were established that consisted of 15 plots each. Each rectangular plot measured 4 feet by 9 feet and contained 50 seedlings planted on a 1 foot by 1 foot spacing with 6-foot buffers on each side of the plot. Within each block, each treatment was applied once to a plot. All seedlings within a plot from each block were clipped in late March of 2011, closely followed by burning of one plot from each block on April 14, 2011. Mid-growing-season burns were completed on July 14, 2011 and late growing-season/early dormant-season burns on November 10, 2011. One control plot from each block that received no treatments was used in the analysis as well.

One inconsistency with the experimental procedures was that the July burn plots were burned twice within a few days of each other using the same methodology because of poor ignition and incomplete burn coverage on the first attempt, which may have affected some of the survival,

height growth and sprouting results. Some seedlings in these plots burned twice, while others were burned once.

Clipped seedlings were cut 1 to 2 inches above ground level. In addition, all root collar sprouts that may have already existed on the stem were cut to ensure uniform starting heights and sprouting conditions. Prior to conducting burns, herbaceous plants and grasses were cut to ground level within plots, and a 1.5 percent solution of glyphosate herbicide (Cornerstone Plus®) was applied to reduce the effects of these fuels on the burns. The fuel source used for the burns was eastern white pine (*Pinus strobus* L.) needles gathered from nearby plantations. Needles were gathered and sifted to remove larger limbs and twigs. The needles were then allowed to dry on a tarp in full sunlight for at least two hours prior to burning to reduce fuel moisture to levels low enough for the needles to carry a fire. Needles were distributed evenly within plots using 5-gallon buckets to ensure equal fuel volumes within plots.

Burns were established in a ring pattern around plots using drip torches. The temperature and duration of each burn was measured and recorded for each plot. Burn temperatures were recorded every 15 seconds until complete flame-out using a Kintrex® Digital Infrared Thermometer. The thermometer sat on a pole 4 feet from the center of a plot, which was the midpoint between the fifth and sixth tree of the third column. The center was used as the measurement point due to the likelihood of hotter interior temperatures than along the edges. The pole measured 3 feet 8 inches tall, and including the height of the thermometer handle, the thermometer rested approximately 70 inches away from plot center. Fire weather data (relative humidity, ambient air temperature, and wind speed) were recorded prior to conducting each of the burns.

Survival percentage, height of the dominant sprout, and number of sprouts were the three measurements completed following treatments. Measurements were recorded in January 2013, one full growing season after treatments were applied to the first-year seedlings. Analysis of variance was used to test for differences among treatments. Data were analyzed as a randomized complete block experimental design using the PROC MIXED procedure in SAS 9.3 (SAS Institute Inc., 2012). Least square means were separated using Fisher's protected least significant difference test with a significance level set at $P = 0.05$. Burn temperature and duration data were included as covariates in the analysis to determine if they had a significant effect on the dependent variables. Mean burn temperature, total burn duration, maximum burn temperature, median burn temperature, and the sum of all temperature readings were all tested as covariates using a significance level of $P=0.05$.

RESULTS

All seedlings that received burn treatments were topkilled. Significant differences in seedling survival occurred among the five treatments (P=0.04). Survival rates were greatest with the control treatment and the clip treatment, which both had a 75.3 percent survival rate (fig. 1). The average survival rates among the three burning times were not statistically different, ranging from 38.7 to 48.7 percent. The clip and control treatments were significantly different from the April and July burn treatments, but similar to the November burn treatment (fig. 1).

The six variables used in covariate analysis did not affect treatment means for dominant sprout height of shortleaf pine seedlings. Significant differences in dominant sprout height occurred among the five treatments (P<0.001). Seedlings averaged 11 inches tall at planting, and the controls, which had the tallest mean height, averaged 48.5 inches after one growing season (fig. 2). The clip treatment seedlings averaged 26.1 inches. This treatment was statistically different from the three burn treatments and the control. There were no statistical differences among the three burn treatments as indicated by their letter groupings, even though numerically, seedlings in the July burn treatment were shorter on average (15.4 inches) than seedlings burned in April (19.2 inches) and November (19.7 inches).

The number of sprouts produced by each seedling was significantly affected by the maximum burn temperature covariate. Maximum burn temperatures ranged from 512 degrees Fahrenheit in one of the March burn plots to greater than 932 degrees Fahrenheit in one of the November burn plots. There were significant differences among treatments with the covariate included (P=0.0089). Differences in the adjusted (for the covariate) and unadjusted (without the covariate) means and standard errors are presented in table 1. The July burn produced the fewest number of sprouts (4.2), while the April burn (7.0) yielded nearly three more sprouts per seedling on average. The November burn produced the most sprouts of any treatment (11.0). The mean number of sprouts produced in the clip treatment (6.0) was statistically similar (letter groupings) to the April burn and not significantly different from the number of sprouts produced by the July burn. The control treatment produced the fewest sprouts (1.3), and this treatment was significantly different from the other treatments (table 1).

DISCUSSION

Several studies have observed poor survival rates after summer burns as compared to dormant season or early growing season burns in shortleaf pine seedlings of various ages (Cain and Shelton 2000, Grossmann and

Kuser 1988, Shelton and Cain 2002) similar to those in this study. The low survival rate of seedlings burned in April was likely a partial result of poor root/soil contact and seedlings not being fully established after their February planting (Grossnickle 2005, Rietveld 1989). Another study with 6-year-old seedlings reported similar survival percentages for an April burn that was assessed one full growing season after the treatment year (Lilly and others 2012). Although some seedlings in the July burn plots were burned twice, survival percentages were not statistically different from the April or November burn plots. More fully established seedlings should attain large enough size for the root collar, develop thicker bark, and produce larger basal crooks, which may increase survival percentages after burning (Little and Somes 1956). Although the survival percentages for the November burn was similar to the two earlier burns, others have observed that as seedling size increases, survival percentage increases (Lilly and others 2012, Mattoon 1915).

The control and clip treatments had the same survival percentage (75.3 percent). The high survival of the clipped seedlings differed from another study in Arkansas that found a survival rate of 48 percent for four-year-old seedlings that were clipped at a similar height above ground level (Campbell 1985). The control seedlings had a somewhat lower one-year survival rate (75 versus greater than 80 percent) than the expected survival rate of shortleaf pine seedlings that are outplanted in Arkansas National Forests by the U.S. Forest Service (Mexal 1992).

The clipped seedlings grew taller than the burned seedlings, as expected. The lack of heat damage to the basal crook and the dormant buds just above the basal crook near the soil line result in a greater likelihood for clipped seedlings to grow taller (Cain and Shelton 2000, Lilly and others 2012, Little and Somes 1956). Because there were no significant differences among the burn treatments, data from seedlings older than one year old may be necessary to detect statistical differences in height growth using these same treatments. The three burn treatments had about a 60 percent or less height reduction as compared to the controls. A similar study in Arkansas found that one-year-old seedlings burned during January were 82 percent shorter than the controls measured one growing season after burns were applied (Cain and Shelton 2000). Height growth following the clip treatment and the burn treatments in this study was in the 1- to 3-foot range expected for this species throughout most of its range when typical weather patterns occur during the growing season (Lawson 1990, Williston 1951).

Although the height of shortleaf pine sprouts in burned plots was about 60 percent less than that in unburned control plots, burning combined with the sprouting ability of shortleaf pine could allow shortleaf pine to be more competitive with other species during the regeneration process. This outcome is reinforced in a site preparation study to create mixed pine-hardwood stands by Mullins and others (1997) when planting loblolly pine following a complete hardwood harvest. The planted loblolly pine seedlings only survived and developed when burning and/or herbicides were used to hinder initial hardwood growth. Those pine seedlings planted in harvested areas without site preparation had poor survival because they were overwhelmed by the hardwood sprout growth. The site preparation burn was conducted following the harvest and before the pine planting. Shortleaf pine probably would have similar growth properties as loblolly pine during establishment. An added advantage is the sprouting ability of shortleaf pine. A burning regime after planting could put shortleaf pine sprouts on a more even footing with sprouting hardwoods. Mixtures of pine (shortleaf) and oak were probably initiated and maintained with a fire regime before fire suppression began in the early 1900s (Brose and others 2001, Elliott and Vose 2005).

The mean number of sprouts per tree produced after burn treatments was less with the maximum temperature covariate included for the April and July burns, whereas the seedlings burned in November produced more sprouts with this covariate included. This is likely a result of the seedlings being better established in November following the February planting. All burning treatments produced more sprouts than clipping except for the July burn. This result is different from a study in New Jersey by Grossmann and Kuser (1988), who found more sprouts on six- to eight-year-old seedlings after spring clippings. The discrepancies in this result could be due to differences in burn intensity or duration, which was not outlined in the New Jersey study. Lilly and others (2012) found more sprouts on average (8.8 +/- 0.7 to 7.51 +/- 0.7 unadjusted) following an April burn applied to six-year-old seedlings. This finding agrees with the axiom that sprouting ability increases with size until a certain size threshold is reached. As expected, the controls produced few sprouts in comparison to the clip and the burn treatments, which has been outlined in previous work by others (e.g., Guldin 1986, Mattoon 1915). Managers interested in obtaining more or fewer sprouts in young shortleaf pine regeneration following burns may want to carefully consider the timing of burning to influence sprouting. Fewer sprouts would likely be more attractive in most situations due to increased vigor. One to three sprouts typically differentiate themselves from the rest and achieve larger size classes (Mattoon 1915).

ACKNOWLEDGMENTS

The authors would like to thank Dr. Kevin Hoyt, director of the UT-FRREC Cumberland Forest, Martin Schubert, manager of the UT-FRREC Cumberland Forest, Randal Maden, and Todd Hamby for their help in establishing and conducting the study.

LITERATURE CITED

Atkinson, K.L. 2010. The shortleaf pine initiative. In: Symposium on Shortleaf Pine Research: Past, Present and Future. Stillwater, OK: Department of Natural Resource Ecology and Management (NREM), Oklahoma State University: 16-18.

Birch, T.W.; Hansen, M.H.; McWilliams, W.H.; Sheffield, R.M. 1986. The shortleaf resource. In: Murphy, P.A., ed. Symposium on the shortleaf pine ecosystem. Monticello, AR: Arkansas Cooperative Extension Service: 9-24.

Brose, P.; Schuler, T. Van Lear, D.; Berst, J. 2001. Bringing fire back: The changing regimes of the Appalachian mixed-oak forests. Journal of Forestry. 99:30-35.

Bukenhofer, G.A.; Neal, J.C.; Montague, W.G. 1994. Renewal and recovery: Shortleaf pine/bluestem grass ecosystem and red-cockaded woodpeckers. Proceedings of Arkansas Academy of Science. 48: 243-245.

Cain, M.D.; Shelton, M.G. 2000. Survival and growth of *Pinus echinata* and *Quercus* seedlings in response to simulated summer and winter prescribed burns. Canadian Journal of Forest Research. 30(11): 1830-1836.

Campbell, T.E. 1985. Sprouting of slash, loblolly, and shortleaf pines following a simulated precommercial thinning. Research Note SO-320. New Orleans: U.S. Department of Agriculture Southern Forest Experiment Station. 3 p.

Coffey, C. 2012. The history of shortleaf pine on the Cumberland Plateau. In: Proceedings of the Shortleaf Pine Conference: East Meets West, Bridging the Gap with Research and Education Across the Range. Huntsville, AL: Alabama Cooperative Extension System and the U.S. Department of Agriculture Forest Service: 2-6.

Elliot, K.J.; Vose, J.M. 2005. Effects of understory prescribed burning on shortleaf pine (*Pinus echinata* Mill.)/mixed-hardwood forests. Journal of the Torrey Botanical Society. 132(2): 236-251.

Fowells, H.A., ed. 1965. Silvics of forest trees of the United States. Washington, DC: U.S. Department of Agriculture Forest Service Agricultural Handbook No. 271. 762 p.

Grossnickle, S.C. 2005. Importance of root growth in overcoming planting stress. New Forests. 30: 273-294.

Grossmann, M.N.; Kuser, J.E. 1988. Rooting primary-leaved sprouts of pitch and shortleaf pine. Northern Journal of Applied Forestry. 5: 158-159.

Guldin, J.M. 1986. Ecology of shortleaf pine. In: Murphy, P.A., ed. Symposium on the shortleaf pine ecosystem. Monticello, AR: Arkansas Cooperative Extension Service: 25-40.

Lawson, E.R. 1990. *Pinus echinata* Mill. shortleaf pine. In: Burns, R.M.; Honkala, B.H., tech. cords. Silvics of North America: Vol. 1. Conifers. Agriculture Handbook 654, Washington, DC: U.S. Department of Agriculture Forest Service: 316-326.

Lilly, C.J.; Will, R.E.; Tauer, C.G. [and others]. 2010. Factors influencing shortleaf pine sprouting after fire. In: Symposium on shortleaf pine research: past, present, and future. Stillwater, OK: Department of Natural Resource Ecology and Management (NREM), Oklahoma State University: 8-9.

Lilly, C.J.; Will, R.E.; Tauer, C.G. [and others]. 2012. Factors affecting the sprouting of shortleaf pine rootstock following prescribed fire. Forest Ecology and Management. 265: 13-19.

Little, S.; Somes, H.A. 1956. Buds enable pitch and shortleaf pines to recover from injury. Station Paper NE-81. Broomall, PA: U.S. Department of Agriculture Forest Service, Northeastern Research Station. 14 p.

Little, S.; Mergen F. 1966. External and internal changes associated with basal-crook formation in pitch and shortleaf pines. Forest Science. 12(3): 268-275.

Mattoon, W.R. 1915. Life history of shortleaf pine. Bulletin 244, Washington, DC: U.S. Department of Agriculture Forest Service. 46 p.

Mexal, J.G. 1992. Artificial regeneration of shortleaf pine: put it all together for success. In: Brissette, J.C.; Barnett, J.P, eds. Proceedings of the Shortleaf Pine Regeneration Workshop. Gen. Tech. Rep. SO-90. New Orleans, LA: U.S. Department of Agriculture Forest Service, Southern Forest Experiment Station: 172-186.

Moser, K.W.; Hansen, M.; McWilliams, W.H.; Sheffield, R.M. 2007. Shortleaf pine composition and structure in the United States. In: Kabrick, J.M.; Dey, D.C.; Gwaze, D, eds. Shortleaf pine restoration and ecology in the Ozarks: proceedings of a symposium. Gen. Tech. Rep. NRS-P-15. Newtown Square, PA: U.S. Department of Agriculture Forest Service, Northern Research Station: 19-27.

Mullins. J.A.; Buckner, E.R.; Waldrop, T.A.; Evans, R.M. 1997. Site preparation methods for establishing mixed pine-hardwood stands in the southern Appalachians. In: Waldrop, T.A., ed. Proceedings of the 9th Biennial Southern Silviculture Conference. Gen. Tech. Rep. SRS-20. Asheville, NC: U.S. Department of Agriculture Forest Service, Southern Research Station: 22-25.

Oswalt, C.M. 2012. Spatial and temporal trends of the shortleaf pine resource in the Eastern United States. In: Kush, J.; Barlow, R.J.; Gilbert, J.C, eds. Proceedings of the shortleaf pine conference: east meets west, bridging the gap with research and education across the range. Huntsville, AL: Alabama Agricultural Experiment Station Special Report No. 11: 33-37.

Rietveld, W.J. 1989. Transplanting stress in bareroot conifer seedlings: its development and progression to establishment. Northern Journal of Applied Forestry. 6: 99-107.

SAS Institute Inc. 2012. SAS version 9.3. Cary, NC: SAS Institute Inc.

Shelton, M.G.; Cain, M.D. 2002. The sprouting potential of shortleaf pines: implications for seedling recovery from top damage. In: Walkingstick, T; Kluender, R.; Riley, T., eds. Proceedings of the 2002 Arkansas Forest Resources Center Arkansas Forestry Symposium, Little Rock, AR: 55-60.

Smalley, G.W. 1982. Classification and evaluation of forest sites on the Mid-Cumberland Plateau. Gen. Tech. Rep. SO-38. U.S. Department of Agriculture Forest Service, Southern Forest Experiment Station. 58 p.

Stone, Jr., E.L.; Stone, M.H. 1954. Root collar sprouts in pine. Journal of Forestry. 52(7): 487-491.

USDA Natural Resources Conservation Service. 2012. Web Soil Survey. http://websoilsurvey.nrcs.usda.gov/app/WebSoilSurvey.aspx. [Date accessed: March 21, 2012].

Williston, H.L. 1951. Height growth of pine seedlings. Journal of Forestry. 49: 205.

Table 1—Mean number of sprouts produced after one full growing season adjusted for the significant covariate maximum burn temperature and means unadjusted for the covariate

Treatment	Maximum covariate P=0.0089 F=6.99			Unadjusted means P=0.0118 F=27.4		
	Mean	SE	LG[a]	Mean	SE	LG
BA	7.01	0.706	B[b]	7.51	0.706	AB
BJ	4.25	0.666	C	4.81	0.663	B
BN	11.09	0.721	A	10.06	0.647	A
CL	—	—	—	6	0.591	B
CO	—	—	—	1.33	0.588	C

[a]LG denotes statistical letter grouping.

[b]Means within each column not followed by the same letter differ significantly at P = 0.05.

Note: BA is the burn in April of 2011, BJ is the burn in July of 2011, BN is the burn in November of 2011, CL is the clip in March of 2011, and CO is the control that received no treatment.

Note: cells with dashes had no maximum burn temperature covariates because these treatment areas were unburned.

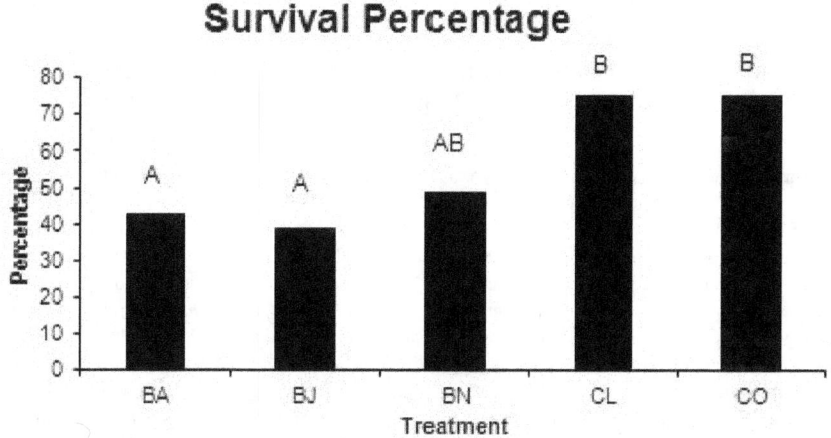

Figure 1—Mean survival percentage by treatment one growing season following treatment. Columns with different letters differ significantly at P = 0.05. BA is the burn in April of 2011, BJ is the burn in July of 2011, BN is the burn in November of 2011, CL is the clip in March of 2011, and CO is the control that received no treatment.

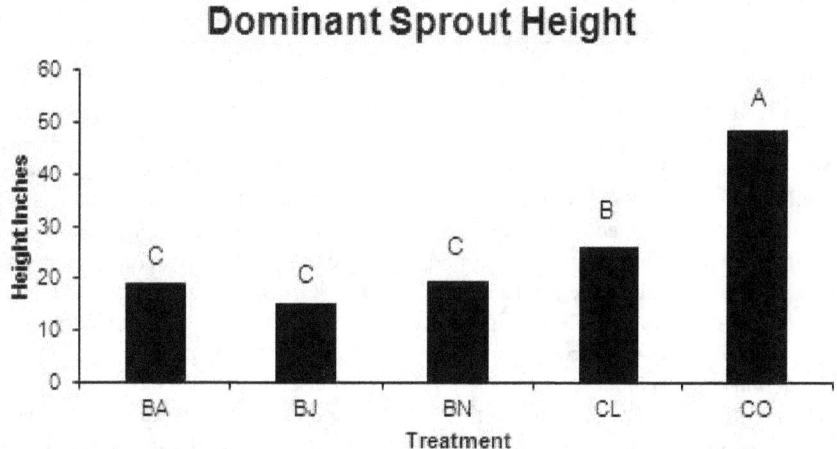

Figure 2—Mean dominant sprout height by treatment one growing season following treatment application. Columns with different letters differ significantly at P = 0.05. BA is the burn in April of 2011, BJ is the burn in July of 2011, BN is the burn in November of 2011, CL is the clip in March of 2011, and CO is the control that received no treatment.

AILANTHUS AND PRESCRIBED FIRE: IS IT A VOLATILE COMBINATION?

Joanne Rebbeck, Todd Hutchinson, Louis Iverson, Matthew Peters, Daniel Yaussy,
Michael Bowden, Greg Guess, and Aaron Kloss[1]

Abstract—Throughout much of the Central Hardwoods region, the use of prescribed fire on public lands has increased rapidly in the last decade to improve oak regeneration. While prescribed fire can favor oak regeneration, its use may also increase risk of invasion and expansion of nonnative invasive species (NNIS). Although fire has often been shown to facilitate the expansion of NNIS in the Western United States, much less in known about the effects of fire on invasives in the Eastern United States. In 2008, a team of Ohio scientists and land managers initiated a Joint Fire Science Program (JFSP) project to study how the distribution and abundance of *Ailanthus altissima* (*Ailanthus*) relates to recent prescribed fires, harvesting activity, seed sources, and other landscape and stand characteristics. We found that recent timber harvest activity was the best predictor of *Ailanthus* presence; prescribed fire was not a good predictor. We also quantified the direct effects of prescribed fire on the demography of *Ailanthus* populations, with and without a pre-burn application of stem-injected herbicide. We found that after one prescribed fire, *Ailanthus* germinants and sprouts from topkilled saplings and trees were poor competitors with faster-growing post-fire woody regeneration as forest floor shading increased over time. This study demonstrates that prescribed fire alone does not appear to facilitate the spread of *Ailanthus*. These findings also suggest that further empirical studies are needed to address the combined impacts of fire and timber harvesting on *Ailanthus* invasions in eastern U.S. forests.

BACKGROUND—FIRE AND INVASIVE PLANT BIOLOGY

To best understand how woody invasives are impacted by fire and other management practices, it is crucial to know the individual life history traits of these plants. Invasive species often are prolific seed producers, which are either wind or animal dispersed; they typically reproduce at a young age; and they can often sprout prolifically (Marinelli and Randall 1996). Rebbeck (2012) summarized the biological and ecological traits of common nonnative invasive trees, shrubs and vines found in Eastern U.S. forests. Important traits to consider when evaluating a species of interest include: (1) level of shade tolerance, (2) dioecious or monoecious reproduction, (3) annual seed production rate, (4) mode of seed dispersal, (5) seed bank viability, (6) annual growth rate, (7) sprouting ability, (8) competitiveness, and (9) successional status. Unfortunately, there are numerous information gaps for many of the species (Gucker and others 2012, Rebbeck 2012).

Limited empirical data are available regarding how many invaders respond to fire in the Eastern United States, though more is known about fire and invasives in Western U.S. forests and grasslands. Huebner (2006) evaluated 17 common nonnative invasive species (NNIS) for their response to fire and their potential to change current fire regimes in eastern oak communities and reported that most of the woody species evaluated have the potential to be resistant of fire at maturity. These included autumn olive (*Elaeagnus umbellate*), common buckthorn (*Rhamnus cathartica*), Japanese and bush honeysuckles (*Lonicera* spp.), kudzu (*Pueraria montana* var. *lobata*), multiflora rose (*Rosa multiflora*), Norway maple (*Acer platanoides*), and privet (*Ligustrum japonicum*). The response of *Ailanthus* to fire was not studied directly, but *Ailanthus* was predicted to endure and/or increase because of its ability to sprout. While updating the U.S. Forest Service Fire Effects Information System, Gucker and others (2012) characterized the information available on fire and invasive plants in the Eastern United States.

[1]Joanne Rebbeck, Research Plant Physiologist, USDA Forest Service, Northern Research Station, Delaware, OH 43015

Todd F. Hutchinson, Research Ecologist, USDA Forest Service, Northern Research Station, Delaware, OH 43015

Louis Iverson, Research Landscape Ecologist, USDA Forest Service, Northern Research Station, Delaware, OH 43015

Daniel A. Yaussy, Research Forester Emeritus, USDA Forest Service, Northern Research Station, Delaware, OH 43015

Matthew Peters, GIS Specialist, USDA Forest Service, Northern Research Station, Delaware, OH 43015

Michael Bowden, Natural Resource Administrator, Ohio Department of Natural Resources, Division of Mineral Resources Management, Columbus, OH 43229

Greg Guess, Land Management Administrator and Fire Supervisor, Ohio Department of Natural Resources, Division of Forestry, Chillicothe, OH 45601

Aaron Kloss, Firewise Coordinator, Ohio Department of Natural Resources, Division of Forestry, Columbus, OH 43229

Citation for proceedings: Waldrop, Thomas A., ed. 2014. Proceedings, Wildland Fire in the Appalachians: Discussions among Managers and Scientists. Gen. Tech. Rep. SRS-199. Asheville, NC: U.S. Department of Agriculture Forest Service, Southern Research Station. 208 p.

They found that often information relevant to fire was anecdotal and that observation-based information was sparse. The group concluded that more experiments and observations are needed, including collecting several years of data in a particular ecosystem, studying different burning conditions at varying times of year with varying fire severities, and varying intervals between burns. The authors' primary message was that "more high-quality information is needed for fire managers to avoid exacerbating problems with invasive plant species." We do know that fires often topkill vegetation that later resprouts prolifically, increase light levels within forest stands, and consume leaf litter, which releases nutrients and exposes mineral soils. These forest floor changes typically favor germination and seedling establishment, with opportunistic NNIS often getting a jump start on the native species if seed sources are present. Soil disturbances resulting from the installment of fire breaks can also promote NNIS establishment. The use of dozers, tankers, and all-terrain vehicles may introduce seeds of NNIS into previously non-infested areas. Because the current state of fire and invasive plant species research in Eastern U.S. forests is very limited, anecdotal information is currently being used by managers.

Adding to the challenge of utilizing prescribed fire and other management practices to promote oak regeneration is the fact that some invasive plants are, like oaks, disturbance-dependent species. They can share similar life history traits (e.g., strong sprouters, well-developed root systems, and drought tolerance), making it a challenge to promote oaks while minimizing the establishment and growth of native and nonnative competitors. *Ailanthus* represents one such woody invasive species. Prescribed fire topkills stems and promotes resprouting of both oaks and nonnatives. When developing a management strategy, it is important to link the timing of treatments to the phenology and energy storage patterns of the targeted species. To be most effective, managers need to find the "Achilles heel" of the target species and treat it when it is most vulnerable. An effective management plan should connect the timing of fire and/or cutting to periods of low energy reserves in roots to reduce or eliminate subsequent sprouting. Since maximum starch accumulation occurs in late summer to early fall for most species, this would not be an effective time to burn. Conversely, rapid mobilization of root starch reserves occurs in the spring when plants are producing new leaves, but successful implementation of spring prescribed fires can be challenging because of typically narrow burn windows. The timing of leaf-out can vary considerably with species. Bush honeysuckles are typically the first to leaf out in the spring and the last to drop leaves in the fall, while oaks are late to leaf out and retain leaves well into late fall. Huddle and Pallardy (1999) investigated the impact of burn season

on survival, growth, and root starch of 1- and 2-year-old red maple, white oak, and red oak seedlings. They found no difference in survival among species after a fall burn (pre-leaf drop). In contrast, red oaks survived spring fires (after leaf-out) better than maple seedlings because of higher resprouting of oaks, which was attributed to higher root starch levels. This same physiological approach is recommended when determining the most effective time to implement a prescribed burn or treat NNIS with herbicides. Late summer and early fall is the ideal time for stem injections to promote translocation of herbicide to roots to prevent resprouting of woody NNIS, but we do not recommend it as an effective season to burn.

Another important component for any land management plan is to have a current inventory of NNIS within the area of interest. Before implementing a harvest or prescribed fire program, it is crucial to be proactive regarding nonnative invasive plants before that first tree is cut or fire line is installed. Managers need to know what nonnative species are present, and where and in what numbers they are found, both within and nearby units where prescribed fires are planned. Unfortunately, managers are often lacking adequate resources to conduct NNIS inventories and to treat infested sites. A worst-case scenario would be the creation of a NNIS monoculture within a landscape with little to no ecological or economic value. In 2003, our group witnessed the abundant establishment of *Ailanthus* seedlings following a thinning and prescribed fire treatment installed in one of three southeastern Ohio State forests as part of the national Joint Fire Science Program (JFSP) Fire and Fire Surrogate Study (Rebbeck 2012, Rebbeck and others 2005). It appears that the combination of an ample seed source in the stand along with soil and canopy disturbances during treatment installation caused the surge in *Ailanthus* seedlings. This was further supported by a post-treatment inventory that found few if any adult female *Ailanthus* present in the two adjacent treatment units (shelterwood only and burn only), where no large post-treatment increase in *Ailanthus* was observed.

We learned valuable lessons from the consequences of that study. First, early detection of NNIS in advance of a disturbance is critical to limit the establishment of invasives after the disturbance. Second, it would have been advantageous to remove the seed source with an herbicide treatment prior to the prescribed burn. Had we known the extent of infestation in advance, those observed impacts could have been mitigated prior to thinning and burning. That post-disturbance increase in *Ailanthus* did, however, initiate the development of an active partnership between land managers and researchers that focuses on learning where *Ailanthus* is found on a large forested landscape, developing a cost-effective mapping tool, identifying predictors of its presence in these forested landscapes, and how *Ailanthus* responds to prescribed fire. Our overarching goal is to develop strategies that will help limit the expansion of *Ailanthus* while also sustaining oak in a managed forest landscape.

SUCCESSFUL MANAGER–RESEARCHER COLLABORATION

In 2008, the JFSP sought research proposals that specifically addressed the interaction of invasive plants and fire in the Eastern United States. We successfully secured funding and developed a series of forest management questions related to the use of prescribed fire and invasive plants focusing on the prolific sprouter and seed producer, *Ailanthus*:

1. Can prescribed fire be used effectively without facilitating the spread of NNIS?

2. Can prescribed fire be used as a surrogate for herbicide treatment of NNIS?

3. Can herbicide and fire treatments be combined to enhance control of NNIS?

4. To what extent does fire interact with timber harvesting and natural disturbances to promote the establishment and spread of NNIS?

Our two research objectives were to determine the distribution and abundance of *Ailanthus* across a managed forest landscape (Tar Hollow State Forest) and quantify the direct effects of prescribed fire on *Ailanthus* populations. The forest has a long history of timber harvesting and farming since European settlement in the late 1700s. Following a Federal land resettlement program in the 1930s, a public forest was established. It is reforested with both artificial and natural regeneration of mixed oak and mixed mesophytic species. It currently has an active timber harvesting program, and since 2001, an active prescribed burn program. Based on dendrochronological records, *Ailanthus* has been present on Tar Hollow since the early 1930s.

The first task of the project was to efficiently identify seed-bearing female trees across the forested study area. We chose to aerially map *Ailanthus* during the dormant season, when the visibility of its persistent seed clusters is most prominent (fig. 1). We utilized a Bell 206 B3 JetRanger helicopter owned by the Ohio Department of Natural Resources (ODNR) Division of Wildlife. ODNR Division of Forestry personnel conducted the aerial survey using georeferenced digital aerial sketch mapping technology developed to conduct forest health surveys (Schrader-Patton 2003) (fig. 2). Approximately 9,600 acres of highly dissected forested land was mapped in a little more than 2 hours. Through a partnership with the ODNR Division of Forestry and the Wayne National Forest, we

continue to refine our mapping tool, and subsequently have identified *Ailanthus* infestations in more than 500,000 acres of public forests in Ohio. Coordinates from these surveys were used to produce infestation maps for further management planning and are easily downloaded to hand-held global positioning system (GPS) units to be used by field crews to locate *Ailanthus* trees for chemical or other treatments. The method is proving to be a highly effective and efficient tool to map the distribution of *Ailanthus* seed sources in large landscapes. A typical survey, including rental of helicopter time, costs approximately $0.40 per acre. A manuscript that describes the mapping methodology in detail is currently in preparation.

In addition to the aerial mapping of seed-bearing female trees, we installed a systematic grid of research plots within the 9,600-acre study area to quantify the following: abundance, size, and age distribution of *Ailanthus*; proximity to *Ailanthus* seed sources; timber harvest history; fire history and intensity; canopy structure; and a suite of landscape features such as slope, aspect, and soil properties. Approximately 2,100 acres of the study area had been burned between 2001 and 2009. Forest Service scientists and research technicians were given full access to ODNR timber harvest records from the study area; records were digitized and incorporated into a geographic information system (GIS) database. Current data analysis includes the development of a GIS-based model of key factors to predict the presence of *Ailanthus*. To date, more than 60 variables have been tested in models. Fire history was not a significant predictor of *Ailanthus* presence; the best predictor of *Ailanthus* presence was whether a timber harvest had occurred within the last 25 years. Canopy structure was also important, with more open mid-canopies favoring *Ailanthus*. Plans are underway to validate the predictive model of *Ailanthus* on the Wayne National Forest in southeastern Ohio.

The second objective of this collaboration was to document the direct effects of prescribed fire on *Ailanthus*. To date, no previous work on the direct effects of fire on *Ailanthus* has been published. We implemented a replicated study at Tar Hollow State Forest to determine if an herbicide treatment in advance of a prescribed burn would limit *Ailanthus* expansion after fire. Treatments included control (no herbicide, no burn), burn only, herbicide only, and herbicide + burn. *Ailanthus* stems (≥1 inch diameter at breast height [dbh]) were stem-injected (hack-n-squirt) with imazapyr (6.25% of Arsenal®AC [53.1% a.i.]) the fall prior to a spring burn. Three years post-treatment, 91 percent of the herbicide-only and 95 percent of herbicide + burn treated *Ailanthus* stems 4 inches dbh and larger were dead with no resprouting. However, in the burn-only plots,

Ailanthus mortality was only 37 percent of stems 4 inches dbh and larger. In the first postfire growing season, small sprouts (up to 1 inch dbh) and newly-germinated *Ailanthus* seedlings increased three- to four-fold in the burn-only and herbicide + burn treatments. After three growing seasons, those numbers dropped to preburn levels because these smaller stems competed poorly with other vegetation such as the nonnative wineberry (*Rubus phoenicolasius*), native blackberry (*Rubus* spp.), and herbs that were also stimulated by the fire. A second prescribed burn is planned for 2014 to assess the impacts of multiple fires on *Ailanthus* populations in mixed oak forests.

SUMMARY

To summarize what we have learned about the interaction of fire and forest management practices and *Ailanthus* from this collaborative project, let us revisit our initial questions:

- What are the direct effects of fire on *Ailanthus*? A single mid-April prescribed fire stimulated both *Ailanthus* seed germination and sprouting. However, new *Ailanthus* germinants and small sprouts did not persist in subsequent years because of competition with other vegetation. We are in the process of studying the impact of multiple burns on *Ailanthus* regeneration.

- Can prescribed fire be used effectively without facilitating the spread of *Ailanthus*? Perhaps, but further long-term study is needed. Timber harvesting within the last 25 years appears to be more important in facilitating the spread of *Ailanthus* than a history of fire, as indicated in our GIS-based modeling.

- Can prescribed fire be used as a surrogate for herbicide treatment of *Ailanthus*? Given the results of this single study, the use of prescribed fire alone should not be considered as an alternative to herbicide to control *Ailanthus*. Although fire topkills *Ailanthus*, postfire sprouting is prolific.

- Can herbicide and fire treatments be combined to enhance *Ailanthus* control? The two treatments combined were very effective in killing and preventing the sprouting of large saplings (>1 inch dbh) and *Ailanthus* trees (≥4 inch dbh).

- How does fire interact with timber harvesting and natural disturbances to promote establishment and spread of *Ailanthus*? We have just begun to study the interactions of timber harvesting and natural disturbances on *Ailanthus* populations. Factors that predict *Ailanthus* presence in forests are emerging. However, more collaborative landscape level studies between land managers and researchers are needed across the Eastern United States.

LITERATURE CITED

Gucker, C.L.; Zouhar, K.; Kapler Smith, J.; Stone K.R. 2012. Characteristics of information available on fire and invasive plants in the Eastern United States. Fire Ecology. 8(2): 57-81.

Huddle, J.A.; Pallardy, S.G. 1999. Effect of fire on survival and growth of *Acer rubrum* and *Quercus* seedlings. Forest Ecology and Management. 118: 49–56.

Huebner, C.D. 2006. Fire and invasive exotic plant species in eastern oak communities: an assessment of current knowledge. In: Dickinson, M.B., ed. Proceedings, Fire in eastern oak forests: delivering science to land managers conference. Gen. Tech. Rep. NRS-P-1. Newton Square, PA: U.S. Department of Agriculture Forest Service, Northern Research Station: 218-232.

Marinelli, J.; Randall, J.M, eds. 1996. Invasive plants: weeds of the global garden. Brooklyn: Brooklyn Botanical Garden. 111 p.

Rebbeck, J.; Hutchinson, T.F.; Long, R.P. 2005. Invasive plants affecting the management of Ohio's forests. In: Proceedings, 16th U.S. Department of Agriculture interagency research forum on gypsy moth and other invasive species. Gen. Tech. Rep. NE-337. Newtown Square, PA: U.S. Department of Agriculture Forest Service, Northeastern Research Station: 68-70.

Rebbeck, J. 2012. Fire management and woody invasive plants in oak ecosystems. In: Dey, D.C.; Stambaugh, M.C.; Clark, S.L.; Schweitzer, C.J., eds. Proceedings, The 4th Fire in Eastern Oak Forests Conference. Gen. Tech. Rep. NRS-P-102. Newtown Square, PA: U.S. Department of Agriculture Forest Service, Northern Research Station: 142-155.

Schrader-Patton, C. 2003. Digital aerial sketchmapping. Interim Project Report RSAC-1202-RPT2. Salt Lake City, UT: U.S. Department of Agriculture Forest Service Engineering, Forest Health Technology Enterprise Team, Remote Sensing Applications Center. 14 p. http://www.fs.fed.us/foresthealth/technology/pdfs/1202-RPT2.pdf. [Date accessed: January 24, 2014].

Figure 1—Dormant growing season view of seed clusters on adult female *Ailanthus* tree.

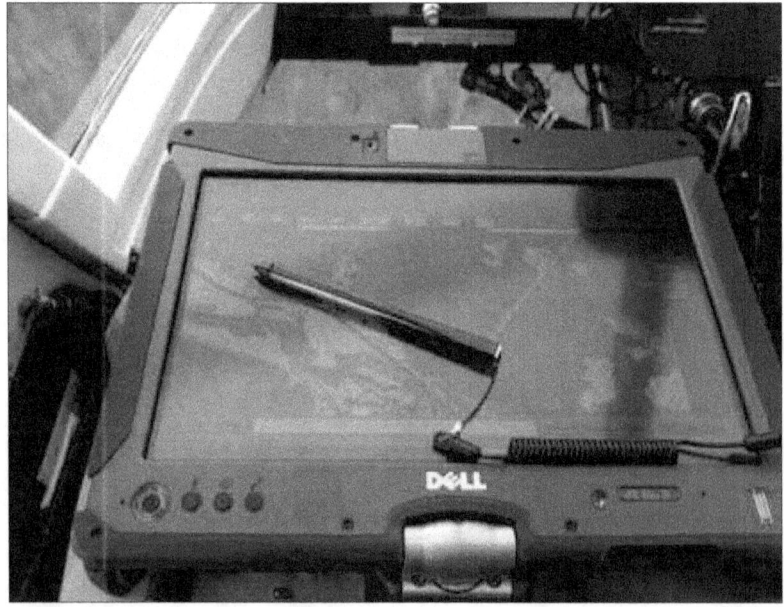

Figure 2—Digital sketch mapping software tablet used to survey female *Ailanthus* during helicopter surveys.

FIRE IN MOUNTAIN BOGS

Adam Warwick[1]

Abstract—Southern Appalachian montane wetlands are rare natural communities. Distributed throughout the Appalachians' high-elevation depressions, valley slopes, and basins, a highly variable combination of abiotic factors shape the character of each "bog." Most unaltered bogs are distinguished by a generally open vegetative structure and diverse herbaceous flora, but with a tendency toward succession to forests. Natural disturbances arrest some bogs in early seres. However, anthropogenic influence has increasingly precluded many such disturbance regimes, resulting in uninhibited succession, habitat homogenization, and the gradual demise of the specialized flora and fauna. To restore and maintain some bogs' naturally open character, land managers such as The Nature Conservancy (TNC) have chosen to mimic disturbance using a variety of methods, including prescribed burning. This paper provides insight into how two TNC-owned sites were historically influenced by fire, presents some of TNC's experience using prescribed fire in bogs, and describes trends in Green Pitcher Plant (*Sarracenia oreophila*) abundance as regular fire regimes were restored to the sites.

INTRODUCTION

Southern Appalachian montane wetlands, collectively known as bogs, are rare natural communities. Forming as small, wet concavities within high-elevation depressions, valley slopes, and basins, bogs contribute greatly to the biodiversity of the Southern Blue Ridge Ecoregion. Individual bogs can vary considerably in terms of geomorphic setting, hydrologic regime, and soil and water chemistry, yet most are characterized by a generally open vegetative structure with diverse herbaceous flora (Schafale 2012). Bogs can vary from permanently wet to intermittently dry, with hydroperiods driven largely by groundwater seepage. Habitat conditions are generally harsh, containing highly acidic, nutrient-poor, anoxic soil characteristics from which unique suites of plants are established. Through time, abiotic processes and disturbances have shaped these wetlands, including flooding driven both by beavers and by weather regimes, ungulate grazing, clearing by native people, and in some cases fire. In the absence of natural disturbance, bogs tend to rapidly succeed with shrub and tree invasion. Challenges commonly encountered with restoration of bogs' early seral conditions include the extirpation of grazers, shorter duration and less frequent flooding, absence of beavers, native and nonnative invasive species, urban and agricultural development, fire suppression, and altered soil and water chemistry from excessive nutrient input. In many cases, a combination of these factors impedes bog restoration and management. Due to the large scale destruction of these unique places, land managers must adapt and mimic these processes to conserve the few remaining sites and inherently rare species.

North Carolina's Department of Environment and Natural Resources Natural Heritage Program recognizes five types of bogs (Schafale 2012) based largely on vegetation composition differences. All are recognized by the Ecological Classification System as Southern and Central Appalachian Bogs and Fens (CES202.300; Federal Geographic Data Committee 2008). Southern Appalachian Fens are herb-dominated wetlands sustained by highly basic groundwater seepage. Swamp Forest Bog Complexes are tree-dominated communities that occur along streams within floodplains (Schafale 2012). French Broad Valley Bogs and Southern Appalachian Bogs are similar, but both contain a greater proportion of herbaceous vegetation, and French Broad Valley Bogs generally contain a proportion of Coastal Plain disjunct wetland plant species (Schafale 2012). The Low Mountain Seepage Bog is distinguished by a unique suite of Piedmont and Coastal Plain disjunct plants (Schafale 2012). It is important to account for these subtle variations when considering management using fire. Variables such as presence or absence of sphagnum and specific plant species can lend important information and likely prevent deleterious outcomes.

While preserve management and conservation easement monitoring are a significant part of The Nature Conservancy's (TNC) mission, TNC is continually building capacity to restore natural fire regimes in the appropriate places with the help of the Fire Learning Network. Similarly, efforts to share bog management experience is continually expanding. In light of the potential Mountain Bogs National Wildlife Refuge establishment, TNC and the U.S. Fish and Wildlife Service have partnered to establish the Bog Learning Network. The aim of the Bog Learning Network is to share experiences and help provide tools and techniques

[1] Adam Warwick, Stewardship Director, The Nature Conservancy, Asheville, NC 28806

Citation for proceedings: Waldrop, Thomas A., ed. 2014. Proceedings, Wildland Fire in the Appalachians: Discussions among Managers and Scientists. Gen. Tech. Rep. SRS-199. Asheville, NC: U.S. Department of Agriculture Forest Service, Southern Research Station. 208 p.

that can be used to restore and manage these unique places. The goal of this paper is to relate information, experiences, and results of burning in a specific type of Southern Appalachian montane wetland and generate dialogue among managers regarding the use of fire in Southern Appalachian wetlands.

TNC manages two Low Mountain Seepage Bogs that occur near the banks of Lake Chatuge (fig. 1). Eller Seep Preserve contains a 2.9-acre wetland that represents North Carolina's only Low Mountain Seepage Bog and supports one of the largest known populations of *Sarracenia oreophila* (Green Pitcher Plant). Just south of the Georgia state line lies Reed Branch Wet Meadow Preserve, which contains a 3.5-acre Low Mountain Seepage Bog and supports Georgia's only naturally occurring *S. oreophila* population. Over the last several thousand years, fire, flooding, and grazing have shaped the flora and fauna of these bogs, and the fact they still exist is a result of continued disturbance. *S. oreophila* and associated herbaceous vegetation indicates open conditions likely occurred here historically, as *S. oreophila* seeds must fall on bare, moist mineral soil in order to germinate and become established. In the absence of such conditions, seedling recruitment decreases, reproduction becomes primarily asexual, and populations inevitably decline (Folkerts 1992).

Prior to the damming of the Hiawassee River and creation of Lake Chatuge Reservoir in 1942, this region contained a series of seepage bogs that supported *S. oreophila* (Carlson 1994), and evidence indicates the region's wetlands withstood periodic fire. Adjacent uplands are comprised of Mesic Oak-Hickory (Simon 2011), and pre-settlement forests suggest low intensity fires occurred every 10-15 years with occasional more intense fires help to maintain and regenerate fire tolerant oaks (Landfire 2010). Both of these sites lie near the base of western-facing slopes within the Hiawassee River Valley. Further, Native Americans inhabited the valley from about 2000 years before present and were known to use fire for agriculture and hunting purposes (Govus 1990). The previous landowner of Eller Seep burned the site annually from 1908-1972 to keep the land open for grazing (Govus 1990). This is perhaps the most critical factor for *S. oreophila* existence at the site. Following his death in 1972, burning ceased until the early 1990's. During this time hydrologic modifications were made in an attempt to drain the site. These activities resulted in rapid hardwood invasion and subsequent decline of *S. oreophila*. Reed Branch was burned annually for at least 20 years until 1990 (Tollner 1997), during which time it was used as a pasture. The hydrology of the area was disturbed when a ditch was installed to drain an adjacent pasture, and at least one tile drain was installed on the property.

TNC's management goals for these bogs are to maintain the open character, increase *S. oreophila* populations, and promote the continued existence of diverse and rare seepage bog plant communities. Thus, the primary strategy is to limit hardwood encroachment to the center of the bog and expand the herbaceous zone. The restoration methods used by TNC are controlled burning every 1-3 years and mechanical and/or chemical treatment of encroaching hardwoods that would otherwise outcompete, such as red maple (*Acer rubrum*) and smooth alder (*Alnus serrulata*).

MATERIALS AND METHODS

Eller Seep

Since the acquisition of Eller Seep in 1992, TNC has conducted seven controlled burns: April 1992, March 1997, April 2002, January 2005, April 2007, April 2009, and April 2011. Approximately 3 months following the burns, the number of *S. oreophila* leaves (i.e., pitchers) and flowers was then counted by sampling along ten permanent belt transects (fig. 2). The beginning of the baseline was marked by a 23-cm diameter at breast height tulip poplar (*Liriodendron tulipifera*) and was established by running a metric tape from this point out at 310°. The ten 5 m by 40 m belt transects ran perpendicular to this baseline. Each transect was divided into 5 m by 5 m sections. Transect sections were labeled based on the starting distance from the baseline. Thus, Section 0 identified the first section 0-5 m from the line. Section 5 is for 5-10 m from the line, etc. (fig. 2). In addition, there was a high density area on transects 7 and 8 which was divided into 2.5 m by 2.5 m sampling plots. This area was located between 0 and 12.5 m from the baseline in a block which includes portions of transects 7 and 8. Separate counts of a subsample of plots were made within this area but not included in the transect counts for years before 2007. More intensive data were collected in these high density plots, including size classes to gather greater detail. However, separate monitoring of the high density area did not provide significant additional information, and it was discontinued in 2007. In 2007–2008, counts for transects 7 and 8 included all plants within the entire length of the transects, including the high density area. Therefore, the total transect counts prior to 2007 are not directly comparable to the total counts for 2007–2008 because they do not include this high density area. In order to compare the older transect data with the more recent data, data for transects 7 and 8 are excluded. While some transect data are lost, the comparison gives a better picture of the trends and changes in the sampled area. To compare data for the portions of the transects in the high density area, comparisons would need to be made between sample counts in earlier years and total counts in 2007 and 2008, which would be of questionable value.

In 1990–1994, only a 5 m by 27.5 m section of transects 7 and 8 was counted, which excluded the high density area from 0 to 12.5 m from the baseline. In 1995–1998, transect data appear to exclude the high density area, but tabular data are not available, only a summary report, so no transect data are presented. Data were not collected from 1999–2001. In 2002–2006, transect data were collected which excluded the high density area. In 2007–2008, the entire 5 m by 40 m length of transects 7 and 8 were counted, including the high density area. Clump counts may not be a reliable measure of population size changes because it is unclear how clumps merge and separate over time.

Reed Branch Wet Meadow

Since TNC acquired Reed Branch in 1992, eight controlled burns have been conducted: September 1998, January 2002, March 2004, March 2006, March 2008, December 2009, March 2012, and October 2013. Monitoring at Reed Branch consisted of complete *S. oreophila* pitcher and flower counts in late spring. From 1998–2008, monitoring occurred annually with one hiatus, 2000–2002. In 2009, monitoring was only conducted in the second growing season following fire to allow comparisons between years, since counts of pitchers and flowers varied greatly between fire years and non-fire years. It also allowed counts of flowers, since flowering is generally suppressed in the season following fire. Lastly, monitoring is easier since numbers of pitchers are high in the season following fire. Monitoring has since taken place in 2011 and 2013. Regression models show that numbers of both pitchers and flowers have steadily increased in the population since management and monitoring began in 1998.

RESULTS

The number of *S. oreophila* clumps at Eller Seep remained relatively stable from 1990 to 1994. However, when monitored again following an eight-year hiatus, the number of clumps had dropped sharply when measured in 2002. The numbers then continually increased through 2007 (fig. 3). Clump count dropped again in 2007 and 2008. However, it was determined that clump counts may not be a reliable measure of population size changes because it is unclear how clumps merge and separate over time.

From an initial count of 777 in 1990, the number of *S. oreophila* pitchers continually increased through 2008, with relatively minor declines in 2002 and 2006 (fig. 4). The number of flowers was variable from 1990–2008, but increased sharply the year after each fire (fig. 5). The number of flowers counted increased from 40 in 1990 to 135 in 2008. Late frosts hinder flowering and thus account for some of the variability

Reed Branch monitoring data show a steady increase in number of pitchers each year in both fire and non-fire years, appearing as linear growth. (fig. 6). There was a sharp increase in number of pitchers from 2006 to 2008, which affected the R^2 value. An exponential model was used, but it only increased the value slightly and it was still below 0.90. There was a steady increase in flowers counted from 1998–2006 (fig. 7). After 2006, however, flower numbers began to decline. There are 250 less flowers counted in 2008 when compared to the next lowest year in 1999. There are 795 less flowers counted in 2008 when compared to 2006. There was a statistically significant increase in number of pitchers during fire years compared to non-fire years ($p = 0.022$). However, there was no statistically significant increase in flower production during non-fire years when compared to fire years ($p = 0.085$).

CONCLUSIONS

Restoration of an appropriate fire regime has effectively reversed the decline of *S. oreophila* populations at both Eller Seep and Reed Branch. *S. oreophila* and native herbaceous species that inhabit Low Mountain Seepage Bogs benefit from controlled burning (U.S. Fish and Wildlife Service 1994) and appear to thrive if burned in one- to three-year intervals. Flowering was noticeably more prolific in the year after burning. Brush cutters have been used to remove hardwoods at Eller Seep, which helps increase continuity of the fuel bed and limits hardwood growth in years when the bog may not burn. The aim at Eller Seep is to further suppress hardwood growth by possibly shifting the timing of controlled burns to the late spring or early summer, in combination with cutting and chemical treatments. These results pertain specifically to Low Mountain Seepage Bogs, a rare type of montane wetland with characteristic fire-adapted species. Implementation of a fire program in sphagnum-dominated wetlands and/or those with other *Sarracenia* species should be approached with caution. TNC staff hopes that this paper will encourage other land managers to share experiences, not only with fire, but with all management techniques that help conserve rare plants and animals supported by bogs.

ACKNOWLEDGMENTS

Thanks to staff from the Georgia Chapter of the Nature Conservancy for their hard work over the years and for providing the data from Reed Branch: David Wilson, Malcolm Hodges, and Erick Brown among others. Thank you to Margit Bucher, Megan Sutton, Andrew Roe, and Phil Croll from the North Carolina Chapter of the Nature Conservancy.

REFERENCES

Carlson, B. 1994. RBWM site conservation plan. Unpublished report. On file with: The Nature Conservancy-Southern Blue Ridge Office, 46 Haywood Street, Asheville, NC 28801.

Faber-Langendoen, D.; Keeler-Wolf, T.; Meidinger, D. [and others]. 2012. Classification and description of world formation types. Part I (Introduction) and Part II (Description of formation types). Reston, VA; Arlington, VA: Hierarchy Revisions Working Group, Federal Geographic Data Committee, FGDC Secretariat, U.S. Geological Survey and NatureServe. 216 p.

Federal Geographic Data Committee. 2008. Vegetation classification standard. FGDC-STD-005. 119 p. http://usnvc.org/wp-content/uploads/2011/02/NVCS_V2_FINAL_2008-02.pdf. [Date accessed: January 20, 2014].

Folkerts, G.W. 1992. Identification and measurement of damage caused by flower and seed predators associated with *Sarracenia oreophila* and recommended management/control measures deemed appropriate. Unpublished Report. On file with: The Nature Conservancy-Southern Blue Ridge Office, 46 Haywood Street, Asheville, NC 28801.

Govus, Thomas E. 1990. Land use history, population study methods and management recommendations for the Eller Preserve, Clay County, North Carolina. Unpublished Report. On file with: The Nature Conservancy-Southern Blue Ridge Office, 46 Haywood Street, Asheville, NC 28801.

Hodges, Malcom. 2013. Conservation Management Plan: Reed Branch Wet Meadow Preserve. Unpublished Report. On file with: The Nature Conservancy-Southern Blue Ridge Office, 46 Haywood Street, Asheville, NC 28801.

LANDFIRE. 2010. [Homepage of the LANDFIRE Program, U.S. Department of Agriculture Forest Service; U.S. Department of the Interior]. [Online.] Available: http://www.landfire.gov/index.php. [Date accessed: January 20, 2014].

NCWRC [North Carolina Wildlife Resources Commission]. 2010. Bogs and Associated Wetlands-Southern Blue Ridge Mountains. http://www.ncwildlife.org/Portals/0/Conserving/documents/Mountains/SBR_Bogs_and_associated_wetlands.pdf. [Date accessed: January 20, 2014].

Roe, Andrew; Croll, Phil. 2009. Monitoring summary of Green Pitcher plant (*Sarracenia oreophila*) at Eller Seep. Unpublished Report. On file with: The Nature Conservancy-Southern Blue Ridge Office, 46 Haywood Street, Asheville, NC 28801.

Schafale, M.P. 2012. Guide to the Natural Communities of North Carolina Fourth Approximation. Raleigh, NC: NC Natural Heritage Program. 208 p.

Simon, S.A. 2011. Ecological zones in the Southern Blue Ridge: 3rd approximation. Unpublished report. On file with: National Forests in NC, 160 Zillicoa Street, Asheville, NC 28801.

Tollner, B. 1997. Report of visit to the Reed Branch proposed site for pitcher plant preservation. Internal report. Athens, GA: The University of Georgia.

U.S. Fish and Wildlife Service. 1994. Green Pitcher Plant Recovery Plan. Jackson, MS: U.S. Fish and Wildlife Service. 23 p.

Wilson, David B. 2008. Data analysis of green pitcher plant (*Sarracenia oreophilia*) at Reed Branch Meadow. Unpublished Report. On file with: The Nature Conservancy-Southern Blue Ridge Office, 46 Haywood Street, Asheville, NC 28801.

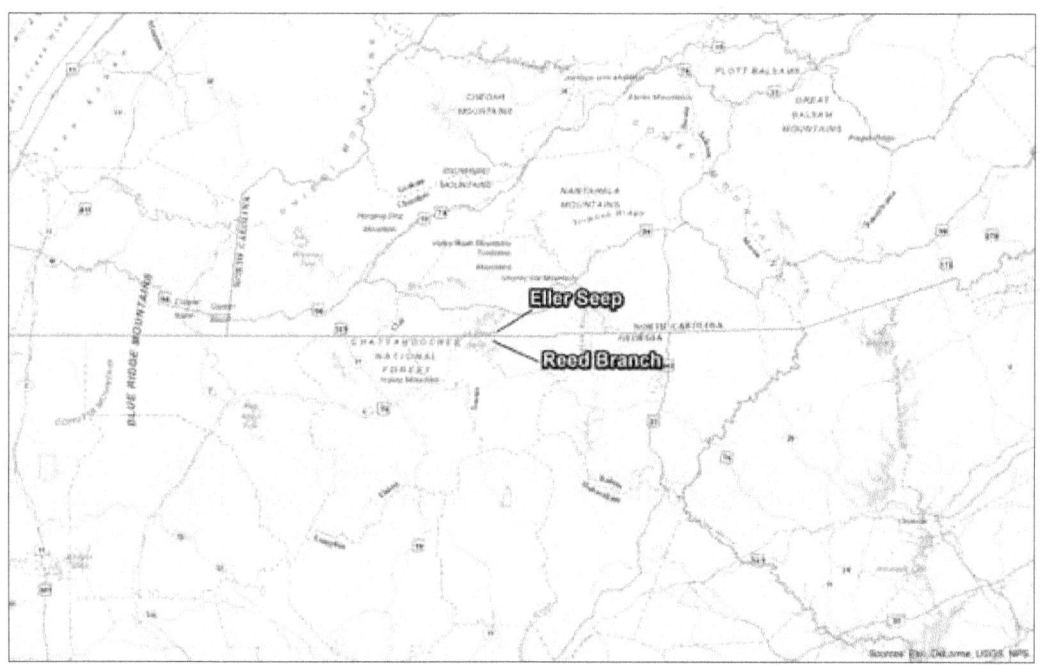

Figure 1—Eller Seep Preserve and Reed Branch Wet Meadow Preserve.

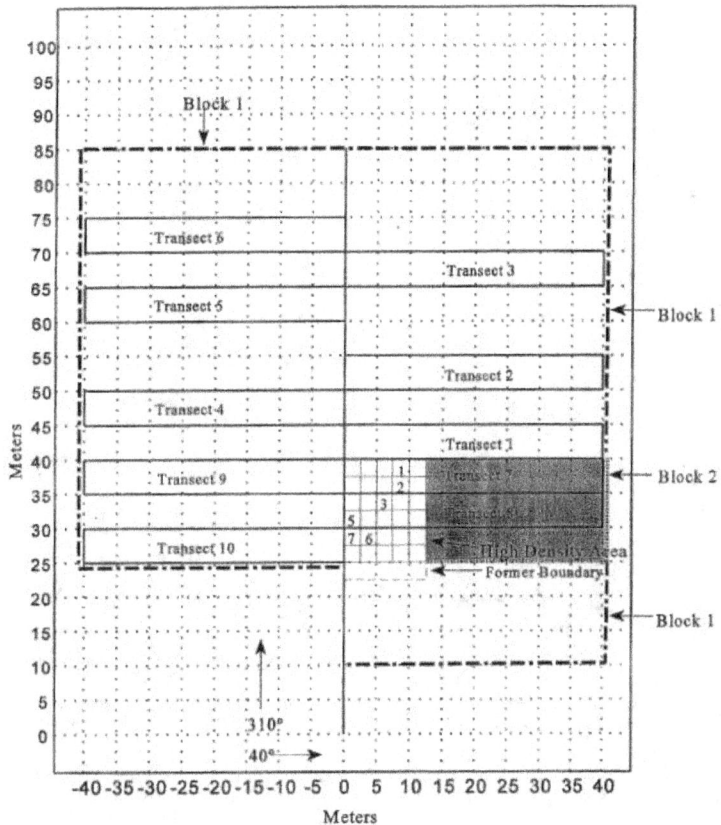

Figure 2—Sampling design at Eller Seep Preserve (from Rudd and Sutter, 1998 Monitoring Report). Low and high density areas sampled with numbered transects and plots, respectively.

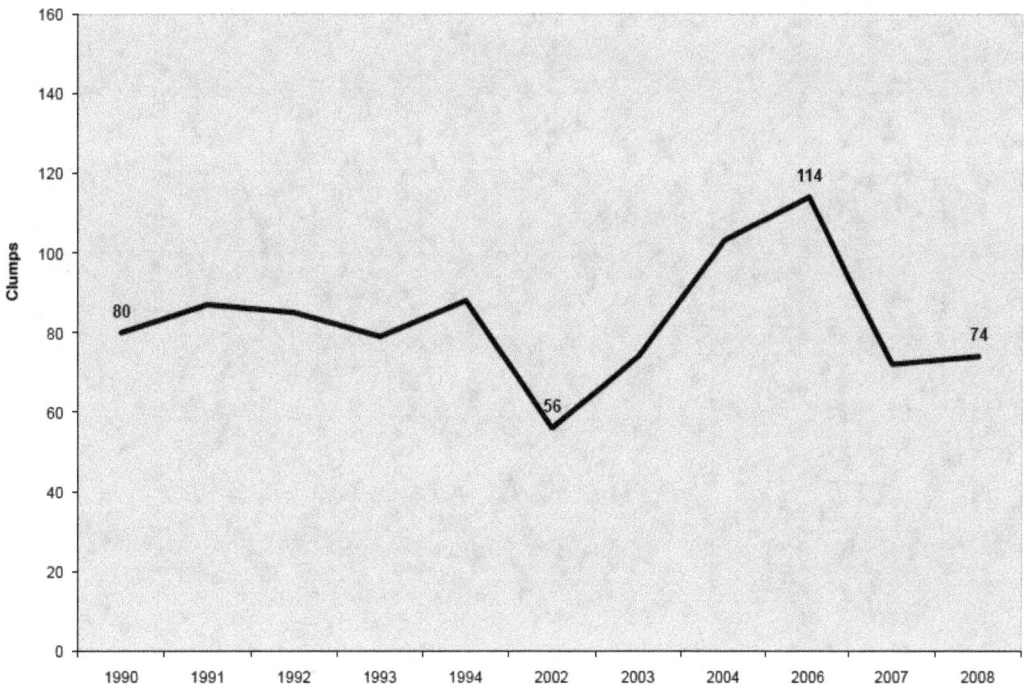

Figure 3—Trend in the number of *S. oreophila* clumps at Eller Seep Preserve (1990–2008). Controlled burns were conducted in 1992, 1997, 2002, 2005, 2007, 2009, and 2011.

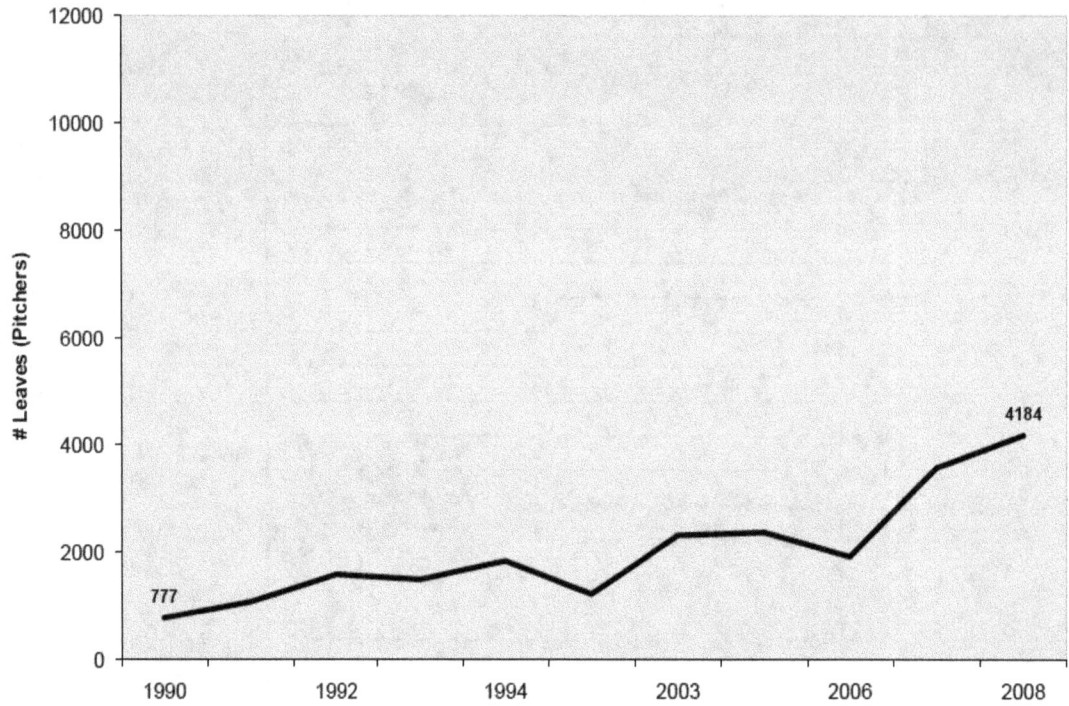

Figure 4—Trend in the number of *S. oreophila* pitchers at Eller Seep Preserve (1990–2008). Controlled burns were conducted in 1992, 1997, 2002, 2005, 2007, 2009, and 2011.

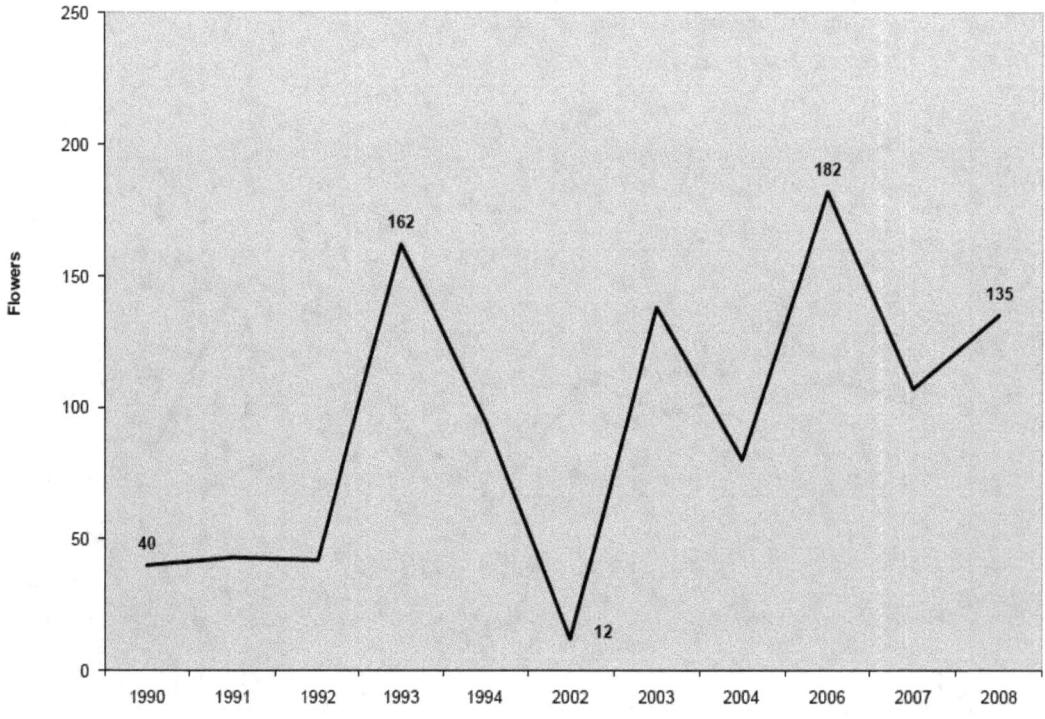

Figure 5—Trend in the number of *S. oreophila* flowers at Eller Seep Preserve (1990–2008). Controlled burns were conducted in 1992, 1997, 2002, 2005, 2007, 2009, and 2011.

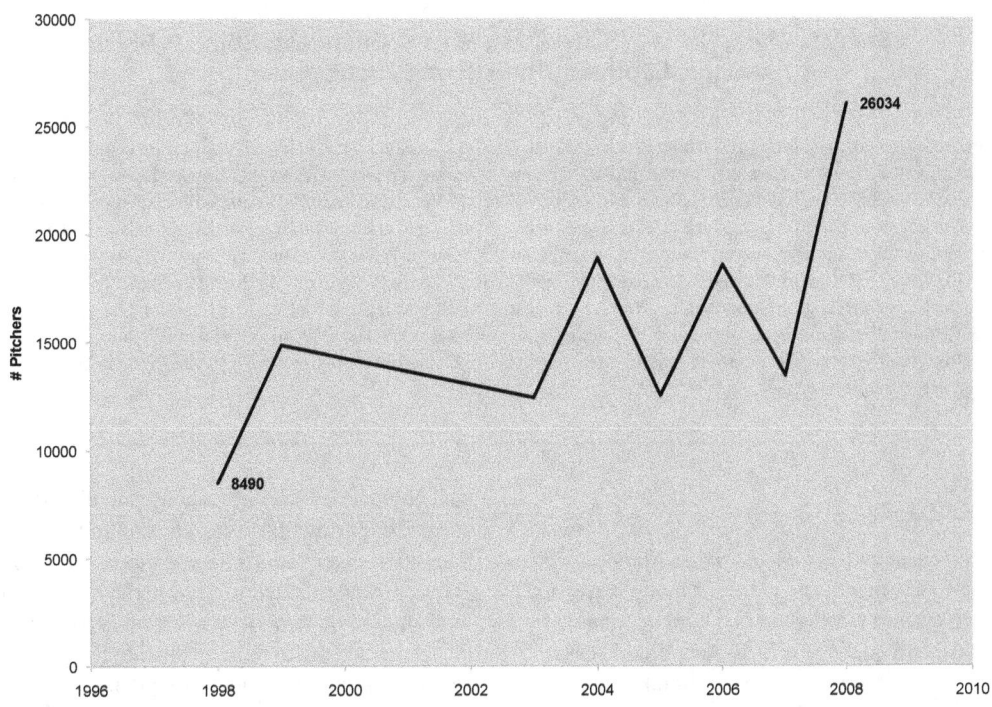

Figure 6—Trend in the number of *S. oreophila* pitchers at Reed Branch Wet Meadow Preserve (1996–2008). Controlled burns have been conducted in 1998, 2002, 2004, 2006, and 2008.

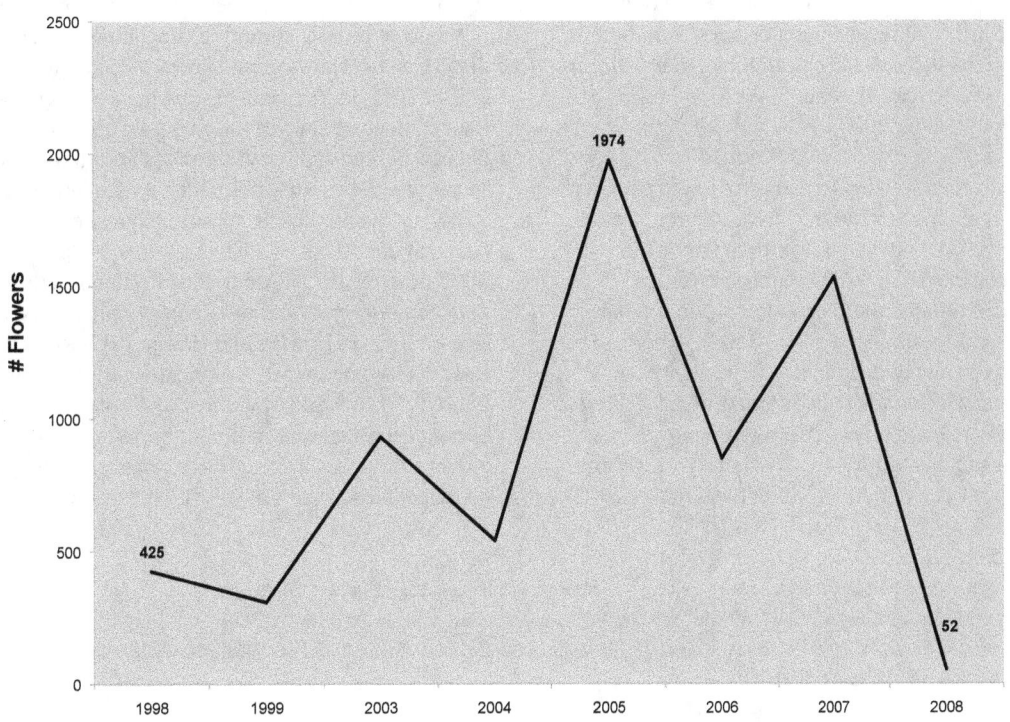

Figure 7—Trend in the number of *S. oreophila* flowers at Reed Branch Wet Meadow Preserve (1996–2008). Controlled burns have been conducted in 1998, 2002, 2004, 2006, and 2008.

THE AMERICAN CHESTNUT AND FIRE: 6-YEAR RESEARCH RESULTS

Stacy L. Clark, Callie J. Schweitzer, Mike R. Saunders, Ethan P. Belair,
Scott J. Torreano, and Scott E. Schlarbaum[1]

Abstract—American chestnut [*Castanea dentata* Marsh. (Borkh.)] is an iconic species with important ecological and utilitarian values, but was decimated by the mid-20th century by exotic fungal species from Asia. Successful restoration will require sustainable silvicultural methods to maximize survival and afford chestnut a competitive advantage over natural vegetation. The study examined effects of prescribed burning and commercial tree harvesting on survival and height growth of planted American chestnut on the mid-Cumberland Plateau in Tennessee. American chestnuts grew best in patch clearcuts compared to areas that had been commercially thinned. A severe drought during the establishment year probably led to decreased survival and growth rates. However, 6-year survival was highest for trees with smaller ground-line diameter and taller stem heights at the time of planting and in units that had lower levels of percent full sunlight in the first year after planting. Prescribed burning did not affect survival or height growth, but browsing by deer was more common in burned versus unburned areas.

INTRODUCTION

The American chestnut [*Castanea dentata* Marsh. (Borkh.)] was a dominant canopy tree in many hardwood forest types in eastern North America until decimated by primarily two exotic pathogens from Asia. Ink disease (causal agent *Phytophthora cinnamomi* Rands) and chestnut blight [causal agent *Cryphonectria parasitica* (Murr.) Barr] reduced the species primarily to recurrent understory sprouts on upland sites with well-drained sandy soils (Anagnostakis 2001, 2012). American chestnut has been extirpated as a canopy tree throughout its former range since the early to mid-20th century. Restoration will require artificial regeneration of trees with durable resistance to ink disease and chestnut blight, as natural resistance in American chestnut to these pathogens is relatively low (Griffin 2000).

American chestnut was extirpated prior to the emergence of modern ecological or forestry research programs. Consequently, little is known regarding American chestnut's response to natural or anthropogenic disturbance. Although the species has shade-tolerant characteristics (Joesting and others 2007), American chestnut was probably disturbance-dependent, with some life-history characteristics similar to oak (*Quercus* L.) genera (Wang and others 2013). Phylogeny studies indicate oaks and chestnuts are closely related within the Fagaceae (Beech) family (Kremer and others 2007), and could share similar responses to disturbances such as fire. Experimental research, exploratory analysis, and long-term observations have established the premise that oaks are well adapted to fire (Abrams 1992), but similar information on American chestnut is lacking. An increase in *Castanea* (Mill.) pollen coincided with an increase in charcoal abundance, suggesting that chestnut was favored by fire and a warming climate in New England forests ca. 1,500 years ago (Delcourt and Delcourt 1998, Foster and others 2002).

Historical literature and studies of remnant trees revealed that American chestnut is a species with one of the most prolific sprouting capabilities following disturbances (Hawley and Hawes 1912, Matoon 1909, Paillet 1984). American chestnut grows faster in height than competing species following disturbances or when planted in high-light environments (Frothingham 1924, Jacobs and Severeid 2004, McEwen and others 2006). Fast growth and prolific sprouting may be an adaption to frequent disturbances, including fire (Foster and others 2002, Russell 1987). American chestnut has thinner bark than oak, however, and fire damage may predispose the tree to disease (Hawley and Hawes 1912, Russell 1987). Baker (1884) described American chestnut as "greatly injured" by fire, and Matoon (1909) noted that American chestnut sprouts were particularly prone to rot if the parent stump was infected with disease. Throughout its range, prescribed fire was often used to facilitate

[1] Stacy L. Clark, Research Forester, USDA Forest Service, Southern Research Station, Knoxville, TN 37996

Callie J. Schweitzer, Research Forester, USDA Forest Service, Southern Research Station, Huntsville, AL 35801

Mike R. Saunders, Associate Professor, Purdue University, Department of Forestry and Natural Resources and the Hardwood Tree Improvement and Regeneration Center, West Lafayette, IN 47907

Ethan P. Belair, Graduate Research Assistant, Purdue University

Scott J. Torreano, Professor, University of the South, Department of Forestry and Geology, Sewanee, TN 37383-1000

Scott E. Scharlbaum, Professor, The University of Tennessee, Department of Forestry, Wildlife, and Fisheries, Knoxville, TN 37996

Citation for proceedings: Waldrop, Thomas A., ed. 2014. Proceedings, Wildland Fire in the Appalachians: Discussions among Managers and Scientists. Gen. Tech. Rep. SRS-199. Asheville, NC: U.S. Department of Agriculture Forest Service, Southern Research Station. 208 p.

gathering chestnuts, and often the fire would escape and damage the timber (Hough 1878). Despite chestnut's apparent susceptibility to fire, these early accounts should be viewed in the context of the era in which they were written, a time when fire was not actively controlled and was often condemned (Brose and others 2001). We can hypothesize from these early accounts that too frequent or severe fire was detrimental to chestnut's ability to gain dominance (Russell 1987). Infrequent, low-intensity fires may have favored species' expansion, particularly in the northern extent of the species' range (Foster and others 2002), suggesting that fire should be evaluated for viability as a process to be used in American chestnut restoration activities.

Regeneration harvests or intermediate stand treatments that reduce overstory stand density increased growth of American chestnut seedlings compared to trees planted under full canopy conditions (Clark and others 2012a, McCament and McCarthy 2005, Rhoades and others 2009). Effects of prescribed burning and interactions with harvesting have only been tested with American chestnut when fire was prescribed prior to direct seeding of nuts (McCament and McCarthy 2005). In particular, only two studies have directly examined the response of planted American chestnut seedlings to fire after seedlings were planted. One study will be described herein, and the other was conducted outside the species range using fire simulation (Belair and others, in press). We discuss effects from various disturbances, including prescribed burning and commercial tree harvesting, on 6-year old planted American chestnuts. We modeled probabilities for survival and deer browse, as well as height predictions for artificially regenerated American chestnut seedlings based on silvicultural treatments, seedling size at planting, and selected environmental influences.

METHODS

This study was established on forest property owned and managed by University of the South, in Franklin County, near the town of Sewanee, TN. The site is on the Weakly Dissected Plateau Landtype Association of the mid-Cumberland Plateau (Smalley 1982), and native American chestnut sprouts were present in the stand. Annual precipitation averages 150 cm per year and is greatest from December through March. Soils can be described as Hartsells-Lonewood-Ramsey-Gilpin and developed in residuum from sandstone. The study site was a 20.2-ha hardwood stand and was subdivided into three approximately equally sized blocks based on topographic characteristics. Site index (base age 50) for northern red oak was approximately 20 m. In the winter of 2006–2007, all three blocks were thinned to 15 m^2 ha^{-1} of basal area using thinning from below, and within each block, two patch clearcuts 0.1 to 0.2 ha in size were harvested. Patch

clearcuts within each block were a minimum of 90 m apart.

Within each block, prescribed burn units of 1.0 to 1.8 ha, including at least one of the patch clearcuts and part of the thinning area, were established, with burns originally slated for March 2007. The original experimental design was a randomized block design with three blocks and a two by two factorial with thinning versus patch clearcuts and burning versus no burning as the two factors. Due to logistical constraints related to a severe drought that created unsuitable burning conditions throughout the desired burn window (U.S. Drought Monitor 2014), only one block was burned in 2007 (table 1). The burn was conducted on March 7 and was moderate in intensity with 0.9 to 1.8 m flame heights. The original experimental design was further compromised when two of the patch clearcuts were entered and hand-thinned in July 2009 (table 1). The hand-thinning consisted of removal of red maple (*Acer rubrum* L.) and sourwood (*Oxydendrum aboreum* L. DC.) seedlings using hand-saws and machetes. In addition, a January 2010 tornado affected two experimental units, a patch clearcut and a thinning unit (table 1). The tornado-affected thinning unit was salvage-logged within a few weeks following the tornado. The tornado and the salvage logging effectively removed all overstory trees in the thinned experimental unit. In March 2010, the original prescribed burn plan was implemented, but the burn did not reach the thinning unit in block 2. Recorded flame heights and tree scorch marks in each experimental unit were used to classify fires into mild (flame heights $\leq$ 0.9 m) and moderate intensity (flame heights > 0.9 m) (table 1). All prescribed burns were set with backing fires ignited with drip torches.

In March 2007, immediately following the prescribed burn, we planted 5 American chestnuts and 35 northern red oak seedlings in each experimental unit. The experimental material was pure American chestnut provided by the American Chestnut Foundation from a Cumberland Plateau seed source. Bare-root (1-0) nursery seedlings were produced in the Georgia State nursery in Bryomville, GA using protocols developed to produce relatively large seedlings with fibrous root systems (Kormanik and others 1994). Evidence of root rot caused by *Phytophthora cinnamomi* was not evident on any seedlings. Seedlings were planted using JIM_GEM® KBC bars modified to increase bar width to 30 cm to accommodate planting of larger seedlings. The American chestnut seedlings were planted on a 3-m by 3-m spacing randomly intermixed with the northern red oak seedlings. Each seedling was measured for ground-line diameter (GLD) and height to the tallest live bud at the time of planting in 2007 and then again in years 2008–2012 after trees had set bud (August through March). Other categorical measurements included survival, presence or absence of deer browse to the terminal bud, dieback of the main stem, and chestnut blight. Blight was identified as a vertical ellipsoid shaped canker on the stem that was sometimes sunken or slightly swollen. The canker had vertical cracking or fissuring of the bark with mycelial fans just below the bark surface (visible with a 5X hand lens), and/or with orange stromata protruding from the bark (cf. Griffin and Elkins 1986). Chestnut blight was recorded on live trees, and we continued to record the presence of blight each year after the tree died. Stem dieback and deer browse were recorded on live trees. We documented if a basal sprout had replaced the original leader as the tallest stem.

During the first growing season (2007), we measured the amount of photosynthetically active radiation (PAR) (μmol m^{-2} s^{-1}) above the terminal bud, and above the widest margins of each live American chestnut and northern red oak seedling's crown using an AccuPar ceptometer. Percent full sun (PFS) was estimated by comparing the average PAR measurements from each seedling to PAR measurements taken at the same time from a ceptometer placed in full sun approximately 0.2 km away. Tree PFS values were averaged across live chestnut and northern red oak seedlings within each experimental unit to give an estimate of the experimental unit's PAR. We did not use individual PFS values taken at each live American chestnut because we had a relatively low sample size within each experimental unit (n $\leq$ 5) that increased variability and gave a relatively poor representation of the amount of sunlight during the first growing season created by the treatments. Additionally, PFS measurements taken above live trees could not be used to model survival probabilities (described below).

We will only discuss results from the American chestnut planting in this paper. Due to the deviation from the original experimental design, data were analyzed with exploratory methods using logistic regression and multiple linear regression model building techniques. All analyses were conducted using SAS (SAS Institute 2009). Logistic regression (PROC LOGISTIC) was used to predict survival and deer browse using the following dichotomous or continuous independent variables: year since planting (1 to 6), burning prior to planting (burn versus no burn), seedling height at planting, ground-line diameter at planting, PFS in 2007, the tornado (yes or no), and chestnut blight (yes or no). We tested three class variables to identify experimental units that were commercially thinned and not hand-thinned, and units that represented commercial patch clearcuts with and without hand-thinning, respectively, within the appropriate years. We also tested three class variables to identify experimental units that had been burned in 2010 with two intensities (not burned, a mild intensity burn, and a moderate intensity burn). Logistic regression models were built

using methods described by Hosmer and Lemeshow (2000) and Menard (2010). The final model was selected after conducting chi-square tests for differences between AIC values of the candidate predictor models; the most parsimonious (model containing the least number of variables with the most explanatory power) was selected as the final model. A Hosmer-Lemeshow goodness of fit statistic was used to test the null hypothesis that the model explained the variation in the data, and p-values of less than 0.10 were interpreted as poorly fit models. We examined the Area Under the ROC (Receiver Operator Characteristic; defined by sensitivity versus 1-specificity) Curve (AUC), which is a measure of explained variation, and we considered models with an AUC value greater than 0.5 to have good explanatory power (Menard 2010). Surviving seedlings and those with deer browse were coded as successful (1), and dead seedlings and seedlings without browse as unsuccessful (0) in the logistic regression models to predict survival and deer browse probabilities.

PROC REG was used to conduct multiple linear regression to predict seedling height. Potential independent variables tested included the same dichotomous and continuous variables used in the logistic regression models in addition to dieback of the main stem (yes or no) and deer browse to the terminal bud (yes or no). The linear regression models were built using methods described by Wasserman and Kutner (1990). The final model was selected after conducting chi-square tests for differences between AIC values of the candidate predictor models; the most parsimonious model was selected as the final model. We used PROC REG to test diagnostics for heteroscedasticity of error terms, and normality assumptions were tested by examining frequency plots of residuals in PROC UNIVARIATE. Parameter estimates and associated p-values for the final model were produced using PROC GLM because, unlike PROC REG, the GLM procedure does not assume data are balanced for categorical variables.

RESULTS

General Trends across Experimental Units

Average height and GLD at planting were 115 cm (SE = 4.6) and 9.5 mm (SE = 0.4), respectively, and varied from 28 to 190 cm in height and from 4.9 mm to 16.7 mm in GLD. PFS in 2007 averaged 31 (SE = 1.7) across all experimental units and ranged from 13 percent (unit 3) to 64 percent (unit 10) (table 1). By the sixth growing season, trees averaged 236 cm (SE=40) in height and had 39 percent (SE = 6) survival across all experimental units (table 1). Experimental units varied greatly in terms of height and survival. Deer browse averaged 42 percent (SE = 8) in year 1, and decreased to 20 percent (SE = 7) and 0 percent in year 4 and 6 after planting, respectively. Stem dieback averaged 23 percent (SE = 7) in year 1, 40 percent (SE = 9) in year 4, and 22 percent (SE = 9) in year 6 after planting. Chestnut blight increased from 2 percent (SE = 2) in year 1 to 41 percent (SE = 6) in year 6 after planting and was present in all experimental units except a thinning unit in block 2. Sprouting occurred in every year, but was lowest in year 6 after planting.

Survival Predictions

The logistic regression model to predict survival adequately explained the variation according to the goodness of fit test (P = 0.97) and the AUC value (0.76). Chestnut blight, prescribed burning, combined effects of harvesting and hand-thinning, and the tornado were not included in the model to predict survival. PFS in 2007 was the most significant predictor of survival probabilities, and survival probabilities decreased as PFS increased (table 2). Year since planting was the second most significant predictor of survival. Height at planting had a weak but positive relationship to survival. Although the main effects of planting height and interactions with GLD and PFS had p-values greater than 0.05, inclusion of these effects in the model significantly lowered the AIC value. The negative effect of increasing PFS values in 2007 on subsequent survival weakened as tree height at planting increased (fig. 1). As GLD increased, survival was predicted to decrease according to the logistic regression model. Taller trees had the best survival despite GLD, particularly for trees taller than approximately 140 cm at planting. Trees predicted to have the highest survival had small GLDs and tall heights at the time of planting and were planted in relatively low light environments.

Deer Browse Predictions

The logistic regression model for deer browse adequately explained the variation according to the goodness of fit test (P = 0.90) and the AUC value (0.79). The effects of GLD, chestnut blight, harvesting, and the tornado were not included in the model to predict deer browse. Year since planting was the most significant predictor of deer browse, and deer were less likely to browse as year since planting increased (table 2). Burning prior to planting and planting height were significant predictors of deer browse probabilities. Deer browse was more frequent in areas that had burned prior to planting and on seedlings with smaller stem heights. Shorter trees planted in burned areas 1 year after planting had the highest deer browse probabilities, and taller trees planted in unburned areas 6 years after planting had the lowest deer browse probabilities.

Height Predictions

The final multiple regression model for seedling height had an $R^2 = 0.51$ (F = 29.95, p < 0.0001). We transformed height using a natural log function to avoid heteroscedasticity. Prescribed burning prior to and after planting, GLD at planting, chestnut blight, and deer browse were not significant predictors of height in the multiple regression model. Year since planting, height at planting, PFS in 2007, stem dieback, the tornado, and harvesting treatments were significant predictors of total height (table 3). Height at planting was positively related to total height, and PFS in 2007 was negatively related to total height. Stem dieback was negatively related and was the most significant predictor of total height. In year 6, dieback was predicted to decrease stem height by approximately 150 cm in patch clearcuts that were hand-thinned and not affected by the tornado (fig. 2). Trees were predicted to be 293 cm tall in patch clearcuts that were hand-thinned, 162 cm tall in patch clearcuts that were not hand-thinned, and 136 cm tall in commercially thinned units by year 6 after planting, given mean PFS (31 percent), mean height at planting (115 cm), and no effect of tornado or dieback (fig. 2). The tornado increased these predicted heights by 129 cm, 71 cm, and 59 cm in the patch clearcuts with hand-thinning, patch clearcuts without hand-thinning, and the commercially thinned units, respectively.

DISCUSSION

Results should be interpreted with caution for two primary reasons. First, sample size was relatively low, restricting the power of the statistical analysis and the ability to test predictions from the models on a subset of data. Low sample size is related to the difficulty in securing American chestnut experimental material (Hebard 2013). Second, deviations from the original experimental design (e.g., alteration of prescribed burning, the unplanned hand-thinning, and the tornado) were sometimes confounding, and also led to difficulty in making inferences. The analysis used individual trees as independent observations, when the individual tree was originally designed to be a subsample of the larger experimental unit. This deviation from the original experimental design may have caused an increase in Type I errors (accepting significance of effects when there was no effect). For example, the tornado affected units that burned the same year as the tornado, making separation of burning intensity and tornado effects on survival and height impossible. Units 10 (patch clearcut) and 12 (commercial thin) in block 3 were the only units that burned prior to planting, and they also had relatively high PFS in 2007. The impacts of the pre-plant burn on PFS in the first growing season could be confounded with effects of localized site conditions because only one block burned prior to planting. Furthermore, a severe drought that occurred the year of planting also complicates interpretation of results. The drought was characterized as exceptional by the end of the first growing season and severe by the end of the second growing season (U.S. Drought Monitor 2014). Despite these limitations, this study gives some insight into the effects of various disturbances on planted American chestnut seedlings.

Survival

Our results are consistent with previous studies that found American chestnut survival was not limited by low light levels (Clark and others 2012a, Rhoades and others 2009). The species has certain shade-tolerant characteristics such as a low light saturation point (~200 μmol m^{-2} s^{-1}) and light compensation point (~30 μmol m^{-2} s^{-1}) (Knapp and others, in press; Joesting and others 2009; Wang and others 2006) that allow seedlings to survive in shaded environments. Survival was limited by high light conditions in this study, in contrast to previous studies that indicate American chestnut was highly productive under an open canopy or full sun conditions (Clark and others 2012a, Latham 1992, Wang and others 2006). However, the relationship between survival and PFS in 2007 was confounded by low replication of the pre-plant burn and a drought. Units 10 and 12 had relatively low 6-year survival rates (0 and 40 percent, respectively) and relatively high PFS values in 2007 (64 and 37 percent, respectively), and appeared to be on a slightly more xeric topographic area compared to other units. These two units were also the only units to have been burned prior to planting. We could not determine if the relatively high PFS values recorded in the first growing season in these two units were related to the effects of the pre-plant burn or to the xeric site conditions. We hypothesize the effect of the 2007 and 2008 drought interacted with site conditions to affect the relationship between PFS in the first growing season and subsequent survival. Trees planted on xeric sites, such as units 10 and 12, would experience more stress during drought compared to trees on more mesic sites, leading to lower survival rates (Gustafson and Sturtevant 2013). The physiological mechanisms that probably mitigate the negative effects of drought in American chestnut may have been compromised as light levels increased. Drought has been shown to decrease stomatal conductance, transpiration, and leaf xylem water potential in northern red oak seedlings (Jacobs and others 2009). These functions would have been further decreased as PFS increased, as has been shown in shade-house studies (Brown 2012, Wang and others 2006).

The negative effect of PFS in the first growing season on seedling survival in subsequent years was partially mitigated if the tree had a relatively large stem height at planting (fig. 1), probably because the tree had more above-ground structure to physiologically compensate for the negative effects of the drought. By year 6, trees planted with the tallest stem heights under the highest

level of PFS had similar survival to shorter trees planted under lower level of PFS. An alternative hypothesis to explain the negative relationship between PFS and survival could be because competition increased over time in units that had high PFS in 2007. However, competition data (not shown) indicated that competition did not increase in density or height in relation to PFS levels in 2007.

Root-collar diameter or GLD can be used as a proxy for root system development, as it has been highly correlated to root volume or number of roots in American chestnut and oak species (Clark and others 2000, 2010, 2012b, Jacobs and others 2004). The negative relationship between GLD and survival was surprising given that seedling size at planting, particularly related to root system morphology, has been positively related to survival in other Fagaceae species such as oak (Dey and others 2008). Large seedling GLD at planting could be a less important indicator for improving survival of American chestnut seedlings compared to oak species. Seedling size at planting did not affect survival after five growing seasons for American chestnut seedlings in high or low light conditions (Clark and others 2012a), after 1 year in shelterwood or clearcut plantings (Clark and others 2010), or after four growing seasons underplanted in a midstory removal (Belair and others, in review). In greenhouse studies, American chestnut's root-to-shoot ratio was lower than oak species across a range of light availability (Latham 1992), suggesting chestnut allocates more energy to the stem growth at the expense of root development. Another study found that the American chestnut seedlings increased root development compared to shoot development as PFS increased (Wang and others 2006). In this study, the negative effect of GLD was only significant in the presence of the PFS variable. Trees were not able to support a larger root system, particularly if planted in low light conditions. At higher light levels, drought conditions appeared to be the primary limiting factor for survival. Height at planting also interacted with GLD, and the negative effect of GLD was partially mitigated if the seedling was tall. Taller seedlings at planting would presumably have more leaf area to assimilate carbon for maintenance of below-ground structures (Wang and others 2006).

Most units that burned in 2010 contained trees that sprouted following the burn (table 1), potentially diminishing the effect of burning on survival. The ability of American chestnut to sprout following topkill has been well documented for sprouts from mature rootstock (Paillet 1984, 1988), but few studies have sought to quantify the response of planted seedlings to topkill (Belair and others, in press).

Deer browse

The negative relationship of seedling height to deer browse was consistent with previous studies that have shown shorter hardwood seedlings are more likely to be browsed (Oswalt and others 2006). The positive effects of prescribed burning on the abundance and exposure of available browse and mast for deer consumption has been documented (Dills 1970, Ivey and Causey 1984). Prescribed burning probably increased browsing to planted seedlings by attracting deer to the burned area. The logistic regression did not show a significant effect of harvest treatments on deer browse in the presence of other significant variables, but the data do suggest that browse on chestnut seedlings was more frequent in thinned areas (39 percent) compared to patch clearcuts (7 percent) 4 years after planting (table 1). Deer browse to planted seedlings was not apparent after 2010, probably because the University of the South instituted new hunting pressure within the forest property that reduced deer population levels. Our results indicate that burning could negatively affect restoration attempts in areas with high deer populations, particularly for smaller size seedlings. Protection measures, such as trees shelters, could reduce browse effects, but they are expensive and might create a microclimate conducive to chestnut blight (Ponder 1995).

Height

Prescribed burning, either before or following seedling planting, did not affect height of seedlings. Our results were not in agreement with a previous study that found prescribed burning prior to planting increased growth of direct-seeded chestnuts in harvested and in unharvested forests (McCament and McCarthy 2005). The lack of replication of the pre-plant burn probably made response to this treatment more difficult to detect. We partially attribute the negligible effect of post-planting prescribed burning on height to the ability of American chestnut to prolifically sprout following topkill (Matoon 1909, Paillet 1984). In addition, prescribed fires are often highly variable and patchy in nature even within a relatively small spatial area (Arthur and others 2012). The fires probably did not affect every planted tree or their competition similarly. This high variation could lead to the inability to detect fire as a significant effect. Other variables besides prescribed burning were more important in influencing height of American chestnut seedlings.

Height at planting was predicted to positively influence total height, suggesting tree size at planting will be important in affecting overall competitiveness of American chestnut seedlings. The importance of seedling quality has been clearly demonstrated with oak species (Dey and others 2008) and has been shown to positively affect growth of American chestnuts planted in regeneration harvests (Clark and others 2012a). The

negative effect of PFS on height was surprising given that American chestnut grows best as percent full sun increases (Latham 1992, Wang and others 2006), but as with survival, we attribute this response to influences from the 2-year drought that occurred at the time of planting. The drought probably interacted with PFS and local site conditions to reduce the ability to assimilate carbon under the highest light levels, particularly on more xeric sites.

Seedlings should be planted in areas where dieback is less likely to occur. While not empirically tested, dieback was more common in thinned stands (43 percent) versus patch clearcut stands (15 percent) after one growing season (table 1). Planting in commercially thinned stands reduced height compared to patch clearcut stands, probably because trees were limited by available light after the first growing season in thinned areas, particularly as drought effects diminished. Trees had higher rates of dieback in thinned areas because they were compensating for low light levels by sacrificing stem growth to maintain existing root structures (Latham 1992). Hand-thinning within the patch clearcuts increased height, similar to other studies that have shown competition control will increase height growth of planted hardwood seedlings (Spetich and others 2002). The tornado positively affected height probably because the tornado and salvage logging acted as a release to trees planted in the affected area.

CONCLUSIONS

This is one of the first empirical studies to document the ability of planted American chestnut seedlings to sprout following topkill by fire. Treatment effects of burning and harvesting were probably influenced and confounded by external disturbances, including a 2-year long drought and a tornado followed by salvage logging. Prescribed burning had a negligible effect on survival and height of planted American chestnut seedlings after 6 years, but burning appeared to attract deer. More browse was documented on seedlings planted in burned versus unburned areas. Given that American chestnut planting stock is difficult to procure and quite valuable, we would not currently recommend using prescribed burning in areas where American chestnut seedlings have been planted in order to avoid losses or injury. Furthermore, injury to seedlings from prescribed burning could potentially interfere with their ability to resist diseases such as blight.

Seedlings in this study were more influenced by harvesting, amount of PFS in the first growing season, and seedling size at planting than by prescribed burning. However, PFS in 2007 was probably reduced by a drought, and its effects should be interpreted with caution. Managers seeking to efficiently use limited resources to artificially regenerate American chestnut should plant seedlings with large stem heights in areas treated using a regeneration harvest, like a patch clearcut used in this study. Planting within commercially thinned areas may not be a viable option in restoration of American chestnut in the short term. Trees may be able to be successfully released several years after being planted in a commercial thinning, but these trees may have stagnate height growth or even dieback in the meantime. This study also suggests that during a severe drought, American chestnut may not be able to survive or grow if planted in environments with relatively high light levels and/or on xeric sites. Future research with more replication is needed to confirm or reject predictions made in this study, particularly regarding seedling response to various environmental conditions and silvicultural treatments, including prescribed burning.

ACKNOWLEDGMENTS

The authors would like to thank the University of the South, Department for Forestry and Geology, including Nicole Nunley, Ken Smith, and Nate Wilson for assistance throughout the study. We also thank the University of Tennessee's Tree Improvement Program for partial support of this study. We thank The American Chestnut Foundation, Kentucky Chapter, for providing experimental material. Ryan Sisk and Nathan Brown with the USDA Forest Service, Southern Research Station, and John Johnson, University of Tennessee, Department of Forestry, Wildlife, and Fisheries, provided valuable assistance in data collection. Todd Hutchinson and Leila Pinchot, USDA Forest Service, Northern Research Station, provided reviews that improved the manuscript.

LITERATURE CITED

Abrams, M.D. 1992. Fire and the development of oak forests. BioScience. 42: 346-353.

Anagnostakis, S.L. 2001. The effect of multiple importations of pests and pathogens on a native tree. Biological Invasions. 3: 245-254.

Anagnostakis, S.L. 2012. Chestnut breeding in the United States for disease and insect resistance. Plant Disease. 96(10): 1392-1403.

Arthur, M.A.; Alexander, H.D.; Dey, D.C. [and others]. 2012. Refining the oak-fire hypothesis for management of oak-dominated forests of the Eastern United States. Journal of Forestry. 110(5): 257-266.

Baker, F.B. 1884. Report upon the lumber and wood trade in certain States. In: Report on Forestry, Volume IV (Egleston, N.H. preparer). Washington, DC: Government Printing Office. 421 p.

Belair, E.P.; Saunders, M.R.; Bailey, B.G. [In review]. Underplanting American chestnut in oak-hickory forests: effects of midstory removal, root trenching, and weeding treatments on growth and survival. Forest Ecology & Management.

Belair, E.P.; Saunders, M.R.; Clark, S.L. [In press]. Effects of simulated prescribed fire on American chestnut (*Castanea dentata*) and Northern red oak (*Quercus rubra*) regeneration. In: Proceedings of the Central Hardwood Forest Conference 2014. Newtown Square, PA: U.S. Department of Agriculture Northern Research Station.

Brose, P.T.; Schuler, M.; Van Lear, D.H.; Berst, J. 2001. Bringing fire back: the changing regimes of Appalachian mixed oak forests. Journal of Forestry. 99: 30-35.

Brown, C.E. 2012. The influence of shade, water stress, and root competition on American chestnut regeneration. West Lafayette, IN: Department of Forestry and Natural Resources, Purdue University. 116 p. M.S. Thesis.

Clark, S.L.; Schlarbaum, S.E.; Kormanik, P.P. 2000. Visual grading and quality of 1-0 Northern red oak seedlings. Southern Journal of Applied Forestry. 24: 93-97.

Clark, S.L.; Schweitzer, C.J.; Schlarbaum, S.E. [and others]. 2010. Nursery quality and first-year response of American chestnut (*Castanea dentata*) seedlings planted in the southeastern United States. Tree Planters' Notes. 53(2): 13-21.

Clark, S.L.; McNab, H.; Loftis, D.; Zarnoch. S. 2012a. American chestnut growth and survival five years after planting in two silvicultural treatments in the southern Appalachians, USA. Forests. 3: 1017-1033.

Clark, S.L.; Schlarbaum, S.E.; Saxton, A.M.; Hebard, F.V. 2012b. Nursery performance of American and Chinese chestnuts and backcross generations in commercial tree nurseries. Forestry: International Journal of Forest Research. 85: 589-600.

Delcourt, P.A.; Delcourt, H.R. 1998. The influence of prehistoric human-set fires on oak-chestnut forests in the southern Appalachians. Castanea. 63: 337-345.

Dey, D.C.; Jacobs, D.F.; McNabb, K. [and others]. 2008. Artificial regeneration of major oak (*Quercus*) species in the Eastern United States-a review of the literature. Forest Science. 54(1): 77-106.

Dills, G.G. 1970. Effects of prescribed burning on deer response. The Journal of Wildlife Management. 34(3): 540-545.

Frothingham, E.H. 1924. Some silvicultural aspects of the chestnut blight situation. Journal of Forestry. 22: 861-872.

Foster, D.R.; Clayden, S.; Orwig, D.A. [and others]. 2002. Oak, chestnut and fire: climatic and cultural controls of long-term forest dynamics in New England, USA. Journal of Biology. 29: 1359-1379.

Griffin, G.J. 2000. Blight control and restoration of the American chestnut. Journal of Forestry. 98: 22-27.

Griffin, G.J.; Elkins, J.R. 1986. Chestnut blight. In: G.J. Griffin, and J.R. Elkins, eds. Chestnut blight, other *Endothia* diseases and the genus *Endothia*. St. Paul, MN: American Phytopathological Society. 803 p.

Gustafson, E.J.; Sturtevant, B.R. 2013. Modeling forest mortality caused by drought stress: implications for climate change. Ecosystems. 16: 60–74.

Hawley, R.C.; Hawes, A.F. 1912. Forestry in New England: a handbook of eastern forest management, 1st ed. London: John Wiley & Sons. 479 p.

Hebard, F.V. 2013. Meadowview notes 2011-2012. The Journal of the American Chestnut Foundation. 27(1): 19-25.

Hosmer, D. W.; Lemeshow, S. 2000. Model-building strategies and methods for logistic regression. In: Applied Logistic Regression, Second Edition. Hoboken, NJ: John Wiley & Sons, Inc.: 91-142.

Hough, F.B. 1878. Report upon forestry, Vol. 1. Washington, DC: U.S. Department of Agriculture. 650 p.

Ivey, T.L.; Causey, M.K. 1984. Response of white-tailed deer to prescribed fire. Wildlife Society Bulletin. 12(2): 138-141.

Jacobs, D.F.; Severeid, L.R. 2004. Dominance of interplanted American chestnut (*Castanea dentata*) in southwestern Wisconsin, USA. Forest Ecology and Management. 191: 111-120.

Jacobs, D.F.; Selig, M.F.; Severeid, L.R. 2009. Drought susceptibility and recovery of transplanted *Quercus rubra* seedlings in relation to root system morphology. Annals of Forest Science. 66: 1-12.

Joesting, H.M.; McCarthy, B.C.; Brown, K.J. 2007. The photosynthetic response of American chestnut seedlings to differing light conditions. Canadian Journal of Forest Research. 37: 1714-1722.

Joesting, H.M,; McCarthy, B.C.; Brown, K.J. 2009. Determining the shade tolerance of American chestnut using morphological and physiological leaf parameters. Forest Ecology and Management. 257: 280-286.

Knapp, B.O.; Wang, G.G.; Clark, S.L. [and others]. [In press]. Leaf physiology and morphology of *Castanea dentata* (Marsh.) Borkh., *Castanea mollissima* Blume, and three backcross breeding generations planted in the southern Appalachians, USA. New Forests.

Kormanik, P.P.; Sung S.S.; Kormanik, T.L. 1994. Irrigating and fertilizing to grow better nursery seedlings. In: Proceedings of the Northeastern and Intermountain Forest and Conservation Nursery Associations. Gen. Tech. Rep. RM-GTR-243. Fort Collins, CO: U.S. Department of Agriculture Forest Service, Rocky Mountain Research Station: 115–121.

Kremer, A.; Casasoli, M.; Barreneche, T. [and others]. 2007. Fagaceae Trees. In: Kole, C., ed. Genome Mapping and Molecular Breeding in Plants, Vol. 7. Berlin Heidelberg: Springer-Verlag: 161-198.

Latham, R.E. 1992. Co-occurring tree species change rank in seedling performance with resources varied experimentally. Ecology. 73: 2129-2144.

Mattoon, W. R. 1909. The origin and early development of chestnut sprouts. Forest Quarterly. 7: 34-47.

McCament, C.L.; McCarthy, B.C. 2005. Two-year response of American chestnut (*Castanea dentata*) seedlings to shelterwood harvesting and fire in a mixed-oak forest ecosystem. Canadian Journal of Forest Research. 35: 740-749.

McEwan, R.W.; Keiffer, C.H.; McCarthy, B.C. 2006. Dendroecology of American chestnut in a disjunct stand of oak-chestnut forest. Canadian Journal of Forest Research. 36: 1-11.

Menard, S.W. 2010. Logistic regression: from introductory to advanced concepts and applications. Los Angeles: SAGE. 392 p.

Oswalt, C.M.; Clatterbuck, W.K.; Houston, A.E. 2006. Impacts of deer herbivory and visual grading on the early performance of high-quality oak planting stock in Tennessee, USA. Forest Ecology and Management. 229: 128-135.

Paillet, F.L. 1984. Growth-form and ecology of American chestnut sprout clones in northeastern Massachusetts. Bulletin of the Torrey Botanical Club. 111: 316-328.

Paillet, F.L. 1988. Character and distribution of American chestnut sprouts in southern New England woodlands. Bulletin of the Torrey Botanical Club. 115: 32-44.

Ponder, F., Jr. 1995. Shoot and root growth of northern red oak planted in forest openings and protected by treeshelters. Northern Journal of Applied Forestry. 12: 36-42.

Rhoades, C.; Loftis, D.; Lewis, J.; Clark, S. 2009. The influence of silvicultural treatments and site conditions on American chestnut (*Castanea dentata*) seedling establishment in eastern Kentucky, U.S.A. Forest Ecology and Management. 258: 1211-1218.

Russell, E.W.B. 1987. Pre-blight distribution of *Castanea dentata*. Bulletin of the Torrey Botanical Club. 114: 183-190.

SAS Institute Inc. 2009. SAS/STAT user's guide. Version 9. 2nd Edition. Cary, NC: SAS Institute Inc.

Smalley, G.W. 1982. Classification and evaluation of forest sites on the mid-Cumberland Plateau. Gen. Tech. Rep. SO-GTR-38. New Orleans, LA: U.S. Department of Agriculture Forest Service, Southern Forest Experiment Station. 58 p.

Spetich, M.A.; Dey, D.C.; Johnson, P.S.; Graney, D.L. 2002. Competitive capacity of *Quercus rubra* L. planted in Arkansas Boston Mountains. Forest Science. 48: 504-517.

Wang, G.G.; Baurle, W.L; Mudder, B.T. 2006. Effects of light acclimation on the photosynthesis, growth, and biomass allocation in American chestnut (*Castanea dentata*) seedlings. Forest Ecology and Management. 226: 173-180.

Wang, G.; Knapp, B.O.; Clark, S.L.; Mudder, B.T. 2013. The silvics of *Castanea dentata* (Marsh.) Borkh., American Chestnut, Fagaceae (Beech family). Gen. Tech. Rep. SRS-GTR-173. Asheville, NC: U.S. Department of Agriculture Forest Service, Southern Research Station. 18 p.

Wasserman, J.N.W.; Kutner, M.H. 1990. Applied linear statistical models: regression, analysis of variance, and experimental designs, 3rd ed. Homewood, IL: Irwin. [Number of pages unknown].

U.S. Drought Monitor. 2014. U.S. Department of Agriculture. [Online]. http://droughtmonitor.unl.edu/MapsAndData/DataTables.aspx. [Date accessed: January 29, 2014].

Table 1—Survival, total height, deer browse, stem dieback, chestnut blight, and sprouting after 1 (2007), 4 (2010), and 6 (2012) growing seasons for American chestnut seedlings planted in experimental units affected by harvesting, prescribed burning in 2007 and 2010, percent full sun in 2007, hand-thinning, and tornado

Block		1	1	1	1	2	2	2	2	3	3	3	3	
Unit Number		1	2	3	4	5	6	7	8	9	10	11	12	All
Harvest Type[a]		PC	PC	T	T	PC	PC	T	T	PC	PC	T	T	
Burning 2007[b]		No	No	No	No	No	No	No	No	No	Mod	No	Mod	
PFS 2007		33	19	13	21	24	24	20	39	40	64	34	37	31
Hand-thinning 2009		Yes	No	No	No	Yes	No	No	No	No	No	No	No	
Tornado 2010		No	Yes	No	Yes	No	No	No	No	No	No	No	No	
Burning 2010[b]		No	Mild	No	Mild	No	Mod	No	No	No	Mod	No	Mod	
Survival (percent)	2007	100	100	80	60	80	100	80	20	80	40	80	60	73
	2010	40	60	80	60	80	40	80	20	40	0	80	40	51
	2012	20	60	20	60	80	40	80	20	20	0	40	40	39
Total Height (cm)	2007	124	148	127	101	130	141	167	18	116	60	122	142	127
	2010	343	254	119	114	263	217	103	110	75	--	149	61	164
	2012	558	408	178	262	343	313	129	127	138	--	57	64	236
Deer browse (percent)	2007	20	60	20	0	20	60	25	0	100	100	0	67	42
	2010	0	33	25	33	0	0	25	100	0	--	0	50	20
	2012	0	0	0	0	0	0	0	0	0	0	0	0	0
Stem Dieback (percent)	2007	20	20	100	0	0	0	0	100	0	50	25	33	23
	2010	0	33	50	67	0	50	75	100	0	--	25	50	40
	2012	0	0	0	0	33	0	25	0	0	--	100	50	22
Chestnut blight (percent)	2007	0	0	20	0	0	0	0	0	0	0	0	0	2
	2010	60	60	20	0	25	60	40	0	20	0	40	20	32
	2012	60	40	80	40	25	60	40	0	40	0	80	20	41
Sprout from base (percent)	2007	20	20	0	0	0	0	0	0	0	50	25	0	9
	2010	0	33	25	0	0	50	25	100	0	--	25	50	20
	2012	0	0	0	0	0	0	0	0	0	--	50	0	4

[a] PC=patch clearcut; T=Commercial thinning; PFS=percent full sun.
[b] Prescribed burns were described as mild or moderate (Mod) in intensity.

Table 2—Parameter estimates (standard errors in parenthesis), Wald chi-square statistics, and p-values for variables and interactions in logistic regression models to predict survival probabilities (n = 354) and deer browse (n = 188)

Variable	Parameter estimate	Wald	p
Survival			
Intercept	1.0050 (0.3045)	10.8937	<0.0001
YSP	-0.3105 (0.0737)	17.7282	<0.0001
HT-115.12[a]	0.0100 (0.0058)	2.4305	0.1190
1/GLD- 0.114	14.6810 (5.7973)	6.4131	0.0113
$(PFS^2/100)$-11.136	-0.1030 (0.0174)	34.9944	<0.0001
(HT-115.12)*(1/GLD- 0.114)	0.2631 (0.1466)	3.2193	0.0728
(HT-115.12)*[$(PFS^2/100)$-11.136]	0.0008 (0.0004)	3.3269	0.0682
Deer browse			
Intercept	1.9002 (0.7559)	6.3193	0.0119
YSP	-0.4556 (0.1281)	12.6419	0.0004
HT	-0.0176 (0.0057)	9.6655	0.0019
Burn 2007	1.9382 (0.6019)	10.3683	0.0013

[a] To avod mut co near ty, cont nuous var ab es were first centered by subtract ng the mean before be ng used n transformat ons. YSP=year s nce p ant ng, HT=p ant ng he ght, GLD=p ant ng ground- ne d ameter, PFS=percent fu sun n grow ng season 2007.

Table 3—Parameter estimates (standard errors in parenthesis) and associated F and p values for a multiple regression model to predict height (n = 187)

Variable	Parameter estimate	F	p
Year	0.0368 (0.0250)	2.16	0.1431
Height at planting	0.0036 (0.0011)	11.57	0.0008
PFS 2007	-0.0141 (0.0042)	11.22	0.0010
Dieback	-0.7126 (0.0807)	78.06	<0.0001
Tornado	0.3623 (0.1466)	6.11	0.0144
Patch Clearcut (PC) without hand-thinning (no HT)			
Intercept	4.8905 (0.1929)	15.92	<0.0001
PC HT	0.5948 (0.1455)	15.92	<0.0001
Thin	-0.1755 (0.0840)	15.92	<0.0001
Patch Clearcut (PC) with hand-thinning (HT)			
Intercept	5.4853 (0.2282)	15.92	<0.0001
PC no HT	-0.5948 (0.1455)	15.92	<0.0001
Thin	-0.7702 (0.1383)	15.92	<0.0001
Commercial thinning (Thin)			
Intercept	4.7150 (0.1939)	15.92	<0.0001
PC no HT	0.1755 (0.0840)	15.92	0.0381
PC HT	0.7702 (0.1383)	15.92	<0.0001

YSP=year s nce p ant ng, PFS 2007=percent fu sun n grow ng season 2007.

Note: He ght was transformed by the natura og. Intercepts and parameter est mates un que to each eve of the harvest ng c ass var ab e are g ven.

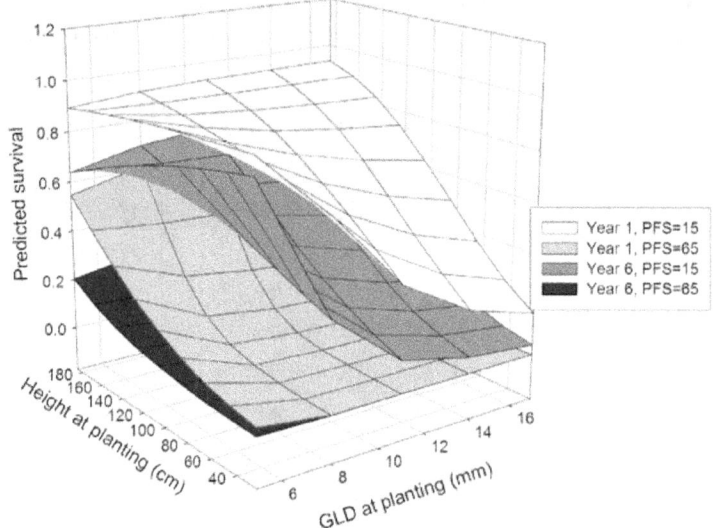

Figure 1—Predicted survival probabilities for American chestnut seedlings based on tree height and ground-line diameter (GLD) at planting for high and low values of percent full sunlight (PFS) at years 1 and 6 after planting.

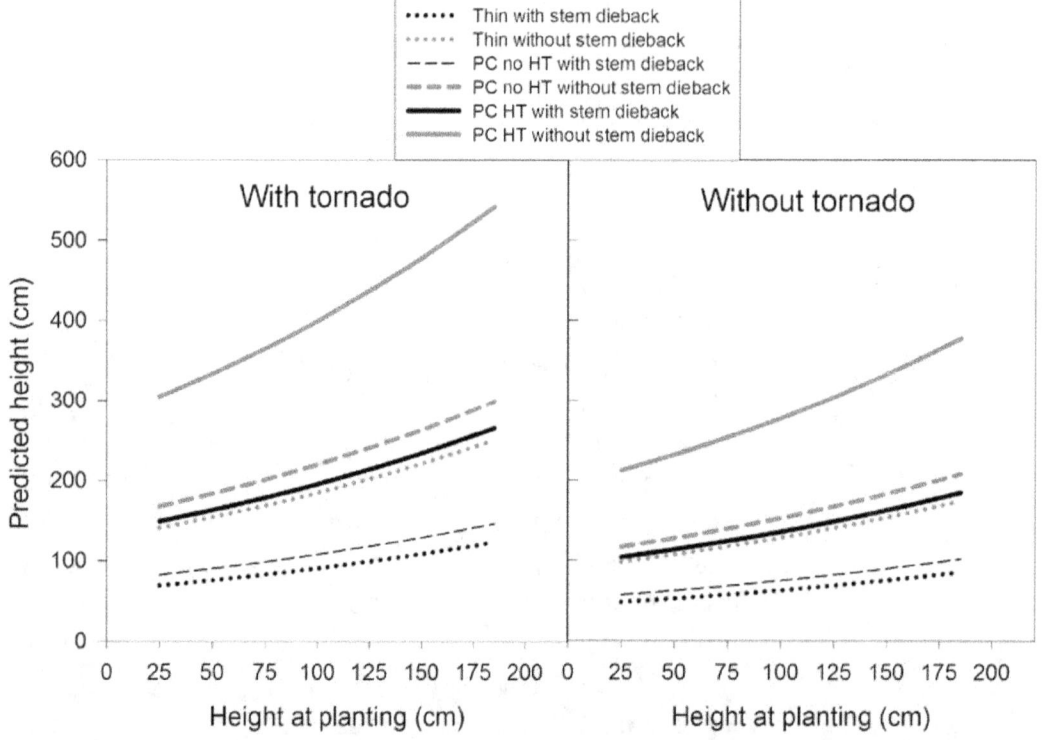

Figure 2—Predicted height 6 years after planting for trees growing under 31 percent full sun in areas affected or not affected by the 2010 tornado. Predictions are shown by planting height and stem dieback occurrence for three harvesting treatments: commercial thinning (Thin), patch clearcuts (PC) with hand-thinning (HT), and patch clearcuts (PC) without hand-thinning (no HT).

Ecology—Wildlife

INDIANA BATS, NORTHERN LONG-EARED BATS, AND PRESCRIBED FIRE IN THE APPALACHIANS: CHALLENGES AND CONSIDERATIONS

Susan C. Loeb and Joy M. O'Keefe[1]

Abstract—The Indiana bat (*Myotis sodalis*) is an endangered species and the northern long-eared bat (*M. septentrionalis*) has been proposed for listing as endangered. Both species are found throughout the Appalachians, and they commonly inhabit fire-dependent ecosystems such as pine and pine-oak forests. Due to their legal status, prescribed burns in areas where these species occur must be conducted to avoid harming or harassing the animals, and managers must consider the effects of their prescribed burning programs on these species. We review what is known about the potential positive and negative impacts of prescribed fire on Indiana and northern long-eared bats throughout their life cycles. Prescribed fire may affect Indiana bats and northern long-eared bats by causing short-term disturbance while they are in their roosts, and this may impact them more during critical points of their life cycle such as post-hibernation and the early pup-rearing phase. Prescribed fires may destroy roosts, although they may also create some. However, several studies suggest that both Indiana bats and northern long-eared bats select areas that have been burned for both roosting and foraging, indicating that prescribed fire may be beneficial for both species. Further, prescribed fire may be critical for the long-term restoration of their preferred habitats. Thus, managers and policymakers must balance the short-term impacts with the long-term benefits of prescribed fire within the range of these species.

INTRODUCTION

Indiana bats (*Myotis sodalis*) and northern long-eared bats (*M. septentrionalis*) are small (~7–10 g) insectivorous bats distributed throughout much of the Eastern United States, including the Appalachian region (fig. 1). The Indiana bat was listed as an endangered species in 1967, primarily due to disturbance to and destruction of their hibernacula. Despite protection and rehabilitation of many of their hibernacula since being listed as endangered, Indiana bat populations continued to decline throughout the latter half of the 20th century (USFWS 2007). The number of Indiana bats appeared to be increasing from 2000–2007, but White-Nose Syndrome (WNS), a newly emerging infectious disease that has resulted in massive deaths of hibernating bats (Blehert and others 2009), has caused renewed declines (Langwig and others 2012, Turner and others 2011). WNS is now found throughout the Appalachian region (Turner and others 2011), and Indiana bat populations are projected to experience severe declines or extirpation throughout their range as a result of it (Thogmartin and others 2013). In contrast, northern long-eared bat populations were considered secure until the introduction of WNS. However, due to high mortality rates associated with WNS (Langwig and others 2012, Turner and others 2011), the northern long-eared bat was proposed for listing as an endangered species in October 2013 (Federal Register 2013). The final decision regarding the status of the northern long-eared bat will be made in late 2014.

The distributions of Indiana bats and northern long-eared bats in the Eastern United States overlap much of the range of fire-dependent pine (*Pinus*) and oak (*Quercus*) forests, and both species roost in pine and oak trees (Lacki and others 2009a). Historically, fires in the Appalachians occurred during the dormant season but at fairly frequent (2–13 years) intervals over large extents (Flatley and others 2013). The close association of Indiana bats and northern long-eared bats with fire-adapted and fire-dependent habitats throughout the Appalachians presents problems for many managers. Due to their legal status, prescribed burns in areas where these species occur must be conducted to avoid "take"—take includes any action that may result in the harassment, harm, pursuit, wounding, or collection of an endangered species, where harm can include habitat modification (Bean 2009). Because prescribed burning may be critical for ensuring future habitat, managers and policymakers must balance the long-term needs for habitat restoration with the potential for short-term negative impacts. Our objective is to review what is known about the potential positive and negative effects of prescribed fire on Indiana and northern long-eared bats throughout their life cycles. We hope that this information can be used to develop science-based habitat management strategies that include prescribed fire and will allow managers to meet their habitat restoration goals and protect these endangered bats.

[1]Susan C. Loeb, Research Ecologist, Southern Research Station, USDA Forest Service, Clemson, SC, 29634-0331

Joy M. O'Keefe, Assistant Professor, Indiana State University, Terre Haute, IN

Citation for proceedings: Waldrop, Thomas A., ed. 2014. Proceedings, Wildland Fire in the Appalachians: Discussions among Managers and Scientists. Gen. Tech. Rep. SRS-199. Asheville, NC: U.S. Department of Agriculture Forest Service, Southern Research Station. 208 p.

BIOLOGY AND ECOLOGY OF INDIANA AND NORTHERN LONG-EARED BATS

Like many temperate bat species, Indiana bats and northern long-eared bats have four distinct phases of their annual life cycle that are important to understand when considering the effects of prescribed fire on their populations. These phases are: 1) the winter hibernation period, 2) spring emergence and migration, 3) the summer maternity period, and 4) fall migration and swarming.

During winter (October or November to March or April), both species hibernate in cold caves and mines, and bats lower their body temperatures to reduce energy expenditures. Indiana bats form large clusters in hibernacula, usually on the cave or mine walls and ceilings. Population sizes of Indiana bats in hibernacula range between 1 and >50,000 (USFWS 2007) with 80 percent of the population residing in just 16 hibernacula (Thogmartin and others 2012). In contrast, northern long-eared bats form small clusters in cracks and crevices, and hibernating populations tend to be small (<300 bats; Caceres and Barclay 2000). However, due to their habit of roosting in inaccessible parts of hibernacula, our knowledge of winter populations of northern long-eared bats is limited.

In spring, Indiana bats and northern long-eared bats emerge from hibernation and migrate various distances to their summer ranges. Depending on sex and possibly geographic region, emergence generally occurs from mid-March to the beginning of May, with females leaving earlier than males (Cacares and Barclay 2000, Hall 1962). In West Virginia, Indiana bats do not leave hibernacula until late April or early May (Hobson and Holland 1995), whereas northern long-eared bats in Indiana emerge in March and early April, somewhat earlier than little brown bats (*M. lucifugus*) and tri-colored bats (*Perimyotis subflavus*; Whitaker and Rissler 1992). Female Indiana bats have been documented to migrate as far as 575 km from their hibernacula to their maternity range (Winhold and Kurta 2006), whereas northern long-eared bats stay within about 60–90 km of their hibernacula (Nagorsen and Brigham 1993).

Once on the summer range, female Indiana bats form maternity colonies that usually contain 30–200 adults (USFWS 2007), whereas northern long-eared bats form maternity colonies that are usually 30–90 adults (Caceres and Barclay 2000). Both species roost in snags and live trees, often between a piece of shedding bark and the bole of snags; however, northern long-eared bats are more likely to use crevices and cavities than Indiana bats (Lacki and others 2009a). In the southern Appalachians, optimal roosting habitat for Indiana bats is dead pine trees near a ridge top in a south-facing mixed pine-hardwood forest

(Hammond 2013). In other parts of the Appalachians, Indiana bats use a variety of roosts, which are primarily hardwoods such as oak, hickory (*Carya*), and maple (*Acer*) species (Brack 2006, Ford and others 2002, Johnson and others 2010). Although northern long-eared bats have broader roosting niches than Indiana bats, they show roosting preferences for a variety of tree species across their range including shortleaf pine (*P. echinata*), oaks, and hickories (Carter and Feldhamer 2005, Foster and Kurta 1999, Perry and Thill 2007). In the southern Appalachians, northern long-eared bats select a variety of oak species as roosts but also roost in dead white pines (*P. strobus*; O'Keefe 2009).

The summer maternity period is a critical period for raising young, restoring fat reserves, and molting, all of which require large amounts of energy. Thus, foraging resources during this period are an important consideration. Indiana bats forage primarily by hawking insects from the air, whereas northern long-eared bats typically glean insects from vegetation (Faure and others 1993). Both species forage in interior or closed canopy forests in the Appalachians and elsewhere (Ford and others 2005, Jantzen and Fenton 2013, Loeb and O'Keefe 2006, Schirmacher and others 2007), although they will also use openings (O'Keefe and others 2013, Sparks and others 2005). They are opportunistic feeders, but Lepidoptera, Diptera, and Coleoptera are prominent orders of insects in their diets in most areas (e.g., Carter and others 2003, Feldhamer and others 2009, Lacki and others 2009b, Tuttle and others 2006, Whitaker 2004).

Starting in mid-August and continuing to October or November, bats migrate to their swarming sites and hibernacula. Swarming is a behavior in which bats gather at hibernacula entrances to familiarize juveniles with hibernacula and to mate (Davis and Hitchcock 1965, Thomas and others 1979). During this period, many bats still roost in trees in the area surrounding the swarming sites (Brack 2006, Gumbert 2001). Bats may either enter the hibernaculum at which they swarm or move to another hibernaculum for the winter.

EFFECTS OF FIRE DURING HIBERNATION

Little is known about the effects of fire on bats during the hibernation period (Perry 2012). Smoke entering the cave is a potential concern because this could cause bats to arouse (Dickinson and others 2009). Bats typically arouse every 2–3 weeks during the hibernation period, but each arousal is energetically costly, and the amount of fat reserves they have at the beginning of the hibernation period is often just sufficient to allow them to make it through the hibernation period (Thomas and others 1990). Because WNS results in frequent arousals during hibernation (Reeder and others 2012), smoke inundation may have a significant impact on bats if it causes additional arousals and energy expenditure. Fire may also alter the vegetation near hibernacula openings which could change airflow and, thus, positively or negatively affect microclimates within the hibernacula (e.g., Richter and others 1993). Only one study has examined the effects of smoke on hibernating bats, finding no response by bats despite slight increases in noxious gases (Caviness 2003). To reduce the risk of impacting bats during the hibernation period, many forests restrict prescribed fires close to hibernacula (e.g., USDA Forest Service 2004). However, more data are needed to determine if these restrictions are needed.

EFFECTS OF FIRE DURING THE SPRING EMERGENCE PERIOD

Late winter-early spring (March through mid-April) is an important period for prescribed fires in the Appalachian region (Brose and others 2013). However, this is also the period when Indiana and northern long-eared bats emerge from hibernation and begin using tree roosts. Thus, there is potential for conflict between conducting prescribed fires during the optimal burn periods and protecting Indiana bats and northern long-eared bats during the emergence period.

Prescribed fire during the emergence period may impact Indiana bats and northern long-eared bats in several ways. When bats emerge from hibernation, they must restore their fat reserves for migration and reproduction. For WNS-affected bats, restoration of fat reserves is even more critical as they may have even fewer fat reserves than non-affected bats (Warnecke and others 2012), and disruption of bats in their tree roosts during this period may add additional stress. Further, bats commonly use torpor as a means for conserving energy even after leaving hibernacula (Willis 2006). In the southern Appalachians, female Indiana bats use daily torpor in June and July, particularly in the morning when air temperatures are lowest (Hammond 2013). Torpor length and depth are negatively correlated with temperature and positively correlated with precipitation (Dzal and Brigham 2013). Thus, torpor bouts during spring will likely be more frequent, deeper, and longer than in the summer months. For example, hoary bats (*Lasiurus cinereus*) use deep, prolonged torpor bouts lasting ~ 4 days/bout during spring rain/snow storms in Saskatchewan, Canada (Willis and others 2006). Indiana bats that have recently emerged from hibernacula in Vermont switch roosts every 4.8 days and only emerge from roosts about 1/3 of the nights (Britzke and others 2006). However, during the summer maternity season, female Indiana bats in the same area switch roosts approximately every day (Watrous and others 2006). This suggests that Indiana bats enter deep torpor for energy conservation during the spring. If torpor

bouts are deep and long during the spring emergence period due to cold snaps, Indiana and northern long-eared bats may not be able to respond as quickly to the presence of fire. Therefore, conducting prescribed fires on warmer days or during warmer periods of the day may allow bats to respond more quickly to the sound and smell of smoke, and to escape the fire (Layne 2009). For example, northern long-eared bats left their tree roosts within 10 minutes of ignition when a fire was lit late in the day (1640 and 1650 EST; Dickinson and others 2009). In contrast, red bats (*Lasiurus borealis*) require >20 minutes to respond when temperatures drop below 50 °F (Layne 2009).

Prescribed fire may also impact the availability of roosts during the emergence period. Although a great deal has been learned about roost site selection of Indiana bats and northern long-eared bats during the summer maternity season (see below), we are not aware of any studies that have examined roost site use or selection by northern long-eared bats in spring, and only a few studies that have examined Indiana bat roost use and selection in spring (Britkze and others 2006, Gumbert 2001, Hobson and Holland 1995). Britzke and others (2006) tracked female Indiana bats from hibernacula in New York to 39 roost trees in New York and Vermont, and noted that bats favored live trees such as shagbark hickories (*C. ovata*) more than is typically observed in summer. In Kentucky, male Indiana bats primarily roost in oaks and hickories during spring, many of which are alive, whereas pines snags are used much more in summer (Gumbert 2001). Further, the number of crevice roosts increases by 20 percent in spring compared to summer and fall. The greater use of live trees in Vermont and Kentucky during spring and the seasonal variation in roost use in Kentucky suggests that basing management actions in spring and fall on our knowledge of roost selection during summer may be misguided. Thus, until more information is gained regarding roost site use and selection by these bats during the spring emergence period, it will be difficult to develop burn programs that avoid disturbing or destroying Indiana bat and northern long-eared bat roosts during spring.

Similar to roosting behavior, little is known about foraging habitat use during the spring emergence period. In particular, it is important to understand how prescribed fires affect prey availability and its distribution during this period. However, we are not aware of any studies that have examined the immediate effect of prescribed fire on spring nocturnal insect abundance and composition. Further, although several studies have examined foraging habitat use during summer, no studies have examined foraging habitat use during spring. Bats may use different habitats during spring in response to either changes in structure (i.e., leaf-off) or insect availability. Thus, bats may respond differently to prescribed fire in spring foraging habitats than to those in summer foraging habitats. More data are needed to determine what habitats these bats use during the spring emergence period and how prescribed fire may affect use of those habitats.

EFFECTS OF PRESCRIBED FIRE DURING THE SUMMER MATERNITY PERIOD

Growing season burns are usually restricted in areas that contain Indiana bats during the maternity season, and they may be restricted in areas with northern long-eared bats in the future. However, prescribed fire conducted during other seasons may still have impacts, both positive and negative on summer habitat use by Indiana and northern long-eared bats. Fire will most likely have its greatest impacts on foraging and roosting habitats.

Prescribed fire may affect foraging habitat by affecting insect prey availability and forest structure. The results of studies that have examined the effects of prescribed fire on nighttime flying insects are equivocal. For example, overall insect abundance and abundance of Coleopterans and Dipterans increased in the 5 months after prescribed fires in Kentucky (Lacki and others 2009b), whereas insect availability is not related to burn history in Missouri (Womack 2011). In Idaho, a high-severity wildfire led to a pulse of nutrients in streams, thereby increasing aquatic insects and bat activity up to 5 years post fire (Malison and Baxter 2010).

Several studies in forested habitats across the world have examined foraging habitat use of bats in response to prescribed fire. In general, bat activity increases in areas that have been burned, particularly for large-bodied species that are less clutter-adapted than smaller, more agile species (e.g., Armitage and Ober 2012, Inkster-Draper and others 2013, Loeb and Waldrop 2008, Smith and Gehrt 2010). Most authors have attributed these changes to a reduction in forest clutter. Unfortunately, only a few studies have been conducted in areas with Indiana bats or northern long-eared bats. Northern long-eared bat occupancy of sites in Missouri is negatively related to saplings/ac, sawlogs/ac, and conifer basal area and positively related to the number of fires within the past 10 years, although these relationships are not statistically significant (Starbuck 2013). In Kentucky, northern long-eared bat forage closer to burned areas than to nonburned areas in the 4 months following a prescribed burn which may be due to reduced clutter in these areas or increased insect availability (Lacki and others 2009b). Five of six Indiana bats with home ranges overlapping low-severity burns selected the burned areas during their foraging bouts; this finding was attributed to more open understories in burned areas (Womack and others 2013). Prescribed fire may also generate early successional conditions in forests; bats that are ecologically similar

to Indiana and northern long-eared bats show neutral or positive responses to moderate- or high-severity fires that created these conditions in California (Buchalski and others 2013). Thus, based on a small number of studies, it appears that prescribed fire has a positive or neutral effect on Indiana and northern long-eared bat foraging habitat. However, far more data are needed to fully understand how prescribed fire affects foraging habitat use of Indiana and northern long-eared bats, particularly in relation to such factors as fire intensity and fire frequency.

Prescribed fire may also affect summer roosting habitat by creating or destroying roost structures and changing the fine-scale structure of the habitat around the roosts that make them more or less desirable to bats (Perry 2012). Most of the data on the effects of prescribed and wildland fire on snag dynamics are from the Western United States. In general, more snags are lost than are created, particularly larger diameter snags (e.g., Bagne and others 2008, Horton and Mannan 1988, Randall-Parker and Miller 2002), although small diameter snags may increase in abundance (Stephens and Moghaddas 2005). In the southern Appalachians, snag basal area is significantly higher in areas that receive high-severity burns compared to areas that have not been burned or have received low- or medium-severity burns (Rush and others 2012). However, the size distribution of these snags is not known. Boyles and Aubrey (2006) also found that snag availability was greater in a burned area compared to an adjacent nonburned area in Missouri. Thus, it appears that prescribed fire may destroy existing snags, but in some cases new snags are created. However, before conclusions can be drawn about the short-term effects of prescribed fire on roost structures, more information is needed on how snag creation and loss varies with factors such as fire frequency, time since burning, species, topography, and fire intensity. Further, if prescribed fire is necessary to create the types of habitat that bats prefer for roosting (see below), then the short-term effects must be balanced against the long-term habitat needs of these animals.

Although only a few studies have examined the effects of prescribed fire on roost use and selection by Indiana bats, these studies suggest that they respond positively to prescribed fire in terms of roosting behavior. For example, Indiana bats (mostly males) use burned areas in proportion to their availability in Kentucky (Gumbert 2001), and male Indiana bats in West Virginia roost in fire killed trees 1–3 years post fire (Johnson and others 2010). Most of the roost trees used in West Virginia are adjacent to canopy gaps, but the roosts in the burned areas are in larger gaps than those in the unburned areas. Bats often choose roosts near edges or canopy gaps because these trees get more solar exposure, allowing the bats to use the warmth of the sun for passive warming (Kalcounis-

Ruppell and others 2005). For example, in Missouri, evening bats (*Nycticeius humeralis*) show strong preference for roosts in burned areas where canopy light penetration is significantly greater (Boyles and Aubry 2006). It appears that changes in forest structure created by prescribed fire, such as the creation of more open canopies or canopy gaps, is beneficial for Indiana bats.

Two studies in the Appalachian region have examined the effects of prescribed fire on northern long-eared bat roosting behavior. In West Virginia, female northern long-eared bats respond positively to prescribed fire, possibly due to an increase in the amount of exfoliating bark on live and dead trees (Johnson and others 2009). Further, cavities in areas that were burned are significantly warmer than cavities in unburned areas, suggesting that roosts in the burned areas receive more solar radiation. Similarly, in Kentucky, female northern long-eared bats select roosts in burned areas over unburned areas within months of a spring prescribed fire (Lacki and others 2009b), and northern long-eared bats in Arkansas select roosts in stands that have been thinned and burned (Perry and others 2007, Perry and others 2008). Thus, although the data are limited, it appears prescribed fire in the Appalachians and surrounding areas results in good summer roosting habitat for both northern long-eared and Indiana bats. In addition to creating beneficial changes in forest structure around roosts, prescribed fire may be needed to promote the regeneration of fire-adapted species such as pines and oaks, both of which are important roosts for Indiana and northern long-eared bats. Pines may be ideal roosts due to their faster growth rates and tendency for exfoliating bark. Although slower growing, oaks can be quite large in diameter and also produce exfoliating bark both when alive and dead.

EFFECTS OF PRESCRIBED FIRE DURING THE FALL MIGRATION AND SWARMING PERIOD

Little is known is about the behavior of Indiana bats and northern long-eared bats during the migration and swarming periods. However, in many respects the fall swarming period is very similar to the spring emergence period. Bats must increase their energy intake to put on fat to make it through the hibernation period as well as mate, both of which demand high levels of resources.

As in spring, there is some evidence that tree roosts used during the fall are somewhat different from those used during the summer. In West Virginia, male Indiana bats use primarily live roosts that have a greater amount of bark, in areas with greater stand basal area and smaller canopy gaps (Johnson and others 2010). In Kentucky, male Indiana bats use live white oaks (*Q. alba*) more in fall than in spring and summer, and use live trees with a

greater amount of bark cover more in fall than in summer (Gumbert 2001). Live trees also comprise the majority of roost trees used by Indiana bats during the fall in Virginia (Brack 2006). Thus, the effects of prescribed fire on fall roost tree use and selection may be different than that observed during summer. At present, there are no data on roost use or selection by northern long-eared bats during the swarming period.

Only one study has examined foraging behavior of Indiana bats during the fall swarming period, and there are no studies on northern long-eared bats. In Virginia, Indiana bats use open deciduous forests which have experienced a disturbance such as harvesting within the past 10–20 years more than expected and more often as the season progresses; developed areas, closed deciduous forests, mixed hardwood-conifer stands are used less than expected in fall (Brack 2006). Due to reduced clutter, it may be more efficient for bats to forage in open versus closed forests, and thus, prescribed fire may have a positive effect on foraging behavior in fall if it creates more open forest conditions.

It is likely that Indiana bats and northern long-eared bats use torpor in fall as in spring, even while roosting in trees. Similar concerns regarding fires during cold periods of the day should be considered when developing burn plans. However, potential effects on bats from differences in day length, weather conditions, and fuel moisture should also be considered.

POTENTIAL EFFECTS OF NOT BURNING

One of the many goals of prescribed fire in the Appalachians is the reduction of fuel loads to prevent wildfire (Reilly and others 2012). Wildfires are not uncommon in areas that contain northern long-eared and Indiana bats, and if they occur during the maternity period, particularly before the pups are volant, they could have a large impact on the reproductive success of these species. For example, between 1998 and 2006 there were 16 lightning-caused fires in Great Smoky Mountains National Park (Cohen and other 2007), an area that contains both northern long-eared bats and Indiana bats (Harvey 2002). In August 2010, a wildfire that began from a lightning strike burned ~300 acres of pine and oak forests on the southwest side of this park. Fire managers adopted a "let it burn" approach to reduce fuel loading in the area, but monitored fire lines and protected potential Indiana bat roosts by clearing fuels and litter around dead pine snags. During wildfires, the probability that bats at roost will experience ear burns should increase (Dickinson and others 2010). Further, if roost trees are destroyed during wildfires or become unusable because of the loss of bark, then it may be difficult for bats to find alternate roost sites, particularly if the fire is large.

Surface fuels, which exacerbate wildfire effects, may increase as a result of drought, either through direct tree mortality or increased prevalence of pathogens and disease (Reilly and others 2012). Because drought is projected to increase in the South in future decades (Liu and others 2013), the probability of more severe wildfires is likely to increase due to heavier fuel loadings. Thus, to reduce the risk of wildfire during seasonally sensitive periods for Indiana bats and northern long-eared bats, it may be important to conduct prescribed fires that reduce fuel loads.

Another consequence of not burning or burning infrequently is the creation of highly cluttered habitats that are not suitable for Indiana bat or northern long-eared bat roosting and foraging habitat. More frequent prescribed fires result in forests with less clutter and greater bat activity (Armitage and Ober 2012). Thus, in the absence of other disturbances, frequent prescribed fires may be necessary to create and maintain suitable habitat for both Indiana and northern long-eared bats in the Appalachians.

CONCLUSIONS

The use of prescribed fire in the Appalachians is critical for fuels reduction as well as habitat restoration. Reconciling these needs with those of endangered bats and other species can be challenging. However, Indiana bats and northern long-eared bats have been part of the Appalachian ecosystem for thousands of years and have adapted to periodic fires on the landscape. In fact, although the data are limited, several studies suggest that prescribed fire may benefit Indiana bats and northern long-eared bats by improving both roosting and foraging habitat. Long-term benefits such as the creation of pine-oak habitats must also be considered and weighed against some short-term effects (e.g., loss of roost trees or disturbance of the roost). Conducting burns during time periods that will minimize disturbance to bats is one way to reduce risk. It is evident that far more research is needed on Indiana bats and northern long-eared bats during the spring, fall, and winter periods. Research should concentrate on potential effects of smoke during the hibernacula period, roosting and foraging behavior during spring and fall, and how prescribed fire during various seasons affects roosting and foraging habitats and behavior in spring and fall. This information will allow managers to develop effective management plans that will permit them to meet their vegetation restoration goals while reducing the risk to these sensitive bat species.

ACKNOWLEDGMENTS

We thank R.W. Perry and L.K. Burns for helpful comments on previous drafts.

LITERATURE CITED

Armitage, D.W.; Ober, H.K. 2012. The effects of prescribed fire on bat communities in the longleaf pine sandhills ecosystem. Journal of Mammalogy. 93: 102-114.

Bagne, K.E.; Purcell, K.L.; Rotenberry, J.T. 2008. Prescribed fire, snag population dynamics, and avian nest site selection. Forest Ecology and Management. 255: 99-105.

Bean, M.J. 2009. The Endangered Species Act: science, policy, and politics. Annals New York Academy of Sciences. 1162: 369-391.

Blehert, D.S.; Hicks, A.C.; Behr, M. [and others]. 2009. Bat white-nose syndrome: an emerging fungal pathogen? Science. 323: 227.

Boyles, J.G.; Aubrey, D.P. 2006. Managing forests with prescribed fire: implications for a cavity-dwelling bat species. Forest Ecology and Management. 222: 108-115.

Brack, V., Jr. 2006. Autumn activity of *Myotis sodalis* (Indiana bat) in Bland County, Virginia. Northeastern Naturalist. 13: 421-434.

Britzke, E.R.; Hicks, A.C.; Von Oettingen, S.L.; Darling, S.R. 2006. Description of spring roost trees used by female Indiana bats (*Myotis sodalis*) in the Lake Champlain Valley of Vermont and New York. American Midland Naturalist. 155: 181-187.

Brose, P.H.; Dey, D.C.; Phillips, R.J.; Waldrop, T.A. 2013. A meta-analysis of the fire-oak hypothesis: does prescribed burning promote oak reproduction in Eastern North America? Forest Science. 59: 322-334.

Buchalski, M.R.; Fontaine, J.B.; Heady, P.A., III, [and others]. 2013. Bat response to differing fire severity in mixed-conifer forest California, USA. PLoS One. 8:e57884.

Caceres, M.C.; Barclay, R.M.R. 2000. *Myotis septentrionalis.* Mammalian Species. 634: 1-4.

Carter, T.C.; Feldhamer, G.A. 2005. Roost tree use by maternity colonies of Indiana bats and northern long-eared bats in southern Illinois. Forest Ecology and Management. 219: 259-268.

Carter, T.C.; Menzel, M.A.; Owen, S.F. [and others]. 2003. Food habits of seven species of bats in the Allegheny Plateau and Ridge and Valley of West Virginia. Northeastern Naturalist. 10: 83-88.

Caviness, M. 2003. Effects of prescribed fire on cave environment and bat inhabitants. Bat Research News. 40: 130.

Cohen, D.; Dellinger, B.; Klein, R.; Buchanan. B. 2007. Patterns in lightning-caused fires at Great Smoky Mountains National Park. Fire Ecology Special Issue. 3: 68-82.

Davis, W.E.; Hitchcock, H.B. 1965. Biology and migration of the bat, *Myotis lucifugus*, in New England. Journal of Mammalogy. 46: 296-313.

Dickinson, M.B.; Lacki, M.J.; Cox, D.R. 2009. Fire and the endangered Indiana bat. In: Hutchinson, T.F., ed. Proceedings of the 3rd fire in eastern oak forests conference. Gen. Tech. Rep. NRS-P-46. Newtown Square, PA: U.S. Department of Agriculture Forest Service, Northern Research Station: 51-75.

Dickinson, M.B.; Norris, J.C.; Bova, A.S. [and others]. 2010. Effects of wildland fire smoke on a tree-roosting bat: integrating a plume model, field measurements, and mammalian dose-response relationships. Canadian Journal of Forest Research. 40: 2187-2203.

Dzal, Y.A.; Brigham, R.M. 2013. The tradeoff between torpor use and reproduction in little brown bats (*Myotis lucifugus*). Journal of Comparative Physiology B. 183: 279-288.

Faure, P.A.; Fullard, J.H.; Dawson, J.W. 1993. The gleaning attacks of the northern long-eared bat, *Myotis septentrionalis,* are relatively inaudible to moths. Journal of Experimental Biology. 178: 173-189.

Federal Register. 2013. Endangered and threatened wildlife and plants; 12-Month finding on a petition to list the eastern small-footed bat and the northern long-eared bat as endangered or threatened species; listing the northern long-eared bat as an endangered species; Proposed Rule, CFR 50, Part 17, Vol. 78, No. 191: 61046-61080.

Feldhamer, G.A.; Carter, T.C.; Whitaker, J.O., Jr. 2009. Prey consumed by eight species of insectivorous bats from southern Illinois. American Midland Naturalist. 162: 43-51.

Flatley, W.T.; Lafon, C.W.; Grissino-Mayer, H.D.; LaForest, L.B. 2013. Fire history, related to climate and land use in three southern Appalachian landscapes in the Eastern United States. Ecological Applications. 23: 1250-1266.

Ford, W.M.; Menzel, J.M.; Menzel, M.A.; Edwards, J.W. 2002. Summer roost-tree selection by a male Indiana bat on the Fernow Experimental Forest. Report NE-378. Newtown Square, PA: U.S. Department of Agriculture, Forest Service, Northeastern Research Station. 7 p.

Ford, W.M.; Menzel, M.A.; Rodrigue, J.L. [and others]. 2005. Relating bat species presence to simple habitat measures in a central Appalachian forest. Biological Conservation. 126: 528-539.

Foster, R.W.; Kurta, A. 1999. Roosting ecology of the northern bat (*Myotis septentrionalis*) and comparisons with the endangered Indiana bat (*Myotis sodalis*). Journal of Mammalogy. 80: 659-672.

Gumbert, M. W. 2001. Seasonal roost tree use by Indiana bats in the Somerset Ranger District of the Daniel Boone National Forest, Kentucky. Richmond, KY: Eastern Kentucky University. 136 p. M.S. thesis.

Hall, J.S. 1962. A life history and taxonomic study of the Indiana bat, *Myotis sodalis*. Volume 12. Reading, PA: Reading Public Museum and Art Gallery. 68 p.

Hammond, K. R. 2013. Summer Indiana bat ecology in the southern Appalachians: an investigation of thermoregulation strategies and landscape scale roost selection. Terra Haute, IN: Indiana State University. 87 p. M.S. thesis.

Harvey, M. J. 2002. Status and ecology of the Indiana bat (*Myotis sodalis*) in the Southern United States. In: Kurta, A.; Kennedy, J., eds. The Indiana bat: biology and management of an endangered species. Austin, TX: Bat Conservation International: 29-34.

Hobson, C.S.; Holland, J.N. 1995. Post-hibernation movement and foraging habitat of a male Indiana bat, *Myotis sodalis* (Chiroptera: Vespertilionidae), in western Virginia. Brimleyana. 23: 95-101.

Horton, S.P.; Mannan, R.W. 1988. Effects of prescribed fire on snags and cavity-nesting birds in southeastern Arizona pine forests. Wildlife Society Bulletin. 16: 37-44.

Inkster-Draper, T.E.; Sheaves, M.; Johnson, C.N.; Robson, S.K.A. 2013. Prescribed fire in eucalypt woodlands: immediate effects on a microbat community of northern Australia. Wildlife Research. 40: 70-76.

Jantzen, M.K.; Fenton, M.B. 2013. The depth of edge influence among insectivorous bats at forest–field interfaces. Canadian Journal of Zoology. 91: 287-292.

Johnson, J.B.; Edwards, J.W., Ford, W.M.; Gates, J.E. 2009. Roost tree selection by northern myotis (*Myotis septentrionalis*) maternity colonies following prescribed fire in a Central Appalachian Mountains hardwood forest. Forest Ecology and Management. 258: 233-242.

Johnson, J.B.; Ford, W.M.; Rodrigue, J.L. [and others]. 2010. Roost selection by male Indiana myotis following forest fires in Central Appalachian Hardwoods forests. Journal of Fish and Wildlife Management. 1: 111-121.

Kalcounis-Rueppell, M.C.; Psyllakis, J.M.; Brigham, R.M. 2005. Tree roost selection by bats: an empirical synthesis using meta-analysis. Wildlife Society Bulletin. 33: 1123-1132.

Lacki, M.J.; Cox, D.R.; Dickinson, M.B. 2009a. Meta-analysis of summer roosting characteristics of two species of *Myotis* bats. American Midland Naturalist. 162: 318-326.

Lacki, M.J.; Cox, D.R.; Dickinson, M.B. 2009b. Response of northern bats (*Myotis septentrionalis*) to prescribed fires in eastern Kentucky forests. Journal of Mammalogy. 90: 1165-1175.

Langwig, K.E.; Frick, W.F.; Bried, J.T. [and others]. 2012. Sociality, density-dependence and microclimates determine the persistence of populations suffering from a novel fungal disease, white-nose syndrome. Ecology Letters. 15: 1050-1057.

Layne, J.T. 2009. Eastern red bat (*Lasiurus borealis*) response to fire stimulus during torpor. Springfield, MO: Missouri State University. 47 p. M.S. thesis.

Liu, Y.; Prestemon, J.P.; Goodrick, S.L. [and others]. 2013. Future wildfire trends, impacts, and mitigation options in the Southern United States. In: Vose, J. M; Klepzig, K.D., eds. Management options: a guide for natural resource managers in southern forest ecosystems. Boca Raton, FL: CRC Press: 85-125.

Malison, R.L.; Baxter, C. 2010. The fire pulse: wildlfire stimulates flux of aquatic prey to terrestrial habitats driving increases in riparian consumers. Canadian Journal of Fisheries and Aquatic Sciences. 67: 570-579.

Loeb, S.C.; O'Keefe, J.M. 2006. Habitat use by forest bats in South Carolina in relation to local, stand, and landscape characteristics. Journal of Wildlife Management. 70: 1210-1218.

Loeb, S.C.; Waldrop, T.A. 2008. Bat activity in relation to fire and fire surrogate treatments in southern pine stands. Forest Ecology and Management. 255: 3185-3192.

Nagorsen, D.W.; Brigham, R.M. 1993. Bats of British Columbia: Royal British Columbia museum handbook. Vancouver, Canada: University of British Columbia Press: 177 p.

O'Keefe, J.M. 2009. Roosting and foraging ecology of forest bats in the Southern Appalachian Mountains. Clemson, SC: Clemson University. 152 p. Ph.D. dissertation.

O'Keefe, J.M.; Loeb, S.C; Gerard, P.D.; Lanham, J.D. 2013. Effects of riparian buffer width on activity and detection of common bats in the Southern Appalachian Mountains. Wildlife Society Bulletin. 37: 319-326.

Perry, R.W. 2012. A review of fire effects on bats and bat habitats in the eastern oak region. In: Dey, D.C.; Stambaugh, M.C.; Clark, S.L.; Schweitzer, C.J., eds. Proceedings of the 4th Fire in Eastern Oak Forests Conference. Gen. Tech. Rep. NRS-P-102. Newtown Square, PA: U.S. Department of Agriculture, Forest Service, Northern Research Station: 170-191.

Perry, R.W.; Thill. R.E. 2007. Roost selection by male and female northern long-eared bats in a pine-dominated landscape. Forest Ecology and Management. 247: 220-226.

Perry, R.W.; Thill. R.E.; Leslie, D.M., Jr. 2007. Selection of roosting habitat by forest bats in a diverse forested landscape. Forest Ecology and Management. 238: 156-166.

Perry, R.W.; Thill. R.E.; Leslie, D.M., Jr. 2008. Scale-dependent effects of landscape structure and composition on diurnal roost selection by forest bats. Journal of Wildlife Management. 72: 913-925.

Randall-Parker, T.; Miller, R. 2002. Effects of prescribed fire in ponderosa pine on key wildlife habitat components: preliminary results and a method for monitoring. In: Laudenslayer, W.F., Jr.; Shea, P. J., Valentine, B.E. [and others], eds. Proceedings of the symposium on the ecology and management of dead wood in western forests. Gen. Tech. Rep. PSW-181. Albany, CA: U.S. Department of Agriculture Forest Service, Pacific Southwest Research Station: 823-834.

Reeder, D.M.; Frank, C.L.; Turner, G.G. [and others]. 2012. Frequent arousal from hibernation linked to severity of infection and mortality in bats with white-nose syndrome. PLoS One. 7:e38920.

Reilly, M.J.; Waldrop, T.A.; O'Brien, J.J. 2012. Fuels management in the Southern Appalachian Mountains, hot continental division. In: LaFayette, R.; Brooks, M.T.; Polyondy, J.P. [and others], eds. Cumulative watershed effects of fuel management in the Eastern United States. Gen. Tech. Rep. SRS-161. Asheville, NC: U.S. Department of Agriculture Forest Service, Southern Research Station: 101-116.

Richter, A.R.; Humphrey, S.R.; Cope, J.B.; Brack, V., Jr. 1993. Modified cave entrances: thermal effect on body mass and resulting decline of endangered Indiana bats (Myotis sodalis). Conservation Biology. 7: 407-415.

Rush, S.; Klaus, N.; Keyes, T. [and others]. 2012. Fire severity has mixed benefits to breeding bird species in the southern Appalachians. Forest Ecology and Management. 263: 94-100.

Schirmacher, M.R.; Castleberry, S.B.; Ford, W.M.; Miller, K.V. 2007. Habitat associations of bats in south-central West Virginia. Proceedings Annual Conference Southeastern Association of Fish and Wildlife Agencies. 61: 46-52.

Smith, D.A.; Gehrt, S.D. 2010. Bat response to woodland restoration within urban forest fragments. Restoration Ecology. 18: 914-923.

Sparks, D.W.; Ritzi, C.M.; Duchamp, J.E.; Whitaker, J.O., Jr. 2005. Foraging habitat of Indiana myotis (Myotis sodalis) at an urban/rural interface. Journal of Mammalogy. 86: 713-718.

Starbuck, C. 2013. Bat occupancy of forests and managed savanna and woodland in the Missouri Ozark Region. Columbia, MO: University of Missouri. 82 p. M.S. thesis.

Stephens, S.L.; Moghaddas, J.J. 2005. Fuel treatment effects on snags and coarse woody debris in a Sierra Nevada mixed conifer forest. Forest Ecology and Management. 214: 53-64.

Thogmartin, W.E.; Sanders-Reed, C.A.; Szymanski, J.A. [and others]. 2013. White-nose syndrome is likely to extirpate the endangered Indiana bat over large parts of its range. Biological Conservation. 160: 162-172.

Thogmartin, W.E.; King, A.; McKann, P.C. [and others]. 2012. Population-level impact of white-nose syndrome on the endangered Indiana bat. Journal of Mammalogy. 93: 1086-1098.

Thomas, D.W.; Dorais, M.; Bergeron, J.-M. 1990. Winter energy budgets and cost of arousals for hibernating little brown bats, Myotis lucifugus. Journal of Mammalogy. 71: 475-479.

Thomas, D.W.; Fenton, M.B.; Barclay, R.M.R. 1979. Social behavior of the little brown bat, Myotis lucifugus. I. Mating behavior. Behavioral Ecology and Sociobiology. 6: 129-136.

Turner, G.G.; Reeder, D.M.; Coleman, J.T.H. 2011. A five-year assessment of mortality and geographic spread of white-nose syndrome in North American bats and a look to the future. Bat Research News. 52: 13-27.

Tuttle, N.M.; Benson, D.P.; Sparks, D.W. 2006. Diet of the Myotis sodalis (Indiana bat) at an urban/rural interface. Northeastern Naturalist. 13: 435-442.

U.S. Fish and Wildlife Service (USFWS). 2007. Indiana bat (Myotis sodalis) draft recovery plan: first revision. Fort Snelling, MN: U.S. Fish and Wildlife Service. 258 p.

U.S. Department of Agriculture (USDA) Forest Service. 2004. Land and resource management plan for the Daniel Boone National Forest. Management Bulletin R8-MB 117A. Winchester, KY.

Warnecke, L.; Turner, J.M.; Bollinger, T.K. [and others]. 2012. Inoculation of bats with European Geomyces destructans supports the novel pathogen hypothesis for the origin of white-nose syndrome. Proceedings National Academy of Science. 108: 6999-7003.

Watrous, K.S.; Donovan, T.M.; Mickey, R. M. [and others]. 2006. Predicting minimum habitat characteristics for the Indiana bat in the Champlain Valley. Journal of Wildlife Management. 70: 1228-1237.

Whitaker, J. O., Jr. 2004. Prey selection in a temperate zone insectivorous bat community. Journal of Mammalogy. 85: 460-469.

Whitaker, J. O., Jr.; Rissler, L. J. 1992. Seasonal activity of bats at Copperhead Cave. Proceedings of the Indiana Academy of Science. 101: 127-134.

Willis, C. K. R. 2006. Daily heterothermy by temperate bats using natural roosts. In: Zubaid, A.; McCracken, G. F.; Kunz, T. H., eds. Functional and Evolutionary Ecology of Bats. New York, NY: Oxford University Press: 38-55.

Willis, C.K.R.; Brigham, R.M.; Geiser, F. 2006. Deep, prolonged torpor by pregnant, free-ranging bats. Naturwissenschaften. 93: 80-83.

Winhold, L.; Kurta, A. 2006. Aspects of migration by the endangered Indiana bat, Myotis sodalis. Bat Research News. 47: 1-6.

Womack, K. M. 2011. Habitat and management effects on foraging activity of Indiana bats (Myotis sodalis) in northern Missouri. Columbia, MO: University of Missouri. 83 p. M.S. thesis.

Womack, K.M.; Amelon, S.K.; Thompson, F.R., III. 2013. Resource selection by Indiana bats during the maternity season. Journal of Wildlife Management. 77: 707-715.

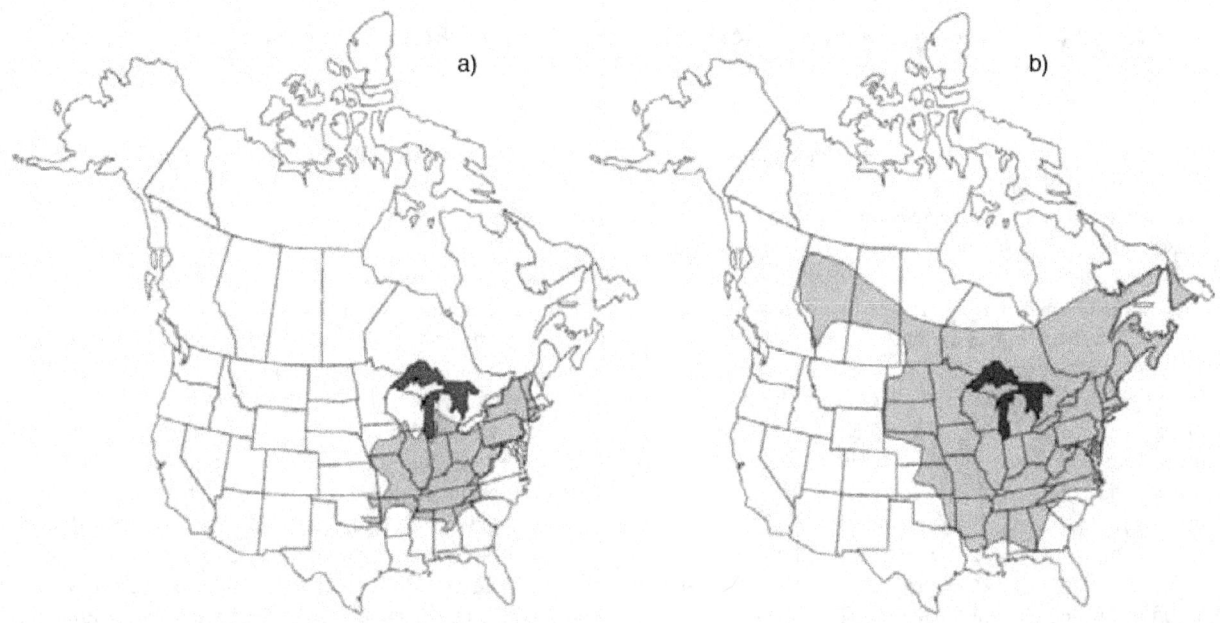

Figure 1—Approximate ranges of a) the Indiana bat and b) the northern long-eared bat.

BIRD RESPONSE TO FIRE SEVERITY AND REPEATED BURNING IN AN UPLAND HARDWOOD FOREST

Cathryn H. Greenberg, Thomas A. Waldrop, Joseph Tomcho, Ross J. Phillips, and Dean Simon[1]

Prescribed burning is a common management tool for upland hardwood forests, with wildlife habitat improvement an often cited goal. Fire management for wildlife conservation requires understanding how species respond to burning at different frequencies, severities, and over time. In upland hardwood forests of the Eastern United States, high-severity fires are rare, and effects on breeding bird communities are not well known. Research indicates that single or multiple low-intensity burns with little tree mortality may have a negligible effect on most bird species, or short-term effect on some species associated with shrub or leaf litter cover (Aquilani and others 2000; Artman and others 2001; Greenberg and others 2007, 2013). In contrast, high-severity fires with heavy tree mortality may create habitat for species requiring open, early successional conditions (Greenberg and others 2011) or snags for nest cavities, while retaining many species associated with closed canopy forests (Greenberg and others 2007, 2013). In this study, we experimentally assessed how breeding bird communities and species responded to fuel reduction treatments, including prescribed fire and a fire surrogate.

Our study was conducted on the 14,400-acre Green River Game Land in Polk County, North Carolina, in the mountainous Blue Ridge Physiographic Province of Western North Carolina. Our experimental design was a randomized block design with repeated measures over years. We selected three study areas (blocks) within the Game Land. We selected blocks to ensure consistency in baseline forest age, type, and management history among the treatments. Minimum size of experimental units (4 within each block; 12 total units) was 35 acres to accommodate 25-acre "core" areas, with 66-foot buffers around each. Treatments were: mechanical understory reduction in 2002 (M); prescribed fire in March 2003 and a second burn in March 2006 (B); mechanical understory reduction (2002) followed a year later (2003) by prescribed fire, and a second burn in 2006 (MB); and compared to controls (C).

We measured density of live trees and snags in each experimental unit before treatments (2001), twice after initial treatments (2003, 2005), and again twice after the second prescribed burns in both burn treatments (2006, 2011). We surveyed breeding bird communities using three, 164-foot radius point counts spaced 656 feet apart in each experimental unit. Each point was surveyed for 10 minutes during three separate visits between 15 May and 30 June during 2001–2005 (after initial fuel reduction treatments) (Greenberg and others 2007), and in 2006, 2007, 2009, and 2011 (Greenberg and others 2013) to study the longer-term effects of fuel reduction treatments that included a second prescribed fire in both B and MB.

During the first prescribed burns (March 2003), flame heights of 3 to 6 feet occurred throughout all burn units, but reached up to 15 feet in localized spots within blocks, where topography or intersecting flame fronts contributed to erratic fire behavior. In the 2003 burns, temperature at 12 inches aboveground averaged 594 °F in B, but patches (6–22 percent of each burn unit) burned at temperatures >1100 °F. In MB, where loading of dead fine woody fuels was approximately double that of C and M, temperatures at 30 cm aboveground averaged 517 °F, and 22–49 percent of each unit burned at temperatures >1100 °F. The second burn (March 2006) was less intense, with flame heights generally < 5 feet. In 2006, measured temperatures 12 inches aboveground were generally < 316 °F on B sites and 433 °F in MB sites, with <3 percent of any burn unit exceeding 1100 °F. A detailed description of fire behavior in this study is given by Waldrop and others (2010).

[1]Cathryn H. Greenberg, USDA Forest Service, Southern Research Station, Bent Creek Experimental Forest, Asheville, NC

Thomas A. Waldrop, USDA Forest Service, Southern Research Station, Clemson, SC

Joseph Tomcho, North Carolina Wildlife Resources Commission, Burnsville, NC

Ross J. Phillips, USDA Forest Service, Southern Research Station, Clemson, SC

Dean Simon, North Carolina Wildlife Resources Commission, Lawndale, NC

Citation for proceedings: Waldrop, Thomas A., ed. 2014. Proceedings, Wildland Fire in the Appalachians: Discussions among Managers and Scientists. Gen. Tech. Rep. SRS-199. Asheville, NC: U.S. Department of Agriculture Forest Service, Southern Research Station. 208 p.

Initial (2003) higher dead fuel loadings and consequently high-severity fires in MB killed trees (fig. 1a) and created open-canopy structure with abundant snags (fig. 1b). These changes to forest structure resulted in much higher species density (fig. 2a) and richness (fig. 2b) of breeding birds in MB compared to other treatments due to a higher occurrence and (or) abundance of species associated with young, open forest and edge conditions such as eastern bluebirds (*Sialia sialis*), indigo buntings (*Passerina cyanea*), eastern towhees (*Pipilo erythrophthalmus*), brown thrashers (*Toxostoma rufum*), chipping sparrows (*Spizella passerina*), American goldfinches (*Carduelis tristis*), mourning doves (*Zenaida macroura*), and pine warblers (*Setophaga pinus*), in addition to most other species that also occurred in the other treatments and control. Abundance of most other species was not affected by the three fuel reduction treatments, even after the second burn.

Although we could not assess whether a second burn contributed additionally to the delayed tree mortality initiated by a single burn, our results indicate that repeated, relatively low-intensity burning with patches of higher intensity fire can affect a gradual, subtle change in forest structure that may, over time, attract breeding bird species associated with young forest conditions. In contrast, a single high-intensity, high-severity fire can create young forest conditions and a heterogeneous canopy structure that can be maintained by repeated burning and increase breeding bird relative abundance and richness by attracting disturbance-adapted species while retaining most other forest species.

ACKNOWLEDGMENTS

This research was funded by the Forest Service, U.S. Department of Agriculture through the National Fire Plan and by the U.S. Joint Fire Science Program (JFSP). We thank the North Carolina Wildlife Resources Commission for their field support, for permitting this study to be conducted on State Game Lands, and for conducting all fuel reduction treatments. Also thanks to Stan Zarnoch, Chris Moorman, and Gordon Warburton for their input.

LITERATURE CITED

Aquilani, S.M.; LeBlanc, D.C.; Morrell, T.E. 2000. Effects of prescribed surface fires on ground- and shrub-nesting neotropical migratory birds in a mature Indiana oak forest, USA. Natural Areas Journal. 20: 317-324.

Artman, V.L.; Sutherland, E.K.; Downhower, D.F. 2001. Prescribed burning to restore mixed-oak communities in southern Ohio: Effects on breeding-bird populations. Conservation Biology. 15: 1423-1434.

Greenberg, C.H.; Livings-Tomcho, A.; Lanham, J.D. [and others]. 2007. Short-term effects of fire and other fuel reduction treatments on breeding birds in a southern Appalachian hardwood forest. Journal of Wildlife Management. 71: 1906-1916.

Greenberg, C.H.; Collins, B.S.; Thompson, F.R. III; McNab, H.R.; 2011. What are early successional habitats, how can they be sustained, and why are they important? In: Greenberg, C.H.; Collins, B.S.; Thompson, F.R. III, eds. Sustaining Young Forest Communities: Ecology and Management of Early Successional Habitats in the Central Hardwood Region, USA. Managing Forest Ecosystems Vol. 21, New York: Springer: 1-10.

Greenberg, C.H.; Waldrop, T.A.; Tomcho, J. [and others]. 2013. Bird response to fire severity and repeated burning in upland hardwood forest. Forest Ecology and Management. 304: 80-88.

Waldrop, T.A.; Phillips, R.A.; Simon, D.A. 2010. Fuels and predicted fire behavior in the Southern Appalachian Mountains after fire and fire surrogate treatments. Forest Science. 56: 32-45.

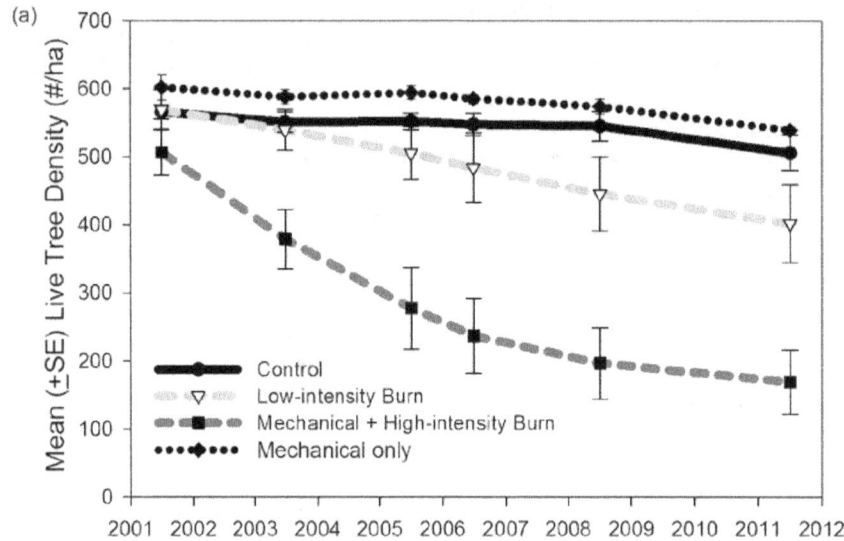

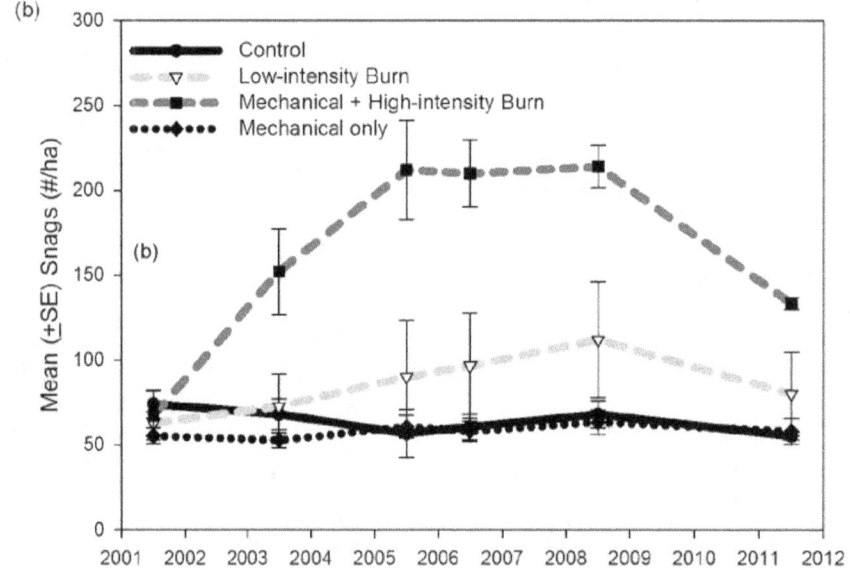

Figure 1—Mean (±SE) total density of (a) live trees and (b) standing snags in 3 fuel reduction treatments: burned (2003 and 2006); mechanical understory reduction (2002); mechanical understory reduction (2002) then burned (2003 and 2006); and untreated controls (n = 3 each), Green River Game Land, Polk County, NC.

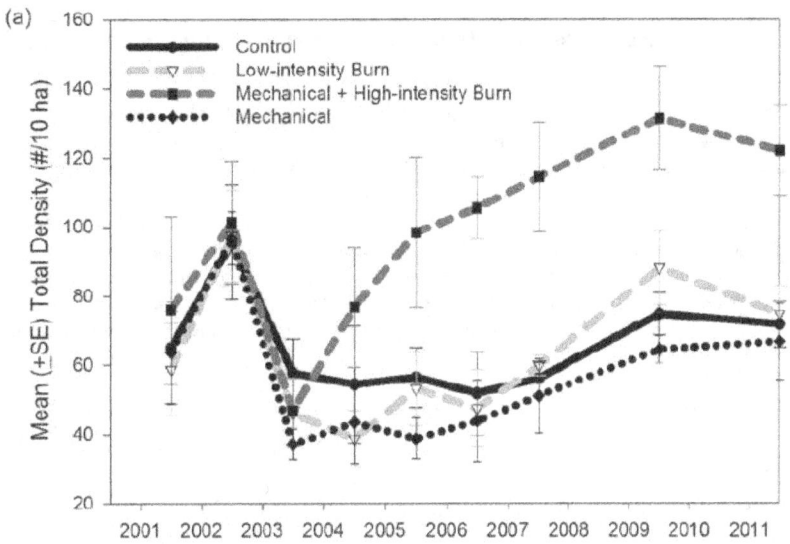

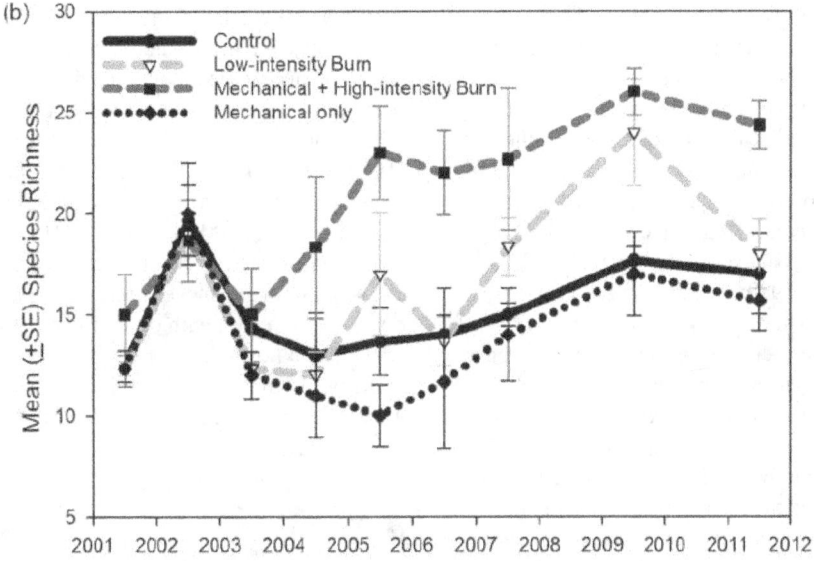

Figure 2—Mean (±SE) (a) total density and (b) species richness of breeding birds in 3 fuel reduction treatments: burned (2003 and 2006); mechanical understory reduction (2002); mechanical understory reduction (2002) then burned (2003 and 2006); and untreated controls (n = 3 each), Green River Game Land, Polk County, NC.

SYNTHESIS OF THE EFFECTS OF FIRE ON SOUTHERN APPALACHIAN FAUNA

Amber L. Pitt, Robert F. Baldwin, Joseph J. Tavano, Thomas A. Waldrop, and Ross J. Phillips[1]

Abstract—We reviewed the effects of prescribed fire on wildlife in the southern Appalachian Mountains and placed our results in the context of regional, national, and global studies. We conducted a Web search of peer-reviewed literature and technical reports to evaluate the number of prescribed fire studies pertaining to geographical regions and taxonomic groups. We obtained 717 relevant, unique studies, the majority of which were from North America (n=513). The most studied taxonomic group globally was birds (n=244). Within the United States, most studies occured in the Southeast region (n=179), including 21 in the southern Appalachians. All southern Appalachian studies with wildlife as dependent variable were of prescribed fire. Our review of the papers specific to the southern Appalachians revealed no strong signals. The lack of strong signals that can be generalized across taxa or ecosystems may be due to the limited number of studies and their short-term, localized, and/or species-centric character. By focusing new research at multiple spatiotemporal scales, we may gain powerful, multi-scale inference.

INTRODUCTION

Fire has been a powerful force structuring ecosystems for millennia. In recent decades, fire and the use of fire for ecosystem management have received much research attention. While the use of fire to restore and maintain plant communities is relatively understood, there is no consensus as to how fire influences fauna, and fire-fauna relationships are more difficult to predict. The southern Appalachian Mountains comprise a globally-significant region of biological diversity that is maintained in part by disturbance; fire may have extensively influenced the distribution of plants and animals (Lorimer 1980, Van Lear and Waldrop 1989). The region has millennia of human occupation that may have, at least in part, played a role in fire maintenance (Delcourt and Delcourt 1997). The southern Appalachians have a number of plant communities known to be strongly influenced to entirely structured by fire. For example, Table Mountain pine (*Pinus pungens*) on dry ridges and southwest-facing slopes 1–4000 feet elevation is largely dependent on burns (Spira 2011). Furthermore, the most predominant fire frequency interval in the region is 11–30 years (fig. 1). Recent decades have seen rapid expansion of urban areas near wildlands, and amenity-based exurban growth directly on the edges of forest areas (Brown and others 2005, Turner and others 2003). Such human settlement alters the extent to which prescribed fire may be used to manage and restore ecosystems.

Prescribed fire has become an essential landscape-level management tool. It is one of the only circumstances in which managers directly manipulate disturbance. Prescribed fire is invoked to mimic disturbance at specific frequencies, intensities, and extents. For example, there are a few but rare examples of flood, grazing, and timber harvest used to recreate non-anthropogenic disturbance (Fuhlendorf and Engle 2001, Seymour and Hunter 1999). Yet, fire is used in a number of ecosystems as a management and restoration tool (Ford and others 2000, Noss and others 2006). A number of studies have been conducted of the effects of prescribed fire on wildlife. We seek to review those studies, compare research effort in the region with other areas of the world, and synthesize knowledge of fire effects on wildlife. We focus our review on effects of prescribed fire on birds, mammals, herpetofauna, and invertebrates in the southern Appalachians.

METHODS

We approached this review using both quantitative and qualitative methods. We conducted a web search of peer-reviewed literature and technical reports to evaluate the number of studies pertaining to geographical regions and taxonomic groups. Our literature searches were done using Google Scholar, Google, and Web of Knowledge search engines. Search terms included "fire"

[1]Amber L. Pitt, Assistant Professor, Department of Biological and Allied Health Sciences, Bloomsburg University of Pennsylvania, Bloomsburg, PA 17815

Robert F. Baldwin, Associate Professor, School of Agricultural, Forest, and Environmental Sciences, Clemson University, Clemson, SC 29634

Joseph J. Tavano, Research Specialist, Clemson University, Clemson, SC 29634

Thomas A. Waldrop, Supervisory Research Forester, Southern Research Station, USDA Forest Service, Clemson, SC 29634

Ross J. Phillips, Ecologist, Southern Research Station, Clemson, SC 29634

Citation for proceedings: Waldrop, Thomas A., ed. 2014. Proceedings, Wildland Fire in the Appalachians: Discussions among Managers and Scientists. Gen. Tech. Rep. SRS-199. Asheville, NC: U.S. Department of Agriculture Forest Service, Southern Research Station. 208 p.

and "prescribed fire", combined in different searches with "wildlife", "bird", "mammal", "reptile", "amphibian", "invertebrate", "insect", "frog", "salamander", "snake", "lizard", "turtle", and "avian". We found a total of 941 references that we initially considered relevant. After further inspection, 226 were omitted due to their nature as conference abstracts, duplicative of other references (same research, different publication), general ecology reviews, or topically unsuitable (mis-classified by search terms).

A total of 717 studies was used to compare numbers of studies by world region, world region X taxonomic group, by North American region, and North American region X taxonomic group. Studies focused on the southern Appalachian region (n=21) were exhaustively read and categorized by effect (direct=behavioral, population/community, mortality; indirect=habitat), type of measurement (nest success/selection, roost selection, habitat selection, abundance, richness, population estimate), and taxonomic group. Southern Appalachian studies were further reviewed and summarized by above categories.

RESULTS

A total of 717 relevant, unique studies was obtained. By a large margin, the majority of studies (n=513) come from North America, followed by Australia (n=104), Europe (n=48), Africa (n=30), South America (n=13), and Asia (n=9; fig. 2). These totals are further subdivided by taxonomic group in figure 3. Worldwide, the most studied taxonomic group with respect to prescribed fire effects is birds (n=244), followed by mammals (189), invertebrates (n=155), and herpetofauna (n=152; fig. 3). Within the United States, most studies have been conducted in the Southeast (n=179), followed by the Midwest (n=98), Southwest (n=83), Pacific (n=64), Rocky Mountain (43), and Northeast (n=11) regions (fig. 4). In the United States, the most studied taxonomic group with respect to prescribed fire is birds (n=189), followed by mammals (n=121), invertebrates (n=91) and herpetofauna (n=90; fig. 5). While most studies from within the United States come from the Southeast region, the majority are in association with Coastal Plain/longleaf pine ecosystems. Relatively few studies have examined the effects of prescribed fire on fauna in the southern Appalachians (n=21; table 1), the majority of which came from a single research site in North Carolina (n=11; fig. 6). Most of the studies for the southern Appalachians were of direct effects at the population/community level, and only one attempted population estimation (small mammals). The preponderance of effects was neutral and positive (table 2). Depending on taxa, positive effects were strong (e.g., browse availability for white-tailed deer; Lashley and others 2011), or weak (e.g., behavioral shifts for myotis to exploit new snags; Johnson and others 2009).

Most studies were neutral in that they indicated no effect (no significant differences) for most taxa. Behavioral adaptations were noted that were not associated with differences in reproductive success (e.g., wood thrush nesting higher off the ground in burned areas). Negative effects were noted for salamanders, shrews, and ground and low-shrub-nesting birds (Matthews and others 2010, Greenberg and others 2007a, 2007b; Artman and others 2001). Interannual variability was large in some cases, outweighing treatment effects (e.g., shrews; Matthews and others 2009).

DISCUSSION

Globally, North America has benefitted from the greatest number of studies of the effects of fire on fauna—the Southeastern United States the best studied region of the continent. Within the Southeastern United States, most research is focused on the formerly extensive and emblematic fire-maintained long-leaf pine ecosystems. These are especially prevalent in coastal systems where habitat fragmentation and over-exploitation has rendered that once-extensive system a major conservation concern (Noss 2013). The southern Appalachians, despite a history of relatively frequent fire in many ecosystems (i.e., not only dry-slope, fire-maintained forests), have received much less research attention as to the effects of that fire on fauna. Of the studied fauna, birds have received the most attention, at habitat, community, population, and behavioral levels.

Our review of the 21 papers specific to prescribed fire in the southern Appalachians revealed no strong signals and mostly neutral effects. Effects of fire on fauna were consistent across the studies, in that there was an absence of strong, negative effects. No study illuminated acute or indirect effects that might result in population degradation to the extent that persistence could be negatively influenced. By contrast, a number of studies indicated positive, short-term effects. Of potential negative effects, reduction in leaf litter (some amphibians) and shrubs available for nesting (some birds) were noted as potential, short-term factors. But at the same time, those studies noted only weak negative effects and often, year-year differences in responses. All 21 studies were short term, covering effects spanning 1–6 years (predominately 1–2 years), and were site-based rather than landscape scale. The bias introduced by site-based, short duration studies was counterbalanced by a number of the studies that resulted from controlled experiments over multiple years (Green River; Wine Spring Creek).

The sample of papers for the southern Appalachians is small, and bias is large because there are few replicates within taxa. As a whole, the southern Appalachian literature suggests that prescribed fire can have many positive effects for a number of organisms (floral visiting insects, beetles, many bird species, deer, shrews, lizards, toads). No strong negative influences were noted, with the exception of terrestrial salamanders. Despite the lack of signal, there is consensus that habitat change happens as a result of prescribed fire; that change may have short-term effects on some taxa. Those changes may be temporarily negative (e.g., leaf litter and some salamander species in some sites, cover for ground nesting birds and shrews), temporarily positive (e.g., floral visiting insects, lizards), or neutral (e.g., bats may exploit gaps and new snags following fire), or strongly positive (e.g., availability of nutrition for white-tailed deer). As many species of wildlife exploit early seral stages, snags, gaps, and other artifacts of fire, the positive signals received for insects, bats, lizards, rodents, some birds, is not surprising. How such patterns would manifest over many years in a shifting mosaic of forest disturbance remains relatively unkown, which is true for forest disturbance generally, not just for fire (Clark 1991). Authors of some of the prescribed burning studies noted scale and timing effects; for example localized, short-term effects on ground nesting birds may be minimal but would intensify if cumulative over many burns in time and space (Artman and Downhower 2003, Artman and others 2001).

Amphibians have often been mentioned as of concern for prescribed burning; in the southern Appalachians there are contrasting results. There is some evidence that terrestrial salamanders should be studied more closely, as reductions in leaf litter and increased drying rates of organic matter may negatively impact these taxa (Matthews and others 2010). However, anurans seem to be little influenced. The most common terrestrial anuran is the American toad; its high capture rates may influence the perception that there is little effect on anurans (Greenberg and Waldrop 2008, Kirkland and Snoddy 1996). A recent telemetry study of toads in response to prescribed fire indicates that long distance breeding movements and high tolerance for dessication may contribute to the ability of this species to persist following that disturbance (Pitt and others 2013). Timing of prescribed burning has the potential to have the greatest influence on amphibians as amphibian movements in terrestrial environments is largely influenced by seasonal migration related to reproduction, and expansion of surface activities due to increased moisture (Baldwin and others 2006, Bellis 1962, Lamoureux and others 2002, Madison 1997, Petranka 1998).

The effect of fire on fauna has become increasingly well-studied; however, the results of studies of prescribed fire on fauna remain ambiguous, casting light on specific responses by individual populations and localities. The literature proves little basis to assess the potential long-

term effects of prescribed fire on distribution of species. There is a preponderance of neutral and/or contradictory effects, indicating that something is missing in how these studies are being conducted. We suggest that missing element is scale. Studies that focus on localized areas are likely to also be short term and not reveal anything but short-term responses. Animals vary in their ability to move or otherwise behaviorally adapt to fires; population and community responses require long-term research to elucidate. Fire intensity, extent, and frequency all influence how severe and long lasting its impacts are on resident fauna (Noss and others 2006). This amount of variability in fire behavior combined with species' adaptations to fire and how those characteristics might interact with a particular burn in a particular time and place make generalizations from existing studies quite difficult. However, there are plant and animal communities that are known to be created and maintained by fire over the long term, easing management concerns somewhat. Fire leads to patchiness at the landscape scale and can change distribution of habitats over time and space (Vickery 2002). The fire regime at the region scale (e.g., fig. 1) has biogeographic effects; and yet this remains the least studied aspects of the effect of prescribed fire on fauna.

We suggest these extended spatial and temporal scales be the focus of new research for the southern Appalachians. Spatial ecology employed at extensive, ecoregional scales, combined with dendrochronological and historical research on past patterns, could reveal how fire has influenced distribution of habitats. Such coarse-grained analysis, when combined with data on faunal distributions could allow some inference as to past effects; when combined with fine-grained field analyses of behavioral and population-level effects, such as the 21 studies from the southern Appalachians, powerful, multi-scale inference may be achieved. And, the planning of future field research on prescribed fire could combine long-term effects (such as the multiple fuel reduction treatments from the Green River, NC studies), with more spatially extensive treatments. Source sink population dynamics are probably very important for understanding how wildlife respond to forest disturbance over time and space; while the design of such field studies is daunting, field study can be augmented with spatial modeling. The southern Appalachians, with its high heterogeneity of habitats at multiple spatial scales, might represent a particularly challenging venue for such research, compared to relatively simpler Western systems.

What may be of concern to forest and wildlife managers is the interaction of habitat fragmentation and climate change with distribution of wildlife populations, in light of fire. Future research could explore how the temporal and spatial distribution of prescribed fire of varying intensity could impact distribution of habitats and animal populations. Understanding more about how prescribed fire can maintain disturbance and diversity in the context of anthropogenic change could inform landscape-scale, ecosystem-based management.

LITERATURE CITED

Artman V.L.; Downhower J.F. 2003. Wood thrush (*Hylocichla mustelina*) nesting ecology in relation to prescribed burning of mixed-oak forest in Ohio. Auk. 120: 874-882.

Artman V.L.; Sutherland E.K.; Downhower J.F. 2001. Prescribed burning to restore mixed-oak communities in southern Ohio: Effects on breeding-bird populations. Conservation Biology. 15(5): 1423-1434.

Baldwin R.F.; Calhoun A.J.K.; deMaynadier P.G. 2006. Conservation planning for amphibian species with complex habitat requirements: a case study using movements and habitat selection of the wood frog *Rana sylvatica*. Journal of Herpetology. 40: 443-454.

Bellis E.D. 1962. The influence of humidity on wood frog activity. American Midland Naturalist. 68: 139-148.

Brown D.G.; Johnson K.M.; Loveland T.R.; Theobald D.M. 2005. Rural land use trends in the conterminous United States, 1950-2000. Ecological Applications. 15: 1851-1863.

Campbell J.W.; Hanula J.L.; Waldrop T.A. 2007a. Effects of prescribed fire and fire surrogates on floral visiting insects of the blue ridge province in North Carolina. Biological Conservation. 134(3): 393-404.

Campbell J.W.; Hanula J.L.; Waldrop T.A. 2007b. Observations of the Diana Fritillary (*Speyeria diana*) utilizing forested areas in North Carolina that have been mechanically thinned and burned. Southeastern Naturalist. 6(1): 179-182.

Campbell J.W.; Hanula J.L.; Waldrop T.A. 2008. Effects of prescribed fire and fire surrogates on saproxylic Coleoptera in the southern Appalachians of North Carolina. Journal of Entomological Science. 43(1): 57-75.

Clark J.S. 1991. Disturbance and population structure on the shifting mosaic landscape. Ecology. 72: 1119-1137.

Delcourt H.R.; Delcourt P.A. 1997. Pre-Columbian Native American use of fire on southern Appalachian landscapes. Conservation Biology. 11: 1010-1014.

Ford W.M.; Menzel M.A.; McGill D.W. [and others]. 1999. Effects of a community restoration fire on small mammals and herpetofauna in the southern Appalachians. Forest Ecology and Management. 114(2-3): 233-243.

Ford W.M.; Rodrigue J.L.; Rowan E.L. [and others]. 2010. Woodland salamander response to two prescribed fires in the central Appalachians. Forest Ecology and Management. 260(6): 1003-1009.

Ford W.M.; Russell K.R.; Moorman C.E., eds. 2000. The role of fire in nongame wildlife management and community restoration: traditional uses and new directions proceedings of a special workshop: U.S. Department of Agriculture Forest Service Northeastern Research Station.

Fuhlendorf S.D.; Engle D.M. 2001. Restoring heterogeneity on rangelands: ecosystem management based on evolutionary grazing patterns. Bioscience. 51: 625-632.

Greenberg C.H.; Forrest T.G.; Waldrop T. 2010. Short-term response of ground-dwelling arthropods to prescribed fire and mechanical fuel reduction in a southern Appalachian upland hardwood forest. Forest Science. 56(1): 112-121.

Greenberg C.H.; Miller S.; Waldrop T.A. 2007a. Short-term response of shrews to prescribed fire and mechanical fuel reduction in a southern Appalachian upland hardwood forest. Forest Ecology and Management. 243(2-3): 231-236.

Greenberg C.H.; Otis D.L.; Waldrop T.A. 2006. Response of white-footed mice (*Peromyscus leucopus*) to fire and fire surrogate fuel reduction treatments in a southern Appalachian hardwood forest. Forest Ecology and Management. 234(1-3): 355-362.

Greenberg C.H.; Tomcho A.L.; Lanham J.D. [and others]. 2007b. Short-term effects of fire and other fuel reduction treatments on breeding birds in a southern Appalachian upland hardwood forest. Journal of Wildlife Management. 71(6): 1906-1916.

Greenberg C.H.; Waldrop T.A. 2008. Short-term response of reptiles and amphibians to prescribed fire and mechanical fuel reduction in a southern Appalachian upland hardwood forest. Forest Ecology and Management. 255: 2883-2893.

Johnson, J.B.; Edwards, J.W.; Ford, W.M.; Gates, J.E. 2009. Roost tree selection by northern myotis (*Myotis septentrionalis*) maternity colonies following prescribed fire in a Central Appalachian Mountains hardwood forest. Forest Ecology and Management. 258: 233-242.

Kirkland G.L.; Snoddy H.W. 1996. Impact of fire on small mammals and amphibians in a central Appalachian deciduous forest. American Midland Naturalist. 135: 253-260.

Klaus N.A.; Rush S.A.; Keyes T.S. [and others]. 2010. Short-term effects of fire on breeding birds in southern Appalachian upland forests. Wilson Journal of Ornithology. 122(3): 518-531.

Lamoureux V.S.; Maerz J.C.; Madison D.M. 2002. Premigratory autumn foraging forays in the green frog, *Rana clamitans*. Journal of Herpetology. 36(2): 245-254.

Lashley M.A.; Harper C.A.; Bates G.E.; Keyser P.D. 2011. Forage availability for white-tailed deer following silvicultural treatments in hardwood forests. Journal of Wildlife Management. 75(6): 1467-1476.

Lorimer C. 1980. Age structure and disturbance history of a southern Appalachian virgin forest. Ecology. 61: 1169-1184.

Love J.P.; Vose J.M.; Elliott K.J. 2007. Effects of restoration burns on macroinvertebrates in southern Appalachian pine-oak forests. Journal of the North Carolina Academy of Science. 123(1): 22-34.

Madison D.M. 1997. The emigration of radio-implanted spotted salamanders, *Ambystoma maculatum*. Journal of Herpetology. 31: 542-551.

Matthews C.E.; Moorman C.E.; Greenberg C.H.; Waldrop T.A. 2009. Response of soricid populations to repeated fire and fuel reduction treatments in the southern Appalachian Mountains. Forest Ecology and Management. 257(9): 1939-1944.

Matthews C.E.; Moorman C.E.; Greenberg C.H.; Waldrop T.A. 2010. Response of reptiles and amphibians to repeated fuel reduction treatments. Journal of Wildlife Management. 74: 1301-1310.

Noss R.F. 2013. Forgotten Grasslands of the South: Natural History and Conservation. Washington, DC: Island Press.

Noss R.F.; Beier P.; Covington W.W. [and others]. 2006. Recommendations for integrating restoration ecology and conservation biology in pondersa pine forests in the Southwestern United States. Restoration Ecology: 4-10.

Petranka J.W. 1998. Salamanders of the United States and Canada. Washington, DC: Smithsonian Institution Press.

Pitt A.L.; Tavano J.J.; Baldwin R.F.; Waldrop T.A. 2013. Effects of fuel reduction treatments on movement and habitat use of American toads in a southern Appalachian hardwood forest. Forest Ecology and Management. 310: 289-299.

Raybuck A.L.; Moorman C.E.; Greenberg C.H. [and others]. 2012. Short-term response of small mammals following oak regeneration silviculture treatments. Forest Ecology and Management. 274: 10-16.

Rush S.; Klaus N.; Keyes T.; Petrick J.; Cooper R. 2012. Fire severity has mixed benefits to breeding bird species in the southern Appalachians. Forest Ecology and Management. 263: 94-100.

Seymour R.S.; Hunter M.L. 1999. Principles of ecological forestry. In: Hunter M.L., ed. Managing Biodiversity in Forested Ecosystems. Cambridge, U.K.: Cambridge University Press: 22-61.

Spira T.P. 2011. Wildflowers and Plant Communities of the southern Appalachian Mountains and Piedmont. The University of North Carolina Press.

Turner M.G.; Pearson S.M.; Bolstad P.; Wear D.N. 2003. Effects of land-cover change on spatial pattern of forest communities in the southern Appalachian Mountains (USA). Landscape Ecology. 18: 449-464.

Van Lear D.H.; Waldrop T.A. 1989. History, use, and effects of fire in the southern Appalachians. Asheville, NC: U.S. Department of Agriculture Forest Service, Southeastern Forest Experiment Station.

Vickery P.D. 2002. Effects of the size of prescribed fire on insect predation of northern blazing star, a rare grassland perrenial. Conservation Biology. 16: 413-421.

Table 1—Studies of effects of prescribed fire on fauna in the southern Appalachian region, USA

Effects	Measurement	Taxa	Relevant studies
Direct			
Behavioral	Nest success/ selection	Birds	Artman and others 2001
	Roost selection	Bats	Johnson 2009
	Habitat selection	Anurans	Pitt and others 2013
Population/ Community	Abundance	Herpetofauna	Ford and others 1999; Greenberg and Waldrop 2008; Love and others 2007; Ford and others 2010; Matthews and others 2010
		Small mammals	Ford and others 1999; Greenberg and others 2006; Greenberg and others 2007a; Matthews and others 2009; Raybuck and others 2012
		Birds	Artman and others 2001; Klaus and others 2010; Rush and others 2012
		Invertebrates	Campbell and others 2007b; Love and others 2007; Campbell and others 2008; Greenberg and others 2010
	Richness	Herpetofauna	Ford and others 1999; Greenberg and Waldrop 2008; Matthews and others 2010
		Small mammals	Ford and others 1999; Raybuck and others 2012
		Birds	Greenberg and others 2007b; Klaus and others 2010
		Invertebrates	Campbell and others 2007b; Campbell and others 2008
	Population estimate	Small mammals	Greenberg and others 2006
Direct Mortality		Anurans	Pitt and others 2013
Indirect			
Habitat			
		Herpetofauna	Greenberg and Waldrop 2008; Matthews and others 2010
		Small mammals	Greenberg and others 2006; Greenberg and others 2007a; Raybuck and others 2012
		Birds	Artman and others 2001; Artman and Downhower 2003; Greenberg and others 2007b; Klaus and others 2010; Rush and others 2012
		Bats	Johnson and others 2009
		Deer	Lashley and others 2011
		Invertebrates	Campbell and others 2007a; Greenberg and others 2010

Table 2—Assessment of the effects of prescribed fire on fauna in the southern Appalachians, from 21 studies, showing negative effects noted for herpetofauna (salamanders), birds (ground nesting birds), and small mammals (shrews)

Taxa	Positive effect	Negative effect	Neutral	Studies
Invertebrates	+,+,+		+,+	Campbell and others 2007a, 2007b, 2008;Greenberg and others 2010; Love and others 2007
Herpetofauna	+,+	+	+,+,+,+	Ford and others 1999, 2010; Greenberg and Waldrop 2008; Matthews and others 2010; Pitt and others 2013
Birds	+,+,+	+,+,+	+,+,+,+,+,+	Artman and Downhower 2003; Artman and others 2001; Klaus and others 2010; Rush and others 2012; Greenberg and others 2007b
Mammals	+,+,+,+	+,+,+,+	+,+,+,+,+,+	Ford and others 1999; Greenberg others 2006, 2007a; Lashley and others 2011; Matthews and others 2009; Raybuck and others 2012; Johnson and others 2009

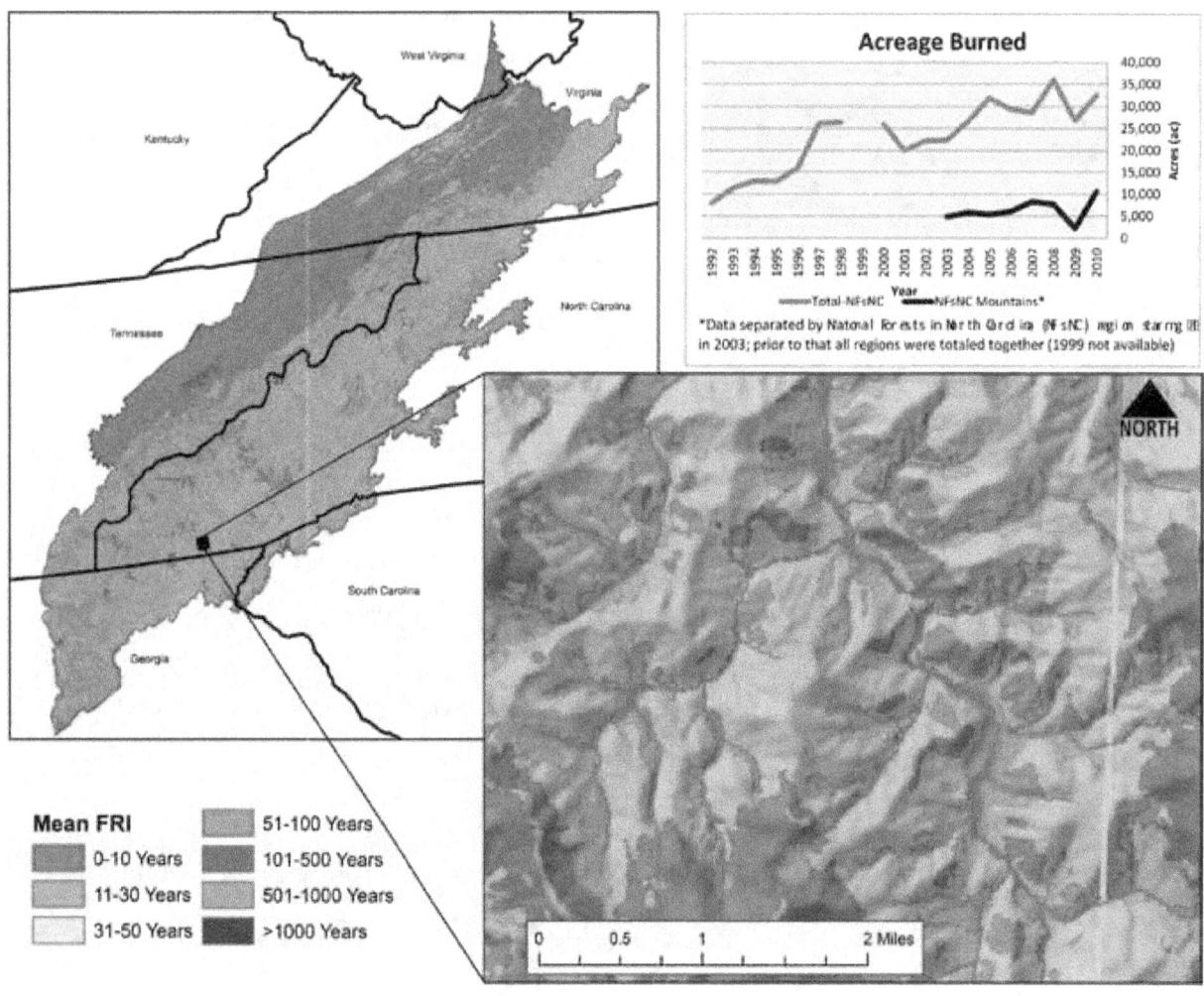

Figure 1—Mean Fire Return Interval estimated for the southern Appalachian region.

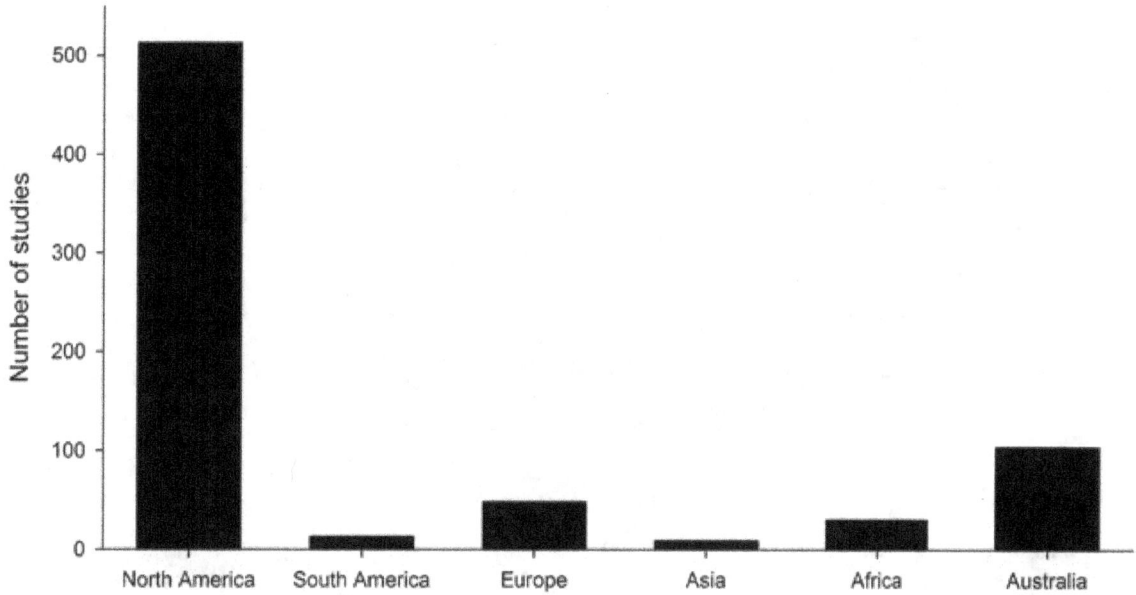

Figure 2—Studies of the effect of prescribed fire on wildlife by continent.

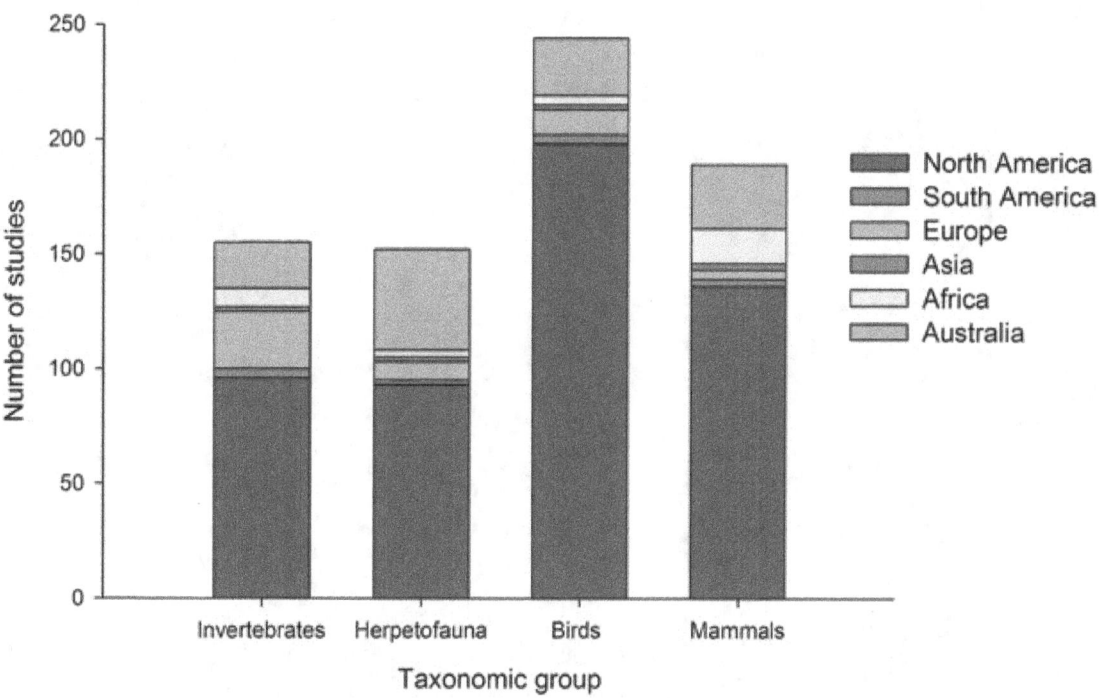

Figure 3—Studies of the effect of prescribed fire by taxonomic group and continent.

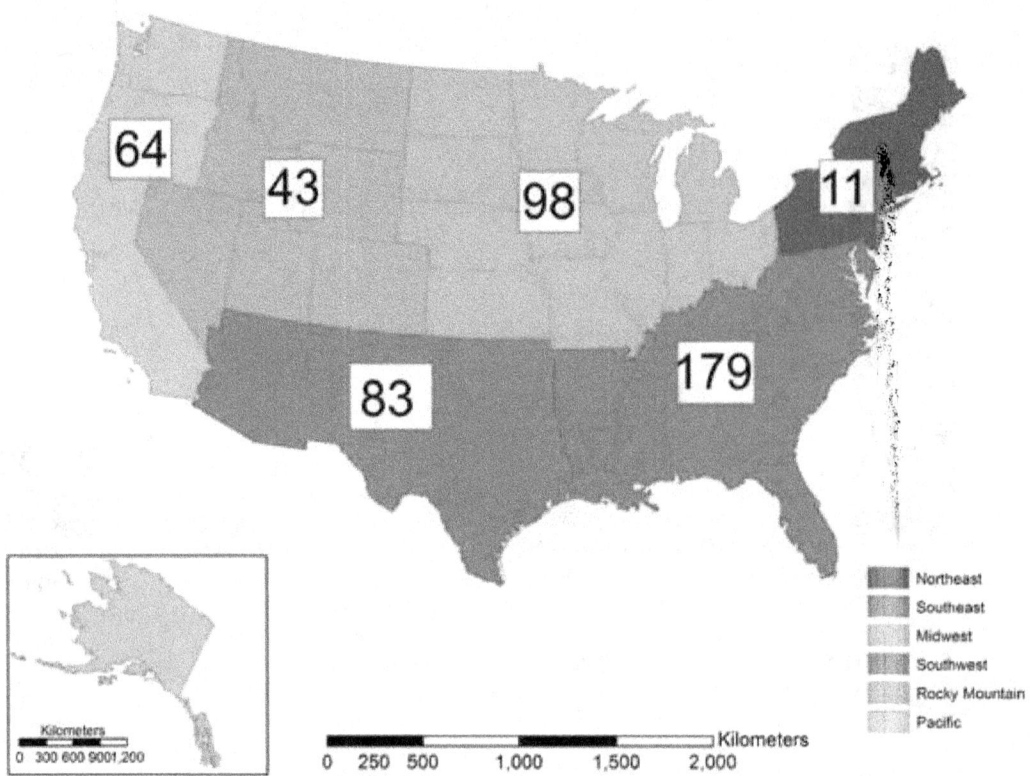

Figure 4—Studies of the effects of prescribed fire on fauna by region of the United States. Numbers represent the number of studies conducted per region.

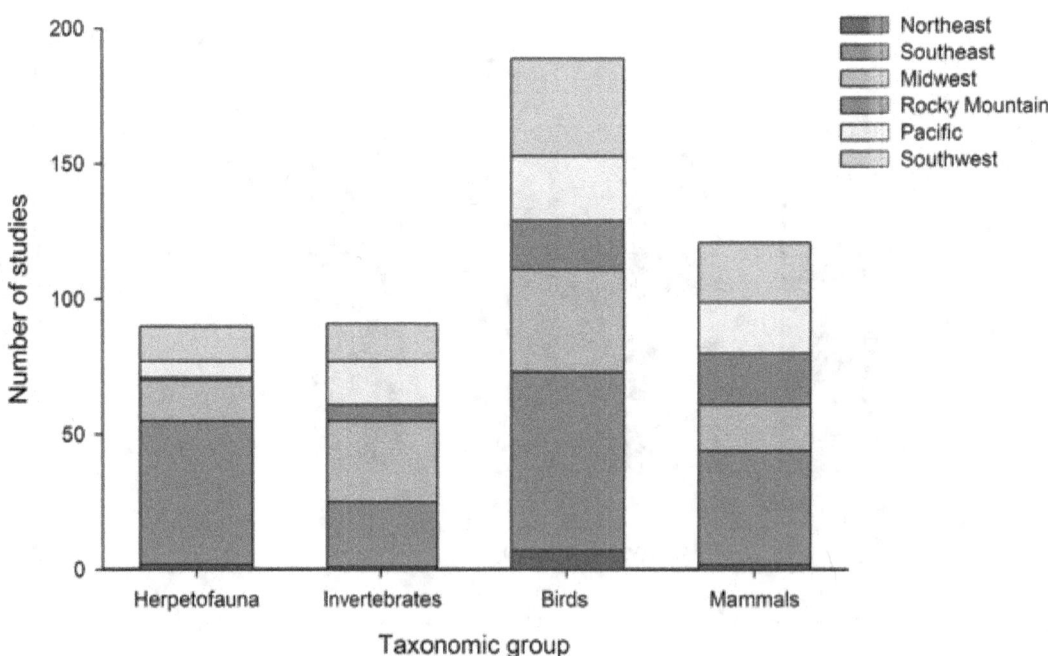

Figure 5—Studies of the effects of prescribed fire by taxonomic group and region of the United States.

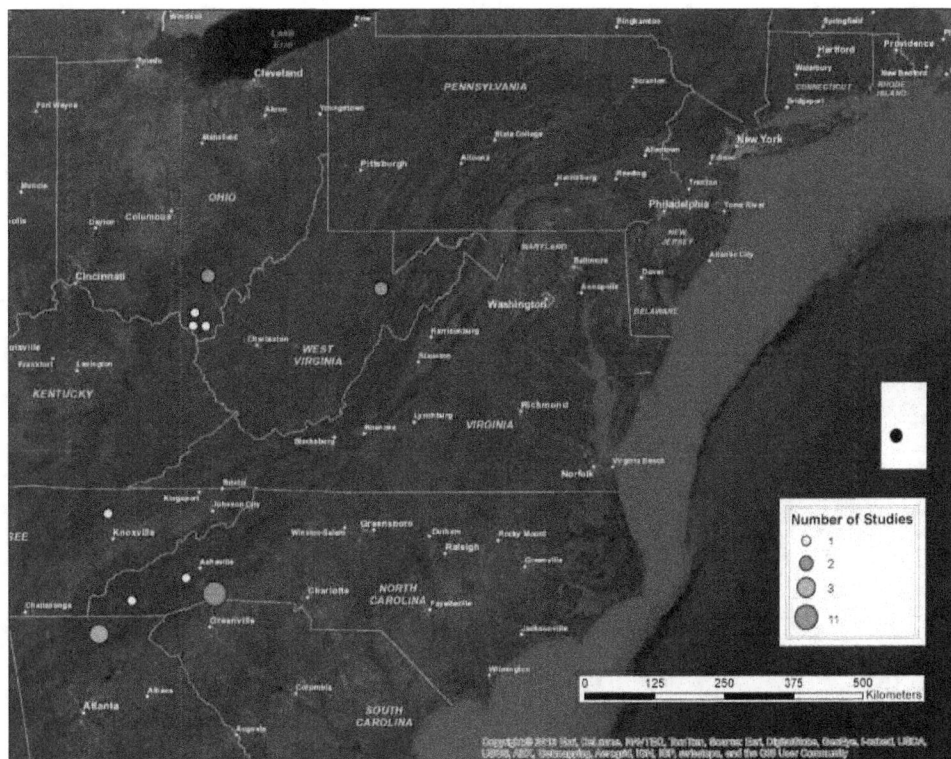

Figure 6—Distribution of studies investigating the effects of prescribed fire on wildlife in the southern Appalachians of the United states.

Fire History and
Fire Effects

THREE CENTURIES OF APPALACHIAN FIRE HISTORY FROM TREE RINGS

Charles W. Lafon, Henri D. Grissino-Mayer, Serena R. Aldrich, Georgina G. DeWeese, William T. Flatley, Lisa B. LaForest, and Jennifer A. Hoss[1]

Abstract—Many researchers and resource managers advocate an increase in fire use to restore fire regimes similar to those under which the vegetation of the Appalachian Mountains developed. Restoring fire implies a need to establish historical reference conditions. We have developed dendroecological reconstructions of fire history and forest dynamics for a network of sites in the Appalachian Mountains of Virginia, North Carolina, and Tennessee. Estimates of fire frequency for these sites indicate that fire typically returned at intervals of 2–19 years. Burning occurred at a relatively steady level under varying land uses until the early twentieth century. Fire activity thereafter plummeted with the onset of organized fire prevention and suppression. Our results suggest fire return intervals that managers might target for restoring communities that developed under the aboriginal and European land uses that preceded widespread logging and fire exclusion.

INTRODUCTION

Over the past two decades, it has become apparent that many ecological communities in the Appalachian Mountains require periodic burning if they are to be maintained (e.g., Brose and others 2001, Williams 1998). Most prominent are those communities in which Table Mountain (*Pinus pungens*) and pitch pine (*Pinus rigida*) dominate. These species exhibit traits, such as cone serotiny, early development of sexual maturity, and thick bark, which enable their populations to persist under periodic burning. These yellow pine stands are widely distributed on dry south- and west-facing slopes at middle and low elevations across the Blue Ridge and the Ridge and Valley provinces between Pennsylvania and Georgia. They are interspersed with hardwood-dominated forests, which predominate on the adjacent slope facets. Various oak (*Quercus*) species are particularly abundant in this hardwood forest matrix (Stephenson and others 1993). Oaks and some of their associates, e.g., hickories (*Carya*) and the once-common American chestnut (*Castanea dentata*), appear to thrive under frequent surface fires, which thwart the establishment of mesophytic trees that have few traits that would enable them to endure frequent burning (Nowacki and Abrams 2008).

Appalachian forests burn infrequently today, a consequence of the effective fire prevention and suppression tactics that have been implemented by State and Federal resource management agencies since the early twentieth century (Lafon 2010). These protection efforts were adopted in response to the widespread, destructive conflagrations that accompanied the commercial logging operations during ca. 1880–1930. At that time, many researchers and managers feared that fire would preclude the development of young forest stands to replace the logged forests. The protection efforts have been so successful, however, that Appalachian forests have developed largely without fire over the past 60–100 years. Today, following this prolonged absence of fire, many fire-associated species and communities are declining in abundance and extent, and appear to be following a successional trajectory toward denser stands abounding in mesophytic, fire-intolerant plant species (Nowacki and Abrams 2008). This situation has led many resource managers to use controlled burning to restore the fire-deprived ecosystems (Waldrop and others 2008).

Restoring fire implies a need to establish historical reference conditions, but the dramatic forest changes of the past century—logging and burning followed by fire exclusion—impede our understanding of how the forests functioned prior to the great logging episode. How frequently did fire occur in the Appalachian forests previously? We have established a network of dendroecological sites to investigate fire history in the Appalachian Mountains of Virginia, Tennessee, and North Carolina. We searched for yellow pine stands that contained old, fire-scarred trees—living and dead—that would document the longest possible record of fire history in the tree-ring record (fig. 1). Pines are especially useful

[1]Charles W. Lafon, Professor, Department of Geography, Texas A&M University, College Station, TX 77843

Henri. D. Grissino-Mayer, Professor, Department of Geography, University of Tennessee, Knoxville, TN 37996

Serena R. Aldrich, Instructor, Geography Faculty, Division of Social Science, Blinn College, Bryan, TX 77805

Georgina G. DeWeese, Assistant Professor, Department of Geosciences, University of West Georgia, Carrollton, GA 30118

William T. Flatley, Postdoctoral Scholar, School of Forestry, Northern Arizona University, Flagstaff, AZ 86011

Lisa B. LaForest, Production Manager, Biology in a Box, Department of Ecology & Evolutionary Biology, University of Tennessee, Knoxville, TN 37996

Jennifer A. Hoss, Manager, Opportune LLP, Houston, TX 77002

Citation for proceedings: Waldrop, Thomas A., ed. 2014. Proceedings, Wildland Fire in the Appalachians: Discussions among Managers and Scientists. Gen. Tech. Rep. SRS-199. Asheville, NC: U.S. Department of Agriculture Forest Service, Southern Research Station. 208 p.

for such work because the resin with which they saturate the fire-injured wood helps preserve the wood from decay, even in dead trees. Many hardwood trees also bear fire scars, but they decay more readily and generally do not preserve as useful a fire history record as do the pines.

METHODS

The study sites are located at several locations within the George Washington National Forest, Jefferson National Forest, and The Nature Conservancy's Narrows Preserve in Virginia; Great Smoky Mountains National Park and House Mountain State Natural Area in Tennessee; and Pisgah National Forest in North Carolina (fig. 2). These sites represent a wide range of the variations in climate and land use history that exist across the Appalachian Mountains. Each site comprises multiple neighboring pine stands (generally four stands) separated by intervening hardwood forest (fig. 3). The spatial configuration of this network enables the most reliable possible estimates of historic fire frequency at the level of the individual stand while also permitting insights into broader (multi-stand and multi-site) patterns of burning. We used standard dendroecological techniques to sample and analyze the fire-scar data. Tree rings were crossdated to permit accurate determinations of the year in which each fire event occurred, and the fire history analyses were conducted using FHX2 software and standard statistical analyses. Details of the study sites, sampling strategies, and analyses performed can be found in Aldrich and others (2010), DeWeese (2007), Flatley and others (2013), Hoss and others (2008), and LaForest (2012).

RESULTS AND DISCUSSION

Analyzing the intervals between successive fires reveals that fires burned often, at intervals typically ranging between about 2 and 19 years (Aldrich and others 2010, DeWeese 2007, Flatley and others 2013, Hoss and others 2008, LaForest 2012) throughout the period of record (generally the 1700s through the early 1900s). For a fire chart that graphically depicts the history of burning at one of the study sites, see Figure 4. The 2–19 year range in fire intervals reflects the differences among sites and between different filtering techniques used for estimating fire return interval. Shorter intervals reflect less conservative estimates obtained on the basis of including all fires recorded at a study site; some of these may have been minor fires that burned only one or two trees in a single stand. Longer intervals reflect more conservative estimates, such as filtering the fires to include only the "major" fires that scarred at least 25 percent of the trees, or only the "area-wide" fires that burned all the neighboring pine stands at a given site during a single year. Regardless of which filtering method is used, a picture of frequent burning emerges.

The results presented here demonstrate that the montane pine stands distributed across the study area burned at short intervals before fire prevention and suppression were implemented during the early twentieth century. Additionally, the short intervals that emerge even for the area-wide fires suggest that the intervening hardwood forests also burned often: for an area-wide fire to occur, it would have had to spread through the hardwood forest to propagate from one pine stand to another (Flatley and others 2013). In fact, we noted numerous hardwood trees that exhibited one or more fire scars (fig. 5). Therefore, our results apply not only to the pine stands but also to the broader mountain slopes across which the pine stands are scattered.

Analyzing temporal variations in fire frequency reveals no long-term trends prior to the era of fire exclusion (Hoss and others 2008, Aldrich and others 2010, Flatley and others 2013, e.g., fig. 6). The fire chronologies that we developed for all the study sites extend back to the period of early European settlement, and for a few of the sites the chronologies reach back further to the period of aboriginal depopulation that preceded European settlement in Virginia, or to the period of Cherokee occupancy that preceded European settlement in Tennessee and North Carolina. Fire appears to have burned these landscapes on a regular basis from the pre-European period through subsequent settlement and agricultural expansion, and also during the episodes of mining and/or logging, which affected each study site in a different manner. The only pronounced change in burning coincided with the advent of active fire prevention and protection in the early twentieth century. We detail our analyses and interpretations more thoroughly elsewhere (Aldrich and others 2010, DeWeese 2007, Flatley and others 2013, Hoss and others 2008, LaForest 2012).

As a basis for restoration, our results suggest that burning at relatively short intervals, similar to the estimates presented here and detailed in our other publications (Aldrich and others 2010, DeWeese 2007, Flatley and others 2013, Hoss and others 2008, LaForest 2012), could be appropriate for maintaining conditions similar to those under which the communities developed during aboriginal and European land uses of the eighteenth and nineteenth centuries. Whether the reintroduction of fire would quickly restore pre-exclusion vegetation properties is an important question. Following several decades of forest development in a nearly fire-free environment, some communities may require intensive management (e.g., multiple/severe fires, mechanical treatment) to initiate a vegetation composition and structure that could be maintained thereafter by regular burning.

ACKNOWLEDGMENTS

This work was funded by the National Interagency Fire Center's Joint Fire Science Program through cooperative agreements with the George Washington and Jefferson National Forests and the Great Smoky Mountains National Park. The research was also enhanced by funding from The Nature Conservancy in Virginia and from two Doctoral Dissertation Research Improvement grants from the National Science Foundation. We thank Steve Croy, Elaine Sutherland, Rob Klein, Judy Dunscomb, and numerous other personnel of Federal, State, and private resource management agencies for their logistical support and many conversations that helped us implement the project. We are especially grateful to the many graduate and undergraduate students who assisted us with field and laboratory work. We thank Tom Waldrop for his support of our research over the years and for granting us the opportunity to contribute to these conference proceedings.

LITERATURE CITED

Aldrich, S.R.; Lafon, C.W.; Grissino-Mayer, H.D. [and others]. 2010. Three centuries of fire in montane pine-oak stands on a temperate forest landscape. Applied Vegetation Science. 13: 36-46.

Brose, P.; Schuler, T.; Van Lear, D.; Berst, J. 2001. Bringing fire back—the changing regimes of the Appalachian mixed-oak forests. Journal of Forestry. 99: 30-35.

DeWeese, G.G. 2007. Past fire regimes of Table Mountain pine (*Pinus pungens* Lamb.) stands in the central Appalachian Mountains, Virginia, U.S.A. Knoxville, TN: University of Tennessee. 308 p. Ph.D. dissertation.

Flatley, W.T.; Lafon, C.W.; Grissino-Mayer, H.D.; LaForest, L.B. 2013. Fire history, related to climate and land use in three southern Appalachian landscapes in the Eastern United States. Ecological Applications. 23: 1250-1266.

Hoss, J.A.; Lafon, C.W.; Grissino-Mayer, H.D. [and others]. 2008. Fire history of a temperate forest with an endemic fire-dependent herb. Physical Geography. 29: 424-441.

Lafon, C.W. 2010. Fire in the American South: vegetation impacts, history, and climatic relations. Geography Compass. 4/8: 919-944.

LaForest, L.B. 2012. Fire regimes of lower-elevation forests in Great Smoky Mountains National Park, Tennessee, U.S.A. Knoxville, TN: University of Tennessee. 279 p. Ph.D. dissertation.

Nowacki, G.J.; Abrams, M.D. 2008. The demise of fire and "mesophication" of forests in the Eastern United States. Bioscience. 58: 123-138.

Stephenson, S.L.; Ash, A.N.; Stauffer, D.F. 1993. Appalachian oak forests. In: Martin, W.H.; Boyce, S.G.; Echternacht, A.C., eds. Biodiversity of the Southeastern United States: Upland Terrestrial Communities. New York: John Wiley & Sons, Inc.: 255-303.

Waldrop, T.A.; Yaussy, D.A.; Phillips, R.J. [and others]. 2008. Fuel reduction treatments affect stand structure of hardwood forests in western North Carolina and southern Ohio, USA. Forest Ecology and Management. 255: 3,117-3,129.

Williams, C.E. 1998. History and status of Table Mountain pine-pitch pine forests of the Southern Appalachian Mountains (USA). Natural Areas Journal. 18: 81-90.

Figure 1—Fire-scarred dead pine in the George Washington National Forest. Multiple fires have injured the tree, as evidenced by the ridges that formed as wood grew over each new fire scar.

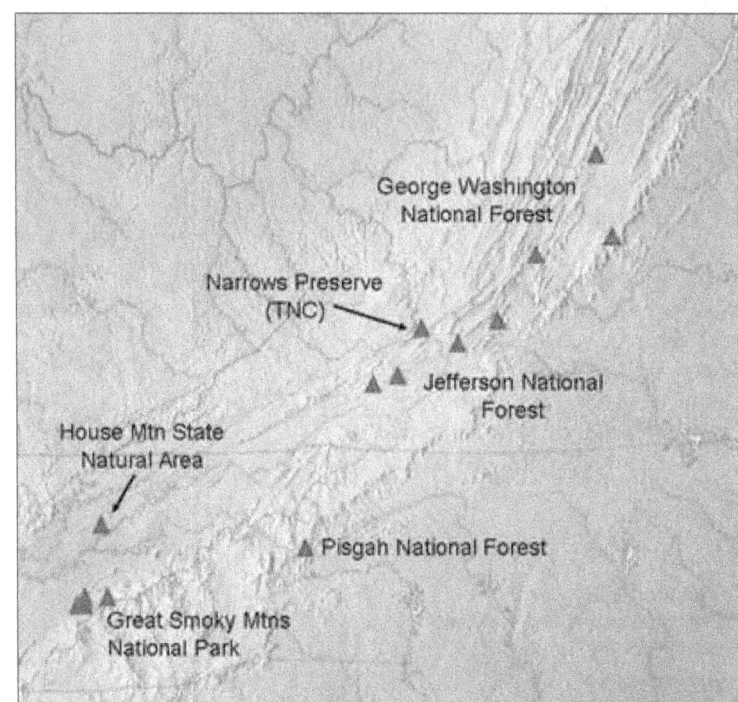

Figure 2—The distribution of fire history study sites (triangles) across the Appalachian Mountains of Virginia, Tennessee, and North Carolina.

Figure 3—A view of the north slope of Brush Mountain, on the Jefferson National Forest. Pine stands occupy the west face (right side in this photograph) of each spur on the dissected mountain slope. The pines in this photograph are evident as darker patches surrounded by the lighter-colored hardwood forests. We collected fire-scarred trees from multiple pine stands at each study site. Many of the fires burned multiple pine stands, suggesting that fires spread across the whole mountain slope, including the hardwood stands that form the forest matrix between pine stands.

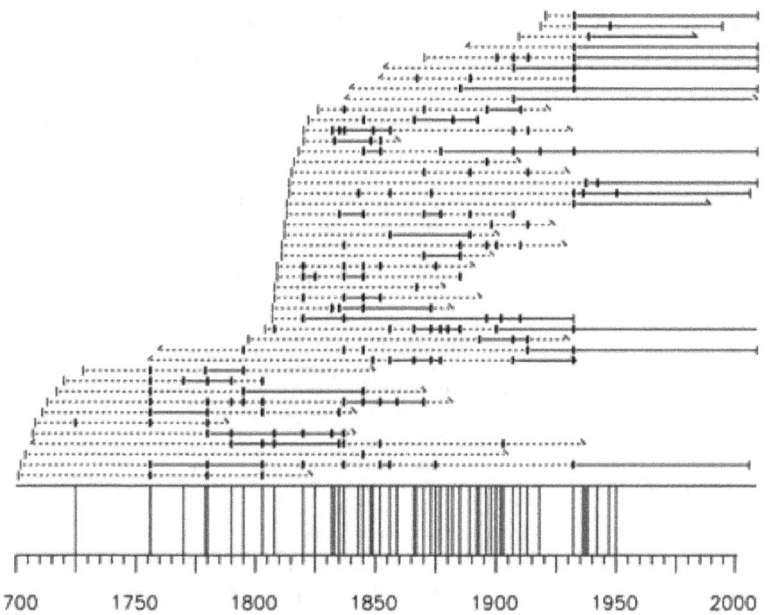

Figure 4—Fire chart from the Linville Mountain study site in the Pisgah National Forest. The timeline at the bottom indicates the period of record, while each horizontal line above it represents the period covered by each of the scarred trees we dated. The vertical tics along each line indicate dated fire scars for each tree, and the longer vertical lines at the bottom of the chart represent the composite fire-scar record for all the trees combined.

Figure 5—A hardwood tree located at Little Mountain in the Jefferson National Forest that exhibited the typical calous wood that formed over an injury caused by a wildfire event at some point in the past. Such fire-scarred hardwoods were found in nearly all sites we examined, but hardwoods decay more rapidly than pines, making them less useful for analyzing fire scars to determine fire history.

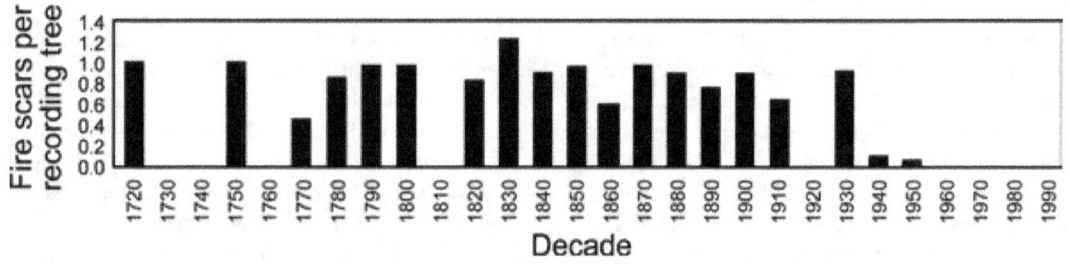

Figure 6—Temporal pattern of fire at the Linville Mountain site, indicated as the mean number of fire scars recorded per tree for each decade. This calculation standardizes the fire record across decades with varying sample sizes, enabling a depiction of temporal trends in fire occurrence. This graph for Linville Mountain reveals little variation in fire frequency from the beginning of the record until the 1930s, after which fire activity declined.

METHODS FOR THE STUDY OF SOIL CHARCOAL AS AN INDICATOR OF FIRE AND FOREST HISTORY IN THE APPALACHIAN REGION, U.S.A.

Sally P. Horn and Christopher A. Underwood[1]

Abstract—Charcoal particles in soils and sediments of the Appalachian region provide evidence of long-term fire history relevant to resource management and to studies of paleoclimate, vegetation history, and the effects of prehistoric and historic humans on the environment. Charcoal records of fire history are of low resolution in comparison to dendrochronological records, but reach well beyond the oldest trees in most areas, providing evidence of fires thousands or tens of thousands of years ago. We focus here on fire history reconstruction from soil charcoal, which provides site-specific evidence of past fires and potentially forest composition. Charcoal > 2 mm may be large enough for taxonomic identification, and of sufficient mass to enable AMS radiocarbon dating of individual particles. Soil mixing due to physical and biological factors creates soil profiles in the southern Appalachians in which charcoal age is not predictable from charcoal depth; soil charcoal records thus require many radiocarbon dates.

INTRODUCTION

The incomplete combustion of plant material during vegetation fires produces charcoal fragments of various sizes. Some of these fragments are incorporated into soils of the burn site, while other fragments are carried away by wind or water, in some cases to later settle on the surface of a lake or wetland. Researchers study charcoal in soils and in sediments of lakes and wetlands at sites around the world to document past fires and to understand long-term relationships between fire, climate, and human activity (Berg and Anderson 2006, Hart and others 2008, Horn and others 2000, League and Horn 2000, Sanford and Horn 2000, Whitlock and Larsen 2001). We focus here on the analysis of macroscopic charcoal in soils of the Appalachian region as an indicator of fire and forest history. The records of past fires that can be obtained from the study of soil or sediment charcoal are coarse (low resolution) in comparison to fire histories developed from dendrochronological analyses of fire-scarred trees, which permit the identification of exact fire years (Flatley and others 2013, Lafon and others 2014). However, the evidence of fire provided by charcoal studies reaches well beyond the oldest trees and tree-ring records in the Appalachian Mountains, providing evidence of fire thousands or even tens of thousands of years ago. For periods of time prior to about 300 years ago, charcoal in soils and sediments is the only evidence we have of wildland fires in the Appalachian region.

Interest is growing in soil charcoal as a proxy for fire history in the Appalachian region. Welch (1999) examined macroscopic charcoal in forests dominated by yellow pines on the Cumberland Plateau. She looked only at the presence or absence of macroscopic charcoal in soil increments, and did not obtain radiocarbon dates. The presence of charcoal in 85 percent of the samples from seven sites documented the importance of fire. Hart and others (2008) quantified macroscopic charcoal in soils of mixed hardwood forests on the Cumberland Plateau. Radiocarbon dates were obtained on five charcoal samples, and several charcoal samples were identified to be from trees with diffuse porous growth rings, possibly maple, beech, or tulip poplar. The weighted means of the calibrated probability distributions of the five radiocarbon dates ranged from 6735 to 174 cal yr BP (calibrated years before present). No overlap occurred within the 2-sigma calibrated age ranges of the dated charcoal samples, indicating a minimum of five unique fire events.

Fesenmyer and Christensen (2010) reconstructed a stand-level fire history in the Nantahala National Forest in western North Carolina from soil charcoal. They sampled a broad array of forest types that included pine forest, xeric-oak hardwood forest, and mesic cove forest. The median probabilities of the calibrated ages of 81 soil charcoal fragments ranged from 4000 to 0 cal yr BP, with one sample returning a date of 10,570 cal yr BP. The prevalence of charcoal from 4000 to 0 cal yr BP demonstrated that fires occurred regularly in the study area during the Late Holocene.

Our soil charcoal work in the Appalachian region has focused on pine and mixed forests in eastern Tennessee and western North Carolina, mainly within Great Smoky Mountains National Park. Within the park we have quantified, identified, and dated charcoal fragments in Table Mountain pine stands and in other stands

[1]Sally P. Horn, Professor, Department of Geography, University of Tennessee, Knoxville, TN 37996

Christopher A. Underwood, Assistant Professor and Program Director for Geography, Lincoln Memorial University, Harrogate, TN 37752

Citation for proceedings: Waldrop, Thomas A., ed. 2014. Proceedings, Wildland Fire in the Appalachians: Discussions among Managers and Scientists. Gen. Tech. Rep. SRS-199. Asheville, NC: U.S. Department of Agriculture Forest Service, Southern Research Station. 208 p.

historically dominated by lower-elevation yellow pine trees (Underwood 2013) to complement and extend analyses of fire-scarred trees in the same study sites (Lafon and others 2014). We have also examined charcoal in soils surrounding a wetland in which we have examined sedimentary charcoal.

CHARCOAL TAPHONOMY AND SOIL CHARCOAL COMPARED TO OTHER EVIDENCE OF PAST FIRE

To use charcoal in soils or sediments as an indicator of past fire requires knowledge of the processes that create, move, and preserve charcoal in different environments (Scott and Dablon 2010). Many of these processes are not yet completely understood, but they are attracting increasing research attention as charcoal in soils is part of the carbon pool and of interest from the perspective of carbon sequestration and cycling (Licata and Sanford 2012, Massielo and Louchouarn 2013), as well as for its value as a paleoenvironmental indicator. The increased use of prescribed fire in Appalachian forests provides an opportunity to test ideas about the production and fate of charcoal in fires. Recent work by Scales (2011) on charcoal distribution following a prescribed fire in Virginia provides a good example of what can be learned from post-fire sampling of charcoal in burn sites.

Although our focus here is large (≥ 2 mm) macroscopic charcoal in soils, consideration of the fate of smaller particles during and after burns provides context for comparing soil charcoal evidence to evidence from studies of charcoal in sediment profiles in lakes and wetlands, which focus on smaller charcoal particles. Studies of charcoal in sediment cores include studies of microscopic charcoal in pollen preparations, sometimes called pollen-slide charcoal, and of larger particles that are sieved from sediments. Charcoal on microscope slides prepared for pollen analysis is generally < 125 or 180 μm, as sieves of this size are commonly used to concentrate pollen. Charcoal that is extracted from sediment cores by sieving is usually ≥ 125 μm, as this is typically the smallest sieve size used in such studies, which often employ nested sieves of 125, 250, and 500 μm, for example (Whitlock and Larsen, 2001). During fires, microscopic charcoal and small particles of macroscopic charcoal are lofted into the air by convection currents. Once aloft, the smallest of these particles may be carried tens of kilometers or more away from the fire. Many charcoal particles present on microscope slides prepared for pollen analysis are < 50 μm and may derive from regional sources (Clark 1988, Whitlock and Larsen 2001), such that their variable abundance through a lake core may reflect the history of burning not just in the lake watershed, but also in a large area upwind from the lake.

In contrast, macroscopic charcoal particles sieved from lake sediments provide evidence of fires within the lake watershed or nearby. If samples for charcoal analysis are taken at a high sampling density, for example in contiguous 1-cm intervals, detailed fire history records can be developed. Depending on the sedimentation rate and the frequency of fires, peaks in charcoal (sediment levels with high charcoal abundance) may represent single past fires, or periods of high fire activity (Whitlock and Larsen 2001). Microscopic charcoal is rarely sampled contiguously in cores, so records can miss fires; thus these records are of lower temporal and broader spatial resolution than macroscopic charcoal records from lake sediments. For both microscopic and macroscopic charcoal records from sediment cores, the ages of charcoal peaks can be estimated from radiocarbon or other dates on bracketing sections of the core. For example, a peak in charcoal half-way between two dated horizons could be interpreted to have an intermediate age. In sediment core studies, radiocarbon dates are sometimes obtained for individual pieces of charcoal, but often dates are obtained for uncharred macrofossils, pooled charred or uncharred organic material, or bulk sediment.

Charcoal that is not blown or washed out of burn sites becomes incorporated in soil horizons by various processes of mixing, or is buried by geomorphic processes. Radiocarbon analyses have demonstrated that charcoal in modern soils and paleosols (buried soils) can persist for thousands to tens of thousands of years, in some cases to beyond the limit of radiocarbon dating, which for typical samples is around 45,000 years ago. In studies of soil and sediment charcoal, a fragment that is too old for radiocarbon dating will have a reported "date" with a greater-than symbol. For example, charcoal in a paleosol in Costa Rica returned a date of > 43,630 years (Driese and others 2007). However, most charcoal particles do not persist this long; if they did, we would be wading through snow-drift like piles of charcoal in fire-prone forests of the world, and soils in these and other frequently burned ecosystems would be black in color.[3] Recently Jaffé and others (2013) demonstrated that charcoal may account for a large proportion of dissolved organic carbon in ecosystems, and suggested that the persistence of charcoal fragments in soils may depend on the material burned and charring temperature, as well as on soil conditions and fauna. These findings deserve more study in the analysis of soil charcoal as they may function as a filter on the information we can obtain from such studies.

---

[3] We credit the idea that fire-prone forests would harbor snow-drift like piles of charcoal, if charcoal was resistant to breakdown, to our colleague Ken Orvis. R. Jaffé was quoted as saying that soils would be black if charcoal in soils was resistant to breakdown in a press release from Florida International University posted by J. Adkins upon publication of the article by Jaffé and others referenced.

Although large charcoal particles can be moved short distances downslope by gravity or overland flow, most of the large charcoal in soils located away from stream courses and floodplains likely reflects the burning of vegetation at or very near the sampling location. Like fire scars on standing trees, charcoal in soils provides evidence of past fire that is highly site-specific, more so than macroscopic charcoal records from lake or wetland sediments, which can document fires within a watershed but not on a particular portion of the watershed. Another advantage of studies of soil charcoal is that charcoal fragments are often massive enough that a radiocarbon date can be obtained on an individual fragment. However, because soils are mixed by biological and geomorphic activity, the age of charcoal cannot be reliably estimated from dates on other charcoal particles in the soil profile.

FIELD METHODS

Researchers obtain soil charcoal samples from the walls of excavations or road cuts, or by collecting soil cores. The number of sites to sample, and the number and arrangement of pits or cores at each site, depends on the specific aims of the research. Collecting cores rather than digging pits in the field offers time efficiency, the ability to work in light rain, and less environmental disturbance, but it is not feasible if the volume of contiguous soil material to be examined is greater than the volume that can be obtained in a single core (e.g., Di Pasquale and others 2008). We favor a cylindrical soil-coring device manufactured by Eijkelkamp© (http://en.eijkelkamp.com/) that allows the collection of successive samples in 10-cm increments to a depth of 1 m or the depth of refusal (Horn and others 1994; fig. 1). The device we use, known as a "single root auger," was developed for use in studies of root growth and was first used for soil charcoal research by Sanford and others (1985) in the Venezuelan Amazon. Despite the name of the device, it does not have a helical shaft commonly associated with augers, but a simple 8-cm diameter cylindrical bucket that allows recovery of soil increments without mixing. The device is pushed down while rotating to collect samples in successive 10-cm increments (0–10 cm, 10–20 cm, and so forth), or 5-cm increments in soils that are difficult to core. Quart-size, zipper-top plastic bags are a convenient size for holding 10-cm soil increments after extrusion from the corer, which can be accomplished by inverting the corer and stepping on the handle.

LABORATORY METHODS

Upon return to the laboratory, charcoal particles are separated from soil by wet-sieving. Soaking samples in water overnight facilitates the sieving process. A simple way to soak the samples is to add water to the plastic bags in which you collected them, and then very gently knead the bag to initiate the disaggregation of the soil sample. Two-pound plastic coffee cans make ideal containers to hold sample bags with water added (one bag per can); the cans keep the bags from falling over and spilling their contents on lab counters and contain leaks if they occur.

In our work in the Appalachian region, we have not found it necessary to use chemical pretreatments before sieving charcoal. Some researchers have used dispersants such as sodium hexametaphosphate to make sieving easier (e.g., Titiz and Sanford 2007). Because of the desirability of obtaining radiocarbon dates on charcoal particles, we recommend against the use of water softeners or dispersants sold for home use, as these may include carbon-containing compounds that might be absorbed by charcoal particles and affect radiocarbon analyses.

Following disaggregation, we wet-sieve soil samples for charcoal analysis using 8-inch diameter sieves with openings of 2 mm. We have selected this sieve size because it will capture particles large enough that it is possible to obtain a radiocarbon date on the individual piece of charcoal, and because fragments of charcoal of this size are potentially identifiable to species or genus. Smaller mesh sizes may be appropriate if large charcoal is sparse and the documentation of the presence or absence of smaller particles is important in the study design. We sieve our samples by holding the sieves under a tap-water faucet. Care should be taken that the force of the flowing water is not so strong that it breaks charcoal or pushes sediment or charcoal over the edge of the sieve. If many samples are to be sieved, the person doing the sieving will be more comfortable if supports are used to hold the sieve. A dishpan should be placed under the sieve to catch heavier sediment to avoid clogging sink drains or filling sink traps.

Charcoal can be distinguished from other materials retained on sieves by its dark black color and sheen and by the way it will usually fracture if a dissecting needle is pressed against it. Dry charcoal will usually leave a streak when gently rubbed on paper, but this test is not recommended if you plan to obtain a radiocarbon date on a specimen, as paper fibers may be transferred to the charcoal that can affect the date obtained. Charcoal can be picked from the surface of the sieve using fine forceps (place wet sieve on a plate or tray to catch drips), or the sieve and its contents can be inverted onto a dish for sorting. A dissecting scope, visor with magnifying lenses, or magnifying light make this task easier. We wash charcoal particles with distilled water before placing them in vials, aiming to remove as much loose soil as possible. We use 20-mL glass scintillation vials that we first treat in a furnace at 550 °C for 1 hour to burn off any organic contaminants. After the scintillation vials have fully cooled, they can be labeled with black marking pens. We use Sharpie®-brand permanent markers with fine points for labeling the sides of glass vials. Extra-fine point markers are good for labeling vial lids, but do not use them on glass vials as the ink will be too thin and will fade over time. We then dry particles at 90 °C overnight in a laboratory oven and subsequently weigh them. We recommend quantifying macroscopic soil charcoal by dry mass.

Following separation from soils and drying, charcoal particles are selected for radiocarbon dating. The material dated depends on the research question. We generally favor getting dates on individual charcoal particles. Hammond and others (2006) obtained radiocarbon dates on randomly selected particles. We have dated from different horizons, with the assumption that different horizons might be of different ages, but from our own work and that of Fesenmyer and Christensen (2010) we now know that depth in the soil profile is a poor predictor of the age of charcoal in soils of Appalachian forests (fig. 2). This is a consequence of the mixing of soil due to various physical and biological factors. Unlike lake sediment sequences, in which ages of charcoal or other components can be estimated from radiocarbon dates that bracket the materials, determining the ages of past fires based on charcoal in Appalachian soils require the dating of large numbers of individual charcoal particles.

Researchers working with soil charcoal obtain radiocarbon dates by submitting samples to one of several private and university laboratories. The standard price for radiocarbon dates obtained using the AMS (accelerator mass spectrometry) method is $500–$600/date. AMS ^{14}C dating allows the dating of individual charcoal fragments with masses of 5–10 mg and sometimes less, depending on the final C in the sample. The charge for AMS radiocarbon analysis includes determination of the ratio of the stable isotopes of ^{13}C and ^{12}C, used to correct for natural isotopic fractionation. Some laboratories offer discounts to researchers with funding from the National Science Foundation or other Federal agencies: ask!

Radiocarbon ages can be converted to estimates of calibrated calendar years using one of several calibration programs. The CALIB program developed by Stuiver and Reimer (1993) has gone through several updates; the latest version is available on the Internet (http://calib.qub.ac.uk/calib/) and can be downloaded for free or used online to determine calibrated age ranges. Researchers generally report the 2-sigma calibrated age range of samples, in cal yr BP, or in cal yr CE or BCE (equivalent to AD/BC; with 0 cal yr BP equal to AD or CE 1950). There is a 95 percent chance that the true age of the charcoal particle falls within this range. Researchers also typically report a point estimate of the calibrated date, such as the weighted mean of the probability distribution function,

or the median (Telford and others 2004). It is important to remember that the date is really not a single value but a probability range. Also, the radiocarbon date reflects the time that the carbon in the plant tissue was fixed by the tree, and not the date of the fire event. The time gap between carbon fixation and the occurrence of a fire is called "inbuilt age" and must be taken into account when compiling fire histories from charcoal (Gavin 2001). In the southern Appalachian region, the estimated inbuilt age is between 50 and 100 years (Fesenmyer and Christensen 2010). The inbuilt-age error needs to be added to the calibrated age range to provide a more realistic range of time during which the fire occurred. For example, if the 2-sigma calibrated age range is 610–470 cal yr BP, adding the maximum estimated inbuilt-age error above would widen this range to 710–470 cal yr BP.

Where possible, the morphological identification of macroscopic charcoal from soils provides an opportunity to identify the type of tree or shrub that burned in the fire. Charcoal fragments must be identified before dating, as the process of radiocarbon analysis is destructive. Charcoal fragments selected for morphological identification should be cut transversely with a razor blade to analyze wood anatomy. Do not use razor blades that are coated with Teflon® or rust-inhibiting oil, as these substances could add carbon contamination to the charcoal sample, and be sure to rinse the blade thoroughly with distilled water before subsequent charcoal fragments are cut. Once a clean, transverse cut has been made, identification is based on the presence and characteristics of anatomical features such as tracheids, resin canals, tyloses, rays, and growth-ring boundaries (fig. 3). Morphological identification of charcoal is best accomplished using reference specimens prepared from plant samples. A variety of methods can be used; we have created reference collections in our lab by igniting samples in crucibles in a muffle furnace (Orvis and others 2005). We have also developed collections by gathering specimens from charred trees in recent burn sites. Charcoal samples can also be identified through comparison with photographs and descriptions in various references on woody anatomy (e.g., Hoadley 1990).

CONCLUSION

Examining soil charcoal in Appalachian forests provides a way to document fires that occurred long before the first written records or tree-ring chronologies. Soil charcoal records are coarse in comparison to dendrochronological records of fire and, because of soil mixing, require many more radiocarbon dates than charcoal records from lake and wetland sediments. However, soil charcoal records provide site-specific evidence of fire that can be useful for forest management and for understanding the long-term development of forest stands. The taxonomic identification of dated charcoal particles provides a way to reconstruct the vegetation that burned as well as the timing of past fires. Soil charcoal studies can also contribute to a better understanding of the carbon cycle and of the role of carbonized wood as a charcoal sink in Appalachian forests.

ACKNOWLEDGMENTS

Our studies of soil charcoal in the Appalachian region have been supported by grants from the National Science Foundation (DGE-0538420, EAR-0822824, BCS-0928508), the Joint Fire Science Program, the Great Smoky Mountains Conservation Association, and the Association of American Geographers, and by a Math and Science Partnership program at the University of Tennessee. We thank our collaborators in charcoal study, in the Appalachians and beyond, for their contributions to the development of the methods described here, most especially Robert Sanford, Jr., Matthew Valente, Ken Orvis, Henri Grissino-Mayer, and Charles Lafon, and the many university faculty, graduate and undergraduate students, and middle school teachers and students who have worked with us to develop charcoal datasets. We also acknowledge support from Great Smoky Mountains National Park, The University of Tennessee Archaeological Research Laboratory, and the University of Tennessee Forest Resources Research and Education Center. Finally, we thank Tom Waldrop for the opportunity to contribute to the conference and this proceedings volume, and for his interest, over more than 20 years, in what we can learn about fire from charcoal in soils and sediments.

LITERATURE CITED

Berg, E.E.; Anderson, R.S. 2006. Fire history of white and Lutz spruce forests on the Kenai Peninsula, Alaska, over the last two millennia as determined from soil charcoal. Forest Ecology and Management. 227: 275–283.

Clark, J.S. 1988. Particle motion and the theory of charcoal analysis: source area, transport, deposition, and sampling. Quaternary Research. 30: 67–80.

Di Pasquale, G.; Marziano, M.; Impagliazzo, S. [and others]. 2008. The Holocene treeline in the northern Andes (Ecuador): first evidence from soil charcoal. Palaeogeography, Palaeoclimatology, Palaeoecology. 259: 17–34.

Driese, S.G.; Orvis, K.H.; Horn, S.P. [and others]. 2007. Paleosol evidence for Quaternary uplift and for climate and ecosystem changes in the Cordillera de Talamanca, Costa Rica. Palaeogeography, Palaeoclimatology, Palaeoecology. 248(1–2): 1–23.

Fesenmyer, K.A.; Christensen, Jr., N.L. 2010. Reconstructing Holocene fire history in a southern Appalachian forest using soil charcoal. Ecology. 91(3): 662–670.

Flatley, W.T.; Lafon, C.W.; Grissino-Mayer, H.D.; LaForest, L.B. 2013. Fire history, related to climate and land use in three southern Appalachian landscapes in the Eastern United States. Ecological Applications. 23(6): 1250–1266.

Gavin, D. 2001. Estimation of inbuilt age in radiocarbon ages of soil charcoal for fire history studies. Radiocarbon. 43(1): 27–44.

Hammond, D.S.; ter Steege, H.; van der Borg, K. 2006. Upland soil charcoal in the wet tropical forests of central Guyana. Biotropica. 39(2): 153–160.

Hart, J.L.; Horn, S.P.; Grissino-Mayer, H.D. 2008. Fire history from soil charcoal in a mixed hardwood forest on the Cumberland Plateau. Journal of the Torrey Botanical Society. 135(3): 401–410.

Hoadley, R. 1990. Identifying wood: accurate results with simple tools. Newton, CT: Taunton Press. 223 p.

Horn, S.P.; Orvis, K.H.; Kennedy, L.M.; Clark, G.M. 2000. Prehistoric fires in the highlands of the Dominican Republic: evidence from charcoal in soils and sediments. Caribbean Journal of Science. 36(1–2): 10–18.

Horn, S.P.; Wallin, T.R.; Northrop, L.A. 1994. Nested sampling of soil pollen, charcoal, and other soil components using a root corer. Palynology. 18: 87–89.

Jaffé, R.; Ding, Y.; Niggemann, J. [and others]. 2013. Global charcoal mobilization from soils via dissolution and riverine transport to the oceans. Science. 340: 345–347.

Lafon, C.W.; Grissino-Mayer, H.D.; Aldrich, S.R. [and others]. 2014. Three centuries of Appalachian fire history from tree rings. In: Waldrop, T., ed. Proceedings, Wildland Fire in the Appalachians: Discussions among Managers and Scientists. Gen. Tech. Rep. SRS-199. Asheville, NC: U.S. Department of Agriculture Forest Service, Southern Research Station: 97–101.

League, B.L.; Horn, S.P. 2000. A 10,000 year record of páramo fires in Costa Rica. Journal of Tropical Ecology. 16: 747–752.

Licata, C.; Sanford, R. 2012. Charcoal and total carbon in soils from foothills shrublands to subalpine forests in the Colorado Front Range. Forests. 3: 944–958.

Massielo, C.A.; Louchouarn, P. 2013. Fire in the ocean. Science. 2013: 287–288.

Orvis, K.H.; Lane, C.S.; Horn, S.P. 2005. Laboratory production of vouchered reference charcoal from small woody samples and non-woody plant tissues. Palynology. 29: 1–11.

Sanford, Jr., R.L.; Horn, S.P. 2000. Holocene rain-forest wilderness: a neotropical perspective on humans as an exotic, invasive species. In: Cole, D.N.; McCool, S.F.; Borrie, W.T.; O'Loughlin, J., comps. Wilderness science in a time of change; Volume 3, Wilderness as a place for scientific inquiry. Proceedings RMRS P-15-Vol-3. Ogden, UT: U.S. Department of Agriculture Forest Service, Rocky Mountain Research Station: 168–173.

Sanford, Jr., R.L.; Saldarriaga, J.; Clark, K.E. [and others]. 1985. Amazon rain forest fires. Science 227: 53–55.

Scales, S.A. 2011. Spatial distribution of charcoal after a prescribed fire on Middle Mountain, Virginia. Blacksburg, VA: Virginia Polytechnic Institute and State University. 58 p. M.S. thesis.

Scott, A.C.; Dablon, F. 2010. Charcoal taphonomy and significance in geology, botany and archaeology. Palaeogeography, Palaeoclimatology, Palaeoecology. 291: 1–10.

Stuiver, M.; Reimer, P.J. 1993. Extended ^{14}C database and revised CALIB 3.0 ^{14}C age calibration program. Radiocarbon. 35: 215–230.

Telford, R.J.; Heegaard, E.; Birks, H.J.B. 2004. The intercept is a poor estimate of the calibrated radiocarbon age. The Holocene. 14(2): 296–298.

Titiz, B.; Sanford, Jr., R.L. 2007. Soil charcoal in old growth rainforests from sea level to the continental divide. Biotropica. 39(6): 673–682.

Underwood, C.A. 2013. Fire and forest history from soil charcoal in yellow pine and mixed hardwood-pine forests in the Southern Appalachian Mountains, U.S.A. Knoxville, TN: The University of Tennessee. 176 p. Ph.D. dissertation.

Welch, N.T. 1999. Occurrence of fire in southern Appalachian yellow pine forests as indicated by macroscopic charcoal in soil. Castanea. 64(4): 310–317.

Whitlock, C; Larsen, C. 2001. Charcoal as a fire proxy. In: Smol, J.P.; Birks, H.J.B.; Last, W.M., eds. Tracking environmental change using lake sediments; Volume 3, Terrestrial, algal, and siliceous indicators. Dordrecht, The Netherlands: Kluwer Academic Press: 75–97.

Figure 1—Using the single root auger to collect soil charcoal in Great Smoky Mountains National Park. The photo on the right shows the extrusion of a 10-cm core increment into a labeled plastic bag. (Photos by Matthew Valente)

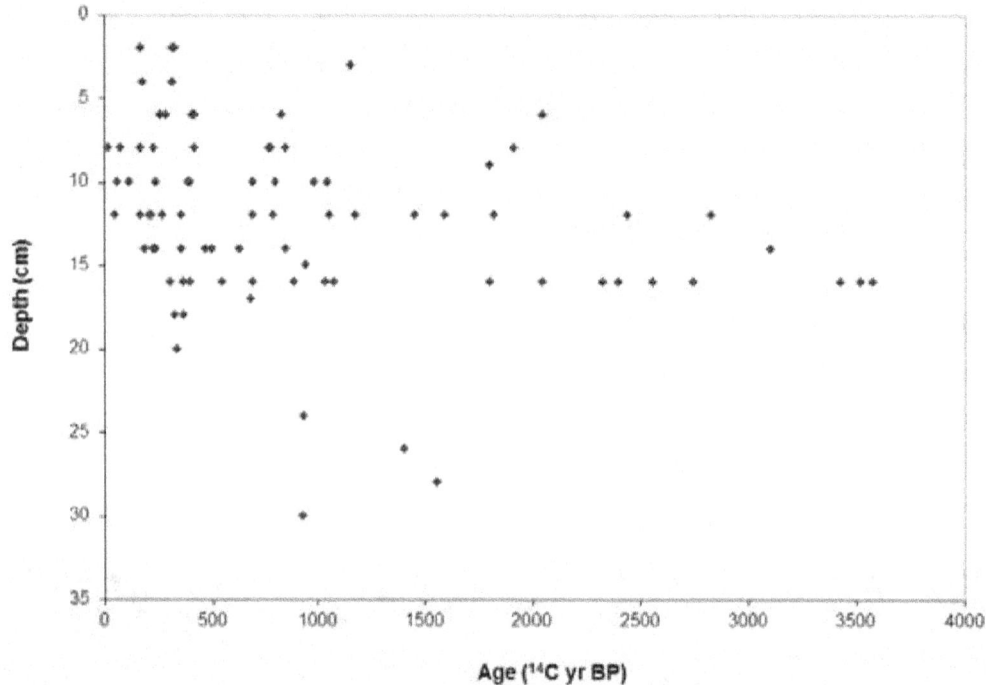

Figure 2—Radiocarbon ages of 81 charcoal fragments plotted against depth of recovery in Nantahala National Forest, from the study of Fesenmyer and Christensen (2010); data available at http://www.esapubs.org/archive/ecol/E091/049/appendix-A.htm. [Date accessed: February 1, 2011].

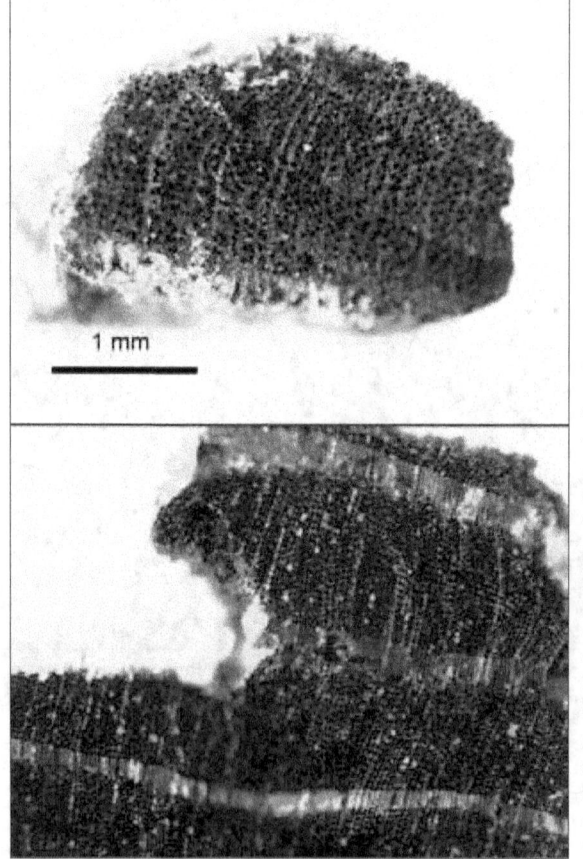

Figure 3—Macroscopic charcoal from study sites in Great Smoky Mountains National Park. The upper photograph shows charcoal from red maple (*Acer rubrum* L.). Anatomical features that allow identification of red maple are narrow rays that are approximately the same width as the widest pores, absence of tyloses, and diffuse-porous wood. The lower photograph shows charcoal from a southern yellow pine (*Pinus*, diploxylon group). Anatomical features that allow identification of southern yellow pine are tracheids, resin canals, and pronounced earlywood to latewood transition at ring boundaries. The wood anatomy of the diploxylon pines that grow in the southern Appalachians is too similar to allow differentiation of charcoal specimens to species. The scale bar is approximate and is for both photographs. (Photos by Chris Underwood)

[Extended Abstract]

RED OAK TIMBER PRODUCT VALUE LOSS DUE TO FIRE DAMAGE

Joseph M. Marschall, Richard P. Guyette, Michael C. Stambaugh, and Aaron P. Stevenson[1]

Fire is increasingly applied as a land management tool toward achieving multiple objectives in eastern North American oak (*Quercus*) communities. Prescribed fire treatments are applied for natural community restoration, hazardous fuel reduction, and multiple silvicultural objectives (Arthur and others 2012, Brose and others 2013, Brose and Van Lear 1998, Burton and others 2011, Dey and Hartman 2005, Pyne and others 1996). In southern Missouri, prescribed fire is used to restore glades, savannas, and woodlands by decreasing the number of woody stems, consuming litter, and creating forest canopy openings, thus promoting fire-tolerant tree and shade-intolerant herbaceous species (Nelson 2005). As land management agencies increasingly move toward landscape-level management processes (e.g., burn units > 1,000 acres), prescribed fire will burn across ecological boundaries more frequently, including into stands of merchantable timber. Currently there is much debate as to whether prescribed fire management for forest community restoration and managing for timber products are mutually exclusive practices. There is a need for improved understanding regarding how prescribed fire affects timber product values in areas containing merchantable sized trees.

We measured the economic loss due to fire-caused injuries (i.e., fire scars) in terms of volume and value in the butt logs of 88 red oak (*Quercus velutina, Q. rubra, and Q. coccinea*) trees harvested from prescribed fire units in southern Missouri. Trees with varying degrees of external fire damage, time since fire, and diameter were harvested and milled into dimensional lumber. Fire scar dimensions and tree size (diameter at breast height (DBH)) were measured prior to tree harvest. Lumber grade changes and volume losses due to fire-related injuries were tracked on individual boards (n=1298, 7754 board feet). Lumber values were assigned using rough, green lumber values reported by the Hardwood Market Report (Southern Hardwoods Category, April 16, 2011).

Overall, value and volume losses were surprisingly low. Volume loss per fire-scarred log averaged 3.9 percent, and the average value loss was 10.3 percent. A large amount of fire-caused defect was removed incidentally during the milling process (fig.1). Statistically significant models ($p < 0.001$) were developed to predict log value loss considering tree size, fire scar size, and fire scar residence time (time between fire damage occurrence and tree harvest). Trees that were mid-sized (i.e., pole size) when injured were most likely to experience higher value loss, while trees that were small or large in diameter at time of injury typically experienced little or no value loss. If fire damage is less than 20 inches in height and/or 20 percent basal circumference injured, then little value loss should occur over 14 years. If these thresholds are exceeded, value loss is likely. Value loss may be very low if trees are harvested within five years after fire damage, regardless of scar size. These findings are applicable for red oak trees which are at least 8 inches DBH at time of fire damage and with fire-scar residence times not greater than 14 years.

ACKNOWLEDGMENTS

This research was funded by the Missouri Department of Conservation.

LITERATURE CITED

Arthur, M.A.; Alexander, H.D.; Dey, D.C. [and others]. 2012. Refining the oak-fire hypothesis for management of oak-dominated forests of the Eastern United States. Journal of Forestry. 110: 257-266.

Brose, P.; Van Lear, D. 1998. Prescribed fire effects on hardwood advance regeneration in mixed hardwood stands. Southern Journal of Applied Forestry. 22: 138-142.

Brose, P.H.; Dey, D.C.; Phillips, R.J.; Waldrop, T.A. 2013. A meta-analysis of the fire-oak hypothesis: does prescribed burning promote oak reproduction in Eastern North America? Forest Science. 59(3): 322-334.

---

[1]Joseph M. Marschall, Senior Research Specialist, University of Missouri, Columbia, MO 65211

Richard P. Guyette, Research Professor, University of Missouri

Michael C. Stambaugh, Research Assistant Professor, University of Missouri

Aaron P. Stevenson, Resource Scientist, Missouri Department of Conservation, West Plains, MO 65775

Citation for proceedings: Waldrop, Thomas A., ed. 2014. Proceedings, Wildland Fire in the Appalachians: Discussions among Managers and Scientists. Gen. Tech. Rep. SRS-199. Asheville, NC: U.S. Department of Agriculture Forest Service, Southern Research Station. 208 p.

Burton J.; Hallgren, S.; Fuhlendorf, S.; Leslie, D. 2011. Understory response to varying fire frequencies after 20 years of prescribed burning in an upland oak forest. Plant Ecology. 212: 1513-1525.

Dey, D.C.; Hartman, G. 2005. Returning fire to Ozark Highland forest ecosystems: effects on advance regeneration. Forest Ecology and Management. 217(1): 37-53.

Nelson, P.W. 2005. The terrestrial natural communities of Missouri. Missouri Natural Areas Committee, Jefferson City, MO. 550 p.

Pyne, S.; Andrews, P.; Laven, R. 1996. Introduction to wildland fire. New York: John Wiley & Sons. 769 p.

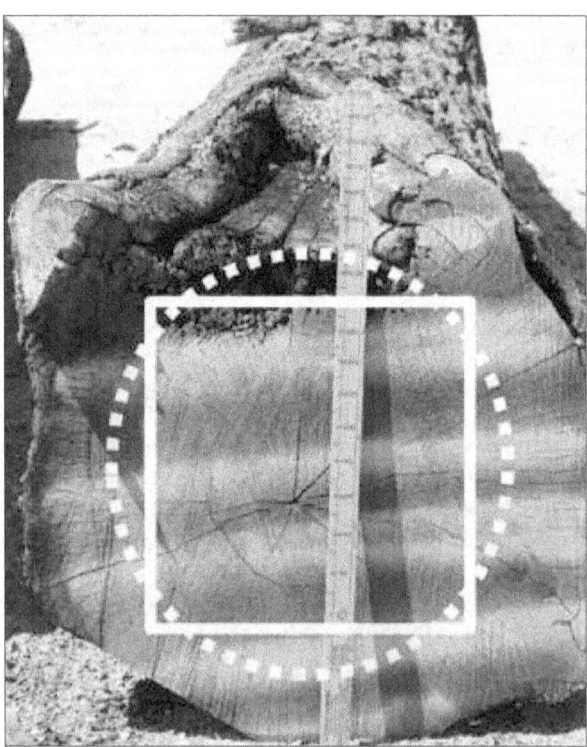

Figure 1—Fire scarred tree pre- and post-harvest. Tree DBH=19.7 inches, fire scar height=27.0 inches, fire scar depth=5.0 inches. The dotted circle on the base of the log depicts (to scale) the log's small end diameter; the solid square represents the portion of the round log that is utilized when manufacturing rectangular dimensional lumber. Though this tree appeared heavily defected while standing, it only experienced 8.0 percent value loss and 2.8 percent volume loss, with much of the fire-caused defect removed during the milling process.

WATER CHEMISTRY OF NORTH BRANCH SIMPSON CREEK AND THE RICH HOLE WILDERNESS FIRE

Daniel M. Downey, Jens Peter Haraldstadt, and Sydney N. Fisher[1]

Abstract—In April 2012, the understory of the Rich Hole Wilderness Area in Virginia including the watershed of North Branch of Simpson Creek (NBSC) was burned in a major wildfire. This fire presented a unique opportunity for the study of effects of forest fires on streams in the Appalachian Mountains. In other locations wildfires have produced changes in soil composition, surface runoff, and water chemistry. As the most dramatic effects of wildfires on streams have been the result of episodic discharge, sampling was conducted May–September 2012 for precipitation runoff events. In addition, synoptic samples were taken in 2012 and 2013 throughout the stream reach. Chemical parameters including pH, acid neutralizing capacity, Na^+, K^+, Mg^{2+}, Ca^{2+}, Cl^-, NO_3^-, SO_4^{2-}, Al, turbidity, and conductivity were measured for comparison to previous data sets. A second stream, Bob Downy Branch, was not affected by the fire and served as a "control" with samples collected coincidentally with those from NBSC. The paper presents the unique combination of forest timber stands, historic and present day land use, acid deposition, geology, and the fire in the observed water chemistry of NBSC.

INTRODUCTION

North Branch Simpson Creek (NBSC) is located on the James River Ranger District of the George Washington National Forest about seven miles east of the Town of Clifton Forge, VA. The stream drains toward the south between the ridges of Mill and Brushy Mountains and enters Simpson Creek (SC). The 1837-acre watershed of NBSC is located within the boundary of the Rich Hole Wilderness Area (RHWA) and is forested primarily with a mixture of chestnut oak (*Quercus montana*), northern red oak (*Q.rubra*), white oak (*Q. alba*), red maple (*Acer rubrum*), and sugar maple (*A. saccharinum*). Rhododendron (*Rhododendron* sp.) and mountain laurel (*Kalmia latifolia*) shrubs are abundant, and there are some pine stands. Water chemistry has been obtained for this stream at a site near the Wilderness boundary (VT 16) from April 1987 to present as part of the quarterly monitoring program of the Virginia Trout Stream Sensitivity Study (VTSSS). On April 9, 2012, a human-caused wildfire occurred within the Rich Hole Wilderness. Since the fire was within a congressionally designed Wilderness, indirect suppression actions were taken including backfire operations, line construction, and limited aircraft support. Otherwise the fire was allowed to burn "naturally;" that is, as it would have done in the era before fire suppression became standard practice. By April 19, 2012, the fire was extinguished by rainfall and containment (fig. 1). It was estimated that 95 percent of

the understory was burned to the forest floor with about 5 percent single and group torching.[2]

It is unusual for an entire watershed in the Ridge and Valley geophysical province of Virginia to be subjected to a "natural" fire, so the Rich Hole fire has provided an opportunity for research. It was suggested by Forest Service, U.S. Department of Agriculture staff that post-fire data for NBSC could provide useful information on the effect of forest fires on stream water. So in May 2012, the Forest Service requested the environmental group at James Madison University to participate in such a study. Limited funds were available so it was decided to limit the study to samples collected by a volunteer and/or Forest Service staff during episodic runoff events. It was thought that any short-term, post-fire changes in water chemistry might be observed in run off. A nearby stream that discharges from an unburned watershed, Downy Branch (DB), was sampled as a "control" in coincidence with NBSC sampling.

GENERAL COMMENTS ON THE EFFECTS OF FIRES ON STREAMS

Forested landscape may be roughly described with three main features: (in order of increasing solar irradiation) the soils and floor of the forest; low height vegetation including shrubs, juvenile trees and other plants called the understory; and an elevated crown of tree limbs

---

[1]Daniel M. Downey, Professor, Department of Chemistry and Biochemistry, James Madison University, Harrisonburg, VA 22807

Jens Peter Haraldstadt, Research Assistant, James Madison University

Sydney N. Fisher, Research Assistant, James Madison University

[2]Personal Communication. 2012. Steve Croy. Supervisor's Office, George Washington and Jefferson National Forests, 5162 Valleypointe Parkway, Roanoke, VA 24019.

Citation for proceedings: Waldrop, Thomas A., ed. 2014. Proceedings, Wildland Fire in the Appalachians: Discussions among Managers and Scientists. Gen. Tech. Rep. SRS-199. Asheville, NC: U.S. Department of Agriculture Forest Service, Southern Research Station. 208 p.

and foliage termed canopy. All three of these features are affected by a forest fire with the extent dependent on seasonal timing, availability of fuel, type of fuel, air temperature, wind, and desiccation. Fire reduction of any of these features can change the physical and chemical nature of water discharging from a burned forest (Tiedemann and others 1978). Studies have demonstrated both short- and long-term changes in physical and chemical attributes of streams. Some changes such as increased sediment loading in discharge may be noted soon after the fire. Other changes such as base cation depletion and carbon balance may be long term. Considerable information on the impact of fires on streams may be found in the literature (Wade 1989). For the NBSC study, any changes in water chemistry that may have occurred from the Rich Hole fire should be evaluated in context of past/present land use and watershed geology.

Rich Hole Wilderness History and Geology

The name "Rich Hole" derives from the drainage holes (hollows) of Brushy Mountain. One of these depressions on the north slope contains a large stand of old growth northern red oak forest that is on the list of National Natural Landmarks (NPS 2009, p. 99). Described as a "cove" or protected virgin forest of large oak and hickory trees, this timber stand was the key to the naming and creation of the RHWA.

Pig iron production was the first major industry that developed in eastern Alleghany County. In 1827, a stone "cold blast" furnace, Lucy Selina (Cappon 1957; Lesley 1859, p. 71), opened on the south bank of Simpson Creek less than a mile downstream from NBSC. In 1854, a second furnace, the "hot blast" Australia Furnace, was built at the site. These furnaces required iron ore, limestone, and charcoal to produce iron metal. Iron was produced from mined deposits of limonite, which is a mixture of iron oxides and hydroxides known as Oriskany iron ore (Lesure 1987, p.11). This ore was 48.2 percent iron, and the two furnaces had the greatest production total of any in the State (Walker 1936, p. 28). Mining of iron ore from the mountain slopes of the then future RHWA caused significant changes and erosion of the landscape. In addition, the mountains were stripped of trees to make charcoal. Pig iron production by the process continued until after the end of the War Between the States. In fact, much of the iron used for Confederate cannon balls and other war material came from these furnaces. Rich Hole is in the headwaters of the James River, and transportation by canals and the river made transport to the forges in Richmond less challenging than other locations. Shortly after the war in 1869, the furnaces were acquired by Longdale Company (Morton, 1923, p. 71). In about 1873, charcoal was replaced by coke for iron production. Coke is made from coal, so it may be

reasoned that the local mountain forests from that time forward were less stressed from harvest and regeneration occurred. Fancy Hill mine on the south slope of Mill Mountain in the RMWA was worked in the late 1800s and early 1900s (Watson 1907, p. 440). Production of iron in Virginia declined in the early twentieth century and by the end of World War I, the production of iron in the vicinity of RHWA became extinct due to competition with western and northern suppliers.

By 1935-36, many acres of the mountain lands of the iron manufacturing industry were purchased by the Federal Government for inclusion in the George Washington National Forest. The unique cove of trees mentioned above that had not been harvested was soon identified as worthy of special protection and the inclusive slopes of Brushy Mountain were designated as "roadless." In 1964, Congress passed the Wilderness Act (PL 88-577) that designated tracts of Federal land as Wilderness Areas. The Forest Service interpreted the act to include only those lands that were historically pristine and free of human disturbance. In 1974, Congress passed the Eastern Wilderness Act (PL 93-622) that extended the opportunity for inclusion of lands in Wilderness Areas previously used for the diverse activities of humanity which could return to a native condition by natural succession. In 1984, Congress passed the Virginia Wilderness Act (PL 98-586) that selected Rich Hole (and three other areas) for detailed study. In 1988, the Rich Hole Wilderness Area was established (PL 100-326).

Lesure (1957) mapped the geology of the ore deposits of the Clifton Forge iron district in Alleghany County, and repeated his interpretation in a mineral survey report done for Rich Hole Wilderness study area (Lesure 1987). In the later study, he mapped the hematite and limonite resources, both of which he termed "subeconomic" and referenced other studies of the geochemistry and geology of the RHWA. The National Geologic Database has provided on-line and downloadable maps of this work (Lesure and Nicholson 1985). Lesure (1987, p. 6) has also identified the sites of abandoned iron mines, charcoaling pits, cuts, and prospect pits. The largest mine site near NBSC, the Fancy Hill mine, was a 20-foot deep open cut 100-feet wide and 150-feet long on the south slope of Mill Mountain. Not indicated was the grade of a narrow gauge railroad that ran from the Fancy Hill mine to the Longdale Furnace site.

An understanding of the geology of NBSC is essential for interpreting its water chemistry (tables 1 and 2). Lesure's explanation (1987, p. 10) of the formation of limonite deposits in RHWA is that acidic groundwater in the Romney Shale dissolved iron sulfides which moved into underlying carbonate rock and precipitated as iron oxides. He describes the general geology as folded marine sedimentary rocks of the Paleozoic age with interbedded shale, siltstone, and limestone of Late Ordovician age, overlaying beds of sandstone, quartzite, and hematitic sandstone to Middle Silurian age and lower Devonium limestone (Lesure 1987, p. 1, 5). The immediate geology of the NBSC was mapped with the stream originating at 3000 feet elevation in Middle Silurian Keefer Sandstone (Sk), passing adjacent to landslide colluvium consisting of Keefer and Rose Hill Sandstone (Qlc) near 2600 feet, then resuming Keefer contact, encountering sandstone colluvium (Qa) near 2200 feet that follows the stream channel down to the confluence with SC near 1400 feet. Near 1800 feet and 1550 feet there are small groups of Lower Devonium and Upper Silurian rocks (DSu) on the west slope, the latter location having been explored for limonite. Near 1700 feet and 1600 feet there are insertions of Romney Sale (Dr) from the west slope. Kozak (1965) mapped the geology of 15 minute Millboro quadrangle that includes the RHWA. His interpretation shows NBSC originating from Clinton Formation (Scl) near 2800 feet elevation and passing Cayuga Group (Scy), Keyser Formation (Sk), Helderberg Group (Dhl), Oriskany Sandstone (Do), Millboro Shale (Dm), and Brallier Formation (Db) at the stream confluence with SC. Alluvium and colluvium are not shown as separate mapped areas. Regardless of which geologic interpretation is used for assessing water chemistry, the upper reach of NBSC drains from acidic sandstone, then encounters shale and basic limestone before entering SC.

Downy Branch Geology and History

The sampling location for Downy Branch (DB) lies 2.6 miles southwest of VT16 on NBSC. This stream is not within the RHWM area and was not included in some of the referenced geological surveys but was included in the Kozak (1965) study. Although DB drains toward the northwest from North Mountain, the geological associations are quite similar to that of NBSC. The same sandstone and limestone formations described above contribute to the watershed geology of DB.

The human use history of DB watershed has not been reported to the same extent as NBSC. The stream enters Blue Suck Branch within the boundaries of an old Civilian Conservation Corps constructed recreation area 0.6 miles upstream of the confluence with SC. There are small dams on DB that may have been built as reservoirs for the recreation area. Any mining or charcoal sites that may have been in the watershed are not identified on the U.S. Geological Survey (USGS) maps.

Coldwater Streams and Water Chemistry

The chemical and physical makeup of a stream is dependent on the watershed from which it discharges. Streams that discharge from high elevation (elevation > 1400 feet) sandstone and shale ridges in the Virginia

Valley and Ridge geophysical province tend to be cold (maximum temperature < 22 °C), free of sediment, and low in dissolved minerals. In Alleghany County, such clean and clear streams support native brook trout (*Salvelinus fontinalis*) and have been included in the VTSSS project. A major goal of VTSSS is establishing the effect of atmospheric acid deposition (acid rain) on the water chemistry of these streams. The primary water quality criterion that is monitored is acid neutralizing capacity (ANC), which is defined as the summation of all titratable bases in the water. The only base of significance in low conductivity headwater streams is bicarbonate ion, which originates from the dissolution of carbonate-bearing minerals in the watershed geology of a stream. In geology where there is little carbonate mineral, the streams are low in ANC, and aquatic life is threatened from acid injections due to rain, snow, etc. Along with ANC, the most common water chemistry parameter is pH, which is the hydronium ion concentration expressed logarithmically. The experimentally found relationship between pH and ANC is illustrated in figure 2. Thus, the observed pH in stream water is the combination of acid from the atmosphere coupled with the ability of geology for a stream to provide neutralizing base (Sharpe and others 1987, Zhi-Jun and others 2000). Although there is no established value for mortality of brook trout and ANC/pH values, it has been observed that streams with negative ANC values and low pH are either devoid of trout or have low population numbers and biomass. Additional water chemistry parameters that are useful for evaluating cold water streams are base cations, acid anions, aluminum, conductivity, and turbidity.

Water Chemistry and NBSC Survey

On September 20, 2012, two Forest Service staff scientists, Dawn Kirk and Fred Huber, hiked the Rich Hole Trail to examine the Wilderness five months after the fire. Water samples were collected from the stream and two tributaries en route from the top of the mountain to the lower boundary. These sites were recorded with a GPS unit (table 3). The single day collection of samples took place two days following a seasonal storm that delivered an estimated 3 inches of rainfall to the NBSC watershed. It is estimated that the discharge peaked on September 18 and was in regression to base flow when the samples were collected. The pH and ANC values found for these samples revealed much about the way water chemistry is influenced by geology. Very low pH and ANC values were obtained for all samples taken more than a mile from the lower Wilderness boundary (table 4, fig. 3) and upstream of 1750 feet elevation. These low values reflect the acidic sandstone geology (Keefer) which constitutes the upper watershed. Near 1 mile upstream, the pH and ANC increase dramatically due to the injection of water from the limestone geology (Helderberg) that provides bicarbonate. On site examination of the 1-mile sampling location suggested that ash from the fire may have been a contributing factor. The pH and ANC decreased downstream from the 1-mile sample location, probably due to the injection of additional acidic water from the east side of the watershed. Aluminum is a metal toxic to fish that can be mobilized under acidic conditions. In this study, all observed aluminum values were low and not threatening for aquatic life.

Fish Populations

Simpson Creek (SC) drains the east side of Brushy Mountain and winds its way nearly 10 stream miles down to the confluence with the Cowpasture River 4 miles east of Clifton Forge. Self-sustaining brook and rainbow trout dominate SC fish populations for about 5 miles from its origin spring near elevation 3000 feet to the historic Longdale Furnace site at 1300 feet. Downstream of Longdale Furnace, the stream temperature increases and warm water fish populations dominate. North Branch Simpson Creek (NBSC) enters SC upstream of Longdale Furnace within the coldwater reach. Blue Suck Branch (BSB) with its tributary Downy Branch (DB) enters SC about 2 miles downstream of Longdale Furnace within the warm water reach. These confluences are important because coldwater fish could migrate from NBSC into SC and vice versa, whereas migration is less likely into/from BSB and DB.

Electrofishing surveys of the above streams have been performed by VDGIF (Fink 2012) with 27 different species of fish found (table 5). Most of these species are native and frequently found in headwater streams in western Virginia. Some species are introduced, e.g., rock bass, smallmouth bass and rainbow trout, either directly into the streams or from migration from the Cowpasture River. The diversity of the fish population is impressive given that for nearly two centuries, the human impact in the watershed has been dramatic. For about 100 years after Colonel John Jordan operated his first iron furnace Lucy Selina [Longdale], "heavy drafts" on the forests to make charcoal (Morton 1923, p. 71) and extensive mining took place along the SC drainage. This was done in an era when no effort was made to avoid sediment movement and damage to the riparian area of streams. Roads and railways were built along the stream, beginning as trails for mining and travel that connected the furnaces along Bratton's Run, the mineral spring resorts along Alum Creek and Jordan's furnaces. By 1832, the Lexington and Covington Turnpike was built over North Mountain, following the trace of the old trails (Morton 1920, p.164). In the late 1920s, the Turnpike became part of US 60, later designated SR 850 North Mountain Road when the interstate and Federal highway conjoined. In 1977, construction of I-64 sandwiched much of the stream between the two roads. An attempt was made to mitigate

streambank erosion after the highway construction was completed (Standage 1986) with semipermeable matting, but recent erosion has continued to introduce sediment into SC.[3] Fish populations for both BSB and DB have been affected by the 1930s construction of dams that are part of a recreation area (Downey and others 2012). These dams are large enough to inhibit fish migration. It is noteworthy that BSB, DB, and NBSC have been listed as Exceptional State Waters-Tier III (VDEQ 2004).

Simpson Creek was included in the VDGIF trout stocking program until the time of construction of I-64. Hatchery raised rainbow trout (RBT) were stocked each year for decades, and it is likely that some of these fish parented the fish collected by VDGIF surveys in recent years. Of the eight different times SC has been surveyed (table 5), four found RBT, one found brook trout (BKT), and three found no trout at all. Unfortunately the location of surveys has varied and was not recorded in the database except those since 2001. For those locations that were identified, l=lower, m=middle and u=upper. The upper location is within the coldwater reach at Longdale Furnace and showed the greatest number of RBT. The other two identified locations are within the warmwater section of SC and did not have any trout. It is likely that the other surveys that didn't show trout in SC and BSB were done in warmwater sections. The survey (1995) for SC that showed BKT but no RBT was from far up in the watershed near 1600 feet elevation.[4] It was thought that the abundance of brook trout may have been due to fingerling stocking in a previous year. In streams in Virginia that have been colonized by RBT, water chemistry generally shows higher pH, ANC, and lower elevation, than in reaches of the same stream that contain BKT. The 1979 and 1995 electrofishing site for NBSC was also unspecified in the database, but VT16 was likely the surveyed site. The NBSC fish data showed BKT and nongame fish populations that matched the SC site surveyed on the same day.

A dramatic difference in water chemistry (table 6) was observed for sites collected near elevation 1444 feet a short distance upstream from NBSC and SC confluence in May 2012. Unlike NBSC, which discharges through sandstone rock for most of its distance, SC discharges mostly from Brallier Formation (Db) for several miles before reaching the confluence of the two streams (Kozak 1965). Thus SC has higher pH, ANC, calcium, and

[3]Personal Communication. 2013. Dawn Kirk. Supervisor's Office, George Washington and Jefferson National Forests, 5162 Valleypointe Parkway, Roanoke, VA 24019.

[4]Personal Communication. 2013. Paul Bugas. Virginia Department of Game and Inland Fisheries, Verona Office, 517 Lee Highway, Verona, VA 24482.

magnesium concentration than NBSC due to the greater contact with limestone and shale geology. This difference in stream chemistry has benefited the RBT that are not only thriving in SC but have replaced the native BKT. As no barrier to fish migration was found, the lower pH, etc. may also be a reason that RBT have not colonized NBSC.

Description of April 2012 Fire

The winter of 2011-2012 was an unusually dry period in western Virginia. At about 5:30 pm on April 9, 2012 (Dooley 2012), a small brush fire was reported along Rich Hole Road (North Mountain Road) near the Rockbridge/Alleghany County line. With dry forest and high winds, the fire soon spread throughout the Simpson Creek valley, resulting in closure of I-64 for nearly 20 hours (Adams 2012). Rich Hole fire was one of six different major wildfires that became known as the Easter Complex due to their occurrence just after Easter Sunday. By April 19, all fires were contained. The Rich Hole fire covered more than 15,454 acres, including 100 percent of the 6450 acre RHWA burned (Inciweb 2012), ending when a sizeable storm front passed through the region delivering about 1 inch rainfall on April 18, 2012.

The Rich Hole fire occurred in the early spring before leaf out for deciduous trees and before most grasses and other plants had emerged from the forest floor. Most of the litter and dead wood that covered the forest floor was partially or totally consumed leaving a layer of gray colored ash. Small trees and bushes were also consumed, but larger trees mostly were not damaged except for minor burn scars in most cases. The fire did not char the soil; in fact, we could find no effect more than 0.8 inch below the surface in the locations we examined. By May, much of the forest canopy had grown out, especially in the riparian area, and throughout the summer the burned area gradually replenished with renewed plant life.

METHODS

Rainfall, Discharge and Sample Collection

Streams often show dramatic changes in water chemistry with changes in discharge that are due to contact time with soils, bedrock geology, and surface materials. During low flow periods, ground water makes up streams, while surface run off is a greater factor during high flows. It would have been worthwhile to measure discharge of the streams as part of this study and collect samples frequently at all stages. However, there was no funding available so sample collection relied entirely on volunteer labor and additional work was not possible. It was thought that the most likely immediate effects of the fire would occur during episodic runoff events, so sample collection was made before and after storms passed through the

area during spring and summer 2012. It was necessary for sample collectors to note storm patterns and predict when to take samples. This was challenging particularly since the summer was relatively dry and some storms turned out to deliver small levels of precipitation that did not substantially change discharge. As things turned out, 15 and 14 water samples were collected from VT16 on NBSC and DB, respectively (table 7). As no stream gauges were in place in the study streams, general discharge was calculated. Eastern Alleghany County receives an average 3 inches rain annually (Citizen Steering Committee 2007). In other studies we have estimated annual yield at about 65 percent for similar rain and forest cover. With these values—stream gradients of 7.6 percent and 9.1 percent and watersheds of 1837 and 990 acres—the average annual discharge is 5.1 and 2.7 cubic feet for NBSC and DB, respectively. The deviation in these averages is near 0.5 cubic feet, ranging from near zero during droughts to more than ten fold the average with high precipitation.

Rainfall and stream discharge for the time when these samples were collected can be estimated from gauges maintained by several governmental agencies. Although no gauge is located right at the study site, the following may serve as surrogates. The IFLOWS network is a system of digital rain gauges located throughout the mountains for warning of potential flooding. The gauges operate with tipple buckets that record rainfall in 0.04-inch increments; data is sent by telemetry to county receivers and made available on the internet. Although the primary purpose of the gauges is public safety, archived rainfall data may be readily downloaded (table 8). Flows or discharge in streams may also be conveniently obtained from internet data for a wide network of stream gauging stations operated by USGS and other agencies. The nearest gauges to RHWA are two IFLOW rain gauges, one on Warm Springs Mountain 10 miles west, and another on North Mountain 3 miles southeast, with a stream gauge located on the Cowpasture River 6 miles southwest near Clifton Forge downstream of the confluence with Simpson Creek (fig. 4).

Efforts were made to begin this project soon after the fire occurred with the first samples collected May 8, 2012 when a rain front was moving through the region. Multiple samples were collected over several days for a storm which gave about 0.75 inches rain total. A large storm passed through about a week later with 1.5 inches rain total. Neither of these storms produced the large flushing event that was desired to determine whether sediment movement and other changes would occur as a result of the fire. Several late May storms and one in July were small and did not result in significant rainfall.

In September, about 3 inches of rain were delivered in a single storm to the NBSC watershed.[5]

Sample Processing

Observations of water temperature, conductivity, turbidity, and pH were made at the time of sample collection in the field. Determination of major ions contributing to charge balance and dissolved trace elements were done in our laboratories. Samples were measured for air-equilibrated pH and acid neutralizing capacity at 68 ° F. After filtration with a 0.2-micron filter (Gelman 4406 LC PVDF), portions of the water samples were measured for acid anions (chloride, nitrate, and sulfate) directly by ion chromatography (Dionex ICS-3000), while a second portion was acidified with high purity nitric acid (Fisher Scientific Co.) and analyzed for calcium, magnesium, sodium, and potassium by flame atomic absorption (Varian SpectrAA 220FS). Other elements (aluminum, copper, iron, zinc, etc.) were analyzed in filtered, acidified samples by inductively coupled plasma–mass spectrometry (ICP-MS) (Agilent 7500). Analytical methods have been described elsewhere (APHA 1998, Downey and others 1994).

RESULTS AND DISCUSSION

Surface soil samples collected for the present study gave values of pH 4.23 and 7.76, respectively for unburned and burned sites. Corresponding alkalinity (bicarbonate) concentrations were 0 and 446 µeq/g. These results indicated a large amount of alkalinity was produced in the ash from carbon combustion by the forest fire. To evaluate whether the bicarbonate or other ash derived chemicals were contributing to post-fire stream water chemistry, data were compared for the results of our analyses to the VTSSS database for NBSC. Average and sample standard deviation values were calculated for all parameters. Fall and winter samples were excluded from the VTSSS set to provide better comparison to the spring and summer samples collected for the present study. At 95 percent confidence, the conductivity (mineral content), calcium, and magnesium increased (table 9). Other values increased but were not statistically significant. It is interesting that both ANC and pH decreased, which is the opposite of what would have been anticipated from the burned soil results, but there was no difference at 95 percent confidence.

Soil erosion was expected to be an important part of the post-fire effects of storms washing sediment into the stream. Turbidity was measured for all post-fire samples and did not increase above baseline values for both NBSC and DB, ranging from 1.0 to 2.5 NTU, except for the

September 18 storm which produced values of 32 and 44 NTU, respectively. Both streams clarified by the second day after this storm. All data indicate that the fire did not create an erosion problem and that NBSC sediment is typical of a Virginia headwater trout stream.

The selection of Downy Branch as the "control" stream was made based on its proximity to NBSC, similarity in watershed size, land use, forest timber stands, etc. However, there are some differences in water chemistry that preclude a direct comparison of the paired samples taken for this study. For example, average values for pH / ANC were 6.18±0.47 / 19.5±6.0 and 6.52±0.15 / 56.7±13.1 for NBSC and DB, respectively. Yet information may be gleaned by comparing *changes* in water chemistry for the paired samples. For each parameter and for each sample collection, a difference (delta) value was calculated for the two streams and several trends were noted. In general, when storms elevate stream discharge dilution causes solute concentrations to decrease and delta values between comparison streams are smaller. However, when storm runoff occurred post fire in the present study, the delta value for ANC either increased (fig. 4) or did not decrease proportionally. This observation supports the observation that ANC for NBSC was reduced after the fire and indicates the decrease was greater with increased discharge. Conversely, both calcium and magnesium delta values increased as a result of concentrations increasing with storm flow. This increase may be due to the two cations flushing from ash. The most dramatic differences were observed during the largest episodic event of the study in September, when the concentrations of discharge calcium and magnesium were greater in NBSC than in DB. These observations may not be conclusive for this study due to the limited size of the data set.

CONCLUSION

The geology of the upper reach for both NBSC and DB consists mostly of sandstone with limited or no natural carbonate. The streams are acidic until they encounter limestone geology low in the watersheds. Mining, charcoaling, logging, and road construction were widespread in the watersheds before acquisition by the Forest Service in the 1930s, with forest timber recovery since that time. Pre- and post-fire data for NBSC indicate that the stream was discharging increased calcium and magnesium during the study period at 95 percent confidence level. These results agree with previous studies (Tiedemann and others 1979, p. 14). Both pH and ANC were lower but not statistically verified at 95 percent confidence. Other parameters also were not statistically different. Paired samples of DB and NBSC supported the observations that calcium and magnesium were increased, with ANC decreased. Soil tests indicated increased pH and bicarbonate due to ash in the burned forest over

---

[5]Personal Communication. 2012. William McNown. 405 Sammys Road Apt 7, Covington, VA 24426.

the unburned samples. It is not known why bicarbonate (ANC) was not released along with the base cations, but charge balance requires some other anions must be discharged as well. A small increase in sulfate was observed but not enough to match the amount of calcium and magnesium. Phosphorus was not measured for this study, and it is possible that phosphate is the "missing" anion.

Limitations of this study included a reliance on discharge and rainfall data information not directly taken at the watershed, a relatively small data set due to a lack of flushing storms during the project period, VTSSS data for which discharge data are not available, dissimilarity between the two streams, and very little pre-fire data for DB. Fire effects to the canopy were variable. There was 75-100 percent mortality in some areas, mostly on rocky dry ridges. While in other areas, there was little to no damage to the canopy. The soil layer was unaffected and in most places the organic duff layer was affected only low to moderate. Stream transport of sediment levels did not change as a result of the fire. It is possible but doubtful that future storms could erode the NBSC, introduce sediment, and change water chemistry. Most likely the landscape will soon recover and the casual visitor will be hard pressed to see that a forest fire occurred in this location.

ACKNOWLEDGMENTS

The authors thank William "Bill" McNown, Forest Service volunteer, for collecting most of the episodic water samples for this study. The information and guidance of Forest Service staff Dawn Kirk, Steve Croy, Fred Huber, and Ed Haverlack are appreciated. Fisheries data provided by VDGIF staff Paul Bugas and Brad Fink proved most useful. Recommendations and maps provided by Dr. Steve Leslie of the James Madison University geology department were invaluable. Participation by the 2012 and 2013 James Madison University Environmental Field Camps and James Madison University students Mike Petit, Keith Burke, Chelsea Barry (sign language interpreter), and Brandon McMillan (Gallaudet University) was appreciated. Partial funding for this work was from James Madison University and National Science Foundation grant CHE-1062629.

REFERENCES

Adams, D. 2012. Firefighters confront a big disadvantage with fires in Alleghany, Rockbridge counties. The Roanoke Times. Posted April 12, 2012 at Roanoke.com. http://www.roanoke.com/news/roanoke/wb/307331.

American Public Health Association (APHA). 1998. Standard methods for the analysis of water and wastewater, 20th ed. Washington, DC: American Public Health Association (APHA), the American Water Works Association (AWWA), and the Water Environment Federation (WEF). [Number of pages unknown].

Cappon, L.1957. Lucy Selina's Charcoal Era. The Virginia Cavalcade. 7(2): 31-39.

Citizen Steering Committee. 2007. Comprehensive plan of Alleghany County, Virginia. June 19, 2007. http://www.alleghenyplaces.com/comprehensive_plan/comprehensive_plan.aspx. [Date accessed: September 22, 2014]

Dooly, M. 2012. Rich Hole fire closes part of I-64. WSLS News 10. Posted April 10, 2012. http://www2.wsls.com/news/2012/apr/10/8/rich-hole-fire-closes-part-i-64-ar-1832609/.

Downey, D.M.; French, C.R.; Odom, M. 1994. Low cost limestone treatment of acid sensitive trout streams in the Appalachian Mountains of Virginia. Water, Air, and Soil Pollution. 77: 49-77.

Downey, D.M.; Burke, K.; Haraldstadt, J.P. 2012. Composition of mortar and concrete samples taken from Longdale Recreation Area: a preliminary archeological study. Report prepared for the U.S. Department of Agriculture Forest Service, George Washington and Jefferson National Forests, December, 2012.

Fink, B. 2012. VDGIF fisheries biologist email communication with DMD 10/16/2012.

Inciweb. 2012. Incident Information System. Updated 4/20/2012. http://inciweb.org/incident/2826/.

Kozak, S. J. 1965. Geology of the Millboro Quadrangle, Virginia. Virginia Division of Mineral Resources. Report of Investigations 8. 19 p.

Lesley, J.P. 1859. The iron manufacturer's guide to the furnaces, forges and rolling mills of the United States, with discussions of iron as a chemical element, and American ore, and a manufactured article, in commerce and in history. New York: John Wiley. 772 p. Available: http://www.clpdigital.org/jspui/handle/10493/158.

Lesure, F.G. 1957. Geology of the Clifton Forge Iron District, Virginia. Virginia Engineering Experiment Station Series Number 118. Blacksburg, VA: Virginia Polytechnic Institute. 130 p.

Lesure, F.G. 1987. Mineral resources of the Rich Hole Roadless Area, Alleghany and Rockbridge Counties, Virginia. U.S. Geological Survey Bulletin B 1667. Denver, CO: U.S. Geological Survey Federal Center. 15 p.

Lesure, F.G.; Nicholson, S.W. 1985. Geologic map of the Rich Hole Roadless Area, Alleghany and Rockbridge Counties, Virginia: U.S. Geological Survey, Miscellaneous Field Studies Map MF-1760-A. http://ngmdb.usgs.gov/ngm-bin/ILView.pl?sid=7494_1.sid&vtype=b&sfact=1.25 and http://ngmdb.usgs.gov/Prodesc/proddesc_7413.htm.

Morton, O.F. 1920. A history of Rockbridge County, Virginia. McClure Co., Inc., Staunton, VA. 574 p.

Morton, O.F. 1923. A centennial history of Alleghany County, Virginia. J.K. Ruebush Company, Dayton, VA. 226 p.

National Park Service (NPS). 2009. National Registry of Natural Landmarks. Washington, DC: National Park Service. http://www.nature.nps.gov/nnl/docs/NNLRegistry.pdf.

Sharpe, W.E.; Leibfried, V.G.; Kimmel, W.G.; DeWalle, D.R. 1987. The relationship of water quality and fish occurrence to soils and geology in an area of high hydrogen and sulfate ion deposition. Journal of the American Water Resources Association. 23(1): 37-46.

Standage, R.W. 1986. Streambank stabilization using geomatrix matting—Simpson Creek, Virginia. Fifth trout stream habitat improvement workshop. Proceedings of the Annual Conference Southeastern Association of Fish and Wildlife Agencies. Lock Haven, PA: Southeastern Association of Fish and Wildlife Agencies: 191-198.

Tiedemann, A.R.; Conrad, C.E.; Dieterich, J.H. [and others]. 1979. Effects of fire on water: a state of knowledge review. National Fire Effects Workshop. Gen. Tech. Rep. WO-10. U.S. Department of Agriculture Forest Service. 28 p.

VDEQ. 2004. Cowpasture River & Simpson Creek Proposed Tier III Waters 3/10 & 3/11/04 Staff Site Visit Summary. Virginia Department of Environmental Quality. http://www.deq.virginia.gov/Portals/0/DEQ/Water/WaterQualityStandards/T3_SITE_VISITSimpson_Crk_tribs_04.pdf. [Date accessed: September 22, 2014]

Wade, D.D. 1989. A guide for prescribed fire in southern forests. Technical Publication R8-TP 11. U.S. Department of Agriculture Forest Service, Southern Region.

Walker, L.W. 1936. An economic and social survey of Alleghany County. Charlottesville, VA: University of Virginia Press.

Watson, T.L. 1907. Mineral resources of Virginia. Lynchburg, VA: J.P. Bell Co.

Zhi-Jun L.; Weller, D.E.; Correll, D.L.; Jordan, T.E. 2000. Effects of land cover and geology on stream chemistry in watersheds of the Chesapeake Bay. Journal of the American Water Resources Association. 36(6): 1349-1365.

Table 1—General description of geologic map units of North Branch Simpson Creek and Downy Branch

ID	Name	Description
Qa	Alluvium (Holocene)	Sandstone sand and gravel
Qlc	Landslide and Colluvium	Quartzite and hematitic sandstone from Keefer and Rose Hill formation
Dr	Romney Shale	Black, pyritic, fissile shale
DSu	Undivided Devonium and Silurian	Contains Ridgeley Sandstone, Licking Creek Limestone, Oriskany iron deposits, Healing Springs sandstone, New Creek limestone, Kesyer limestone, several other sandstones and limestones all undivided
Sk	Keefer Sandstone	White and light gray sandstone quartz

Source: Lesure and N cho son (1985).

Table 2—Comparison of sampling sites and heads of North Branch Simpson Creek and Downy Branch

Site	Latitude	Longitude	Elevation	Reach	Lesure	Kozak
			feet	miles		
NBSC VT16	N 37° 49.210	W 79° 40.296	1444	0.04	Qa	Db
NBSC head	N 37° 52.080	W 79° 39.054	2961	3.8	Sk	Scl
DB sample	N 37° 47.296	W 79° 41.865	1362	0.4	–	Db
DB head	N 37° 46.490	W 79° 40.400	2700	2.8	–	Scl

–These are data that were not co ected by the study c ted here.

Table 3—September 20, 2012 waypoints of sample sites on North Branch Simpson Creek in order of increasing elevation

Site	Latitude	Longitude	Elevation	Reach	Lesure	Kozak
			feet	miles		
NBSC009	N 37° 49.210	W 79° 40.296	1444	0.04	Qa	Db
NBSC008	N 37° 49.554	W 79° 40.241	1541	0.4	Qa	Dm
NBSC007	N 37° 50.076	W 79° 40.108	1749	1.0	Qa	Dhl
NBSC006	N 37° 50.431	W 79° 39.984	1877	1.6	Qa	Sk
NBSC005	N 37° 51.195	W 79° 39.654	2269	2.6	Sk	Scl
NBSC004	N 37° 51.513	W 79° 39.400	2579	3.1	Sk	Scl
NBSC003	N 37° 51.664	W 79° 39.220	2748	3.5	Sk	Scl
NBSC002	N 37° 52.080	W 79° 39.054	2961	3.8	Sk	Scl
Start 001	N 37° 52.198	W 79° 37.502	2279	trailhead	–	–
DB	N 37° 47.296	W 79° 41.865	1362	0.4	–	Db

Note: Downy Branch and the tra head are ncuded. The geoogy of the coect on stes was dentfied by Lesure (1985) and Kozak (1965).

–These are data that were not coected by the study cted here.

Table 4—September 20, 2012 North Branch Simpson Creek water chemistry results

Elevation	pH	ANC	Cl	NO3	SO4	Na	K	Ca	Mg	Al	Con
feet											
1444	6.48	24.8	20.9	0.3	72.7	17.3	13.0	96.1	48.3	0	19.5
1541	6.36	25.6	20.8	0.5	73.0	17.4	12.1	97.9	48.1	0	20.2
1749	7.37	287.9	28.5	0.1	208.0	19.5	18.8	513.7	75.8	1	72.0
1877	5.03	-6.5	18.1	0.3	64.8	15.6	9.3	29.9	43.8	16	17.2
2269	4.90	-11.0	17.9	0.3	64.2	16.1	8.5	24.0	34.1	26	17.7
2579	4.79	-17.9	18.6	0.0	89.5	17.5	13.5	19.3	48.9	37	24.3
2748	4.86	-11.0	29.0	0.3	54.6	27.4	7.6	19.8	25.8	25	18.6
2961	4.90	-13.4	286.5	0.2	51.2	245.8	7.4	16.3	19.4	35	65.6

Table 5—Electrofishing information for streams near Longdale Furnace, VA

Stream	Date	SpDiv	BKT	RBT	BKD	FAD	MTS	TOS
Blue Suck	19860724	6	0	0	14	6	2	2
Blue Suck	19950731	5	0	0	10	10	0	4
Downy	19790131	3	1	0	9	0	2	0
Downy	19860724	4	3	0	25	0	2	2
Downy	19950731	4	3	0	40	1	0	4
NBSC	19760915	4	4	0	26	0	3	4
NBSC	19950731	3	13	0	12	0	0	2
Simpson	19790208	3	0	0	29	0	9	2
Simpson	19790808	9	0	7	10	4	0	4
Simpson	19850827	10	4	26	281	19	?	243
Simpson	19850828	19	0	39	128	?	?	?
Simpson	19950731	3	24	0	19	0	0	4
Simpson-l	20010710	12	0	0	0	0	16	3
Simpson-m	20010711	9	0	0	0	0	12	3
Simpson-u	20060811	9	2	48	13	1	3	7

Dates are prov ded as yearmonthday, SpD v nd cates the tota number of d fferent fish spec es found for a ocat on and numbers of fish of se ected spec es (a ages) found: BKT=brook trout, RBT=ra nbow trout, BKD=b acknose dace, FAD=fanta darter, MTS=mott ed scu p n, TOS=torrent sucker (F nk 2012).

Note: quest on marks nd cate that spec es dent ficat on and numbers are uncerta n.

Table 6—Comparison of North Branch Simpson Creek and Simpson Creek water chemistry

Site	pH	ANC	Ca	Mg	Cond	SO4	Na	Cl
NBSC	6.48	24.8	82.3	48.4	20	72.7	15.8	18.9
SC	7.17	351.1	759.1	130.8	106	180.3	215.5	190.5

Note: samp es were co ected May 11, 2012 about 200 feet upstream of confluence. Ca c um, magnes um, and ANC are produced from carbonate d sso ut on; conduct v ty s due to tota on c compos t on; and su fate s from pyr te and ac d ra n. NaC s most ke y from road sa t used on SR 850 and I-64. Un ts are same as tab e 4.

Table 7—Dates and times of sample collection from North Branch Simpson Creek (NBSC) and Downy Branch (DB) taken for the present study

Stream	Date	Time	Stream	Date	Time
NBSC	5/8/2012	930	DB	5/8/2012	1015
NBSC	5/9/2012	815	DB	5/9/2012	930
NBSC	5/9/2012	1600	DB	5/9/2012	1510
NBSC	5/10/2012	940	DB	5/10/2012	910
NBSC	5/11/2012	1000	DB	5/11/2012	1130
NBSC	5/15/2012	915	DB	5/15/2012	940
NBSC	5/15/2012	1515	DB	5/15/2012	1435
NBSC	5/16/2012	1100	DB	5/16/2012	1020
NBSC	5/22/2012	930	DB	5/22/2012	910
NBSC	5/25/2012	850	DB	5/25/2012	820
NBSC	5/30/2012	1000	DB	5/30/2012	920
NBSC	7/9/2012	1115	DB	7/9/2012	1145
NBSC	9/18/2012	1440	DB	9/18/2012	1400
NBSC	9/19/2012	830	DB	9/19/2012	900
NBSC	9/20/2012	1500			

Note: date s mon/day/yr; t me s m tary.

Table 8—Rainfall recorded at North Mountain and Warm Spring Mountain IFLOW gauges

Date	Time	North Mountain	Warm Springs
	military	*inches*	*inches*
5/8/2012	930	0.04	0.00
5/9/2012	815	0.36	0.68
5/9/2012	1600	0.60	0.76
5/10/2012	940	0.16	0.12
5/11/2012	1000	0.00	0.00
5/15/2012	915	1.32	0.40
5/15/2012	1515	0.80	0.08
5/16/2012	1100	0.00	0.00
5/22/2012	930	0.20	0.00
5/25/2012	850	0.04	0.00
5/30/2012	1000	0.68	0.40
7/9/2012	1115	0.44	0.16
9/18/2012	1440	0.04	1.68
9/19/2012	830	0.08	1.28
9/20/2012	1500	0.08	0.00

Source: http://72.66.190.197/V rg n a IFLOWS/. [Date accessed 1/22/2013].

Table 9—Virginia Trout Stream Sensitivity Study (VTSSS) values for the period 1987-2010 and post-fire values for NBSC: comparison of average and sample standard deviation for water chemistry parameters

Parameter	April/July	Post-Fire	$P < 0.05$
pH	6.21 ± 0.15	6.18 ± 0.47	No
ANC (bicarbonate)	24.5 ± 7.5	19.5 ± 6.0	No
Conductivity	15.7 ± 1.0	23.3 ± 5.0	Yes
Sulfate	74.7 ± 9.3	76.3 ± 6.9	No
Chloride	17.5 ± 1.7	18.3 ± 2.0	No
Calcium	60.9 ± 4.6	89.0 ± 12.5	Yes
Magnesium	35.9 ± 2.1	48.8 ± 2.5	Yes
Potassium	13.6 ± 1.6	13.8 ± 2.7	No
Sodium	14.5 ± 0.9	16.6 ± 2.8	No

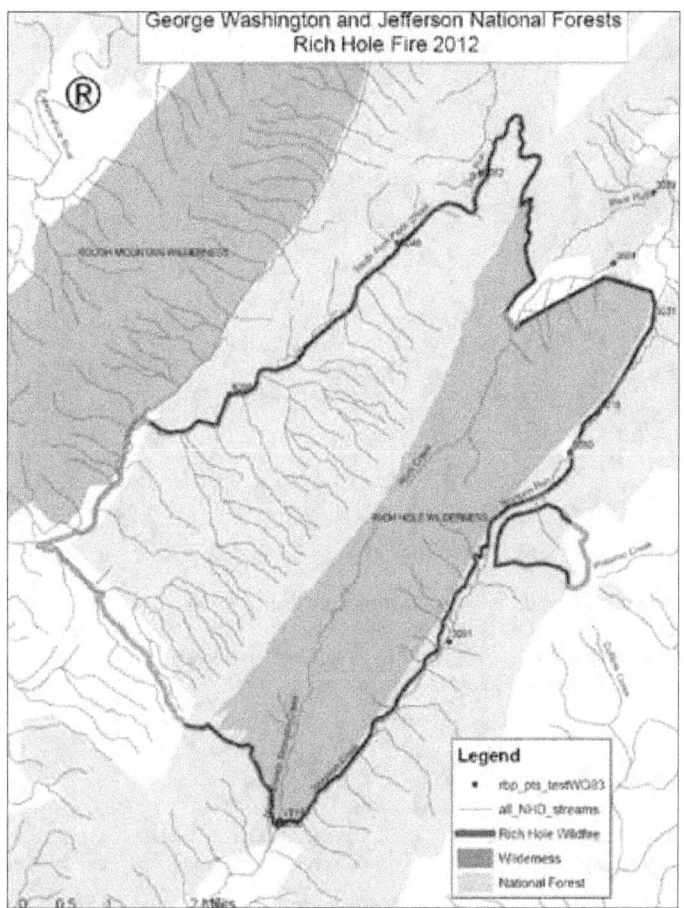

Figure 1—Map of 2012 Rich Hole fire. The 6000-acre fire burned within the areas bounded by bold lines. North Branch Simpson Creek VTSSS sampling location VT16 is located at the southern boundary of the fire. Downy Branch is located south of the mapped area. Map was provided by staff of the Forest Service, George Washington and Jefferson National Forests.

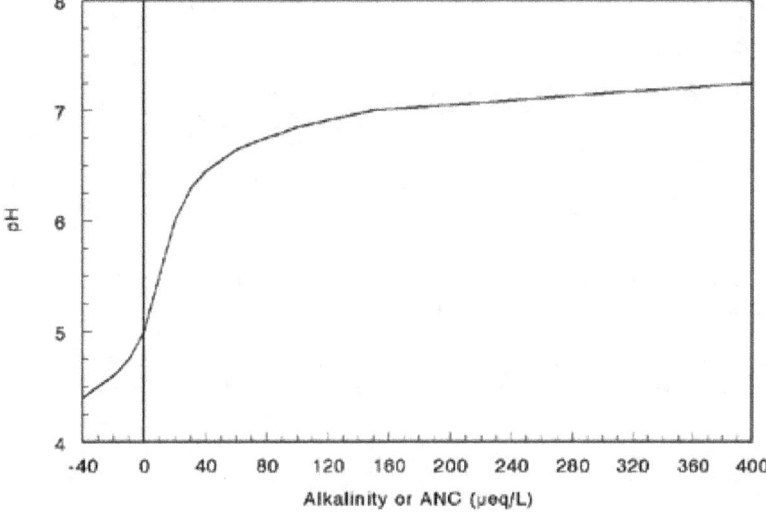

Figure 2—Plot of observed pH values for streams of varying ANC. Since ANC is mathematically determined from a two-endpoint titration method, it is possible for low pH streams (pH < 5.5) to have a negative value.

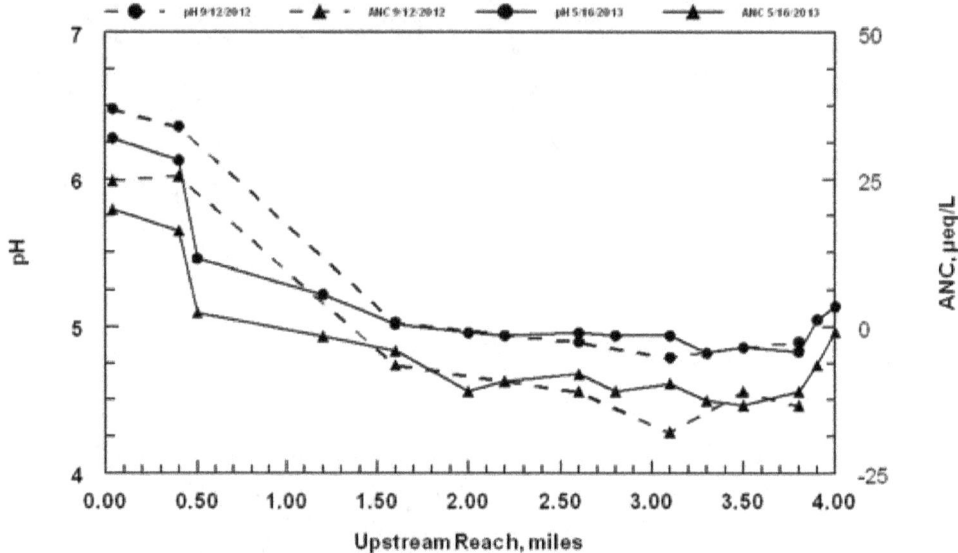

Figure 3—Observed pH and ANC values versus upstream stream distance for two synoptic sample collections for NBSC. The data points are connected for clarity of display and interpretation. Circle and triangle markings represent pH and ANC values, respectively. Broken and solid lines represent September 2012 and May 2013 values, respective

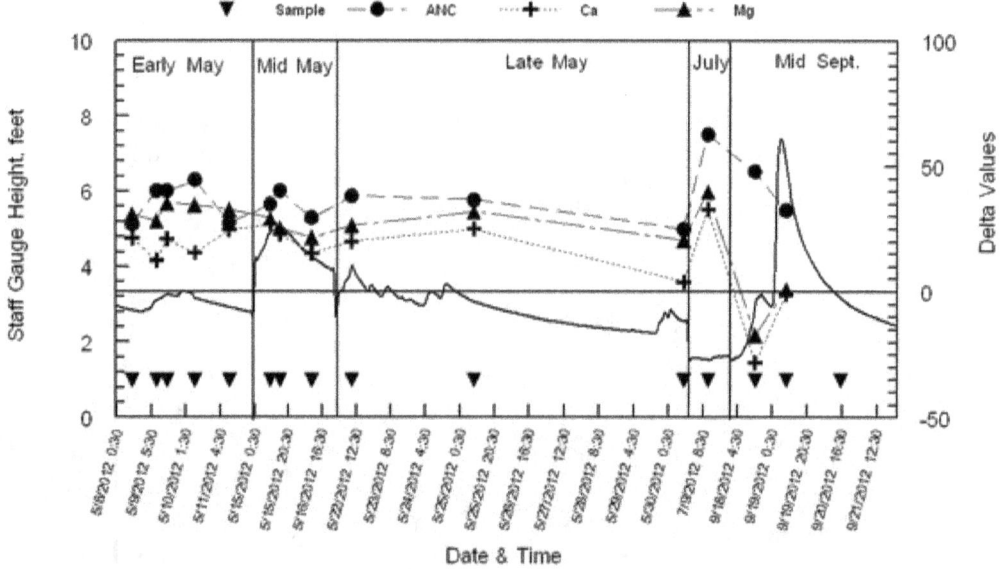

Figure 4—USGS staff gauge height for Cowpasture River and delta values for ANC, calcium, and magnesium for Downy Branch–North Branch Simpson Creek versus time for the project period. The downward triangles mark the dates of sample collection from North Branch Simpson Creek. Delta points are connected for clarity. Timeline is discontinuous. Discharge data obtained for USGS 02016000: http://waterdata.usgs.gov/va/nwis/uv/?site_no=02016000&PARAmeter_cd=00065,00060,62620,00062. [Date accessed: 2/1/2013].

Tools for
Fire Management

[Extended Abstract]

LANDFIRE IN THE APPALACHIANS

James L. Smith, Randy Swaty, Kori Blankenship, Sarah Hagen, and Jeannie Patton[1]

CONTEXT OF THE LANDFIRE PROGRAM

LANDFIRE is approaching its' 10th birthday, and moving forward. A partnership between the U.S. Department of the Interior; the Forest Service, U.S. Department of Agriculture; and The Nature Conservancy, LANDFIRE delivered national spatial data sets representing conditions in 2000, 2008, and 2010, and the first comprehensive descriptions of all major ecosystems in the United States. The impetus of the LANDFIRE Program (formerly the LANDFIRE Project) was to provide foundational information that could support regional and national fire and natural resource management planning programs, such as Fire Programs Analysis (FPA), and the Hazardous Fuels Prioritization and Application System (HFPAS). However, LANDFIRE as it exists today is more than originally envisioned and may serve as complementary or supplementary information for more local applications as well.

WHY SHOULD YOU BE INTERESTED IN LANDFIRE?

Given the context above, what makes LANDFIRE unique? There are five key characteristics of the LANDFIRE program that may make it useful and interesting to anyone involved in natural resource management and wildland fire planning, namely:

- LANDFIRE is comprehensive: every acre in the United States, including Alaska, Hawai'i and the island territories, is included in the product suite, regardless of ownership.

- LANDFIRE is consistent: every attempt was made to treat every acre consistently to allow for regional comparisons, and only procedural changes that improved the usability of the product suite were made over time between the various temporal versions.

- LANDFIRE products are internally compatible: the vegetation models match the BpS product; all tools work with all relevant spatial layers in all versions; all layers 'match' spatially and thematically. LANDFIRE products are ready-to-use from the moment you receive them.

- LANDFIRE delivers many one-of-a-kind products: LANDFIRE produces more than 20, 30-meter raster data layers. Many of these products are unique, such as Pre-European settlement vegetation maps, historic mean fire return intervals, and annual and compiled disturbance layers. In addition, LANDFIRE created and made available quantitative, dynamic vegetation models for every major ecological system in the United States. Where else can you obtain this type of information?

- LANDFIRE is regularly updated: the original version of LANDFIRE represented landscape conditions circa 2001, but vegetation and fuels layers have been updated and delivered twice since, once representing conditions in 2008 and once in 2010. LANDFIRE 2012 production is underway.

WHAT SHOULD YOU REMEMBER AS YOU CONSIDER USING LANDFIRE PRODUCTS?

All users should remember that LANDFIRE products were designed to be used for very large landscape-level, regional or national scale analyses. LANDFIRE may be used to complement or supplement local data, but should not be assumed to represent local conditions faithfully as delivered, i.e., "out-of-the-box." The applicability of LANDFIRE data at the local level will depend on which products will be used, the specific application, and the geography of interest. It requires local review to determine the usability of LANDFIRE spatial products

[1]James L. Smith, TNC LANDFIRE Project Lead, The Nature Conservancy, Jacksonville, FL 32259

Randy Swaty, Ecologist, The Nature Conservancy, Marquette, MI 49855

Kori Blankenship, Fire Ecologist, The Nature Conservancy, Bend, OR 97701

Sarah Hagen, Spatial Ecologist, The Nature Conservancy, Minneapolis, MN 55415

Jeannie Patton, Communications Coordinator, The Nature Conservancy, Boulder, CO 80302

Citation for proceedings: Waldrop, Thomas A., ed. 2014. Proceedings, Wildland Fire in the Appalachians: Discussions among Managers and Scientists. Gen. Tech. Rep. SRS-199. Asheville, NC: U.S. Department of Agriculture Forest Service, Southern Research Station. 208 p.

and models, and while it is possible that unedited LANDFIRE spatial data and models will be useful as-is, that should NOT be the user's expectation. All data, regardless of its source, should be reviewed prior to acceptance and use.

LANDFIRE PERFORMANCE AND APPLICATION IN THE APPALACHIANS

A variety of LANDFIRE Program products have been used in the Appalachian region. A few highlights and links to learn more are presented below. Note that these tidbits of information are based upon personal conversations or investigations of all types—informal, formal, first-hand, second-hand, and reviewing reports. However, we endeavor to pass along any information we think is reliable and potentially of interest to our user community.

- According to some local users, LANDFIRE Existing Vegetation Type (EVT) map accuracy is not sufficient at smaller scales (small geographies). This is disappointing, but it is not unexpected given the design criteria (regional/national scope) for LANDFIRE, and the difficulty of mapping the rather complex hardwood mixtures ubiquitous in the mountains. Also, users should understand that LANDFIRE spatial products are not post-processed to improve their visual appeal—what you see is the raw output of a classification algorithm.

- A good alternative to LANDFIRE EVT may be the Terrestrial Habitat Map created by The Nature Conservancy Eastern Region Science Team. While not perfect (and there have been some legend issues with this product as well), this map has been relatively well received in its coverage area.

- An analysis in the Southern Blue Ridge landscape by Steve Simon indicated that LANDFIRE mapped too much area as "fire dependent" in the BioPhysical Settings (pre-European Settlement vegetation) layer. For instance, fire dependency went too far downslope into the "Coves" according to Simon.

- The LANDFIRE Ecological System legend created some problems in the Appalachian region; for instance, there is only one type of "Cove" in the LANDFIRE BpS and EVT layers. There were some additional omissions as well, and some overlaps between ecological systems that did not exactly match local expectations.

- Eastern West Virginia was mapped 'too mesophytic' in the EVT layer. We remember hearing about this issue from at least one individual, but could not find any specific backup documentation or additional information.

- Where it has been investigated and used, the Percent Forest Cover spatial layer has held up well. It shows the right kind of landscape variation, but does tend to miss very small openings (individual tree gaps, for instance). Typically, large disturbances and small anthropogenic disturbances are visible and relatively well mapped if the time since disturbance is not too great.

- A stakeholder group involved with the Cherokee National Forest North District localized LANDFIRE National Dynamics Vegetation models to develop relevant reference conditions to support local planning. The models were also used with current vegetation condition data developed from a combination of local inventory data and LF2008 Existing Forest Cover to evaluate the costs and benefits of management activities.

- The TNC LANDFIRE Team is currently supporting a Central Appalachians Assessment facilitated by The Nature Conservancy in Virginia and the National Forests of Virginia, primarily utilizing LANDFIRE quantitative vegetation models at this time.

- At a meeting in Asheville, NC, a group of interested individuals modified LANDFIRE vegetation models to develop relevant reference conditions for the important ecosystems in the Pisgah/Nantahala National Forest region. These models, coupled with current vegetation condition information derived from LIDAR, were used in an ecosystem assessment led by Josh Kelly, estern North Carolina Alliance.

- The TNC LANDFIRE Team is currently working with the National Forests of Georgia and partners in the Warwoman landscape in Northeast Georgia to develop local reference conditions for the major ecosystems extant in that watershed.

- The LANDFIRE Program and The Nature Conservancy supported the development of local information in the Southern Blue Ridge region of North Carolina and the Copper Creek watershed in North Georgia.

Check out the LANDFIRE Web Hosted Applications Map for more information on how LANDFIRE has been used across the Nation.

WHERE IS LANDFIRE GOING?

- LANDFIRE vegetation and fuels products updated to represent conditions at the end of CY2010 are available (LF 2010).

- LF2012 production is underway, and incremental delivery is expected to begin in the summer of 2014. We expect to complete all production and deliveries by 1Q of 2015. The Appalachian region will likely be delivered near the end of CY2014 or early CY2015.

- LANDFIRE is considering a complete remap of some spatial layers in the future, either before or after a 2014 update depending on budgets and user needs.

- Finally, LANDFIRE and other national-scale mapping programs are investigating their joint interests and how we can work together to be more effective and efficient. For instance, a formal MOU between GAP and LANDFIRE has been approved.

WHAT CAN YOU DO?

The LANDFIRE user community plays a key role in the future of LANDFIRE, especially helping the program improve the usability of its products. Your investment should be minimal, with incredible potential returns. We are not asking for anything you don't already have or know, just that you provide what you have to us!

- The LANDFIRE update process is driven by disturbance information, be they human-caused or natural. Any disturbance information, called Events" by LANDFIRE, are used in the LANDFIRE update/ change detection process. More information is available on the LANDFIRE program Web site www. landfire.gov.

- LANDFIRE will use geo-referenced vegetation plots to support a future remapping process or to assess the accuracy of current products. Quality field data are critical to LANDFIRE, so consider providing what you have following the guidelines available on the program Web site.

- Tell us what you learn or see when you review or use LANDFIRE Program products—good and bad. Any information is appreciated, but the more specific the more useful it is to us. What did you see and where did you see it? How are you using LANDFIRE Program products? We are working to create an online feedback capability, which will be announced when available. Communicate with LANDFIRE using helpdesk@ landfire.gov for now, or contact a LANDFIRE team member.

- Finally, as you consider using LANDFIRE, think deeply about what you really need (not just what you would like to have), and remember that LANDFIRE is a national/regional scale product suite by design. The LANDFIRE Team will help you determine if/how our program products can be used in your situation. You should not assume they will or will not.

TAKE HOME MESSAGES

LANDFIRE is in the business of providing data and information to the fire, resource management, and conservation communities. This is a difficult 'row to hoe'

because building data sets for other people and programs is like trying to raise their children—you never do it like they would. While LANDFIRE spatial data and models are not perfect, LANDFIRE has proven its worth across the country for regional- or landscape-scale application and can often support more local applications following review and local adjustment. The LANDFIRE Program has evolved the product suite and procedural processes to better meet user requirements—both fire and non-fire. Users can contribute to this process, and indeed enable it, by providing geo-referenced vegetation plots, spatial information on man-made or natural disturbance events, and by communicating what they see and learn to the LANDFIRE Program. Visit the Contribute Data Section on the program Web site (see below) and send us a message at helpdesk@landfire.gov.

ACKNOWLEDGMENTS

The TNC LANDFIRE Team would like to acknowledge our wonderful partners, U.S. Forest Service Fire and Aviation Management, Missoula Fire Science Laboratory (Rocky Mountain Research Station), DOI Office of Wildland Fire Fire Coordination, and the U.S. Geological Survey EROS Center. This work was conducted under Cooperative Agreement 10-CA-11132543-054.

LINKS TO EXPLORE

- Explore real applications of LANDFIRE Program products across the country on the Web Hosted Applications Map! (WHAM!). Full link: maps.tnc.org/ landfire/

- Watch LANDFIRE presentation, learn new methods and tools, and understand LANDFIRE products by viewing videos on our YouTube channel. Full link: www.youtube.com/user/landfirevideo?feature=results_ main

- Join the LANDFIRE discussion community on our Twitter site. Full link: twitter.com/nature_LANDFIRE

- Obtain more details about the LANDFIRE Program and access products at the official program Web site. Full link: www.landfire.gov

- Discover new tools that can use LANDFIRE data developed by the Wildland Fire RD&A team. Full link: www.niftt.gov

- Review additional LANDFIRE application and find support materials on The Conservation Gateway. Full link: www.conservationgateway.org (search for LANDFIRE)

MAPPING FIRE REGIMES FROM DATA YOU MAY ALREADY HAVE: ASSESSING LANDFIRE FIRE REGIME MAPS USING LOCAL PRODUCTS

Melissa A. Thomas-Van Gundy[1]

Abstract—LANDFIRE maps of fire regime groups are frequently used by land managers to help plan and execute prescribed burns for ecosystem restoration. Since LANDFIRE maps are generally applicable at coarse scales, questions often arise regarding their utility and accuracy. Here, the two recently published products from West Virginia, a rule-based and a witness tree-based model, are compared to LANDFIRE fire regime groups. A cell-by-cell comparison of fire regime groups revealed a 56-percent correspondence between the rule-based map and LANDFIRE and a 61-percent correspondence with the witness tree-based map and LANDFIRE. All three maps assign the same fire regime group on about 45 percent of the study area with most of the agreement in wetter areas where fire regime group V predominates. Subsectional boundary differences are distinct in the LANDFIRE map compared to the local products which placed a greater emphasis on forest composition. The intent of this work was to describe alternative means of estimating fire regime groups where LANDFIRE products may not represent local conditions.

INTRODUCTION

The determination of fire regime and condition class (FRCC) on federally owned land is needed for prescribed fire and wildland fire management. Determining fire regimes for large areas, particularly natural or historic fire regimes can be difficult without fire-scar or dendrochronogical records from old-growth forests or sediment charcoal from paleoecological sites. Few old-growth stands remain in eastern forests, and while there is success in establishing disturbance regimes at specific locations (Abrams and others 1995, Aldrich and others 2010, Cutter and Guyette 1994, Guyette and others 2002, Guyette and others 2006a, Schuler and McClain 2003, Shumway and others 2001), determining fire histories over a large area remains difficult. Even with a fire-scar record, fires at both ends of the severity spectrum may be missed as low-intensity fires may not damage the cambium of mature trees (McEwan and others 2007) and high-severity fires, by definition, remove most existing trees. When direct measures are unavailable, other methods can be used to infer historical fire, including paleoecology, witness tree studies, historical documents, and ethnographic records (Egan and Howell 2001, Ruffner 2006).

Recently, large-scale efforts to map fire regimes have been made incorporating fire ecology of tree species to assign fire regimes (Nowacki and Abrams 2008), fire scars from dendrochronology studies (Guyette and others 2006b), and climate and chemistry (Guyette and others 2012). Early nation-wide maps incorporated many lines of evidence to map the role of fire in forested ecosystems. Frost (1998) compiled fire histories from across the contiguous United States and, combined with landform characteristics, created a map of pre-European settlement fire regimes. Where fire history studies were lacking, Frost (1998) used additional lines of evidence to infer fire regimes including charcoal deposits, oral histories, tree species in old land surveys, presence of fire-adapted vegetation, vegetation response to reintroduced fire, and vegetation responses to fire exclusion. Using current and potential vegetation, ecological regions, and expert opinion Schmidt and others (2002) mapped historical natural fire regimes for the contiguous United States at a coarse resolution. The authors stressed that this was not a reconstruction of exact historical conditions, but represented typical fire frequencies expected in the absence of fire suppression (Schmidt and others 2002). Unfortunately, the fine-scale detail required by fire ecologists, land managers, and conservationists for field application was lacking in these nation-wide efforts.

To help identify areas where prescribed burning is appropriate for restoration purposes, two local mapping products were created for the Monongahela National Forest. The first was a rule-based map (Thomas-Van Gundy and others 2007), which applied a simple weighted-averaging technique of fire-adapted scores to polygon data in a GIS. The resultant map of fire-adapted vegetation was directly converted to a fire regime group map (see figs. 5 and 7 of Thomas-Van Gundy and others 2007). The second was a witness tree-based map that converted point-based witness trees from early land surveys into a continuous surface depicting percentage of pyrophilic species (Thomas-Van Gundy and Nowacki 2013). The pyrophilic percentage map was converted

[1]Melissa A. Thomas-Van Gundy, Research Forester, USDA Forest Service, Northern Research Station, Parsons, WV 26241

Citation for proceedings: Waldrop, Thomas A., ed. 2014. Proceedings, Wildland Fire in the Appalachians: Discussions among Managers and Scientists. Gen. Tech. Rep. SRS-199. Asheville, NC: U.S. Department of Agriculture Forest Service, Southern Research Station. 208 p.

to a fire-adapted vegetation map for comparison with the rule-based map, but not into a fire regime group map; that conversion will be made in this paper. In this paper, fire regime groups derived from both mapping products will be compared to LANDFIRE fire regime groups for assessment and comparison. LANDFIRE fire regime groups and other products are a consistent and scientifically reliable set of mapped fire and vegetation characteristics to be used for national, regional, and sub-regional planning. LANDFIRE is not meant to replace local data; however, for this analysis it is being used as a comparison for the locally-derived fire regime groups created with different methods.

STUDY AREA

Fire-adapted vegetation was mapped for the Monongahela National Forest (MNF) (fig. 1). The proclamation boundary of the MNF covers about 1.7 million acres in east-central West Virginia, with national forest land making up about 919,000 acres. The study area includes portions of the Allegheny Mountains and the Northern Ridge and Valley (Cleland and others 2005), two ecological sections with distinct geomorphologies and climates.

The Allegheny Mountains Section has a wet and cool climate, with 39 to 54 inches of precipitation per year (about 20 percent as snow; 30 percent at higher elevations), an annual average temperature of 46 to 52 °F, an average annual maximum temperature of 58 to 63 °F, an average annual minimum temperature of 36 to 39 °F, and a growing season of 126 to 155 days in the study area (Cleland and others 2005). The vegetation of the Allegheny Mountains is strongly influenced by elevation, forming four broad zones: oak, mixed mesophytic, northern hardwoods, and red spruce. The lowest elevations (valleys and foothills) are dominated by oaks (*Quercus* spp.), with sycamore (*Platanus occidentalis*), river birch (*Betula nigra*), and various mesophytes along riparian corridors and in floodplains. Upslope, the vegetation transitions into mixed mesophytic forests, which include yellow-poplar (*Liriodendron tulipifera*), basswood (*Tilia americana*), white ash (*Fraxinus americana*), sugar maple (*Acer saccharum*), and northern red oak (*Quercus rubra*). The northern hardwood group is found on upper slopes and ridge tops and features sugar maple, yellow birch (*Betula alleghaniensis*), American beech (*Fagus grandifolia*), eastern hemlock (*Tsuga canadensis*), and black cherry (*Prunus serotina*). Red spruce (*Picea rubens*) forests occur at the highest elevations (above ~3,000 feet), often mixing with northern hardwoods.

Much of the Northern Ridge and Valley Section lies in the rain shadow of the Allegheny Mountains and supports vegetation reflective of drier conditions (Abrams and McCay 1996, McCay and others 1997). Annual precipitation ranges from 39 to 42 inches (Cleland and others 2005). Annual temperature ranges from 50 to 54 °F, with an average annual maximum temperature of 63 to 66 °F, an average annual minimum temperature of 39 to 41 °F, and the growing season ranges from 149 to 170 days (Cleland and others 2005). In general, northern red oak and white oak (*Quercus alba*) occur on productive mesic sites, often intermixed with eastern white pine (*Pinus strobus*) on side slopes. Increases in scarlet (*Q. coccinea*) and black oak (*Q. velutina*) occur on progressively drier sites. On the driest sites, pitch (*P. rigida*), Table Mountain (*P. pungens*), or Virginia (*P. virginiana*) pines predominate, either in pure stands or mixed with scrub oak (*Q. ilicifolia*) or other oak species.

METHODS

A map of fire-adapted vegetation was created from multiple GIS-based data sources through assigning fire-adapted scores to attributes and calculating a weighted average (for details see: Thomas-Van Gundy and others 2007). Data input included existing vegetation (forest type), potential natural vegetation (primary and secondary plant associations as separate inputs), and landtype association (a mid-level ecological hierarchical unit, essentially giving the biophysical setting). For each dataset, existing literature on species-fire relationships were reviewed to assign a fire adapted score of 1 (most adapted) to 5 (least adapted) to each forest type, plant association, and landtype association. If a fire relationship was unknown or unclear, a 5 was assigned. The data inputs were assigned weights for the calculation of an average fire-adapted score with primary potential vegetation and current vegetation weighted equally and higher than landtype association and secondary plant associations. Fire-adapted scores were converted to standardized fire regime groups (FRGs) as used in LANDFIRE (Barrett and others 2010; see table 1 for definitions) by expert opinion. Considering the dominant vegetation, annual rainfall, and elevation range of the study area, the existence of fire regime group II (stand replacement fires with a return interval of 0-35 years) was unlikely. The fire regime assignments were; fire adaptation score of 2 = FRG I, fire adapted score of 3 = FGR III, fire adapted score of 1 = FRG IV, and fire adapted scores of 4 and 5 = FRG V.

The creation of a map of fire-adapted vegetation from witness tree data is documented in Thomas-Van Gundy and Nowacki (2013). Briefly, the tree species listed in early deeds from the MNF (Thomas-Van Gundy and Strager 2012) were categorized as pyrophilic or pyrophobic based on current literature and assuming recurring fire of low to moderate intensity. At each deed corner, this categorization was used to calculate a percent pyrophilic species value. These values were interpolated between points through ordinary kriging to create a continuous surface. Maps were created displaying the percentage of pyrophilic species in classes, and these classes were translated into fire-adapted scores used in the previous fire-adapted vegetation map.

The percentage pyrophilic values were simply binned by 20-percent classes with 0-20 percent = fire adapted score of 5, 20-40 percent = fire adapted score of 4, 40-60 percent = fire adapted score of 3, 60-80 percent = fire adapted score of 2, and 80-100 percent = fire adapted score of 1. Since FRGs were not approximated from the witness tree data in the 2013 publication, fire-adapted scores similar to the methods used in the rule-based map were assigned to percent pyrophilic classes and assigned an FRG. With further consideration of the standard FRGs and considering characteristics of the study area such as the dominant forested conditions, main tree species, annual rainfall, and elevation range, I do not believe FRGs II and IV (stand replacement fires with a return intervals of 0-35 and 35-200 years, respectively) are appropriate for the study area at the scale of this analysis. Therefore, in this analysis, fire-adapted scores of 1 and 2 (60-100 percent pyrophilic) were assigned to FRG I, score of 3 (40-60 percent pyrophilic) was assigned to FGR III, and scores of 4 and 5 (0-40 percent pyrophilic) were assigned to FRG V.

With these FRG assignments, the rule-based and witness tree-based maps were compared to the most recent LANDFIRE FRG map (LANDFIRE 2013). The locally derived maps were converted to ~98-foot (30-m) grids for these comparisons. All maps were compared on a cell-by-cell basis in ArcMap 10 to spatially display and calculate FRG departure. All three maps were also compared directly in ArcMap 10 through calculating the number of unique values (variety) for fire regime group between the three maps for each cell.

RESULTS

The three estimates of FRG (table 1; figs. 2a, 2b, and 3a) are very different and it is not surprising that differences were found. The cell-by-cell comparison of the rule-based map and LANDFIRE shows that the two versions of FRGs agree exactly on about 57 percent of the area (table 2; fig. 2c). Most of the departures (about 36 percent of the area) were positive 2 or 4 meaning the rule-based map FRGs were greater than LANDFIRE; about 8 percent of the area was in departures of negative 2 or 4.

Creating FRGs from the witness tree-based map resulted in about 30 percent of the study area classified as FR I,

about 14 percent as FR III, and about 56 percent as FR V (table 1, fig. 3a). The fire regime groups inferred from the witness tree data matched LANDFIRE on about 61 percent of the area (table 2). Departures from LANDFIRE from the witness tree-based map were more evenly distributed above and below zero (compared to departures between LANDFIRE and the rule-based map) with about 22 percent of the area with a difference of positive 2 or 4 and about 17 percent in negative 2 or 4 differences.

The grids resulting from these calculations spatially depict where the agreements and departures occur (figs. 2c and 3c). All three versions of FRGs for the study area identify the higher elevations in the mountainous center of the study area as an area of low fire frequency. The influence of subsection boundaries (Cleland and others 2005) is more obvious in the LANDFIRE estimation of FRG (fig. 2b) and is a main contributor to departures from the two locally-derived maps. Also, the influence of river corridors is more defined in the LANDFIRE FRGs than either the rule-based or witness-tree based maps.

The simultaneous comparison of the three maps shows that all three maps agree on FRG assignments on about 45 percent of the study area, and mostly agree on the location of FRG V (38 percent; table 3). Two of the three maps agree on about 46 percent of the study area and areas of no agreement make up only 9 percent of the study area. When viewed spatially, with FRG estimations for the witness tree-based map as background (fig. 4), all three maps have greatest agreement in areas where fire is not likely to be used as management tool or be re-introduced as a disturbance (FRG V, table 3). These areas are the highest elevations and receive higher inputs of precipitation relative to other parts of the MNF.

DISCUSSION

In creating the FRG map from witness tree data, the cut-off values of percent pyrophilic witness tree species were subjectively set based on knowledge of the general ecology of the study area. Using 0-40 percent pyrophilic species to create the FRG V group may have included areas where fire may have occurred more frequently than the national definition would suggest. Other break-point values were considered; however, to remain consistent with published comparisons between the rule-based and witness tree-based maps (Thomas-Van Gundy and Nowacki 2013), the break points were retained. This also demonstrates the difficulty in applying a nation-wide standard. The witness tree data could easily be used without conversion to FRGs to aid managers in planning and designing projects.

The LANDFIRE FRGs were mapped similarly to the methods of Schmidt and others (2002), incorporating existing and potential vegetation and the biophysical setting. The rule-based mapping effort (Thomas-Van Gundy and others 2007) attempted to mirror the methods of Schmidt and others (2002); however, the choice of landtype association as the biophysical setting limited fire score inputs as binary, aiding in the resulting conservative nature of the inferred FRGs (fig. 2a). In the witness tree-based map, no biophysical setting was included. The distinct breaks between FRGs in LANDFIRE (especially the western edge of the MNF, fig. 2b) correspond to subsection boundaries (fig. 1). The potential natural vegetation for the Western Allegheny Mountains subsection is 38 percent mixed mesophytic, 35 percent northern hardwoods, and 27 percent Appalachian oak; and for the Eastern Coal Fields, 52 percent mixed mesophytic, 28 percent Appalachian oak, and 20 percent northern hardwoods (Cleland and others 2005). The representation of these two subsections within the MNF may not be typical of the subsection as a whole as these areas are at either the extreme northern (Eastern Coal Fields) or extreme southern (Western Allegheny Mountains) end of the larger subsection. For these reasons, the methods for estimating FRGs in LANDFIRE may have overstated the role of fire in these two subsections. However, the two locally-derived FRG estimations may have understated the role of fire in these areas. The areas where either local estimate differs greatly from LANDFIRE are likely areas where more field-based information is needed.

Although LANDFIRE data are best suited for national, regional, and sub-regional questions, the FRGs from LANDFIRE are useful for comparison with locally-derived fire regimes since LANDFIRE data are consistent across boundaries and supported by science. While LANDFIRE products are not a substitute for local products, these inferred fire regime groups from fire-adapted vegetation are not a substitute for stand-level data but are useful for local planning and placing fire in a larger context. Although issues with witness tree data are known, for example they do not represent a random sample or a systematic sample, the witness tree-derived map appears to be an improvement and refinement over the rule-based map.

The mapped differences between the two locally-derived FRGs and LANDFIRE FRGs are a useful starting point for detailed, site-specific reviews for project planning. The methods described here are applicable to other landscapes and should be useful for others trying to define areas to restore fire-adapted vegetation. Managers should not limit themselves to one product—witness trees, historical records, potential natural vegetation mapping, fire scars, responses to prescribed fire—all can inform options for restoring fire as a disturbance regime.

ACKNOWLEDGMENTS

I thank John Kabrick and Greg Nowacki for technical reviews of the manuscript.

LITERATURE CITED

Abrams, M.D.; McCay, D.M. 1996. Vegetation-site relationships of witness trees (1780-1856) in the presettlement forests of eastern West Virginia. Canadian Journal of Forest Research. 26: 217-224.

Abrams, M.D.; Orwig, D.A.; DeMeo; T.E. 1995. Dendroecological analysis of successional dynamics for a presettlement-origin white pine-mixed oak forest in the southern Appalachians, USA. Journal of Ecology. 83: 123-133.

Aldrich, S.R.; Lafon, C.W.; Grissino-Mayer, H.D. [and others]. 2010. Three centuries of fire in montane pine-oak stands on a temperate forest landscape. Applied Vegetation Science. 13: 36-46.

Barrett, S.; Havlina, D.; Jones, J. [and others]. 2010. Interagency fire regime condition class guidebook. Version 3.0 [Homepage of the Interagency Fire Regime Condition Class website, USDA Forest Service, U.S. Department of the Interior, and The Nature Conservancy]. [Online], Available: http://www.frcc.gov/. [Date accessed: February 5, 2014]

Cleland, D.T.; Freeouf, J.A.; Keys, J.E. [and others]. 2005. Ecological subregions: sections and subsections for the conterminous United States. Washington, DC: U.S. Department of Agriculture Forest Service. [Map, presentation scale 1:3,500,000; colored].

Cutter, B.E.; Guyette, R.P. 1994. Fire frequency on an oak-hickory ridgetop in the Missouri Ozarks. American Midland Naturalist. 132: 393-398.

Frost, C.C. 1998. Presettlement fire frequency regimes of the United States: a first approximation. In: Pruden, T.L.; Bennan, L.A., eds. Fire in ecosystem management, Tall Timbers Fire Ecology Conf. Proc. No. 20. Tall Timbers Research Station: 70-81.

Guyette, R.P.; Muzika, R.M.; Dey, D.C. 2002. Dynamics of an anthropogenic fire regime. Ecosystems. 5: 472-486.

Guyette, R.P.; Spetich, M.A.; Stambaugh, M.C. 2006a. Historic fire regime dynamics and forcing factors in the Boston Mountains, Arkansas, USA. Forest Ecology and Management. 234: 293-304.

Guyette, R.P.; Dey, D.C.; Stambaugh, M.C.; Muzika, R. 2006b. Fire scars reveal variability and dynamics of eastern fire regimes. In: Dickinson, M.B., ed., Fire in eastern oak forests: delivering science to land managers, proceedings of a conference; 2005 November 15-17; Columbus, OH. Gen. Tech. Rep. NRS-P-1. Newtown Square, PA; U.S. Department of Agriculture Forest Service, Northern Research Station: 20-39.

Guyette, R.P.; Stambaugh, M.C.; Dey, D.C.; Muzika, R. 2012. Predicting fire frequency with chemistry and climate. Ecosystems. 15: 322-335.

Egan, D.; Howell, E.A. 2001. The Historical Ecology Handbook. Washington, DC: Island Press. 469 p.

LANDFIRE. 2013. LANDFIRE Fire regime groups layer. (2013, June - last update). U.S. Department of the Interior, Geological Survey. [Online]. Available: http://landfire.cr.usgs.gov/viewer/. [Date accessed: 2013, September 17].

McCay, D.H.; Abrams, M.D.; DeMeo, T.E. 1997. Gradient analysis of secondary forests of eastern West Virginia. Journal of the Torrey Botanical Society. 124(2): 160-173.

McEwan, R.W.; Hutchinson, T.F.; Ford, R.D. 2007. An experimental evaluation of fire history reconstruction using dendrochronology in white oak (*Quercus alba*). Canadian Journal of Forest Research. 37: 806-816.

Nowacki, G.J.; Abrams, M.D. 2008. The demise of fire and "mesophication" of forests in the Eastern United States. BioScience. 58(2): 123-138.

Ruffner, C.M. 2006. Understanding the evidence for historical fire across eastern forests. In: Dickinson, M.B., ed. 2006. Fire in Eastern Oak Forests: Delivering Science to Land Managers, Proceedings of a Conference. Gen. Tech. Rep. NRS-P-1. Newtown Square, PA: U.S. Department of Agriculture Forest Service, Northern Research Station: 40-48.

Schmidt, K.M.; Menakis, J.P.; Hardy, C.C. [and others]. 2002. Development of coarse-scale spatial data for wildland fire and fuel management. Gen. Tech. Rep. RMRS-87. Fort Collins, CO: U.S. Department of Agriculture Forest Service, Rocky Mountain Research Station. 41 p. + CD.

Schuler, T.M.; McClain, W.R. 2003. Fire history of a ridge and valley oak forest. Res. Pap. NE-724. Newtown Square, PA: U.S. Department of Agriculture Forest Service, Northeastern Research Station. 9 p.

Shumway, D.L.; Abrams, M.D.; Ruffner, C.M. 2001. A 400-year history of fire and oak recruitment in an old-growth oak forest in western Maryland, USA. Canadian Journal of Forest Research. 31: 1437-1443.

Thomas-Van Gundy, M.A.; Strager, M.P. 2012. European settlement-era vegetation of the Monongahela National Forest, West Virginia. Gen. Tech. Rep. NRS-101. Newtown Square, PA: U.S. Department of Agriculture Forest Service, Northern Research Station. 39 p.

Thomas-Van Gundy, M.A.; Nowacki, G.J. 2013. The use of witness trees as pyro-indicators for mapping past fire. Forest Ecology and Management. 304: 333-344.

Thomas-Van Gundy, M.A.; Nowacki, G.J.; Schuler, T.M. 2007. Rule-based mapping of fire-adapted vegetation and fire regimes for the Monongahela National Forest. Gen. Tech. Rep. NRS-12. Newtown Square, PA: U.S. Department of Agriculture Forest Service, Northern Research Station. 24 p.

Table 1—Fire regime groups derived from the rule-based map and from the witness tree-based map of fire-adapted vegetation of Monongahela National Forest maps and from 2010 LANDFIRE data

Fire regime group	% total area rule-based map	% total area witness tree map	% total area LANDFIRE
I - ≤ 35 yr return interval, low & mixed severity	13.9	29.8	30.6
II - ≤ 35 yr return interval, stand replacement severity	0	0	0
III - 35-200 yr return interval, low & mixed severity	13.9	13.8	20.9
IV - 35-200 yr return interval, stand replacing severity	0.3	0	0.3
V - >200 yr return interval, any severity	71.9	56.4	48.1

Table 2—Results of cell-by-cell comparisons of the rule-based map and the witness tree-based map of fire regime groups to LANDFIRE

Difference from LANDFIRE	2007 version % total area	Witness tree version % total area
-4	1.3	3.8
-3	0.0	0.0
-2	6.2	13.0
-1	0.0	0.1
0	55.6	60.8
1	0.3	0.2
2	20.6	15.1
3	0.1	0.0
4	15.8	7.0

Table 3—Results (percent of study area) of three-way comparison of rule-based, witness tree-based, and LANDFIRE estimations of fire regime groups

Agreement	FRG I	FRG III	FRG V	Total
All three	7.0	0.5	38.0	45.4
Two maps	18.6	9.1	17.9	45.6
None	4.3	4.2	0.5	9.0

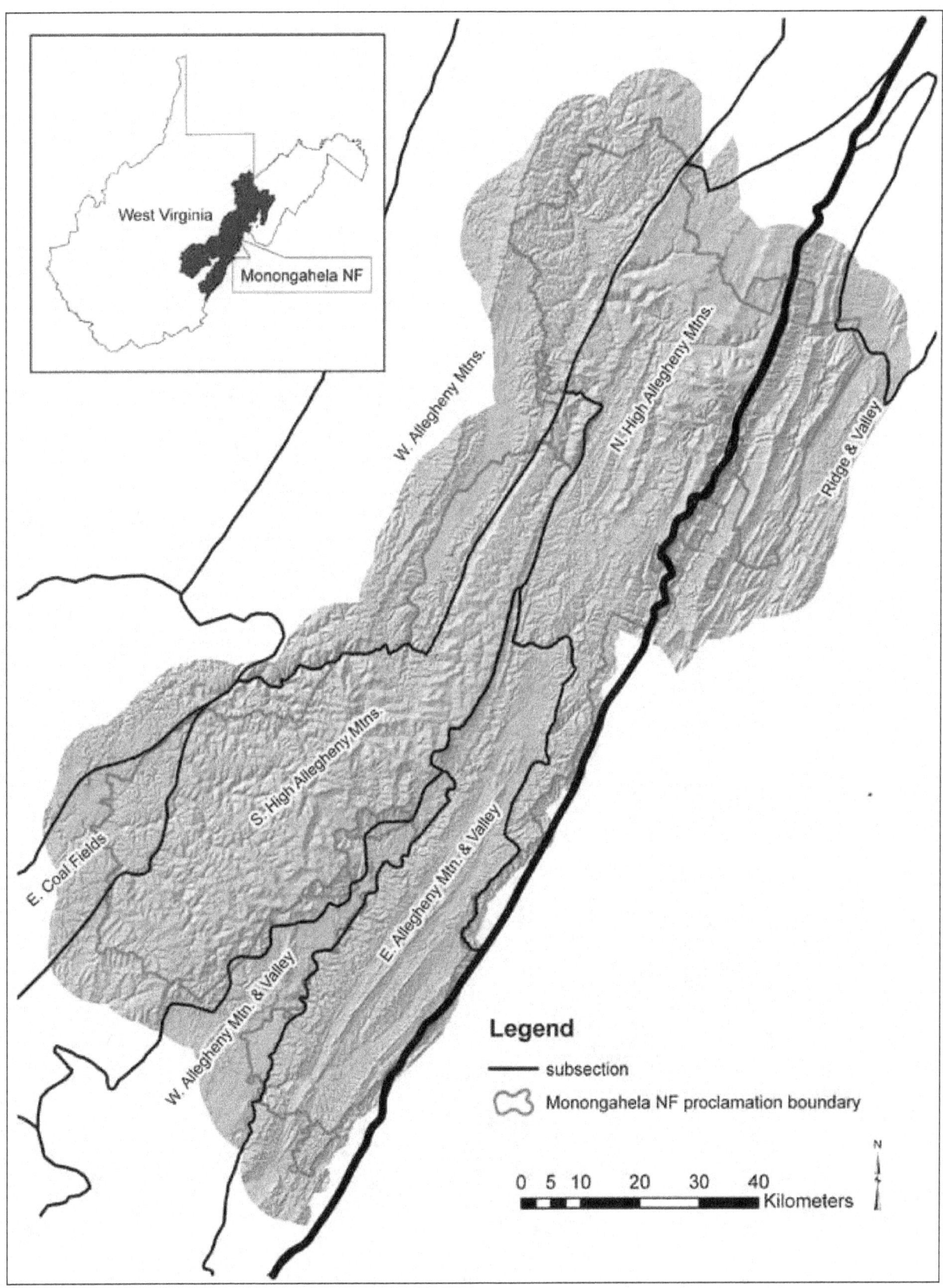

Figure 1—Study area; bold line is the boundary between Northern Ridge and Valley (east) and Allegheny Mountains (west).

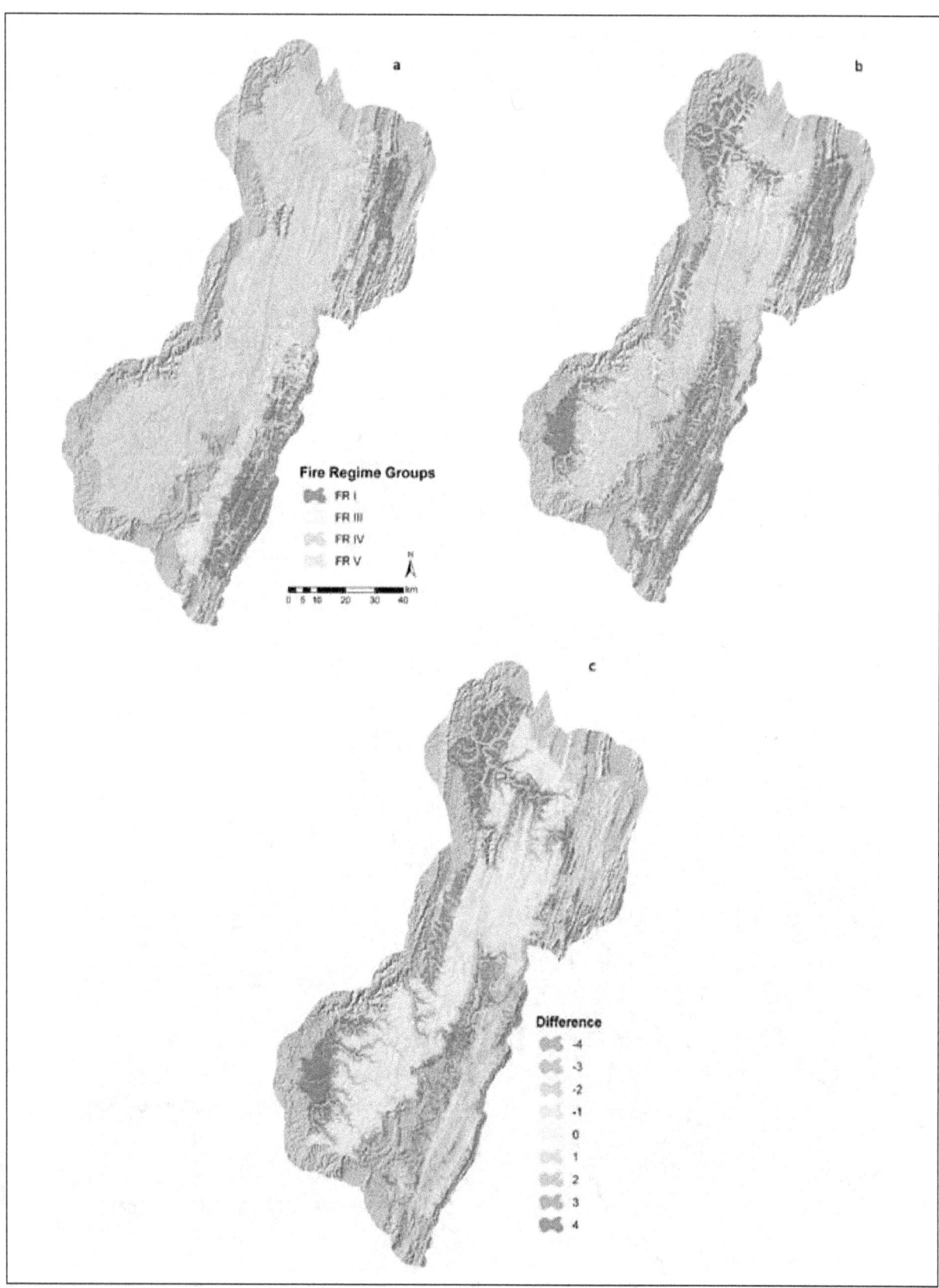

Figure 2—Fire regime group maps derived from (a) the rule-based map (Thomas-Van Gundy and others 2007), (b) LANDFIRE, and (c) the difference between them.

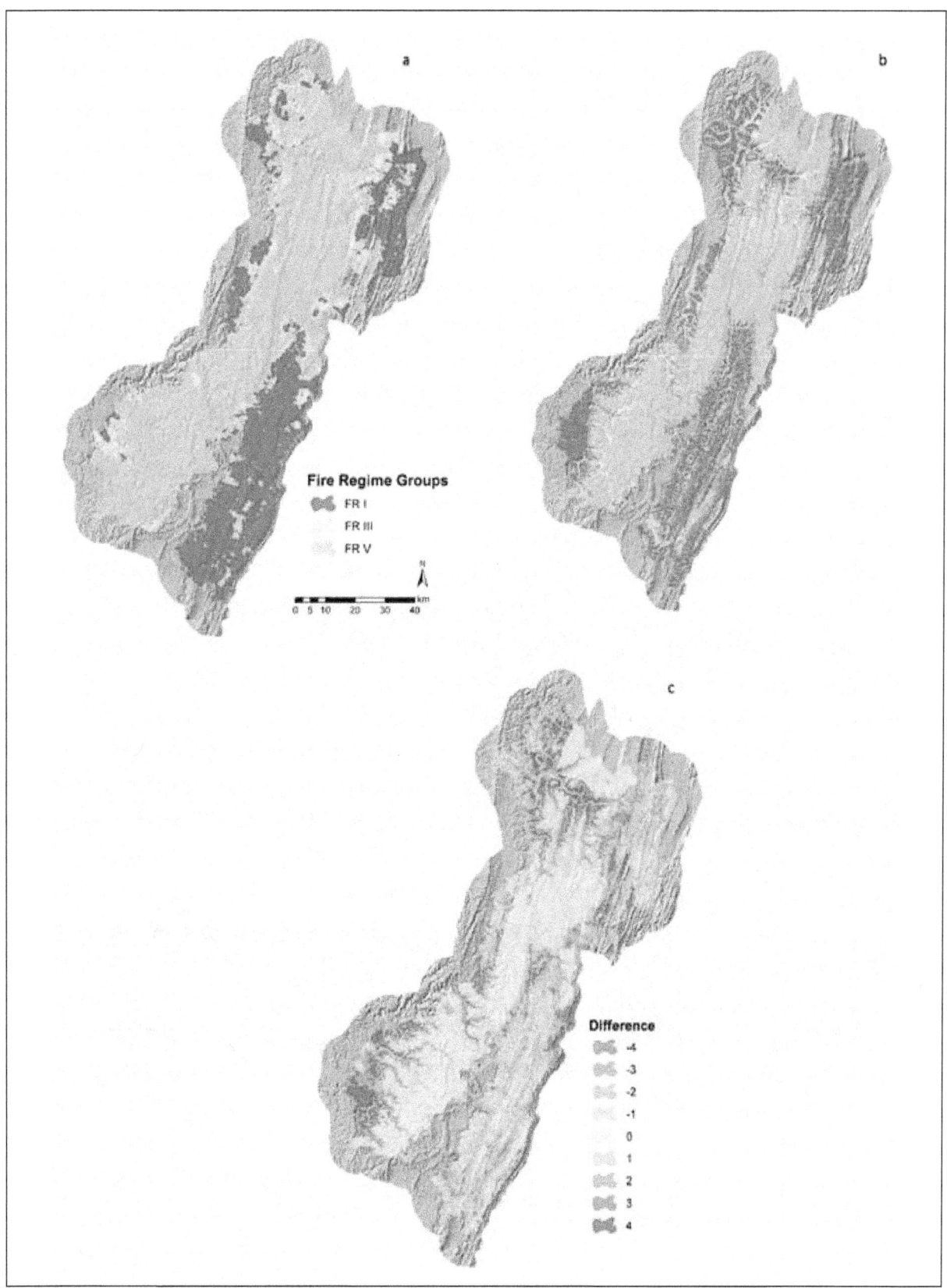

Figure 3—Fire regime group maps derived from (a) the witness tree-based map (Thomas-Van Gundy and Nowacki 2013), (b) LANDFIRE, and (c) the difference between them.

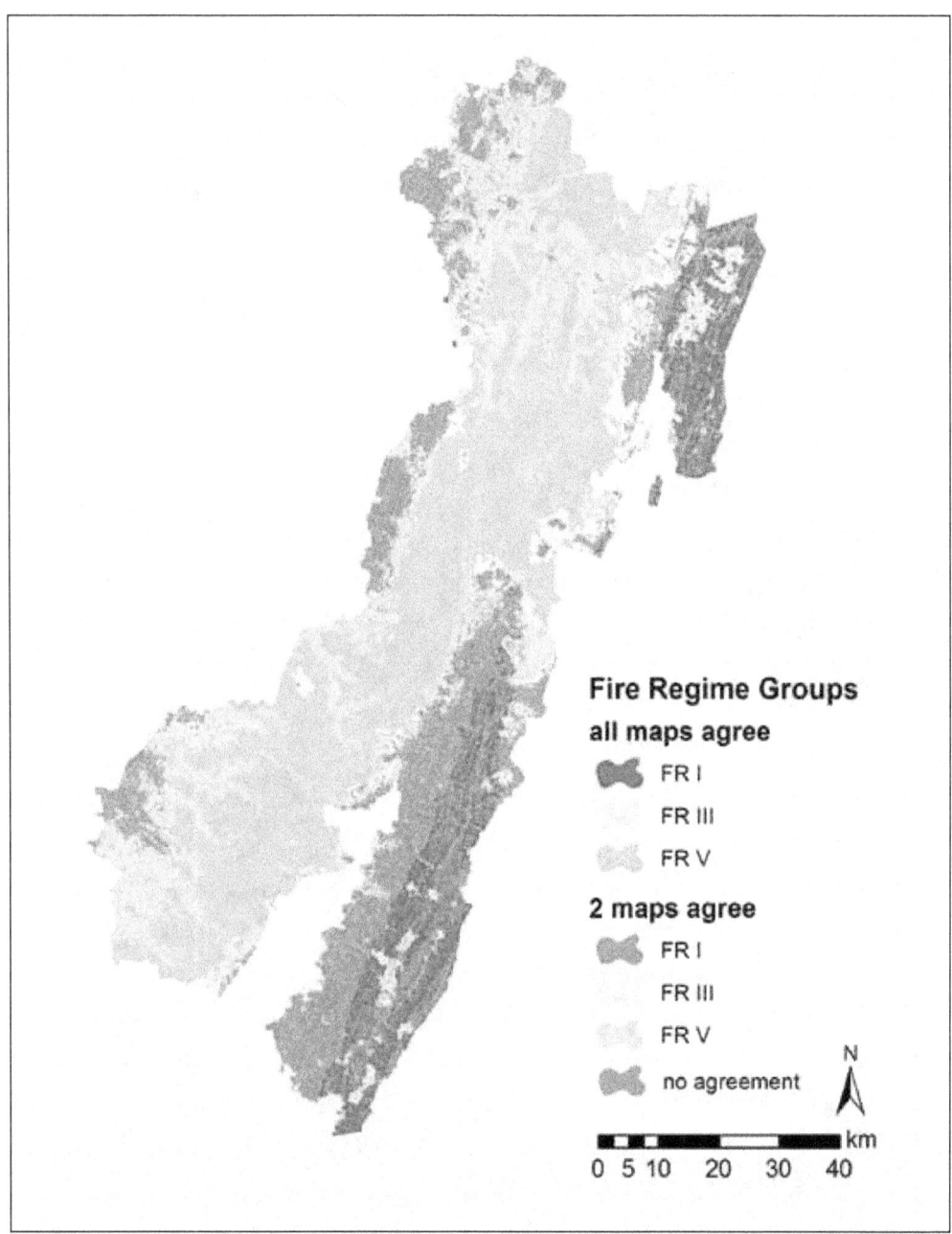

Figure 4—Three-way comparison of all three maps. Areas of full color indicate agreement between all three maps, faded colors represent areas where two maps agreed, and grey areas represent areas of no agreement between the three maps. Fire regime groups from the witness tree-based map are shown.

[Extended Abstract]

A BRIEF INTRODUCTION TO THE INTERAGENCY FUELS TREATMENT DECISION SUPPORT SYSTEM (IFTDSS)

H. Michael Rauscher and Stacy A. Drury[1]

INTRODUCTION

The last decade saw a dramatic proliferation of software systems intended to help fire and fuels managers in the United States. Funding for these software systems came from a variety of sources without any central control or vision. A governance process with stated requirements on how to transition a research-grade software application to an operationally ready one was never created. This resulted in a fuels management environment with numerous, fragmented, stand-alone tools; system and data access issues; decentralized planning and support; minimal security; and ad-hoc training.

To help mitigate this problem situation, the Joint Fire Science Program (JFSP), working in conjunction with the National Wildfire Coordinating Group (NWCG) Fuels Management Committee (formerly the National Interagency Fuels Coordinating Group), initiated the Software Tools and Systems (STS) study in 2007. Between 2010 and 2012, the JFSP released a series of pilot versions of IFTDSS that demonstrated growing functionality and conformance with field user needs. These pilot versions were made available to a large body of test users in an active program to gather user feedback. The most current version of IFTDSS (Beta version 2.0) was released in October 2012. The IFTDSS software integration framework is available at iftdss.sonomatech.com. All project documentation, including a detailed final report, is available at www.frames.gov/iftdss.

WHAT IS IFTDSS?

The Interagency Fuels Treatment Decision Support System (IFTDSS) is an existing service integration platform, currently with over 100,000 lines of software code, that provides command and control for software modules and datasets executing from within a common user interface. It provides capabilities for use and integration of standardized and custom datasets, supports treatment unit- and landscape-scale analyses, data visualization functionality, estimates of fire behavior and first-order fire effects, and quantitative hazard and risk assessments. It allows users to choose pre-designed solution pathways for the most commonly performed fuels treatment tasks. These pre-designed solution pathways, called workflows, were designed and reviewed by members of the user stakeholder community to ensure that offered functionality matched real needs. It is important to understand that IFTDSS is not another new fuels treatment system. It is a service integration framework that organizes and makes available a large number of pre-existing software modules through a single, Web-based graphical user interface.

HOW CAN IFTDSS HELP FIRE AND FUELS MANAGERS AND SOFTWARE DEVELOPERS?

IFTDSS transforms a chaotic, ungovernable set of stand-alone, stove-piped software applications into a consolidated, manageable single software application focused on helping users solve their mission critical business needs. The primary orientation is to support local, project-scale analyses but as part of a landscape area of interest that could be up to 2 million acres in size. IFTDSS takes the model processing power of many different systems and brings them together into one place. The IFTDSS process is easy to understand and use. Users no longer need to learn and to use multiple tools with different interfaces, thus reducing training and re-familiarization time. Users no longer need to spend most of their time on data transformation issues from one software system to another. Users can use the collaboration features of IFTDSS to share data and project analyses with other professionals. Finally, for the first time, users of IFTDSS have access to a credible, yet easy to learn and apply risk assessment process that they can perform themselves at their local office.

[1] H. Michael Rauscher, Science Advisor to Joint Fire Science Program, Rauscher Enterprises LLC, Leicester, NC 28748
Stacy A. Drury, Senior Ecologist, Sonoma Technology Inc., Petaluma, CA 94954

Citation for proceedings: Waldrop, Thomas A., ed. 2014. Proceedings, Wildland Fire in the Appalachians: Discussions among Managers and Scientists. Gen. Tech. Rep. SRS-199. Asheville, NC: U.S. Department of Agriculture Forest Service, Southern Research Station. 208 p.

HAS IFTDSS BEEN TESTED AND EVALUATED?

IFTDSS has been developed with the intimate involvement of numerous members of the fire and fuels community since its inception in 2007. Users were involved at the design state and the early testing stages. Their suggestions and critical comments were a dominant guiding force throughout the development process. In 2013, IFTDSS had over 400 users all across the United States. IFTDSS has also been subjected to an independent evaluation by members of the Software Engineering Institute of Carnegie Mellon University located in Pittsburgh, PA. The report of that evaluation concluded that IFTDSS represented a significant improvement in the software support available to fire and fuels managers (Bennett and others 2013). In general, IFTDSS is well aligned with the interagency Wildland Fire Information and Technology strategic vision as described by Douglas and Phipps (2012). IFTDSS provides a significantly improved platform for the integration of data and models in fire and fuels when compared to the current situation. Eleven workshops, eight in person and three virtual, on-line sessions, were held across the United States. Ninety-eight workshop attendees completed the same post-workshop survey, which was a response rate of 98%. Given the notional size of the fuels management community of approximately 1,000, the survey responses represent approximately 10% of the target community. The users were overwhelmingly positive about IFTDSS (Bennett and others 2013).

WHAT FUNCTIONALITY DOES IFTDSS MAKE AVAILABLE?

Five workflows have been identified and implemented in IFTDSS Version 2.0. Each workflow provides a logical, step-by-step process of using the various tools needed to perform the tasks of that workflow. IFTDSS field-user designed workflows are a set of business-oriented modeling pathways intended to capture the problem-solving needs of the fuels treatment analysis and planning community. They provide access to scientific models in a stepwise, intuitive pattern, reducing the emphasis of individual models. These workflows were developed based on direct user input from JFSP-sponsored fuels treatment working group and other test user groups.

The Data Acquisition and Editing Workflow is used to identify the appropriate vegetation, geophysical, and weather data for IFTDSS that will be needed for a project. The Hazard Analysis Workflow is used to identify potentially hazardous areas across a landscape. The Risk Assessment Workflow provides a first-approximation probabilistic risk assessment for fuels treatment planning. The Fuels Treatment Workflow (a) simulates fuels treatment placement in areas of high fire hazard within an area of interest, and (b) simulates post-treatment influences on fire behavior and fire effects potentials. The Prescribed Burn Planning Workflow provides the information needed to plan and document a proposed prescribed fire.

REFERENCES

Bennett, C.M.; Brown, N.; Doney, D. [and others]. 2013. Final Report of the Interagency Fuels Treatment Decision Support System (IFTDSS) Evaluation Study. Special Report CMU/SEI-2013-SR-017. [Place of publication unknown]: Software Engineering Institute, Carnegie Mellon University. 142 p. Available at: http://www.frames.gov/documents/iftdss/IFTDSS_SEI_FINAL_07-01-2013.pdf.

Douglas, J.; Phipps, J. 2012. Wildland fire information and technology: strategy, governance, investments. Unpublished Interagency report. http://www.frames.gov/documents/iftdss/Signed_IT_Report_March_23_2012.pdf.

[Extended Abstract]

USING THE ADAPTIVE MANAGEMENT PROCESS TO DEVELOP A MONITORING PROGRAM ON THE GEORGE WASHINGTON AND JEFFERSON NATIONAL FORESTS AND THE NATURE CONSERVANCY'S WARM SPRINGS MOUNTAIN PRESERVE

Lindsey A. Curtin and Beth Buchanan[1]

Abstract—The George Washington and Jefferson National Forests (GWJNF) in collaboration with The Nature Conservancy began planning a monitoring program utilizing adaptive management methods to guide prescribed burning in 2008. The development of a successful monitoring program requires extensive research, planning, and cooperation between fire management officers and ecologists to establish measurable burn objectives. Working together, the GWJNF and The Nature Conservancy developed monitoring protocols then utilized the database Feat and Firemon Integrated (FFI), free software developed by the Forest Service, U.S. Department of Agriculture to promote data storage easily used and shared between multiple agencies. The data, once collected in the field and entered into the FFI database, is statistically analyzed, and those objectives identified in the burn plan are reviewed. Management action alteration is dependent upon the results generated from data collection. As management adapts, the cycle continues, allowing land managers to apply scientific principles and knowledge in restoring landscapes to historical fire regimes.

INTRODUCTION

The George Washington and Jefferson National Forests (GWJNF) span 1.8 million acres along the Appalachian and Blue Ridge Mountains, sharing a 13-mile long border with the Warm Springs Mountain Preserve owed by The Nature Conservancy (TNC) in Bath County, VA. The Forest Service, U.S. Department of Agriculture and TNC first came together in 2006 to develop a fire management program for the preserve. This collaboration helped spark the creation of the Alleghany Highlands Fire Learning Network (FLN). The FLN comprises several Federal and State cooperators from Virginia and West Virginia, allowing multiple agencies to meet and work together in achieving fire restoration and management goals. In 2008, the GWJNF and TNC joined forces again to create a monitoring protocol, Forest Composition and Structure Monitoring (FCS), for the prescribed burn programs on the forest and the preserve in an effort to establish land management activities implementing the adaptive management cycle.

An important element of decisionmaking in any land management program is the use of current and applicable scientific information. The adaptive management cycle is one process which continuously incorporates new information through the concept of "learning by doing" (Haney and Power 1996). Adaptive management comprises six steps: researching the system, developing objectives, planning and conducting monitoring, implementing management actions (burning), conducting post-burn monitoring, and analyzing results. As new information is gathered through monitoring, it is fed back into the system and the cycle repeats; managers can then change burn objectives to meet more realistic goals or may decide to change implementation techniques to achieve desired results on the landscape. Additionally, adaptive management benefits land managers by supporting National Environmental Policy Act, or NEPA, claims, proving especially useful if appeals are made to management actions. Those who question or doubt the use of fire in land management are provided with tangible numbers and photos of objective-driven changes taking place in the landscape.

THE ADAPTIVE MANAGEMENT CYCLE

Research the System

Successful land management cannot begin without a thorough understanding of the ecological systems and associated disturbance regimes found on the landscape. Fire management officers and ecologists must understand vegetation type and occurrence, terrain, climate and fire regimes to begin to understand how the landscape has deviated from pre-European settlement and even pre-

[1]Lindsey A. Curtin, Fire Ecologist Trainee, USDA Forest Service, Natural Bridge Station, VA 24579

Beth Buchanan, R-8 Southern Region Fire Ecologist, USDA Forest Service, Roanoke, VA 24019

Citation for proceedings: Waldrop, Thomas A., ed. 2014. Proceedings, Wildland Fire in the Appalachians: Discussions among Managers and Scientists. Gen. Tech. Rep. SRS-199. Asheville, NC: U.S. Department of Agriculture Forest Service, Southern Research Station. 208 p.

fire suppression conditions. Fire regime comprises the general patterns of fire periodicity, seasonality, intensity, and size that emerge over time (Lafon and others 2005). This principle information serves as the foundation for management, giving insight to landscape conditions that will promote a healthy ecosystem.

As the monitoring program was being developed, the Forest Service and TNC cooperators shared their knowledge and expertise of the central Appalachian landscape, fire regimes and characteristics, and the diverse vegetation types found in the mountains. In order to more easily group and describe the ecological systems, the expansive landscape owned by the two agencies was condensed into ecological zones, units of land that can support a specific plant community or plant community group based on environmental factors (Simon 2011). The FLN combined and compared various ecological types using a crosswalk between Simon's Ecological Zone Modeling and the George Washington Forest Plan Systems, establishing three broad system types where fire typically has the greatest effect: mesic, dry-mesic and dry. Prescribed burning efforts on the forest and preserve focus on ecological zones where fire is beneficial to restoring the systems' ecological integrity or condition to their historic range of variability. Using Simon's model, the agencies began planning and prioritizing burn units in landscapes that would likely benefit from fire (table 1).

Develop Objectives

Treating the landscape with prescribed fire requires each burn unit to have obtainable objectives outlined prior to ignition. These objectives guide ignition implementation and techniques, driving burn bosses to conduct firing in ways which achieve specific results on the unit. Additionally, objectives in a burn plan also relate directly to data collected during monitoring. Burn plans across the GWJNF and the preserve have incorporated specific, measurable, achievable, relevant, and timely (SMART) objectives. Specific infers that an objective should clearly define its purpose and subject. A measurable objective is one that can be quantitatively measured through data collection. Relevance ensures objectives are appropriate and feasible for the burn. Timely sets deadlines for results and data collection. For example, one burn objective may call for a 40-percent reduction in red maple (*Acer rubrum*) saplings less than 1 inch dbh within one year post burn. This objective specifically states species, size class, and percent reduction desired then can be measured using protocols developed for the monitoring program. It is relevant to a burn unit with the presence of shade-tolerant red maple and the mortality should be visible on the unit one year post burn. To achieve this objective, the burn boss would conduct firing on the unit with enough intensity to reduce the maple saplings.

Plan and Conduct Monitoring

Objectives cannot be measured in the field without consistent and quantitative data collection. A structured monitoring program is an essential component to the adaptive management cycle because it gives a way to measure changes seen on the landscape after fire. The FCS Protocol, first created in 2008, was revised in 2013. It includes guidelines for plot design, placement within burn units, and specific instructions for data collection. This guides consistent and accurate collection methods across the forest and preserve. The monitoring program uses randomly stratified, circular hundredth-acre plots across burn units to collect data in ecological systems of concern, such as Central Appalachian Dry Oak-Pine Forests (table 1). Each plot is visited before and after a burn at specific intervals to collect data (table 2). The plots are permanently retained through the use of visible paint markers, rebar stakes driven at plot center, and recorded GPS coordinates. Pre-burn or baseline data is collected prior to implementation of a burn to establish a "control" from which change following fire will be measured in the following visits.

Implement Monitoring Actions

Management actions are treatments applied to the landscape, such as timber harvesting, thinning, prescribed fire, or use of herbicides. Both the GWJNF and TNC utilize prescribed burns across large portions of the landscape and multiple ecosystems. Burns are typically conducted in the spring, dependent upon weather conditions, personnel availability, and ongoing wildfires in the area. Fire management officers, including burn bosses and firing bosses, work to burn the unit in a way that achieves desired objectives (fig. 1). Communication both pre-burn and throughout the burn is essential for firing the unit to meet objectives. The burn boss must explain the objectives during briefing, clearly outlining how those objectives should be met to all personnel on the fire, not simply firing bosses. This ensures all personnel have an understanding of why the burn is taking place and may better understand how certain techniques are used to create results. As the burn is conducted, the burn boss must ensure that firing is appropriate to meet objectives. This may include instructing firing bosses to increase or decrease intensity by using various firing methods.

Conduct Monitoring

As mentioned previously, FCS plots are permanent, allowing data to be recorded post burn at the same location. Within six months following a burn, each plot on the unit will be visited and immediate post-burn photos are taken to show immediate fire effects. A full visit is made after one full growing season post burn. Collected data includes photographs of north and south views from plot center, canopy cover measurements taken along four transects using a Densitometer, density quadrats to determine ground cover and seedling abundance, stem count and size of sapling tree/shrub species, and basal area of overstory trees using a Basal Area 10 prism (fig. 2). The plots are visited again five years post burn if the unit is not burned again within that time. If the unit is burned again within five years, immediate post-burn photos and a one-year post burn visit are made for the second entry. This process is continued for the duration the burn unit is treated. Data, once collected, is entered into Feat and Firemon Integrated (FFI). This database program acts to store data that can be shared between cooperators (including those outside Virginia) and performs statistical analyses.

Analyze Results

The analysis and informed use of monitoring data ultimately feeds back into the adaptive management cycle. As new information becomes available, managers and ecologists continue to revise and implement objectives in prescribed burns, using the monitoring program to study future burns. Using Forest Service-developed FFI or other programs, such as Microsoft Excel®, the data can be analyzed on large or small scales. The questions posed by burn objectives (e.g., did we kill 40 percent of red maple saplings under one inch dbh?) are answered. The analyzed data can be easily used by fire management officers to read results of their burn treatments, enabling them to make informed decisions for future burns. New burn objectives may be developed with the new information and/or firing techniques may be altered to achieve different results in the future. For example, if only 20 percent of red maple saplings were killed after one year, fire management officers may decide to burn the unit with more intensity in the next entry and will alter the firing plan to achieve those results. Alternatively, the data may show managers that the burn objectives are unobtainable, prompting them to revise them to more accurately reflect changes that occur on the landscape after a burn.

CONCLUSION

The adaptive management process has become a major focus of the prescribed burn program on the GWJNF and TNC's Warm Springs Mountain Preserve. Through the development of a monitoring program, both the forest and TNC have the ability to use relevant research and data to modify burn plans and firing techniques to best meet predetermined burn objectives. The use of a monitoring program not only provides feedback to fire management officers, but has also established a close working relationship between the Forest Service and TNC. It further supports NEPA claims and provides the public with quantitative evidence of how prescribed burning influences the landscape by improving ecological integrity in different community types.

ACKNOWLEDGMENTS

Steve Croy, Forest Ecologist/Fire Planner & Aviation Officer USDA Forest Service, Roanoke, Virginia; Marek Smith, Director, Alleghany Highlands Program, The Nature Conservancy, Warm Springs, Virginia; Nikole Swaney, Alleghany Highlands Restoration Coordinator, Alleghany Highlands Program, The Nature Conservancy.

REFERENCES

Haney, A.; Power, R.A. 1996. Adaptive management for sound ecosystem management. Environmental Management. 20(6): 879-886.

Lafon, C.W.; Hoss, J.A.; Grissino-Mayer, H.D. 2005. The contemporary fire regime of the Central Appalachian Mountains and its relation to climate. Physical Geography. 26(2): 126-146.

Simon, S.A. 2011. Ecological zones on the George Washington National Forest: first approximation mapping. The Nature Conservancy, Virginia Field Office. On file with:[The Nature Conservancy, Virginia Field Office, 530 East Main St, Ste. 800, Richmond, VA 23219-2428].

Table 1—Plant community groups used to describe changes from a narrow to broad range of ecological communities across the landscape at the introduction and use of prescribed fire[a]

Simon's Ecological Zones	George Washington systems (Forest Plan)	Fire Learning Network systems
Spruce	Spruce Forest	Mesic
Northern Hardwood Slope	Northern Hardwood Forest	
Northern Hardwood Cove	Cove Forest	
Acidic Cove		
Spicebush Cove		
Rich Cove		
Alluvial Forest	Floodplains, Wetlands, and Riparian Areas	
Floodplain Forest		
High Elevation Red Oak	Oak Forests and Woodlands	Dry-Mesic
Montane Oak Rich		
Montane Oak Slope		
Montane Oak Cove		
Colluvial Forest		
Dry Mesic Oak		
Dry Mesic Calcareous Forest		
Dry Oak Evergreen Heath		
Dry Oak Deciduous Heath		
Low Elevation Pine	Pine Forests and Woodlands	Dry
Pine-Oak Heath (eastside ridge)		
Pine-Oak Heath (westside ridge)		
Pine-Oak Heath (ridgetop)		
Pine-Oak Shale Woodlands		
Shale Barren	Cliff, Talus and Shale Barrens	
Alkaline Woodland	Mafic Glade and Barrens and Alkaline Glades & Woodlands	Dry-Mesic
Mafic Glade and Barren		

[a] Plant community groups are defined by Simon (2011), the George Washington National Forest Plan, and the Alleghany Highands Fire Learning Network.

Table 2—Monitoring statuses with descriptions of appropriate use in the Forest Composition and Structure Monitoring Program[a]

Monitoring status	Comment (description and appropriate use)
Pre Burn01	Most appropriately used when unit has not burned in (recent) past. Will be "baseline" data, collected before the first burn.
Baseline	Used in situations where the first data collected is not collected at the beginning of fire reintroduction. Used in lieu of "Pre Burn" data, since it is not technically "pre" burn.
Burn01ImmedPost	Data collected immediately after the 1st burn. Usually is limited to fuels, severity and photos, unless dictated by additional objectives.
Burn01 Year 1	Data collected one full year after the 1st burn, preferably during growing season (which may be 2nd growing season post-burn). Overstory and midstory tree diameters do not need to be re-collected at this time, unless dictated by objectives.
Burn01 Year 5	Data collected 5 full years after the 1st burn. If unit is re-burned before this time, start monitoring sequence over (for example, Burn02 Year1, Burn02ImmedPost) without using this status.
Burn02ImmedPost	Data collected immediately after the 2nd burn. Usually is limited to fuels, severity and photos, unless dictated by additional objectives.
Burn02 Year 1	Data collected one full year after the 2nd burn, preferably during growing season (which may be 2nd growing season post-burn). Overstory and midstory tree diameters do not need to be re-collected at this time, unless dictated by objectives.
Burn02 Year 5	Data collected 5 full years after the 2nd burn. If unit is re-burned before this time, start monitoring sequence over (for example, Burn03 Year1, Burn03ImmedPost) without using this status.

[a] These statuses are also used in FFI to separate and compare data taken at different times on plots.

Figure 1—Implementation of prescribed burn on the Warm Springs Ranger District on the Hidden Valley burn unit. The burn was conducted alongside of personnel from The Nature Conservancy in the Alleghany Highlands Fire Learning Network.

Cover- Points by Transect
(Canopy Cover Estimates using a Densiometer)

Plot Name and Number: _____   Date: _____

Data Collector(s): _____

Monitoring Status: Baseline   Pre Burn   Burn #___   ImmedPost   <1YR   YR 1   YR 5   Other:
(Circle One)

	Distance from Center						
Transect 1 (North)	2'4"	4'8"	7'2"	9'6"	11'9"		Total
CC-Deciduous							___/5
CC-Evergreen							___/5
CC-Sky							___/5
Transect 2 (East)	2'4"	4'8"	7'2"	9'6"	11'9"		Total
CC-Deciduous							___/5
CC-Evergreen							___/5
CC-Sky							___/5
Transect 3 (South)	2'4"	4'8"	7'2"	9'6"	11'9"		Total
CC-Deciduous							___/5
CC-Evergreen							___/5
CC-Sky							___/5
Transect 4 (West)	2'4"	4'8"	7'2"	9'6"	11'9"		Total
CC-Deciduous							___/5
CC-Evergreen							___/5
CC-Sky							___/5

Directions: Using a GRS (Geographic Resource Solution) densiometer, determine canopy cover (deciduous, evergreen, sky) at 20 points within each plot. Beginning 2'4" from the plot origin, face North and walk along transect taking a reading every 2' 4", tallying canopy cover in table above (1 tally per 2'4" interval). Record total hits per canopy cover type for each transect. Repeat facing East, South and West. Reference Appendix III for directions on GRS Densiometer use.

FFI Information	
Number of Transects	4
Transect Length	11.9 (feet)
Number Points/Transect	5

Cover_Frequency
(3.5' x 3.5' Quadrats Understory Cover including Woody Stems up to 3.5' Tall)

Plot Name and Number: _____   Date: _____

Data Collector(s): _____

Monitoring Status: Baseline   Pre Burn   Burn #___   ImmedPost   <1YR   YR 1   YR 5   Other:
(Circle One)

If % Cover is:	0	>0-5	>5-25	>25-50	>50-75	>75-95	>95-100
then record as:	0	2.5	15	37.5	62.5	85	97.5

FFI Note: The recorded % cover is referred to as the Daubenmire scale in the Cover pull-down menu.

Transect/Quadrat	Lifeform	% Cover	Comments	Transect/Quadrat	Lifeform	% Cover	Comments
1 (North)/ 1	C-Grass			3 (South)/ 3	C-Grass		
1 (North)/ 1	C-Forb			3 (South)/ 3	C-Forb		
1 (North)/ 1	C-Invasive			3 (South)/ 3	C-Invasive		
1 (North)/ 1	C-Woody			3 (South)/ 3	C-Woody		
1 (North)/ 1	C-Vine			3 (South)/ 3	C-Vine		
2 (East)/ 2	C-Grass			4 (West)/4	C-Grass		
2 (East)/ 2	C-Forb			4 (West)/4	C-Forb		
2 (East)/ 2	C-Invasive			4 (West)/4	C-Invasive		
2 (East)/ 2	C-Woody			4 (West)/4	C-Woody		
2 (East)/ 2	C-Vine			4 (West)/4	C-Vine		

Directions: Estimate percent aerial cover of grasses (including sedges & rushes), forbs (broad leaved plants, non-woody), trees/shrubs, woody vines and priority non-native invasive species by cover class. Only determine aerial cover of lifeforms up to 3.5' tall. Aerial cover is defined as the percentage of ground obscured by vegetation. Measure the area of ground cover by the outermost perimeter of the natural spread of plant leaves. Small openings within the canopy are included. Record the name of any priority non-native invasive species under the comments column on the data sheet. Reference Appendix V for definitions of lifeforms.

Note: Determine which non-native invasive species are of priority concern for each burn unit. Each unit may have a different list of priority non-native invasive species.

FFI Information	
Number of Transects	4
Transect Length	11.9 (feet)
Number of Quadrats/Transect	1
Quadrat Length	42 (inches)
Quadrat Width	42 (inches)

Figure 2—Datasheets used in Forest Composition and Structure monitoring. Data is transferred into FFI after collection in the field.

DEVELOPMENT OF AN ARCGIS FIRE FREQUENCY, FUEL ACCUMULATION, SEASONALITY AND PRIORITIZATION TOOL TO FACILITATE PRESCRIBED FIRE DECISIONMAKING ON THE TALLADEGA NATIONAL FOREST, ALABAMA

Jonathan M. Stober and Geoff Holden[1]

Abstract—Prescribed fire is used widely to mitigate wildfires and restore ecosystems. However, there are few tools developed to evaluate fire's cumulative impact, calculate frequency, examine seasonality, and estimate fuel accumulation to facilitate decisionmaking in targeting successive prescribed fire application. An ESRI shapefile of all wildfire and prescribed fire events was assimilated from 1978 to 2012 for the 235,000-acre Talladega Division in east central Alabama. A python script-based tool was developed for ArcGIS10 to calculate the annualized average fire return interval, years of fuel accumulation (i.e., date last burned), and frequency of growing to dormant season fire events. Development of a comprehensive fire database that can calculate generalized fuel accumulation will allow for more targeted pairing with appropriate smoke dispersion and better smoke management. Calculations of fire frequency will determine if adequate fire return intervals are occurring on the landscape and focus on areas that need increased effort to meet frequency targets for restoration.

INTRODUCTION

Prescribed fire is a fundamental tool for land managers to mitigate wildfires and restore ecosystems (Costanza and others 2013, Melvin 2012). While individual fire events are often the focus of managers, it is the cumulative impact of successive fires that lead to ecosystem restoration particularly in the Southeast. Fire frequency is the critical metric to determining if fire management goals are being achieved, whether the manager is managing fuels in a wildfire landscape of the West or a prescribed fire landscape of the Southeast. Such calculations have been made with Landsat data, ArcGIS model builder, or in Oracle databases (Hiers and others 2003), but each requires substantial time and resources, pose a steep learning curve, and often do not use specific recorded fire events in the calculation. ArcGIS is a commonly used program by most fire planners and managers; so, we developed a python script-based tool to evaluate our fire management program on the Talladega Division in east central Alabama.

The Talladega Division is the largest remaining tract of montane longleaf located among the highest points in Alabama on the terminus of the Appalachian chain. The Division is mandated with endangered species recovery and currently has 30 active red-cockaded woodpecker clusters. It is projected to have 230 clusters by 2050 to achieve recovery. Fire management is central to restoration of this unique ecosystem, and fuels management in the wildland-urban interface is also of concern. The Talladega's proximity to large metropolitan areas creates smoke management issues not unique to National forests throughout the Southeast. Currently only 150,000 acres or 60 percent of the Division has experienced active fire management in the last 22 years, and the frequency of fire is not achieving historic return intervals to create desired future conditions or manage smoke.

In 1823, cartographers of the day noted that the area consisted of an "extensive pine forest" (fig. 1). Subsequent land surveys circa 1832 (Shankman and Wills 1995), prior to settlement, indicate slopes and ridge tops were dominated by pines with steeper slopes dominated by longleaf, transitioning to shortleaf pine on more gentle slopes and broad ridge tops to loblolly pine in the bottoms. Fire-adapted hardwoods were intermixed in this pine matrix on differing slopes and aspects. Bale (2009) examined the fire scar dendrochronology record on two ridge systems on the Shoal Creek Ranger District and revealed that from 1653 to 1831, prior to Native American extirpation, the fire return interval was 2.7 to 3.2 years. After settlement, the fire frequency increased to a range of 2.5 to 2.6 years from 1832 to 1940. Bale also found that 97 percent of the fires occurred during the dormant season and that fuel bed analysis showed that three years post fire the fuel bed was saturated and capable of carrying a fire. The Forest Service, U.S. Department of Agriculture began acquisition in 1937 and

[1]Jonathan M. Stober, District Biologist, Shoal Creek Ranger District, Talladega National Forest, Heflin, AL 36264

Geoff Holden, Forest Geospatial Program Manager, Francis Marion and Sumter National Forests, Columbia, SC 29212

Citation for proceedings: Waldrop, Thomas A., ed. 2014. Proceedings, Wildland Fire in the Appalachians: Discussions among Managers and Scientists. Gen. Tech. Rep. SRS-199. Asheville, NC: U.S. Department of Agriculture Forest Service, Southern Research Station. 208 p.

promptly began controlling and suppressing all wildland fire, effectively removing fire out of a fire-dependent ecosystem. Prescribed fire began in the mid to late 1980s to manage fuels and comply with management for endangered species. Managers have utilized prescribed fire since then but had never systematically evaluated the fire program's extent or ability to achieve a fire frequency to manage fuels or mimic the natural disturbance regime. To evaluate the fire program, fire records were digitally recorded and an ArcGIS tool developed to summarize the cumulative effect of fire events through time.

METHODS

An ESRI shapefile of all wildfire and prescribed fire events from 1978 to the present was gathered for the Division by assimilating paper and digital records. The master shapefile with all fire records must have a 'date' field in the ESRI date field format. The master shapefile attributes included fire weather conditions, objectives, date, fire type, and location. From the master file, the fire history time period of interest was exported into a new shapefile and the Integrate tool in ArcGIS was used to unify concomitant roads, streams, and burn block boundaries to reduce polygon slivers. The tool was executed in ArcCatalog by identifying the shapefile, an output folder, and the beginning and ending dates of the growing season for the area. The result was a geodatabase containing a feature class that can be brought into ArcMap for display and interpretation of the frequency, seasonality, and recency of the fire program.

The output gives the user the total number of fire events in each polygon to calculate the annualized average fire return interval or fire frequency, years of fuel accumulation (i.e., date last burned), and frequency of growing and dormant season fire events and the relative dates they were last burned during those seasons. The tool also records the last date a fire occurred in each polygon, which can be used to create a fuel accumulation map with annualized rough accumulations. Further calculations can be made by examining the total acreage under fire management, the relative percentages of the fire frequencies across intervals. The extent of the fire program less the boundary of ownership will also illustrate areas missing fuels management. Going back to the master file summaries can be made for the timing of prescribed fires and wildfires to further expose trends in fire management history.

RESULTS AND DISCUSSION

By gathering and summarizing the fire management on the Talladega Division, we were able to see several critical trends. Figure 2 illustrates the annualized rough accumulation on the Division. This information can be used by managers in identifying areas in need of fuels treatment and pairing the relative fuel load with the best atmospheric conditions. For example, the middle of the Division has not been burned since before the year 2000. The liabilities of a fuel load in excess of 13 years and its proximity to highways, parks, and the public may merit that the area either falls out of fire management or that they are only attempted if frequent firing can be sustained into the future to reduce fuel loads and smoke emissions. The areas without fire history also illustrate the ecological and fuel management need to mitigate future wildfire events, a full third (36 percent) of the ownership has no record of fire management. The tool also identifies areas where fuel loads are diminished and moving towards maintenance conditions. For the manager and the decisionmaker, the tool illustrates the trade-off and aids in illustrating the decisions to be made in managing fuels and focusing management. Ultimately, fuels management works by reducing fire intensity and extent which is illustrated on the Division with a declining trend in dormant season (October to March) wildfire events from 1985 to 2012 (fig. 3).

Based on Bale's (2009) analysis, fires were considerably more common during the dormant season. However, lightning ignitions are a common event on the Division, and there is a place for periodic growing season fire events on the Talladega for site prep or top killing and shifting understory vegetation from shrubby hardwood to a more grassy herbaceous community. Growing season prescribed fires were first tested in 1998 and used in earnest since 2003 with a third of all prescribed fires occurring during the growing season. Seasonality expands the fire management window and has its place with current "fire deficit" across the landscape. Ultimately, the more important metric of successful fire management is fire frequency rather than seasonality.

Looking back over 22 years of fire management on the Division, the fire deficit on the landscape becomes apparent but the lack of frequent fire is of greater concern if smoke is to be mitigated and if ecosystem restoration is to be achieved. Table 1 shows a breakdown of annualized fire rotations across two-year intervals on a 150,000-acre basis (prescribed and wildfire fire extent) and under the entire ownership. On the 150,000-acre basis, only 40 percent is receiving prescribed fire on a return interval less than six years. Sixty percent has greater than a six-year fire return interval, is not restoring the ecosystem, and is marginally helpful with fuel and smoke management. When looking across the entire ownership on a 235,000-acre basis, the same pattern is illustrated with a third of the forest without any fire management, another third with very marginal fuel management, and a final third—where fire frequency is approaching historic norms—ecosystem restoration is eminent, fuel loads are being managed, and smoke is mitigated (fig. 4). Moving forward using this tool to summarize cumulative effect of fire events, managers will be able to improve decisions on where prescribed fire is utilized by concentrating resources where restoration can be achieved then expanding outward from a core of fire maintained habitats.

Fire management is constrained by resources, weather, personnel, air sheds, and smoke management concerns. In order to address these limitations, it is useful to know the legacy of previous fire management actions and a generalized knowledge of fuel accumulation, fire frequency, and seasonality of previous prescribed fire events when planning. Monitoring the extent and condition of fire events is critical information that can be used to make better decisions and focus limited resources to achieve desired future conditions.

Go to www.cafms.org/fft to download the tool.

ACKNOWLEDGMENTS

Thanks to Carl Beyerhelm for devising the best code. Eric Schmeckpeper, Blake Morris, Stanley Glover, Mary Rodgers, and Karen McKenzie aided and abetted this project.

LITERATURE CITED

Bale, A. 2009. Fire effects and litter accumulation dynamics in a montane longleaf pine ecosystem. M.S. Thesis. Columbia, MO: Univerity of Missouri-Columbia. 114 p.

Costanza, J.K.; Weiss, J.; Moody A. 2013. Examining the knowing-doing gap in the conservation of fire-dependent ecosystem. Biological Conservation. 158: 107-115.

Heirs, J.H.; Laine, S.C.; Bachant, J.J. [and others]. 2003. Simple spatial modeling tool for prioritizing prescribed burning activities at the landscape scale. Conservation Biology. 17: 1571-1578.

Melvin, M.A. 2012. 2012 National prescribed fire use survey report. [Place of publication unknown]: Coalition of Prescribed Fire Councils, Inc. Technical Report 01-12. 19 p.

Shankman, D.; Wills, D.K. 1995. Pre-European settlement forest communities of the Talladega Mountains, Alabama. Southeastern Geographer. 35: 118-131.

Table 1—Percentage of average annualized fire frequency by 2-year intervals for the 150,000 acres under fire management from 1990 to 2012 and for the entire 235,000 acre ownership

Fire frequency	150K	235K
	---- percent ----	
< 2 years	1	1
2.1-4.0 years	16	10
4.1-6.0 years	17	10
6.1-8.0 years	30	19
8.1-12.0 years	2	1
12.1-22 years	34	22
No fire	0	36
	100	100

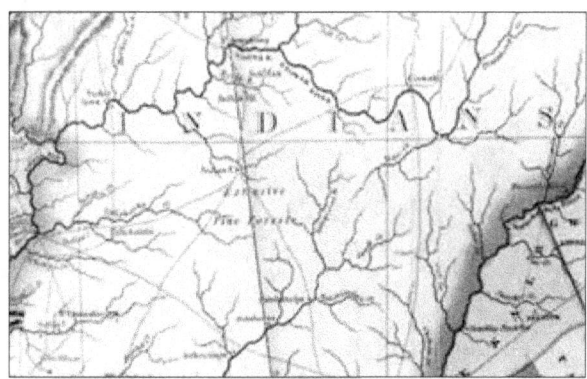

Figure 1—Map in 1823 prior to extirpation of Creek and Cherokee Indian Nations identifying the area as an "extensive pine forest."

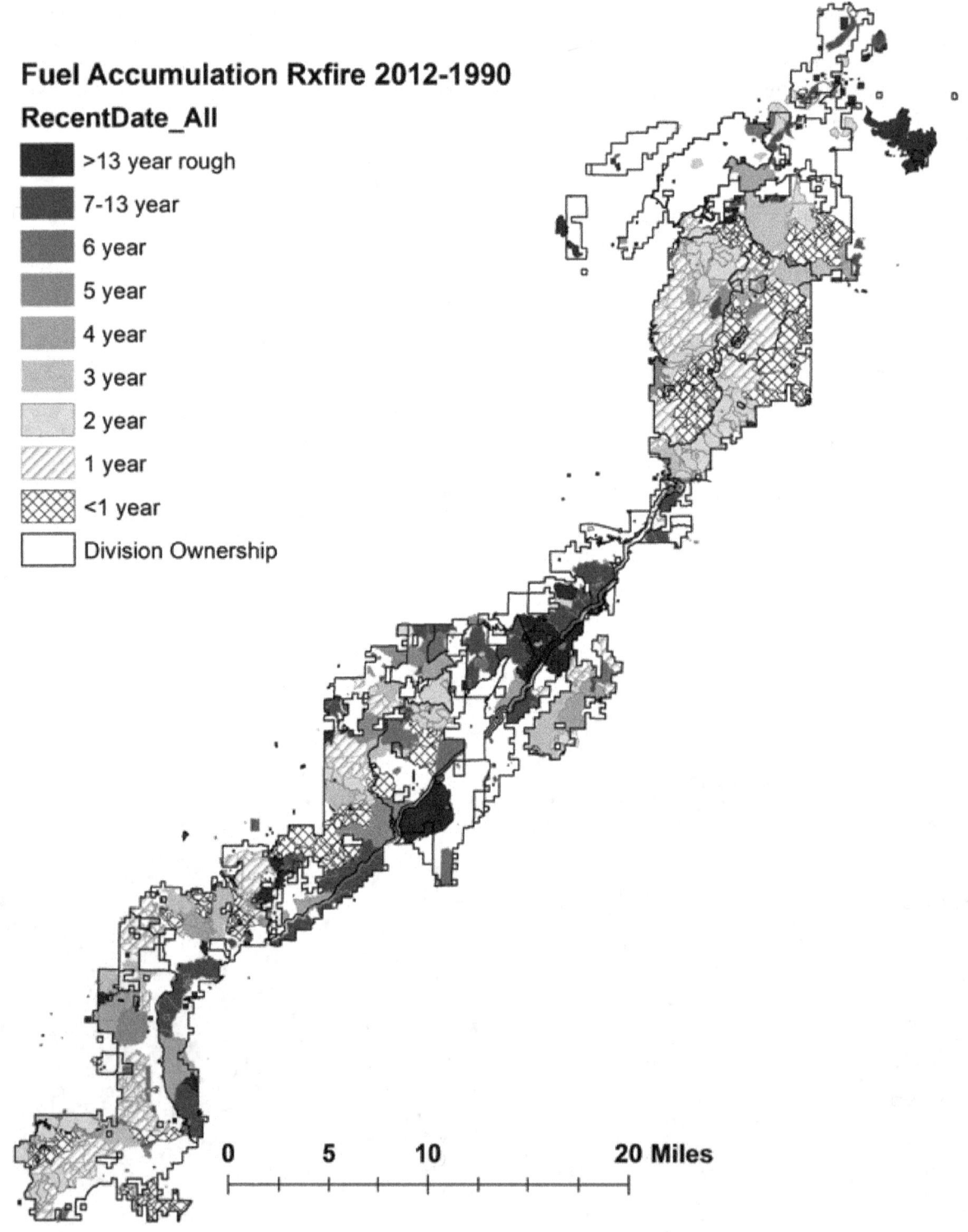

Fuel Accumulation Rxfire 2012-1990

RecentDate_All

- ■ >13 year rough
- ■ 7-13 year
- ■ 6 year
- ■ 5 year
- ■ 4 year
- ■ 3 year
- ☐ 2 year
- ⧅ 1 year
- ⊠ <1 year
- ☐ Division Ownership

0   5   10   20 Miles

Figure 2—Fuel accumulation (rough accumulation) illustrated as time since last fired from 1990 to 2012.

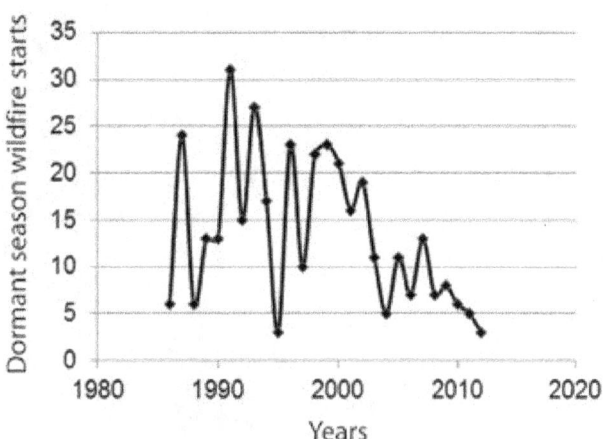

Figure 3—Declining trend in dormant season (October-March) wildfires from 1985 to 2012 illustrating the impact of fuels management on the Talladega Division.

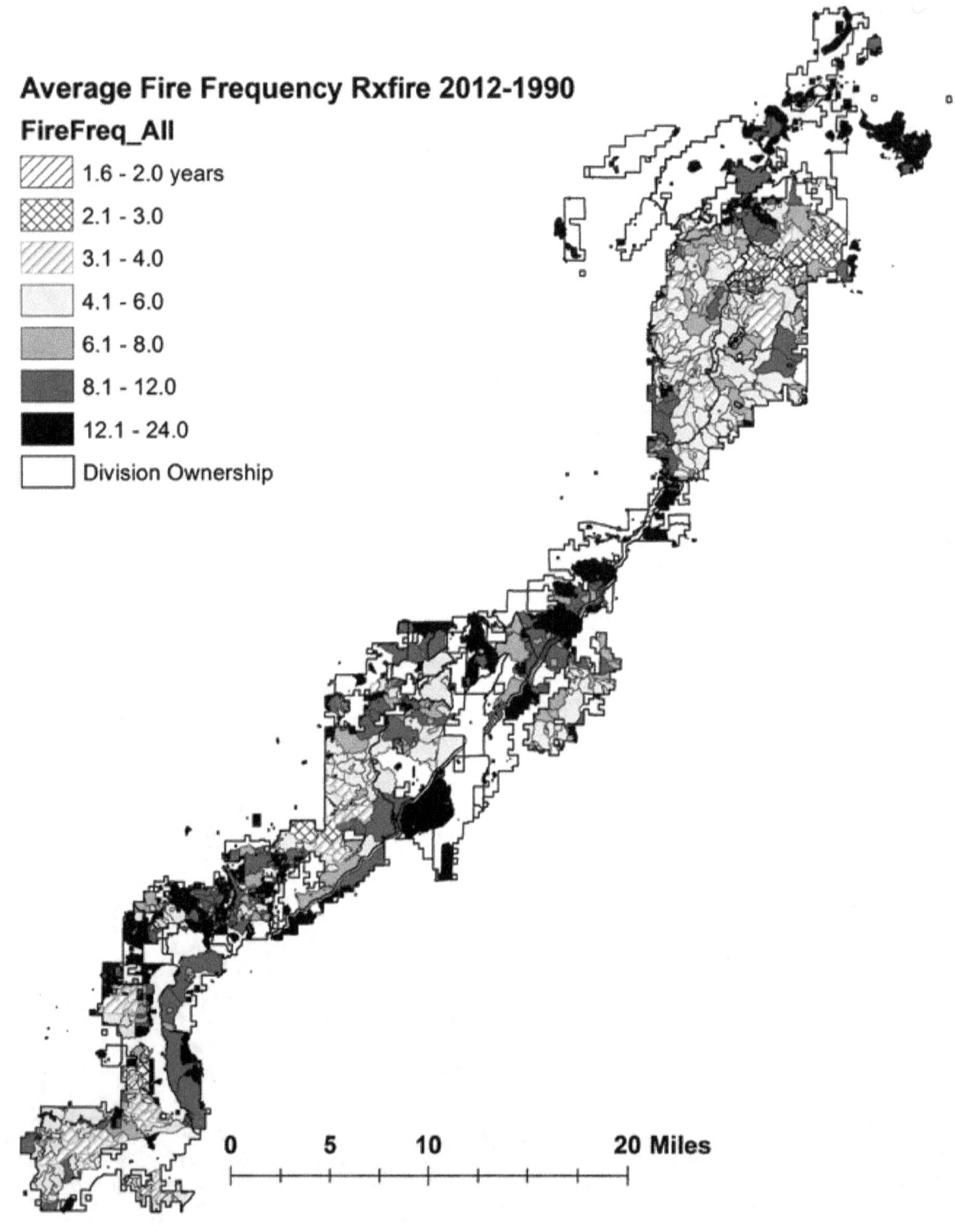

Average Fire Frequency Rxfire 2012-1990

FireFreq_All

- 1.6 - 2.0 years
- 2.1 - 3.0
- 3.1 - 4.0
- 4.1 - 6.0
- 6.1 - 8.0
- 8.1 - 12.0
- 12.1 - 24.0
- Division Ownership

0   5   10   20 Miles

Figure 4—Annualized average fire frequency for the Talladega Division from 1990 to 2012.

USE OF MULTI-SENSOR ACTIVE FIRE DETECTIONS TO MAP FIRES IN THE UNITED STATES: THE FUTURE OF MONITORING TRENDS IN BURN SEVERITY

Joshua Picotte, Michael Coan, and Stephen Howard[1]

Abstract—The effort to utilize satellite-based MODIS, AVHRR, and GOES fire detections from the Hazard Monitoring System (HMS) to identify undocumented fires in Florida and improve the Monitoring Trends in Burn Severity (MTBS) mapping process has yielded promising results. This method was augmented using regression tree models to identify burned/not-burned pixels (BnB) in every Landsat scene (1984–2012) in Worldwide Referencing System 2 Path/Rows 16/40, 17/39, and 1839. The burned area delineations were combined with the HMS detections to create burned area polygons attributed with their date of fire detection. Within our study area, we processed 88,000 HMS points (2003–2012) and 1,800 Landsat scenes to identify approximately 300,000 burned area polygons. Six percent of these burned area polygons were larger than the 500-acre MTBS minimum size threshold. From this study, we conclude that the process can significantly improve understanding of fire occurrence and improve the efficiency and timeliness of assessing its impacts upon the landscape.

INTRODUCTION

Beginning in 2006, the Monitoring Trends in Burn Severity (MTBS) project was tasked to map and assess burn severity for all "large" fires across the United States from 1984 to the present using 30-meter Landsat imagery (Eidenshink and others 2007). Federal fire occurrence data (FOD) from 2004 were used to estimate the magnitude of the nationwide fire occurrence as well as the staffing and data resources required to meet MTBS project objectives. Based upon this analysis, minimum size constraints were imposed: 1000 acres in the West and 500 acres in the East. At the outset of the MTBS project, Landsat imagery was not free, so there were constraints the on the number of Landsat scenes that could be purchased in a given year. Consequently, many fires identified in the FOD could not be reliably mapped because optimal imagery could not be obtained.

Since 2004, the annual number of fire occurrences in the FOD has grown because of better fire event reporting, which has led to more fires being mapped and the subsequent need for more resources to map fires (table 1). Some of these wildfire and prescribed fire records were duplicates as multiple agencies reported the same fire. As awareness of the MTBS program grew, State fire management agencies, primarily in the Southeastern

United States began to provide records of fire occurrence. However, due to the magnitude of the additional fire events, the project decided to postpone assessment of the State reported prescribed fires until all historical Federal fires had been completed. By 2010, the yearly FOD contained many more fire records in comparison with the 2004 (table 1). Of the 1,249 mapped fires for 2010, 1,134 were mapped as "initial" assessments (i.e., using imagery collected shortly after the fire was out because the fire scar quickly fades from the landscape), and 115 were mapped as "extended" assessments (i.e., using postfire imagery acquired usually in the year following the fire in order to assess recovery and delayed mortality).

In 2008, the Landsat archive was opened for free distribution. This provided an opportunity to investigate thousands of historical fire records that were originally declared "unmappable" due to imagery constraints. It became apparent that MTBS processing methods need to be improved to efficiently process large numbers of fires for both current and future fire assessments and for a better assessment of historical fire occurrence. More specifically:

1. There needed to be an automated method for identifying fire events. Each year, MTBS uses the FOD information from the previous year to guide the

[1] Joshua Picotte is Fire Specialist, ASRC Federal InuTeq, Contractor to the U.S. Geological Survey (USGS), Earth Resources Observation and Science (EROS) Center, Sioux Falls, SD 57198. Worked performed under USGS contract G13PC00028.

Michael Coan is Senior Scientist, Stinger Ghaffarian Technologies, Contractor to U.S. Geological Survey (USGS), Earth Resources Observation and Science (EROS) Center, Sioux Falls, SD 57198. Worked performed under USGS contract G10AC00044.

Stephen Howard is Geographer, U.S. Geological Survey (USGS), Earth Resources Observation and Science (EROS) Center, Sioux Falls, SD 57198

Citation for proceedings: Waldrop, Thomas A., ed. 2014. Proceedings, Wildland Fire in the Appalachians: Discussions among Managers and Scientists. Gen. Tech. Rep. SRS-199. Asheville, NC: U.S. Department of Agriculture Forest Service, Southern Research Station. 208 p.

mapping program. This time lag is due to the need for individual agencies to finalize the current year's fire records and for MTBS to compile the finalized records. Mapping, review, and preparation for distribution take more time. Therefore, it can be almost two years before the annual burn severity products are available. This delay is problematic for users who depend on MTBS fire records to evaluate important fire-related disturbance and ecological change.

2. A complete record of fire events is needed. When mapping known fires, MTBS is required to map any "discovered" fires, i.e., those meeting MTBS size requirements but not reported in the FOD. Since 2006, over 17,000 fires have been mapped by MTBS and more than 2,200 were discovered during the process of mapping known fires. These discovered fires may actually be undocumented or exist in the FOD but have an error of location and/or date. Because we only look at scenes for fires identified within the FOD, we suspect there are many fires yet to be discovered, especially in the historical era. Early historical fire record keeping was inconsistent, error prone, and not comprehensive. The latter is an issue especially in the southeastern States, which have a long tradition of widespread prescribed burning. Therefore, a method that does not rely upon human-recorded tabular data is needed.

3. A more efficient method is needed for the selection of imagery to complete the burn severity assessment. The MTBS mapping protocol involves an analysis of a prefire image in conjunction with a postfire image acquired up to one year postfire in order to assess the impacts of the fire, allowing for postfire recovery or mortality to be expressed. The current scene selection process is very labor intensive and compromised by online browse imagery with low resolution: fires near the MTBS size threshold are difficult to see, so it is hard for an analyst to confirm that the FOD point actually falls on a fire in the image.

4. The MTBS protocol must be applicable for all fires. Local land managers and fire ecologists are interested in fires that are below MTBS size thresholds. They will need a way to find and assess these fires.

METHODS

Study Area

We obtained the historical fire records for three national forests in Florida: the Apalachicola, Osceola, and Ocala (fig. 1). These forests were chosen because of their complete burn histories (1984–2012) and because of the large number of prescribed burns conducted during this time frame. They are located within three Landsat Path/Rows in the Southern Coastal Plain, a region with a long history of prescribed burning for clearing undergrowth, reducing hardwood encroachment into pinelands, and promoting various wildlife species (fig. 1). Hundreds of prescribed fires occur each year within this area.

Inputs

Hazard Mapping System Fire Detections— The National Oceanic and Atmospheric Administration (NOAA) Hazard Mapping System (HMS) utilizes satellite-based fire and smoke detections that are collected daily by GOES, AVHRR, and MODIS sensors. The detections are logged as point locations and utilized by NOAA's Air Resources Laboratory to model the next 48 hour's potential smoke emissions and dispersion across North America (Ruminski and others 2006). Frequent observations, as often as every 15 minutes (Zhang and others 2011), allow for a more timely and spatially complete record of fire occurrence than is available from Federal and State fire records. Daily HMS observations have been archived since 2003, which will support retrospective assessments. Operationally, the daily observations are quality checked by NOAA HMS analysts to remove commission errors and add fires visible within the imagery that were not detected by the sensors (Ruminski and others 2006). These data are posted weekly and available online for six months. All post-2011 HMS data were downloaded from the HMS website (http://satepsanone.nesdis.noaa.gov/FIRE/fire.html). HMS data prior to 2011 were obtained from NOAA.

Landsat-Derived Burned Area Polygons—During the development phase of this project, the burned/not-burned (BnB) methodology was developed to automatically generate burned area perimeters from Landsat imagery. A number of previously mapped MTBS fires in the three Paths/Rows of interest were selected. The fires events chosen represented a variety of vegetation types, phenological seasonality, burn severity ranges, and geographic distribution over these Path/Rows. Landsat imagery was chosen that best represented the freshly burned extent of each fire. MTBS burn severity images, produced by the methodology described in Eidenshink and others (2007), were used to identify areas of low, moderate, and high severity within each fire event. Each fire was sampled throughout its range of burn severity as well as was surrounding unburned vegetation. All samples were combined into a training dataset to create a regression tree model, which is a collection of multivariate linear models (Cubist; Rulequest Research 2004). The regression tree model was then run using selected Landsat imagery to create a "likelihood estimate" that each pixel was recently burned. The continuous estimate (1-100) was thresholded at a selected value (i.e., 95 and above) to standardize all the image estimates and create a binary thematic product identifying burned pixels in each Landsat image (1984–2012). Because clouds and shadows in Landsat imagery can obscure portions of fire perimeter, our approach combines all available Landsat imagery to fully delineate a fire perimeter.

The accurate fire perimeters are delineated using Landsat, validated by the presence of an HMS point, and labeled with the correct fire date determined by the HMS record. The burned area polygons provide spatially accurate data, but the temporal resolution is limited to 16 or 8 days depending on satellite availability. Using the capabilities of spatially enabled open source PostgreSQL/PostGIS software, we combine the temporal strengths of the HMS data and the spatial strengths of Landsat imagery to determine the start date and spatial extent of a fire.

Open Source Software—One goal of this effort is to freely distribute data processing scripts developed for this project. We utilized open source (http://www.osgeo.org) PostgreSQL/PostGIS (http://www.postgresql, http://postgis.net) to process all data and Quantum GIS (QGIS; http://www.qgis.org) to view the data. PostgreSQL is a relational database that can be spatially enabled by coupling it with the PostGIS extension. Complex queries can be performed in PostgreSQL to determine the spatial relationships of objects.

Data Processing

Landsat image processing methods currently used by MTBS involves several steps. Each terrain-corrected (L1t) scene is downloaded from the U.S Geological Survey (USGS) Earth Resources Observation and Science (EROS) Center's image archive by the analyst. The imagery is then corrected to top of atmosphere reflectance, reprojected from UTM to Albers Equal Area, and processed to create a Normalized Burn Ratio (NBR) image. To increase our image processing throughput, the USGS Land Satellites Data System Science Research and Development Project and the EROS Science Processing Architecture (ESPA) system used processing scripts to process 1,800 Landsat scenes covering our study area. All Landsat 5 TM and Landsat 7 ETM+ reflectance images, water, cloud, and cloud shadow masks were created by ESPA. This Landsat imagery was used to determine possible burned areas using the Landsat burned area delineation described above.

To accurately date each burned area, we utilized PostgreSQL/PostGIS queries to determine whether HMS points were within 1,500 m of the Landsat-derived fire perimeters and if they were correctly associated with the proper Landsat acquisition (i.e., dated no more than 8 days prior to the Landsat acquisition first showing the burned area polygon). It is likely that a fire could be obscured by clouds in several Landsat overpasses before it is visible. More sophisticated queries can be created to

determine precise HMS dates; however, the burned area polygons are sufficient to identify a "probable" fire.

PRELIMINARY RESULTS AND DISCUSSION

Approximately 1,800 Landsat images (1984–2012) and 88,000 HMS points (2003–2012) were assessed for Paths/Rows 16/40, 17/39, and 18/39. Within these Paths/Rows, we identified approximately 300,000 burned area polygons. The average size of these fires was 257 acres, and almost 18,000 fire polygons exceeded the MTBS 500-acre minimum threshold. By comparison, MTBS mapped 1,400 fires covering the 1984–2011 time period. This suggests there are many unreported prescribed fires above the MTBS size thresholds. However, the southeast region is probably a "worst case scenario" as prescribed fires are not nearly as common in the Western United States. Additionally, it is clear this approach identifies many smaller fires; however, we have not yet determined the minimum fire size threshold that can be reliably delineated and mapped.

To determine the reliability of the results, we visually compared the data to the U.S. Forest Service National Forests of Florida (Apalachicola, Ocala, and Osceola) fire records. We found the fires identified by the burned area delineation process closely matched National Forest records. We identified potentially more MTBS-sized fires than were assessed by MTBS (fig. 2), and for the post-2003 fires, the dates of occurrence were effectively determined by HMS (fig. 3). Further, the burned area perimeters better represented the overall fire patterns and should provide more accurate estimates of burned acreage because MTBS does not delineate unburned islands within the overall perimeter (fig. 2).

After reviewing the burned area products, we determined that some of the burned pixels were detected within urban areas, harvested cropland, and seasonally flooded areas. MTBS is not concerned with cropland, but these areas can be set aside for anyone who has interest in burnable agriculture. Some actual commission errors occurred, apparently due to confusion with freshly plowed agricultural ground, clear cuts, and special types of wetland vegetation in senescence. No effort was made at this time to separate these from the truly burned areas. A refinement of burned croplands vs. plowed ground, and burned emergent wetlands vs. senescent vegetation, are potential problems. A majority of the urban area confusion appears to have a seasonal (solar angle) component that might be addressed by application of a seasonally tuned regression tree model.

For MTBS, it is necessary to identify the best prefire and postfire Landsat images in order to create the burn severity assessments. In the past, MTBS analysts reviewed low resolution browse imagery. This has been improved utilizing ESPA processing system, which searched the Landsat archive and retrieved candidate scenes and clipped them based upon a bounding box derived from the automatically generated burned area perimeter. The full resolution image subsets provide analysts with a more detailed view of the data than was previously possible with the low resolution browse images.

MTBS Viewer Tool and Automation

All the candidate full resolution Landsat image clips are loaded into a Google Earth® KML and viewed with the MTBS QuickLook tool (fig. 4). The QuickLook tool allows analysts to rapidly review the Landsat clips to determine if the detection is in fact a fire and then to record the optimal scenes for the severity assessment, whether the assessment type will be initial (within several months) or extended (at peak of green the following season), and the vegetation type in which the fire occurred. All information entered into the QuickLook tool is stored in a PostgreSQL database.

ESPA processing eliminates many of the image preprocessing steps outlined in the "Processing" section above. Currently, MTBS burn severity processing scripts are run manually after analysts select and order the optimal scenes and make other critical processing decisions (e.g., initial vs. extended). These critical analyst processing decisions are collected by the MTBS QuickLook tool and will be used to automatically drive the MTBS process using the existing scripts: creation of the differenced NBR (dNBR) and Relativized dNBR (RdNBR) images which form the basis of the thematic burn severity map.

Furthermore, we have completed regionally based analyses of all 1984–2010 historical MTBS analyst-determined burn severity breakpoints for each vegetation type (Fry and others 2011) throughout the Unites States to determine the regional average burn severity breakpoints for each vegetation type. These breakpoints will be used to automatically create preliminary MTBS burn severity products. MTBS analysts will then review preliminary/default burn severity products with the next iteration of the automation process.

Potential Improvements to Current MTBS Process

This project has the potential to improve the MTBS fire perimeter and burn severity mapping process. The overall effect of these improvements is to enable the processing of many more fires that would have been previously too time-consuming and expensive to undertake. Further testing of the automated procedures and subsequent product outputs still needs to be completed; however, the basic automated processing framework has been developed. This current project worked on a small subset of the total footprint of the United States that will need to be processed if burn perimeters and severity are to be mapped on a nationwide scale. The methods will be tested in other regions as resources are available.

We anticipate that the previously described automated fire perimeter mapping, creation of thresholded burn severity images, and subsequent review of all products should increase the MTBS mapping capabilities. MTBS will be able to map and review fires more quickly, thereby reducing production time and cost. MTBS may subsequently be able to decrease the current fire mapping thresholds 1,000 acres in the Western United Staes to increase its mapping capabilities. Overall, this would result in the production of a more complete fire history within the United States.

Generally, MTBS fire products become available within two years after fire occurrence. This production timing is purposely structured in this manner to allow for the mapping of extended fire assessments and a rigorous quality control process to ensure that all mapped fires meet MTBS's stringent mapping requirements. If the MTBS project is able to complete the current mapping output in less time, it may be possible to map initial assessments of fires in near real-time. Under this paradigm, MTBS would use HMS fire detections in conjunction with recent postfire Landsat BnB fire perimeters to automatically map fire perimeters. Automated processes would generate thresholded burn severity products. All products would be reviewed for accuracy and revised as needed by MTBS analysts using the QuickLook viewer. This process would be different from the current MTBS mapping process because it would create initial assessments of burn severity for the entire United States. Subsequent extended assessments of burn severity for the United States would be mapped using the original MTBS protocols.

In addition to improving the MTBS process, we expect that the HMS and BnB combined fire perimeter mapping protocols will generate products useful to managers of public and private lands. Many more mapped fires will subsequently become available. Better geospatial records should inform land managers' decisions when attempting to reduce wildfire risk and managing fire-adapted ecosystems with prescribed fire.

CONCLUSION

Our protocols provide a useful methodology for determining previously unknown burned areas within the Southeastern United States. These products will provide MTBS with potential fire perimeters that can then be used to drive the semi-automated procedures that result in the more efficient identification of suitable Landsat imagery and production of burn severity products. Although MTBS will not assess fires that are less than 500 acres, these fire perimeters can provide land managers with a more complete resource then is currently available to monitor the actual extent and acreage of wildfires and prescribed fires on their lands. In the future, there is the potential that these project methodologies could be used to identify potential fire perimeters at near real-time as new Landsat images become available for the continental United States. This would work towards the creation of a national fire atlas.

ACKNOWLEDGMENTS

Funding for this work was provided by NASA ROSES grant NNH11ZDA001N and MTBS. We would especially like to thank Jason Drake and the U.S. Forest Service National Forests of Florida for their help in providing base data and product evaluation, Krishna Bhattarai for testing the capabilities of the MTBS QuickLook tool, and Jeffrey Eidenshink and Birgit Peterson for reviewing this manuscript.

LITERATURE CITED

Eidenshink, J.; Schwind, B.; Brewer, K. [and others]. 2007. A project for monitoring trends in burn severity. Fire Ecology. 3(1): 3-21.

Fry, J.A.; Xian, G.; Jin, S. [and others]. 2011. Completion of the 2006 national land cover database for the conterminous United States. Photogrammetric Engineering and Remote Sensing 77: 858-864.

Rulequest Research. 2004. Data mining tools. http://www.rulequest.com/ [Online] (verified 23 September, 2014).

Ruminski, M.; Kondragunta, S.; Draxler, R. [and others]. 2006. Recent changes to the hazard mapping system. In: Reinventing Inventories: New Ideas in New Orleans: Proceedings of the 15th International Emission Inventory Conference [Online]. [Place of publication unknown]. http://www.epa.gov/ttn/chief/conferences.html. [Date accessed: January 17, 2014].

Zhang, X.; Kondragunta, S.; Quayle, B. 2011. Estimation of biomass burned areas using multiple-satellite-observed active fires. IEEE Transactions on Geoscience and Remote Sensing. 49(11): 4469-4482.

Table 1—FOD tallies and total number of MTBS fires that were assessed in 2004 and 2010

FOD year	Federal fire records	Total fires mapped	Wildfires mapped	Prescribed fires mapped
2004	1,257	427	326	101
2010	3,164	1,249	309	940

Figure 1—Location of the Apalachicola (A.), Osceola (B.), and Ocala (C.) National Forests (red). Dashed gray lines indicate the approximate Landsat WRS2 Path/Row locations for 18/39 (nearest A.), 17/39 (nearest B.) and 16/40 (nearest C.).

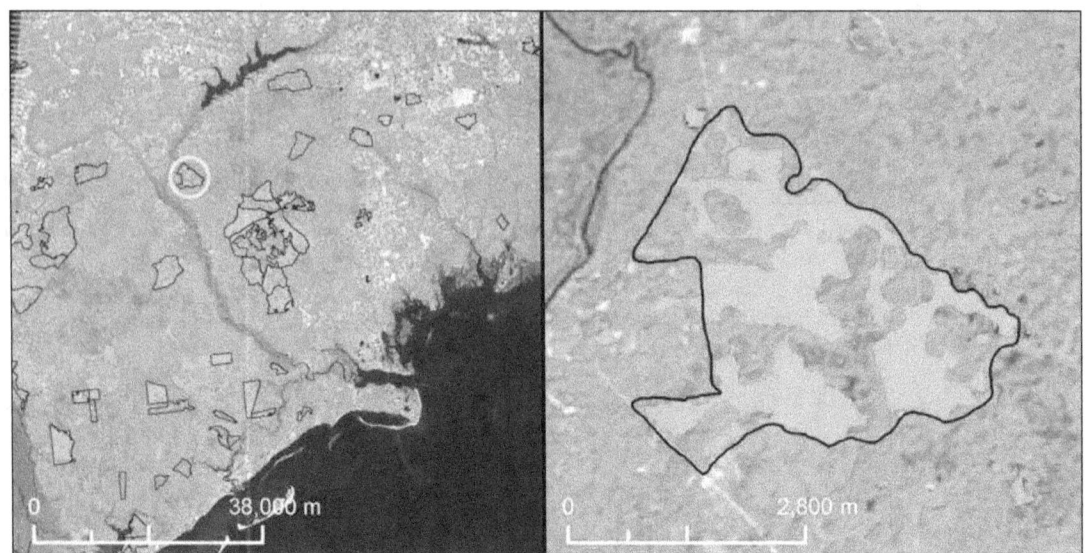

Figure 2—Example of 2011 compiled burned area fire polygons (orange) and their proximity to the MTBS Fire Occurrence Database (FOD) fire perimeters (black). MTBS fire perimeters without any associated orange polygons result from the FOD fire perimeters being derived from 2012 Landsat imagery. The yellow circle in the left image denotes the location of the enlarged fire perimeter shown in the right image and a more precise delineation of the burned area when compared to the MTBS perimeter.

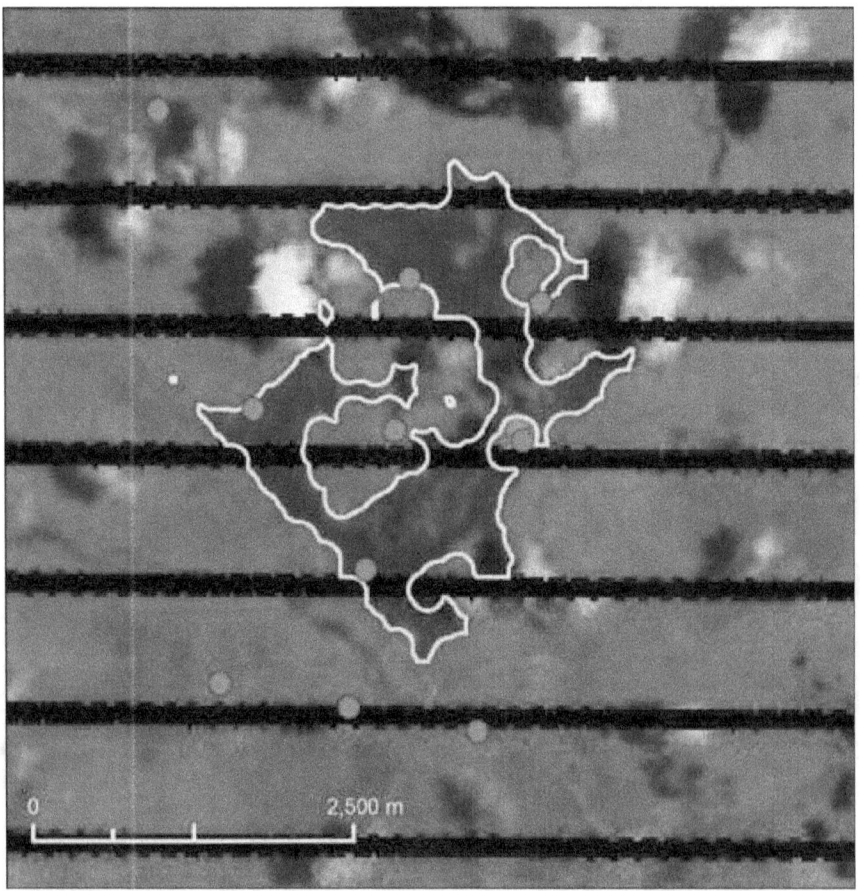

Figure 3—Example of 924-acre burned area polygon (yellow) derived from Landsat scene dated 7/6/2012 and corresponding HMS fire detections (red dots) from 6/29/2012.

Figure 4—Screen shot of the MTBS QuickLook Web-enabled viewing and analyst data entry tool used to store information about each fire assessment.

MULTI-PARTY MONITORING—A GOOD TOOL FOR MANAGERS

Beth Buchanan[1]

Abstract—The use of prescribed fire has increased dramatically over the last 15 years in the Appalachian Mountains; managers are interested in tracking the effects of their fire programs. Since the mid-1990s, Southern Region National forests have been required to collect data on fuels and vegetation in permanent plots. However, lack of personnel dedicated to this effort has limited the number of plots each forest is capable of maintaining. Thus, National forests are encouraged to work across boundaries and share information with neighboring districts, National forests, and agencies with similar burn prescriptions and monitoring types to increase the size of datasets. We discuss the results of this endeavor, including recommendations for improving this approach. In general, data collected in such a manner can be used at least to document trends, which can be used to supplement the more-rigorous research projects which now are becoming more commonplace. Fire effects monitoring completed internally by firefighters and other employees offers multiple benefits to the local units.

INTRODUCTION

The U.S. Department of Agriculture, Forest Service manages 193 million acres of forests and grasslands. The Southern Region of the Forest Service encompasses 13 States and Puerto Rico, including 14 National forests and two special units. Unlike some other areas of the country (e.g., the Western United States), most of the South is privately owned. The Forest Service manages only 13.3 million acres in this region, which is also referred to as Region 8. Across the agency, prescribed fire is a common management tool and nowhere is it more prevalent than in the Southern Region. In 2012, Region 8 burned 885,112 acres.[2] In comparison, the rest of the agency burned 84,448 acres (National Interagency Fire Center 2014). The region that makes up about seven percent of the agency's land base burned more than 91 percent of the total prescribed fire acres. State agencies in the south ignited millions more. Controlled burning is critical in the fire-adapted South because fire is an essential disturbance for natural systems and when intentionally applied also helps protect landowners from the threat of damaging wildfires.

While the South is very fire-adapted, it is also vegetatively diverse. Region 8's States are covered by Braun's (1950) southeastern evergreen, oak-pine, oak-chestnut, mixed mesophytic, western mesophytic, and oak-hickory forest regions (Puerto Rico is not a focus of this discussion). Within Region 8's physiographic regions—including the Gulf and Atlantic Coastal Plains, Piedmont, Appalachian Mountains, and the Interior Highlands—plant composition varies greatly. Coastal plain communities were historically dominated by longleaf pine; piedmont by shortleaf pine and a variety of oaks; and upland areas were or still are oaks, mesic hardwoods, and yellow pines. But even within these general groups, diversity is the rule rather than the exception. Topography, precipitation, historic land use, and disturbance regimes, including fire, contribute to the patterns of vegetation across the landscape.

National forests are located in each of the vegetative and physiographic divisions. Each forest currently prescribe-burns anywhere from a few thousand to more than a hundred thousand acres annually. However, in most of the region, fire had been absent as a landscape-scale disturbance for decades before being reintroduced. Managers recognize the need for fire, but because it is a relatively new management practice for this generation, they often are unsure of the nuances of fire application and effects. In the time since fire was removed from the landscape, vegetation has changed; simply putting fire back at a certain return interval does not necessarily achieve a desired future condition. Fire management officers (FMOs) track changes over time and movement towards desired conditions. Until recently, there was a paucity of fire ecology research in the Eastern United States. FMOs indicated that existing research often was not specific to the situations found on a particular forest. Effective land management is difficult without utilizing current and applicable monitoring or research.

---

[1]Beth Buchanan, Regional Fire Ecologist, USDA Forest Service, Roanoke, VA 24066

[2]Personal Communication. 2013. Calvin L. Miller, Operations Coordinator-Aviation, Southern Area Coordination Center, 1200 Ashwood Parkway, Suite 230, Atlanta, GA 30338.

Citation for proceedings: Waldrop, Thomas A., ed. 2014. Proceedings, Wildland Fire in the Appalachians: Discussions among Managers and Scientists. Gen. Tech. Rep. SRS-199. Asheville, NC: U.S. Department of Agriculture Forest Service, Southern Research Station. 208 p.

Because of the diversity of vegetation, fuels, fire regimes, and fire behavior, fire personnel need to understand fire effects in relation to fire prescription. In 2003, Region 8 FMOs asked for direction with regard to internal data collection within permanent plots in order to document local changes as well as to educate new employees with regard to fire effects. Ultimately, they wanted local data that answered their questions, in language they understood.

Monitoring the effects of prescribed fire is essential for documenting movement toward a desired future condition and tracking changes. Data provide the scientific basis for planning and implementing future burn treatments. Monitoring is a critical part of the adaptive management cycle, an iterative feedback loop that allows prescribed fire managers to alter management if objectives are not achieved. It is, in effect, learning by doing.

FIRE EFFECTS MONITORING IN FOREST SERVICE REGION 8

In 2003, a regional team recommended a program of monitoring prescribed fire effects to be implemented within the Southern Region. The team developed monitoring direction for National forests across Region 8, facilitating a uniform standard of data collection associated with prescribed fire. Those standards include methods to evaluate fuel reduction and vegetative effects.

The recommended protocols allow flexibility within National forests and geographic areas to determine the amount and extent of monitoring needed to meet local issues of concern, while still maintaining a minimum standard dataset. Most protocols and datasheets rely heavily on those described in the National Park Service's Fire Monitoring Handbook (FMH) (USDI National Park Service 2003). Since 2004, fire effects monitoring has been required work on National forests in Region 8 (USDA Forest Service 2011a).

National forests receive direction on where to install plots, how many to install, and what data shall be collected (USDA Forest Service 2011b). Collecting the data via standard protocols and using the recommended plot size are encouraged, although National forests have the option to use different protocols and plot sizes, as long as the minimum data are collected.

Plots are installed in a stratified random method. Strata are defined as "monitoring types," or areas of similar vegetation, fuels, burn prescription, and management history. Plots are installed randomly within monitoring types. National forests are encouraged to work together to define monitoring types, to facilitate data sharing

across unit boundaries. Each forest district is instructed to install two permanent monitoring plots per year, in the monitoring types of their choice. The agency recognizes that such a small number of annual plots generates concern in that the vegetation and weather conditions inherently vary from year to year, but the Forest Service does not employ dedicated monitoring personnel; monitoring is but one of many job duties for each data collector. Thus, the number was a compromise that would allow some data to be collected with minimal interference with other duties. Trends can be documented in these burn units, even if the monitoring results cannot prove statistically valid changes.

Vegetation and fuel data are collected at each visit. Trees are documented by species, density, diameter at breast height (dbh), mortality, and damage. Live tree seedling (all trees <2 inches at dbh or less than 4.5 feet tall) density is also tracked by species. Understory cover in classes is recorded by lifeform, including grass and grass-like, ferns, other forbs, woody shrubs, and vines. Individual species and/or species groups of special interest are also recorded. Examples are mountain laurel (*Kalmia latifolia*) and great rhododendron (*Rhododendron maximum*), which are important because of their role in fire behavior, and nonnative invasive species including *Microstegium vimineum*. National forests track dead and down fuels in size classes and also record litter and duff depth. A minimum of four photos is taken at each visit. Plots are visited the growing season before each burn, and then revisited multiple growing seasons following the burn. In addition, plots are visited immediately post-burn to document fuel consumption and severity.

PARTNERSHIPS

Over half the National forests in Region 8 have joined the U.S. Fire Learning Network (FLN), a federally-funded initiative to decrease barriers to restoring fire on the landscape. Collaborative planning, implementation, adaptive management, and the sharing of lessons learned are at the core of the FLN. One of the most commonly cited barriers is the lack of local fire ecology data to inform the fire management program, and consequently the National forests often also work with partners on monitoring projects. Districts are encouraged to work together internally (intra- and inter-forest) in order to improve the expertise level and increase the workforce, as well as sample size. Additionally, some National forests work with external agency partners in the FLN including The Nature Conservancy (TNC); the National Park Service, which employs permanent monitoring crews; and other agencies who are similarly strapped for time and funding.

Some National forests have dedicated a position to oversee fire effects monitoring on the districts. Those National forests and districts that recognize the value of monitoring tend to devote the most resources toward this program. For example, the Cherokee National Forest (Tennessee) has installed about 40 0.2-acre plots beginning in 2002. The plots are mainly in oak and yellow pine monitoring types and have been tracked through several prescribed fire applications. Program oversight, including data entry, quality control, and plot visit scheduling, comes from the forest level. The Unaka District shares the workload with National Park Service partners from the Southern Appalachian fire effects monitoring crew based in neighboring Great Smoky Mountains National Park (GSMNP, North Carolina and Tennessee). Since datasheets and collection methodologies are very similar, there is quick adaptation to the work assignment. In addition to more expedient data collection, the forest personnel exchange valuable fire behavior and effects observations with partners. Both the Cherokee National Forest and GSMNP are active members of the Southern Blue Ridge FLN, which allows both sets of data to be incorporated into a much larger dataset encompassing the same monitoring types across the southern Appalachians.

The Southern Blue Ridge FLN partnership includes, along with previously mentioned units, the Nantahala and Pisgah National Forests (North Carolina), the Chattahoochee-Oconee National Forest (Georgia), and the Francis Marion-Sumter National Forest (South Carolina). Other major partners include TNC and several State agencies in each of these States (in particular, North Carolina Wildlife Resources Commission), and Land Trust for the Little Tennessee, a conservation owner working in the same landscape. In addition to data being collected by these agencies and organizations, the FLN funds Forest Stewards, Inc. (FSI), to more than double the number of permanent plots on these lands. FSI is headed by a professor at Western Carolina University (North Carolina), who is working with the Forest Service Southern Research Station to analyze the data for the four-state area.

The neighboring George Washington and Jefferson National Forests (GWJNF, Virginia), in the central mountains, is a member of the Appalachian FLN. This network is active in Virginia and West Virginia. The GWJNF is similarly working with their primary fire effects monitoring partner, TNC of Virginia. Through a cost-share agreement, TNC employees work closely with all the districts of the GWJNF, using identical protocols, datasheets, and plot placement decisions. Their interagency monitoring working group had a very productive 2013 with progress made on a number of projects, especially revision of the collaboratively-developed Forest Structure and Composition (FSC) monitoring protocol and data forms. Revisions included editing monitoring goals and measureable objectives that can be referenced in burn plans and development of standardized data entry forms for Feat and Firemon Integrated (FFI) (Lutes and others 2009). FFI is a free software program for ecological monitoring which includes components for data entry, data storage, Geographic Information System, summary reports, and analysis. The most current versions of the FSC protocols and data forms can be found on the Conservation Gateway Web site. Significant progress was also made entering a backlog of previously collected data, with 55 percent of pre- and/or post-burn visits to the 0.01-acre plots monitored by TNC and the GWJNF into FFI. After five years of plot installation, the partnership has 330 plots in three monitoring types analogous and easily cross-walked to the monitoring types used in the Southern Blue Ridge. A next step for this network will be to determine whether more plots should be installed in any of the monitoring types.

The Ozark and Ouachita National Forests (Arkansas and Oklahoma) are active members in the South Central FLN, and have been working with TNC of Arkansas and many other partners to collect data since 2003. For example, more than 120 fire effects monitoring plots have been established across the Big Piney and Pleasant Hill Ranger Districts. Plots also have been established on the Sylamore and Boston Mountain Ranger Districts. Data is entered into FFI and may be combined in the future with data from similar monitoring types in the central and southern Appalachians for a meta-analysis across the oak and yellow pine systems.

Regardless of land ownership, burn plans include objectives such as reducing litter depth, increasing density of oak and pine seedlings, and reducing small dbh non-fire-adapted trees. Across all three Fire Learning Networks, data analysis is under way. Data in the South Central FLN indicate that fire is moving landscapes toward desired future conditions. Analysis is less complete in the other two FLNs, though managers observe positive changes across their landscapes.

SUMMARY

Prescribed fire is being increasingly reintroduced across the southern landscape. Only within the last ten years have managers had access to much fire ecology literature for landscapes outside the Coastal Plain, to help inform their fire management decisions. Even now that research is much more widely available, managers often would prefer to have data collected on their own unit and to be involved with the process. In 2004, National forests in the Southern Region received direction to collect fire effects monitoring data for vegetative strata ranging from the understory to the canopy, as well as for dead and down fuels. Managers also were advised to capture change using photo points. Plots are permanent and are re-measured on a schedule which is dependent on time since last treatment. All data is entered into FFI in order to facilitate sharing and also because this program provides basic statistical analyses that are easily interpreted by managers.

It has become apparent that regardless of good intentions, some National forests are unable to dedicate a position to oversee the fire effects monitoring at the forest level. Thus, the regional program has become one in which the units with the time, personnel, and interest are the ones with quality datasets. Additionally, National forests recognize that sharing data across unit borders is critical to increase the size of datasets and correspondingly reduce the variability within them. With the help and encouragement of partners—the FLN in particular—units work together to describe monitoring types, establish desired future conditions, define protocols, synchronize monitoring visits, and enter and analyze data. Each time managers work across boundaries, relationships are strengthened, trust is garnered, and information is exchanged. When they are collecting data, firefighters are given the chance to observe the changes to the landscape, without needing to focus attention on other management tasks. They can visually connect the fire effects to the fire application techniques, and their sense of ownership of and commitment to the project increases. When managers compare notes, whether in the field or via analyses, they improve the corporate fire

ecology knowledge base amongst all their partners. In the near future, fire effects databases will be merged and analyzed, and compared with research projects in similar monitoring types, thus expanding our understanding of fire effects in the Southern United States.

LITERATURE CITED

Braun, E.L. 1950. Deciduous forests of eastern North America. Philadelphia: Blakiston Co. 596 p.

Lutes, D.C.; Benson, N.C.; Keifer, M. [and others]. 2009. FFI: a software tool for ecological monitoring. International Journal of Wildland Fire. 18: 310-314. http://www.frames.gov/files/6213/6631/8579/FFI_Overview.pdf. [Date accessed: January 9, 2014].

National Interagency Fire Center. 2014. [Homepage of National Interagency Fire Center]. http://www.nifc.gov/fireInfo/fireInfo_stats_prescribed.html. [Date accessed: January 9, 2014].

U.S. Department of Agriculture (USDA) Forest Service. 2011a. [Homepage of Forest Service Manual Southern Region], [Online]. (2011, December 20). FSM 5100, Chapter 5140 Fire Management. R8-5140-2011-1. http://fsweb.r8.fs.fed.us/spf/fire/. [Date accessed: January 9, 2014].

U.S. Department of Agriculture (USDA) Forest Service. 2011b. [Homepage of Forest Service Manual Southern Region], [Online]. (2011, December 20). FSM 5100, Chapter 5140 Fire Management. R8-5140-2011-1, Included by reference. http://fsweb.r8.fs.fed.us/spf/fire/documents/2011/SOUTHERN%20REGION%20PRESCRIBED%20FIRE%20EFFECTS%20MONITORING%20GUIDEBOOK%202011.pdf. [Date accessed: January 9, 2014].

U.S. Department of the Interior (USDI) National Park Service. 2003. Fire Monitoring Handbook. Boise, ID: Fire Management Program Center, National Interagency Fire Center. 274 p.

[Extended Abstract]

A CUMULATIVE FIRE SEVERITY INDEX
FOR THE 2000-2008 LINVILLE GORGE WILDFIRES

Matthew Reilly, Donald Hagan, and Thomas A. Waldrop[1]

INTRODUCTION

The acreage of land burned annually in the Appalachian region has increased steadily over the last thirty years, with the rate of increase nearly doubling in recent years (Lafon and others 2005). Projected increases in fire activity in the southeast due to climate change strongly suggest the area of recently burned land in the southern Appalachian Mountains is likely to continue increasing (Bachelet and others 2001). As a result, there will be a growing need for managers to understand the effects of fires returning to recently burned stands in relation to how repeated fire affects management goals. Unfortunately, information on re-burns in the southern Appalachian Mountains is limited (Arthur and others 1998), and managers in the region can only use inference from past studies from the Western United States for insights into effects of previous fires on re-burn severity (Romme 1982, Thompson and others 2007). With little information available from within the region, it is difficult for land managers in the southern Appalachian region to understand variability and predict wildfire effects.

Past studies on areas subject to re-burn in the Western United States indicate that fire severity depends on the response of live fuels to carry fire (Romme 1982, Thompson and others 2007). The abundant pine regeneration and vigorous sprouting of hardwood trees and ericaceous shrubs typical after fire in the southern Appalachian Mountains suggest that live fuels may respond rapidly and are likely capable of carrying severe fire soon after an initial burn. In this scenario, young pine and oak regeneration may be destroyed prior to reaching maturity, and subsequent regeneration will depend on input of seeds from outside areas. However, if mature pines and oaks can survive them, higher severity re-burns may be more successful than initial burns at eliminating understory shrubs and saplings and reducing litter and duff depth. These effects would further promote regeneration of desirable species [e.g., Table Mountain Pine (*Pinus pungens*)] as well as promoting diversity in the understory.

The occurrence of several large fires from 2000 to 2008 in and around Linville Gorge, North Carolina afforded a unique opportunity to study how landscape characteristics and recent burn history (including sites that burned twice) interact to influence fire behavior in the southern Appalachian Mountains. The specific objectives of this study were to:

- Develop a field-based Composite Burn Index (CBI), based on readily obtainable litter and vegetative characteristics, to quantify fire severity.

- Use the CBI to examine severity patterns in areas subject to initial and repeated wildfire across major environmental gradients.

MATERIALS AND METHODS

Linville Gorge is in the Appalachian Mountains of western North Carolina and contains a 10,843-acre federally designated wilderness area. Steep slopes and complex topography within the gorge create a wide range of environmental gradients, which results in an extremely diverse landscape. From 2000 to 2008, five wildfires burned a large portion of the area in and surrounding Linville Gorge (fig. 1; table 1). The 2000 fire (a.k.a. the Linville Gorge Fire) was the first major surface fire in the area since the 1950s and burned approximately 4,000 acres. In spring 2007, three separate fires (Pinnacle, Dobson Knob, Shortoff Mountain) burned a large portion of the landscape previously burned in 2000, as well as much of the remaining unburned area surrounding Linville Gorge. Another large wildfire (Sunrise) occurred in 2008 and burned much of the area immediately adjacent the area that burned in 2000 and 2007.

A Composite Burn Index (CBI) was applied in 57 plots established across gradients of burn severity in Linville Gorge. The goal was to capture the full spectrum of fire impacts, from low to high severity, in sites burned once or twice. We used a modified version of the Fire Effects

[1]Matthew Reilly is a PhD candidate in the Department of Forest Ecosystems and Society, Oregon State University, Corvallis, OR 97331

Donald Hagan is a Lecturer in the School of Agricultural, Forest, and Environmental Sciences, Clemson University, Clemson, SC 29634

Thomas A. Waldrop is a Supervisory Research Forester, USDA Forest Service, Southern Research Station, Clemson, SC 29634

Citation for proceedings: Waldrop, Thomas A., ed. 2014. Proceedings, Wildland Fire in the Appalachians: Discussions among Managers and Scientists. Gen. Tech. Rep. SRS-199. Asheville, NC: U.S. Department of Agriculture Forest Service, Southern Research Station. 208 p.

Inventory and Monitoring (FIREMON) protocol (Lutes and others 2006) to visually estimate fire effects in four categories within a 50-foot radius of plot center on a 300 point scale. This slight modification of the FIREMON protocol allows variables of local importance to be used. The four categories were percent duff consumption, percent mortality of shrubs, percent mortality of subcanopy trees, and percent mortality of overstory trees. We then summed the fire effects scores for each category (maximum score=1200) to calculate CBI values for each plot. In order to test how well our remotely sensed estimates of fire severity predicted actual fire effects, we created regression models using RdNBR values and estimated wildfire effects for each year. A regression model was created for each year using the RdNBR and CBI values. The models were then applied to the RdNBR raster data for each year to create a spatial model of CBI values within each wildfire. All pixels in each wildfire were then sampled for CBI, elevation, slope, and aspect. We compared the distributions of CBI values across each of these gradients in each landscape.

RESULTS AND DISCUSSION

All wildfires resulted in extremely heterogeneous patterns of fire severity across the landscape, ranging from low levels of litter consumption to total litter and duff consumption and complete midstory and canopy mortality. The distributions of CBI values over major environmental gradients were similar among each of the five burn units, although they were highly variable within each landscape. CBI values were generally higher in landscapes subject to repeated fire and showed similar patterns along gradients in elevation, slope, and aspect (figs. 2-4). Severity was highest at mid to upper elevation on steeper southwestern facing slopes in both cases but was generally higher in re-burned forests.

We propose that re-burn severity in the southern Appalachians is higher due to the rapid response of live vegetation following initial fire. Abundant regeneration of conifers from serotinous cones, a dense layer of sprouting ericaceous vegetation, and large increases in herbaceous cover provide the fine fuels necessary to carry fire. Elevated amounts of dead and downed woods from mortality in the first fire provide larger fuels which increase residence time and heat output. However, if the second fire is soon enough after the first, the forest floor may not have had sufficient time to reach pre-burn levels, thus exposing soil and creating conditions of greater severity.

CONCLUSIONS

The results of this study highlight the utility of linking a field-derived burn severity index with remote sensing for assessing wildfire severity in the southern Appalachian Mountains. Estimates of fire severity were easily generated based on simple field observations, yet they facilitated robust comparisons across a complex mountain landscape. Overall our findings suggest that landscape heterogeneity is a major driver of spatial patterns of fire severity, and that higher severity fires may occur when an area is burned for the second time. This information will benefit land managers as it will help them identify area most severely impacted by wildfire, thereby enabling a more efficient allocation of resources for post-fire rehabilitation and restoration.

LITERATURE CITED

Arthur, M.A.; Paratley, R.D.; Blankenship, B.A. 1998. Single and repeated fires affect survival and regeneration of woody and herbaceous species in an oak-pine forest. Journal of the Torrey Botanical Society. 125: 225-236.

Bachelet, D.; Neilson, R.P.; Lenihan, J.M.; Drapek, R.J. 2001. Climate change effects on vegetation distribution and carbon budget in the United States. Ecosystems. 4: 165-185.

Lafon, C.W.; Hoss, J.A.; Grissino-Mayer, H.D. 2005. The contemporary fire regime of the central Appalachian Mountains and its relation to climate. Physical Geography. 26: 126-146.

Lutes, D.C.; Keane, R.E.; Caratti, J.F. [and others]. 2006. FIREMON: fire effects monitoring and inventory system. Gen. Tech. Rep. RMRS-GTR-164-CD. Fort Collins, CO: U.S. Department of Agriculture Forest Service, Rocky Mountain Research Station. 1 CD.

Romme, W.H. 1982. Fire and landscape diversity in subalpine forests of Yellowstone National Park. Ecological Monographs. 52: 199-221.

Thompson, J.R.; Spies, T.A.; Ganio, L.M. 2007. Reburn severity in managed and unmanaged vegetation in a large wildfire. Proceedings of the National Academy of Sciences. 104: 743-748.

Wimberly, M.C.; Reilly, M.J. 2007. Assessment of fire severity and species diversity in the southern Appalachians using Landsat TM and ETM+ imagery. Remote Sensing of Environment. 108: 189-197.

Table 1—Area impacted by zero, one, or two wildfires between 2000 and 2008 in Linville Gorge Wilderness Area, North Carolina, USA

Fire history	Area (acres)
Unburned	5,017
Burned once in 2000	4,031
Burned once in 2007 or 2008	3,957
Burned twice, 2000 and 2007	6,118

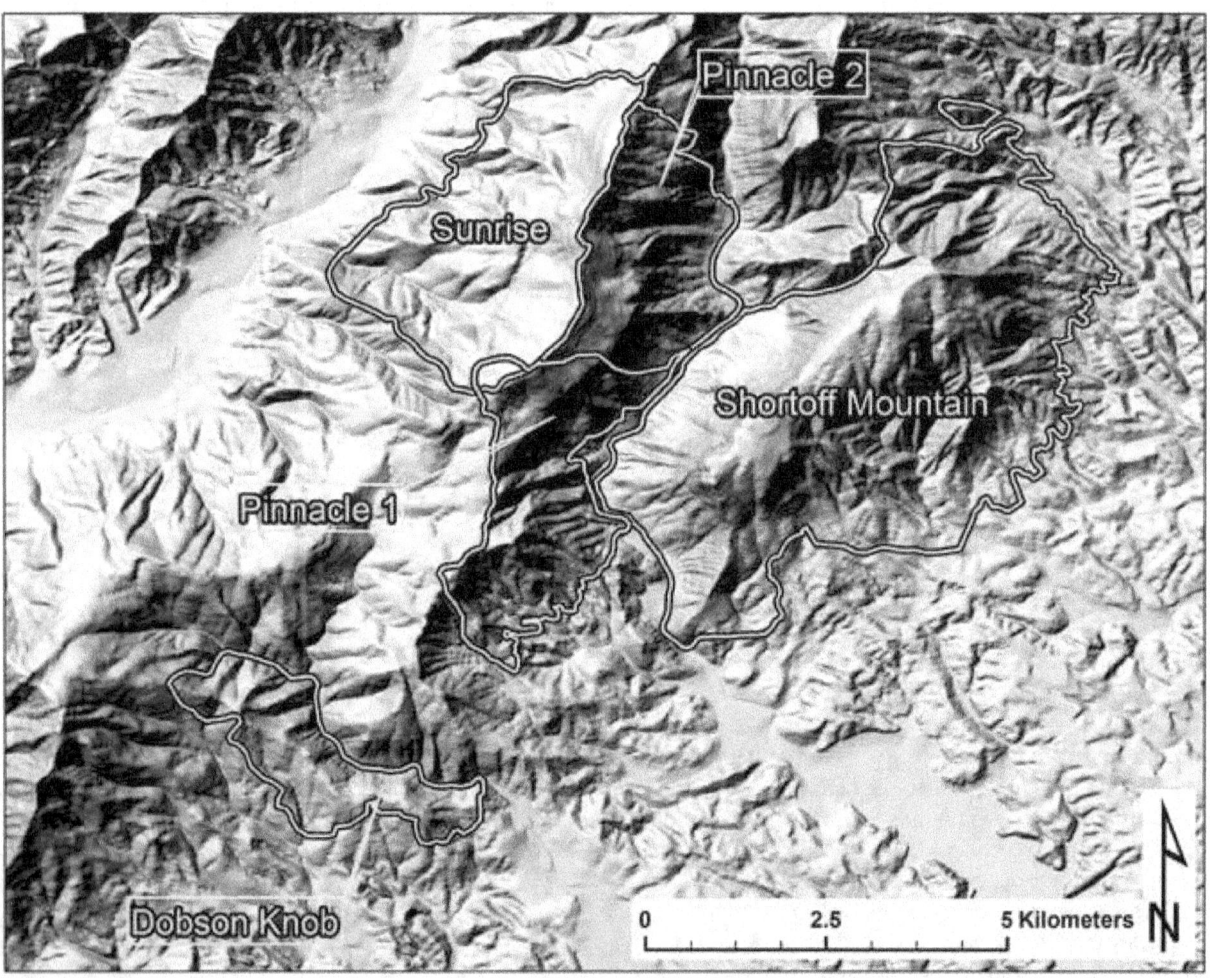

Figure 1—Map of the study area showing burn histories and plot locations. "Pinnacle 2" indicates an area previously burned by the Sunrise fire that was re-burned by the Pinnacle fire. "Pinnacle 1" indicates the portion of the Pinnacle fire that did not impact a previously burned area.

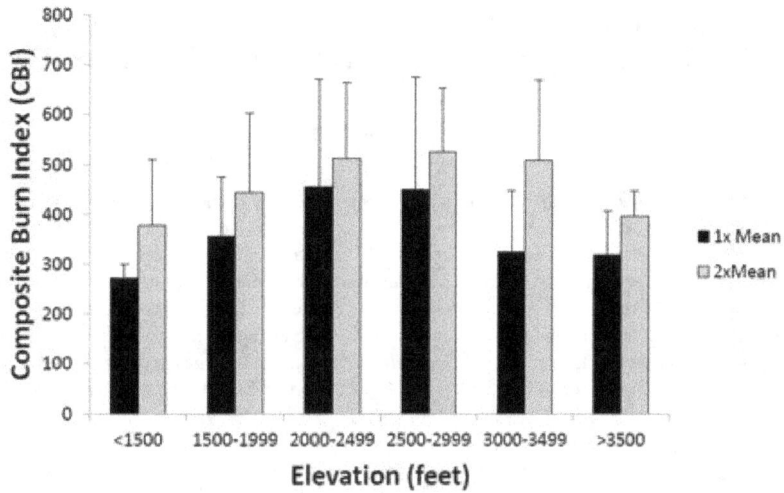

Figure 2—Distribution of CBI values across an elevation gradient for areas burned 1x and 2x in Linville Gorge, North Carolina.

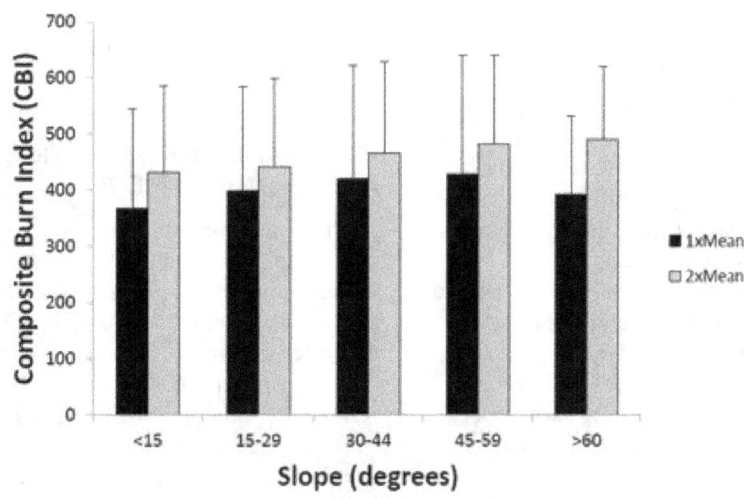

Figure 3—Distribution of CBI values across a slope gradient for areas burned 1x and 2x in Linville Gorge, North Carolina.

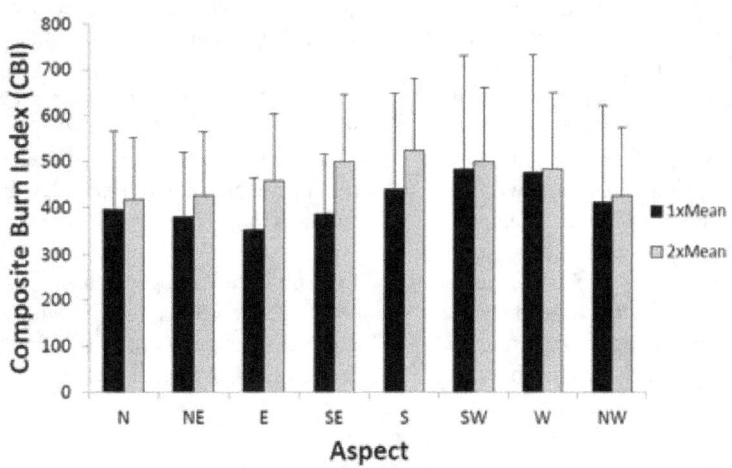

Figure 4—Distribution of CBI values across an aspect gradient for areas burned 1x and 2x in Linville Gorge, North Carolina.

PYROGANDA: CREATING NEW TERMS AND IDENTITIES FOR PROMOTING FIRE USE IN ECOLOGICAL FIRE MANAGEMENT

Timothy Ingalsbee[1]

Abstract—Much of the language used by the wildland fire community and news media has implicit anti-fire bias that perpetuates anti-fire attitudes. In order to promote greater fire use for ecological fire management, new words need to be created; existing words should be redefined; and new identities for fire management workers must be developed. FUSEE presents some examples of the new words, symbols, and slogans it uses in its public education and policy advocacy work to nurture pro-fire attitudes and help support a paradigm shift in fire management. This paper argues that other agencies, organizations, and institutions in the wildland fire community will have to engage in an explicit pro-fire "pyroganda" campaign to help counter its historic anti-fire propaganda and inspire necessary changes in consciousness and behavior in the public and fire management workforce. As part and parcel of this effort, FUSEE proposes renaming wildland firefighters as fire rangers.

INTRODUCTION

Defined in neutral, objective terms by sociologists, propaganda refers to the deliberate, systematic attempt to shape public perceptions, manipulate cognitions, and direct behavior to achieve desired social goals. A classic in-group/out-group double standard exists in the use of propaganda, however. Government agencies' public service announcements and corporations' advertisements are rarely viewed as propagandistic, while the statements and slogans of foreign governments or nonprofit advocacy groups are often labeled as propaganda. Hence, propaganda has become a pejorative term in American society; however, the historic efforts by Federal land management agencies and the news media to affect the American public's beliefs and behaviors in support of wildfire prevention and suppression rightfully should be acknowledged as propagandistic.

Beyond public campaigns to gain citizen support for fire prevention or suppression programs, much of the terminology used in wildland fire management lends itself to propaganda in that it is not unbiased or value-neutral, but rather, heavily slanted by militaristic discourse and terminology that foments anti-fire attitudes. Suppression terms like fire fighting, initial attack, strike teams, aggressive suppression, etc. represent concepts and a mindset that suited 20th century attitudes about wildfire as an enemy or threat to natural resources and human communities. But these words fail to accurately describe emerging pro-fire policies and practices to use fire as a management tool—and respect wildfire as a natural process—to further goals of protecting communities and restoring ecosystems. Accordingly, if the wildland fire community wants to help society forge a new relationship with wildland fire and garner more public support for fire use, then new words, symbols, and identities will have to be consciously created as part of a paradigm shift towards ecological fire management.

PYROGANDA BY GOVERNMENT AGENCIES AND THE NEWS MEDIA

I will use the word pyroganda to refer to efforts to propagandize the public and workers to influence their attitudes and actions in regard to wildland fire. Pyroganda can be used to stimulate anti-fire beliefs and behaviors to further wildfire prevention and suppression goals, or pro-fire beliefs and behaviors to further fire use and restoration goals, and I will be offering suggestions for the latter. Historically, most pyroganda has been State-sponsored and intended to create anti-wildfire attitudes in the general public. The clearest example is the Smokey Bear campaign and its gallery of wildfire prevention posters and slogans. The Smokey Bear campaign was a joint creation of the U.S. Forest Service and the War Advertising Council—a propaganda organ that was part of mobilizing the American people to support the war effort of the 1940s. World War II era posters that said "Forest Fires Aid the Enemy" provided a conceptual bridge to the notion that forest fires are the enemy (fig. 1). Long after the Second World War ended, the war on wildfire continued.

State-sponsored pyroganda has been echoed and amplified by corporate news media. Sensationalistic headlines constantly depict wildfires as catastrophes, associating them almost exclusively with disaster, death,

[1]Timothy Ingalsbee, Executive Director, Firefighters United for Safety, Ethics, and Ecology (FUSEE), Eugene, OR 97405

Citation for proceedings: Waldrop, Thomas A., ed. 2014. Proceedings, Wildland Fire in the Appalachians: Discussions among Managers and Scientists. Gen. Tech. Rep. SRS-199. Asheville, NC: U.S. Department of Agriculture Forest Service, Southern Research Station. 208 p.

and destruction. Journalists often emulate the style of war reporting in their stories, using dramatic terms and images that focus on firefighters bravely battling blazes. The constant framing of wildfires as catastrophes and suppression operations as fire fighting obscures the social and ecological benefits of fire and thwarts the use of alternative management techniques such as fire use. Unfortunately, what most people know and believe about wildfires comes via news stories, so if the bulk of news coverage is slanted by the use of anti-fire language, then it is not surprising that anti-fire attitudes persist despite the recent efforts of some fire professionals to explain the benefits of natural fire ecology processes or progressive fire use policies.

As an intentional State policy to manipulate the behavior of citizens to prevent wildfires, and as a deliberate strategy by the news media to attract more readers and viewers, State-sponsored and media-supported anti-fire pyroganda has been very successful. However, now that fire management agencies desire to use more prescribed and wildland fires to restore and maintain fire-adapted ecosystems, many fire managers are bemoaning the "Smokey Bear syndrome" that prompts public complaints to prescribed burning and politicians' pressure for aggressive wildfire suppression. In essence, fire management agencies have become victims of their past success as propagandists. If agencies are to cultivate public support for greater fire use in land management, then they will have to conduct a deliberate fire promotion campaign with as much vigor and commitment as they conducted their fire prevention campaign. That campaign will require new pro-fire language.

FIREFIGHTERS UNITED FOR SAFETY, ETHICS, AND ECOLOGY (FUSEE)

Firefighters United for Safety, Ethics, and Ecology (FUSEE) is a nonprofit organization founded in 2005. Our members are current, retired, and former wildland firefighters from Federal and State agencies, private companies, and rural volunteers; fire researchers and managers; educators and students; and other interested citizens. Our mission is to do public education and policy advocacy to promote greater firefighter and public safety, ethical use of taxpayer funds and resources, and ecological protection and restoration of fire-adapted ecosystems. Our ultimate goal is to help nurture a paradigm shift in fire management policies and practices that changes society's relationship with wildland fire.

FUSEE produces white papers and press statements into which we devote significant creative energy to deconstruct conventional fire management terminology and rearticulate or invent new concepts or phrases that

we hope will help shift public consciousness and agency behavior. FUSEE focuses its public education projects mainly on re-educating journalists about fire ecology and management, believing that if we can alter the way the news media talk about fire then this will have a larger impact on changing public attitudes and opinions. FUSEE has produced a series of manuals and tipsheets called *A Reporter's Guide to Wildland Fire*. We encourage reporters to go beyond the war reporting approach to covering wildfire events and offer suggestions for alternative words, angles, and frames to use in writing news stories about wildfire events and the full breadth of fire management issues and activities beyond firefighting.

The Reporter's Guide contains a section that we call "All the Words Fit to Print." It displays a table of terms ranging from what we consider to be "loaded" terms (i.e., official words that are biased or slanted to induce anti-fire attitudes), "neutral" terms (i.e., less biased or more objective terms), and "new" terms (i.e., words that could nurture pro-fire attitudes). For example, we present "natural disaster" as a loaded term, "natural disturbance" as more neutral, and "ecological stimulus" as a preferred new term. *The Reporter's Guide* encourages journalists to discard loaded terms and start using what we call neutral or new terms in their stories. Admittedly, our proposed new terms are as, if not more, loaded as conventional terms, but the difference is that we are consciously trying to craft pro-fire language to counter the anti-fire bias in current official fire management terminology.

OLD SYMBOLS AND NEW MEANINGS IN LOGOS AND SLOGANS

In addition to creating new words and redefining old words, FUSEE aims to shift consciousness through the use of symbols and slogans. Symbols offer a means of conveying messages and meanings, and the most powerful persuasive messages come from traditional symbols that are rearticulated with new meanings. A traditional symbol used in fire management is the fire combustion triangle (heat, oxygen, fuel) and the fire environment triangle (weather, topography, fuel). Triangles are used in several logos of fire-related organizations (fig. 2). For example, the U.S. Forest Service Fire and Aviation Management, the Fire Research and Management Exchange System, and the Society of Fire Protection Engineers all utilize the triangle as core graphical elements of their logos.

FUSEE has also incorporated the triangle in its organizational logo, and we use it to symbolize our concept of the "FUSEE triad." The three legs of our triangle refer to safety, ethics, and ecology, and represent our core belief that firefighter safety is fundamentally interconnected with professional and public service ethics, and ecological protection and restoration. If you compromise the integrity of one leg of that triad, the system fails or collapses. Thus, for example, if ecological integrity is compromised through inappropriate land management or fire suppression actions, then these will ultimately negatively impact firefighter safety on future wildfire incidents. The symbol of the triangle is a deliberate part of our pyroganda to persuade the fire community to manage wildfires in ways that link firefighter safety with ethical and ecological management actions.

In general, organizations doing propaganda should pay attention to the spelling and phonetics of their organizational acronyms, and where these acronyms symbolize meaningful words or images, they are more likely to rally community or public support. FUSEE spent some effort creating a name for our organization that has an acronym that also symbolizes a meaningful word to firefighters. FUSEE (pronounced "FEW-zee") represents a fusee, the hand-held torch used by wildland firefighters. Hotshots and smokejumpers consider fusees to be safety items they can use to burn out safety zones in situations where they may face entrapment or burnover. They are also used to ignite burnouts or backfires to contain or control wildfires. FUSEE works to shift the primary use of fusees from stopping wildfires to be more associated with starting controlled fires for prescribed burns or wildland fire use. Reintroducing fire and restoring fire-adapted ecosystems—the occupational environment of firefighters—would proactively enhance the safety of fire crews. We have found that the fusee symbol usually prompts a smile among folks in the wildland fire community who appreciate its meaning; among citizens with no experience in fire management, it sometimes prompts confusion and a fair amount of mispronunciation (e.g. "fussy"). The real utility of our acronym, however, is its use as a symbol for the torchbearer.

The torchbearer is a traditional symbol that refers both to pathbreakers (or "trailblazers") and advocates for social change. For example, the Statue of Liberty is a torchbearer who lights the path toward freedom and democracy in America, and advocates for the spread of freedom and democracy to other countries abroad. FUSEE has displayed a torchbearing hand in its logos and developed a motto that functions like our organizational tagline: "We're torchbearers for a new fire management paradigm!" This symbolizes our unashamed role as advocates promoting fire use in safe, ethical, ecological fire management. We formed our nonprofit organization in large part to enable fire professionals working in government agencies or private companies to anonymously engage in progressive policy advocacy without facing job reprisals. The fusee torchbearer symbol thus works for

us in multiple ways to advocate for pro-fire policies and recruit more fire professionals as advocates (fig. 3).

PRO-FIRE MESSAGES AND FIRE PRO MESSENGERS

Effective propaganda creates memorable messages that articulate ideas and information in ways that inspire change in consciousness or behavior. FUSEE crafts messages that often revise, redefine, or reword existing messages from other organizations and agencies conducting their own pyroganda. For example, we believe that the official phrase "community wildfire protection" conveys an anti-fire message. It focuses on wildfire while excluding other kinds of fire (e.g., controlled burning, fire use), and adopts a defensive posture (i.e., wildfire is a threat we must protect ourselves from) while excluding other possible responses and relationships to fire.

Consequently, we revised that phrase to become "community fire preparation" because we feel it is a more inclusive message that opens up people to be prepared for fire in all its forms—prescribed fire, wildfire, and fire use. And preparation means not just defensively warding it off, but also taking proactive steps to possibly welcome it in! If homeowners have proactively prepared their properties using FireWise[2] principles, then wildfire may not be a threat, and prescribed burning may be a viable tool for managing fuels within the wildland-urban interface zone. Thus, we crafted the slogan, "The sooner communities are prepared for fire, the sooner ecosystems can be restored with fire." The use of words like "for" and "with" denote a new non-antagonistic relationship with wildland fire and add to the implicitly pro-fire message that we hope will be persuasive with homeowners.

FUSEE continues to experiment with messages that we hope will resonate with the public, and equally if not more importantly, inspire fire management workers and managers. Referring to the FUSEE triad of safety, ethics, and ecology, people usually have clear ideas about the concepts of fire safety and fire ecology, but often ask what we mean by "fire ethics?" In response, FUSEE crafted a message to address this question, drawing upon the beloved figure of Aldo Leopold and his renowned concept of a land ethic. Paraphrasing Leopold, we articulated our own fire ethic:

"A thing is right when it contributes to the safety of firefighters and the public, ethical use of public resources, environmental protection of fire-affected landscapes, and ecological restoration of fire-dependent ecosystems. It is wrong when it tends otherwise."

---

[2]National Fire Protection Association. 2014. FireWise Communities. http://www.firewise.org/?sso=0. [Date accessed: September 2014]

We also use Leopold's metaphor of "green fire" as a symbol of wildness to create our slogan, "Keep the Greenfire burning!" Our use of green fire is intended to represent fire use for ecological restoration and a rewilding of landscapes altered by past fire suppression. Our hope is that such clear references to a beloved messenger will help make fire professionals more receptive to our message.

Research demonstrates that often the messenger is as important as the message itself in effective communication. In that respect, we founded FUSEE with the belief that wildland firefighters would make persuasive spokespersons for advocating change in fire management policies and practices. FUSEE has leveraged the iconic image of firefighters as heroes to bravely say what our supporters would not or could not say publicly for fear of job retributions from their employers, or political backlash from industry representatives and elected officials. FUSEE has produced several white papers and press statements that critique the safety risks to firefighters, economic costs to taxpayers, and ecological impacts to public wildlands that result from aggressive suppression actions. The news media are particularly keen to quote a firefighters' group speaking out against controversial firefighting policies or incidents. Compared to other messengers like industry lobbyists or environmental activists, veteran firefighters can raise these criticisms and speak out on controversial fire issues with much more credibility.

PARTNERS IN FIRE EDUCATION

I was invited to a workshop in Boise in 2008 called, "Partners in Fire Education" (PIFE). Two major public opinion polling companies had just completed a national survey and a series of focus groups on public attitudes about the ecological role of fire and the role of fire management. After an hour-long presentation to professional fire educators and agency officials describing the survey sample, methods, and margins of error in their study that cost several tens of thousands of dollars, the polling companies boiled down their analysis to two recommendations for agencies to conduct more successful fire-related messaging:

1) When talking about fire issues to the public, if you can lead with safety-related messages, then this makes people more receptive to additional messages about fire issues.

2) In the eyes and ears of the public, firefighters are the most credible and persuasive messengers to deliver those messages because they are the ones on the front lines dealing with the full risks and consequences of fire.

At that point, several heads turned to look at me. I was more than embarrassed not only because I did not anticipate the sudden attention, but also because I knew that the name "Firefighters United for Safety..." was dreamed up by myself and a couple friends for the mere cost of a round of beers, a far cry from the companies' expensive survey!

The recommendations of the PIFE pollsters seem to be validated by the excellent success that our young, small organization has enjoyed with the news media and policymakers. Measured both in terms of the quantity and quality of news articles that have quoted FUSEE members, we have had great success, indeed. We occasionally provide provocative statements that are intended to induce "shock and awe" that we hope will make people stop and think. For example, FUSEE criticized one of the dominant symbols and iconic media images of firefighting—fire retardant dumped by air tankers—because we were concerned about the environmental effects and economic costs of these toxic chemicals. The Los Angeles Times' editors selected FUSEE's statement to be the "pull quote" for their Pulitzer prize-winning story on the costs and impacts of aerial fire suppression.[3]

We believe that our success in getting high-profile quotes in the media is due as much to the novel messenger we are presenting—the voice of wildland firefighters—as it is due to the messages we are communicating that critique specific firefighting actions that are unsafe, expensive, or ecologically damaging. Our media messages sometimes get through to policymakers. For example, in response to increased public scrutiny and press coverage over aerial retardant, companies are redesigning the chemical composition of fire retardants, and the Forest Service has developed new policies to more carefully target retardant drops to avoid waterways.[4]

NEW IDENTITIES FOR FIRE MANAGEMENT WORKERS

Some people have pointed out the contradiction that our organization has firefighters in its name when, in actuality, many of our members are highly critical of certain firefighting policies and practices. Our philosophical opposition to the use of the war metaphor

[3]Cart, Julie, and Boxall, Bettina. 2008. Air tanker drops in wildfires are often just for show. The bulky aircraft are reassuring sights to those in harm's way, but their use can be a needless and expensive exercise to appease politicians. Fire officials call them 'CNN drops.' Los Angeles Times. July 29.

[4]U.S. Department of Agriculture (USDA) Forest Service. 2014. Interagency Policy for Aerial and Ground Delivery of Wildland Fire Chemicals Near Waterways and Other Avoidance Areas. http://www. fs.fed.us/fire/retardant/. [Date accessed: September 2014].

in fire management should logically extend to the term, "firefighter" and admittedly, we look forward to the day in the future when that word will become as obsolete and anachronistic as the word "smokechaser" is today. Consequently, we are striving to create a new word and identity for ecological fire management workers that will encompass the broad array of duties and functions they will be performing. Ideally, this new identity will be attractive to the fire community at the same time as it captures the news media's and public's imagination and maintains the high social esteem that people feel towards firefighters.

Fire-Lighters, Fire-Guiders, and Pyrotechnicians

In the early days of our organization's founding, we initially experimented with using the terms "fire-lighters" and "fire-guiders." They both rhyme with firefighters and more accurately describe the role of fire use workers starting prescribed fires and steering wildfires. But our supporters commented that these words conjured up images of arsonists, cigarette smokers, or New Age fire-walkers rather than fire use workers. We also tried out the term "pyrotechnicians." This described our vision of fire use workers as high-skill/high-wage professionals using the best science and advanced technology to manage wildfire. However, too many people heard "pyro" as meaning arsonists and failed to hear "technicians," so we stopped promoting that term, too. Besides, the word pyrotechnicians already refers to those that work with fireworks, and we want to see fire artfully applied down on the ground rather than up in the sky.

Firefighters as Cowboys or Native Americans?

For propaganda purposes, the best symbols to use are ones already embedded in the dominant culture and generating positive emotional responses. So what existing images could we adopt that would be positively accepted by wildland firefighters and the public and would nurture pro-fire attitudes in support of ecological fire management? How about cowboys? In fact, the image of loose-herding fires comes close to our vision of managing wildfires with fire use tactics. However, the cultural image and historical legacy of cowboys are mixed: they lived and worked on the land, but they also played an active role in domesticating western wildlands. This is not exactly the image we want to associate with fire restorationists.

How about Native Americans? Indeed, there is much that society could relearn about sustaining habitats from Native American burning practices. In fact, we have promoted the slogan, "Native forests need Native fires!" to symbolize our view that we need to reintroduce indigenous burning practices for both cultural and ecological restoration purposes. However, we are wary of cultural appropriation of Native Americans, so in our view likening firefighters to Native Americans would be inappropriate.

Firefighters as Shepherds or Stewards?

FUSEE wants to link ecological fire management with the concept of land stewardship, so what other cultural images might make that connection? Would shepherds or stewards work well as new identities for firefighters? Although these identities may better symbolize the monitoring work of fire use tactics, images of shepherds passively watching over tender flocks of flames misses something important to many individuals attracted to present-day firefighting: the adventure and adrenaline rush of working alongside uncontrolled flames. They enjoy the adventure of jumping out of airplanes, flying in helicopters, hiking in rugged country, cutting and digging line alongside wild fire. A kind of macho militarist bravado endures in firefighter culture that is sustained by agency terminology (e.g., one of the Ten Standard Orders is to "fight fire aggressively…") and the news media's penchant for portraying firefighters as brave heroes. We doubt that firefighters would accept trading away their heroic warrior identity for that of a shepherd or steward. Besides, if the objectives of a given fire change from fire use for ecological restoration to full suppression for community protection, then workers will need an empowering identity that addresses the extra risk and need for bravery that comes from suppressing rather than stewarding flames. There must be some alternative to an aggressive soldier or passive steward type of identity that empowers active fire management for ecological restoration with all the adventure and hard work that will entail, but discards images of machismo or militarism.

Firefighters as Rangers?

According to the PIFE poll, after wildland firefighters the occupations with the most public credibility on wildfire issues were park and forest rangers. What if firefighters were identified as rangers? While the National Park Service (NPS) is comfortable identifying its seasonal employees as rangers, the U.S. Forest Service reserves that identity for its District line officers and does not share it with other permanent or seasonal employees. Regardless, most citizens identify workers in the NPS and Forest Service as "rangers." Rangers in the Forest Service have long been focused on firefighting, while rangers in the NPS have long been focused on law enforcement. There is nothing essentialist about social identities; rather, each identity must be consciously defined and articulated. Simply renaming firefighters as rangers could continue to be linked in peoples' minds with firefighting or policing rather than fire use for ecological restoration.

In FUSEE's opinion, re-identifying firefighters as fire rangers has the most potential for symbolizing the full spectrum of possible roles and duties needed by fire use workers in ecological fire management, but it all depends on how this identity is articulated. For example, Ontario, Canada has been calling its firefighters "fire rangers" since the late 1800s, but their work is exclusively focused on fire prevention and suppression. There is nothing essential about social identities—they all must be carefully defined and articulated—so as important as it is to make careful use of language, we cannot assume that simply changing the name to fire rangers will help shift the fire management paradigm from firefighting to fire-lighting and fire-guiding. The fire ranger concept must be part and parcel of a wider pyroganda campaign that promotes fire use for ecological fire management.

FIRE RANGERS USE FIRE FOR ECOLOGICAL FIRE MANAGEMENT

FUSEE's conception of fire rangers is a work in progress, and we welcome input from other fire professionals. In our vision, natural ignitions will trigger opportunities for fire rangers to use fire for ecosystem restoration. Using the latest technology for monitoring, mapping, and modeling fire behavior and effects, fire rangers will actively manage wildland fires to accomplish preplanned restoration objectives, and dynamically shift their tactics and strategy according to current and expected conditions. They will be guiding fires as they range across the landscape, steering fires into places they want to burn and away from places that should not burn, slowing down or speeding up fire spread as the weather and fuel conditions warrant, stopping fires when they must, but starting them wherever they can. In essence, fire rangers will be doing something like a hybridized form of "prescribed natural fire use."

For individuals who cherish the hard work and adventure of wildland firefighting, there will still be plenty of that in a job whose description is changed from fighting to managing and using fire. There will be lots of fire line construction; however, instead of reactively cutting fire lines in a suppression state of emergency, many fire lines will be proactively built as fuel breaks to facilitate the creation of firesheds for managing fire and fuels at landscape scales. And we will still need the ability to rapidly deploy crews in remote wildlands to manage ignitions, so smokejumpers, helitacks, helirappellers, and hotshot crews may become the vanguard of the fire rangers corps. While firefighters might lose some of their current status as heroes, we believe fire rangers may gain even more respect as healers—public servants doing the hard work of landscape stewardship and ecosystem restoration. They may even maintain that heroic image as they strive to ward off environmental disasters resulting from climate change.

CONCLUSION

On November 1, 2013, at the "Words on Fire: Toward a New Language of Wildland Fire" Symposium, renowned fire historian and keynote speaker, Dr. Stephen Pyne, argued that the words used by wildland fire management is out of sync with the needs of fire managers to increase the use of fire for ecological and cultural restoration goals. Although the National Wildfire Coordinating Group has repeatedly revised the official glossary of Federal fire management terms, some of these revisions have not always been well received by managers or effectively described the changing goals and objectives, strategies, and tactics of wildfire operations. Much of the current terminology of fire management unwittingly conveys an implicit anti-fire bias that historically functioned as propaganda to guide public and professional beliefs and behaviors toward wildfire. But now that fire ecology science and progressive policy changes are leading society towards a new relationship with wildland fire, the fire community must develop new language with deliberate intent to nurture changes in consciousness and behavior. Whether or not fire professionals can acknowledge this, this reeducation campaign will involve creating new propaganda or pyroganda.

Most fire management workers would rather be working with fire than fighting against it, would prefer to protect and restore the land than damage or degrade it. In the future, fire will change from being an adversary to an ally, a valuable management tool, and a respected force of nature. The wildland fire community will need to re-envision and rearticulate the identity of its workforce that will be more focused on ecosystem restoration than wildfire suppression, serving more as stewards than soldiers. Thus, continuing to call these workers firefighters wrongly perpetuates anti-fire attitudes and plainly misrepresents the nature of their work.

FUSEE proposes that we change the identity of crews from the explicitly anti-fire name of firefighters to the implicitly pro-fire name of fire rangers. Selling this new image and identity to the public will require designing creative logos, symbols, and slogans that communicate how fire rangers are as skilled, brave, wise, hardworking and adventurous as is the reputation of contemporary firefighters. But it will not be enough to simply change workers' job titles. The wildland fire community needs to change its entire discourse—jettison all loaded anti-fire or militaristic terms, and consciously promote neutral/new pro-fire management terms—in order to nurture and sustain public support for fire use in ecological fire management. Ultimately, however, it will matter less the kind of language, logos, messages, and messengers we use than the kind of actions on the ground that we implement. In that respect, fire rangers' pyroganda of the deed as torchbearers will be the most decisive element in shifting the paradigm.

ACKNOWLEDGMENTS

The author wishes to acknowledge the FUSEE Board of Directors, in particular Joseph Fox, Tom Ribe, Rich Fairbanks, and Julie Rogers for our numerous conversations and collaborations that influenced my thoughts about ecological fire management and inspired many of the concepts described in the paper.

Figure 1—Examples of State-sponsored anti-fire pyroganda.

Figure 2—Pyroganda in logos: images as symbols used to create meanings and motives for action.

Figure 3—Examples of FUSEE graphics displaying torchbearer and the triangle symbols.

TORCHBEARERS FOR A NEW FIRE MANAGEMENT PARADIGM: FIREFIGHTERS UNITED FOR SAFETY, ETHICS, AND ECOLOGY (FUSEE)

Timothy Ingalsbee[1]

Firefighters United for Safety, Ethics, and Ecology (FUSEE) is a national nonprofit organization promoting safe, ethical, ecological wildland fire management. FUSEE members include current, former, and retired wildland firefighters; fire managers, scientists, and educators; forest conservationists; and other interested citizens who support FUSEE's holistic fire management vision.

FUSEE's primary mission is to provide public education and policy advocacy in support of a new, emerging paradigm that seeks to holistically manage wildland fire for social and ecological benefits instead of simply 'fighting' it across the landscape. We seek to enable fire management workers to perform their duties with the highest professional, ethical, and environmental standards. Our long-term goal is the creation of fire-compatible communities able to work safely and live sustainably with wildland fire.

FUSEE Promotes a Fire Ethic

Inspired by Aldo Leopold's *land ethic*, FUSEE advocates a new *fire ethic* in fire management policies and practices:
> "*A thing is right when it contributes to the safety of firefighters and the public, ethical use of public resources, environmental protection of fire-affected landscapes, and ecological restoration of fire-dependent ecosystems. It is wrong when it tends otherwise.*"

FUSEE Informs and Empowers the Fire Management Community

FUSEE calls for a renewed professionalism, public service ethos, and environmental conscience among fire management workers. We provide a safe forum for firefighters to stand up and speak out for safe, ethical, ecological fire management.

FUSEE Educates Rural Communities How to Prepare for Wildland Fire

FUSEE advocates an expansive program of public education and community preparation to support the full range of fire management: prescribed fire, fire use, and fire suppression. The sooner communities are prepared for fire, the sooner ecosystems can be restored with fire.

FUSEE Educates People about Safety Risks, Economic Costs, & Environmental Impacts of Firefighting

FUSEE opposes endlessly 'attacking' and 'fighting' fires with costly and environmentally harmful suppression actions that put firefighters at extra risk. We advocate for proactive fire and fuels management that restore wildland ecosystems. We believe every fire management action, including suppression, should be based on ethical, efficient use of taxpayer resources and pre-planned ecological restoration objectives.

FUSEE Promotes Restoring Our Cultural Legacy as Torchbearers Using Fire on the Land

FUSEE advocates a new role and identity for wildland firefighters as fire rangers. It is safer and more effective for fire management workers to start prescribed fires or steer wildfires for desired fire effects than it is to stop wildfires. FUSEE works to instill a renewed public service ethos and professional pride among firefighters as dedicated wildland stewards and skilled ecosystem restorationists.

FUSEE Educates Journalists about Fire Ecology and Management Issues

FUSEE critiques the news media's 'catastrophe mentality' and overuse of the 'war metaphor' that frames the majority of news coverage of wildfire events. FUSEE offers alternative words, angles, and frames for reporters to write informative and investigative stories about a wide range of fire issues beyond the narrow focus on wildfire suppression incidents.

Check out FUSEE's fire reports:
- Getting Burned: A Taxpayer's Guide to Wildfire Suppression Costs
- Smoke Signals: The Need for Public Tolerance and Regulatory Relief for Wildland Smoke Emissions
- Fire Watch: A Citizen's Guide to Wildfire Monitoring
- Collateral Damage: The Environmental Effects of Firefighting—The 2002 Biscuit Fire Suppression Actions and Impacts
- A Homeowner's Guide to Fire-Resistant Home Construction
- A Reporter's Guide to Wildland Fire

Find them all at www.fusee.org.

---

[1]Timothy Ingalsbee, Executive Director, Firefighters United for Safety, Ethics, and Ecology (FUSEE), Eugene, OR 97405

Citation for proceedings: Waldrop, Thomas A., ed. 2014. Proceedings, Wildland Fire in the Appalachians: Discussions among Managers and Scientists. Gen. Tech. Rep. SRS-199. Asheville, NC: U.S. Department of Agriculture Forest Service, Southern Research Station. 208 p.

Manager/Scientist
Success Stories

MANAGEMENT–RESEARCH PARTNERSHIPS FROM A MANAGER'S PERSPECTIVE

Dean M. Simon[1]

Abstract—Natural resource managers have long desired to obtain user friendly, management directed answers from research results. Through partnerships with researchers, cooperative projects, and management hosted endeavors, mutually beneficial outcomes have been accomplished that provide quantifiable data and applicable direction for both research and management professionals. Often times, projects conducted by managers are further facilitated by having research associated elements, which provide support and justification through science-based monitoring and assessment to evaluate outcomes and results. This information transfer from researchers to managers has been an evolving relationship cultured through understanding by both parties of needs, limitations, feasibility, and applicability. Flexibility and compromise by managers and researchers have been an integral part of this process as well. Numerous examples of successful ventures between managers and researchers have occurred, where research has been facilitated by the managers hosting these projects, while managers have benefited by site-specific data of implemented management actions.

NC WILDLIFE RESOURCES COMMISSION MANAGEMENT

Natural resource managers have long desired to obtain user-friendly, management-directed answers to guide their efforts in pursuing goals and objectives for lands they manage. The North Carolina Wildlife Resources Commission (NCWRC) has been mandated, since its creation in 1947, to "conserve and sustain the State's fish and wildlife resources through research, scientific management, wise use, and public input." But the NCWRC is also a regulatory agency, and a primary part of its mission is providing opportunities for public use of these natural resources. The NCWRC manages more lands than any other State agency in North Carolina, totaling over 2 million acres in its Game Lands program, about one forth of which is owned by the NCWRC, making it also the largest landowner agency among State agencies in North Carolina. Providing "an optimally sustainable yield of forest products where feasible and appropriate as directed by wildlife management objectives" is also a very important Game Lands program mission objective because of the importance of this revenue, along with the sale of hunting, fishing and trapping licenses, to the agencies budget and financial support. And, while the NCWRC has authority and ability to manage these lands actively, especially the State-owned areas as needed to meet agency goals and objectives, hosting and implementing research along with managing habitats and regulating game harvest and protection and conservation of wildlife resources is sometimes a challenging endeavor.

The NCWRC has long considered the sportsmen and women of North Carolina (those that buy licenses to hunt, fish, and trap) its primary constituents. So, right from the start, the agency faces the issue of conducting research in and among this primary user group and all the associated user conflict and safety issues. Add to this the numerous other public use demands on these lands such as hiking, biking, bird watching, and kayaking to name a few, and it becomes apparent that there is a lot for a manager to juggle. Also, keep in mind that $3.3 billion in total were spent on wildlife-related recreation in North Carolina last year. It's no wonder that NCWRC managers find that fitting in opportunities for research and filling the needs and requests to host studies and provide adequate sites, replications, and accommodating suitable spatial distribution of sampling to meet study design needs and satisfy statistical significance needs for the research and also dealing with user conflicts can be challenging, to say the least.

Routine infrastructure maintenance (such as work on roads, gates, and other access issues) along with regular habitat management operation schedules related to prescribed burning, forestry and timber harvest, creating, planting, and maintaining wildlife openings, and other land management projects, don't always accommodate timely implementation of research projects without some flexibility, tweaking, and give and take among managers and researchers. Compromise by managers and researchers has been an integral part of this process as well. This is especially true with prescribed burning, which has seen a huge increase (nearly triple)

[1]Dean M. Simon, Mountain Region Wildlife Biologist/Forester, North Carolina Wildlife Resources Commission, Lawndale, NC 28090

Citation for proceedings: Waldrop, Thomas A., ed. 2014. Proceedings, Wildland Fire in the Appalachians: Discussions among Managers and Scientists. Gen. Tech. Rep. SRS-199. Asheville, NC: U.S. Department of Agriculture Forest Service, Southern Research Station. 208 p.

in landscape-level application on NCWRC mountain region Game Lands for forest restoration, fuels reduction, maintenance of wildlife openings, site preparation, general habitat improvement over the past decade, and issues related to the limited suitable and appropriate burning days available in the mountains. Issues associated with wildland-urban interface and smoke management have certainly complicated its implementation. But often times, projects conducted by managers are further facilitated by having research associated elements, which provide support and justification through science-based monitoring and assessment to evaluate the outcomes and results. The days of using anecdotal observation as a sole source of support for implementing landscape-level habitat management projects are long gone on public lands and questions and challenges from stakeholder groups, various organizations, and the general public are more and more common, thus further emphasizing the need to justify management actions based on scientific, research-based quantifiable data and knowledge.

Providing habitat diversity across the landscape and accommodating a diversity of wildlife while managing appropriately for the rare plant and animal species and associated communities that occur on the Game Lands is also a vital part of NCWRC's management direction. An important function for research on NCWRC lands is documenting, studying, and providing information to managers on locations and needs for these natural resources. While this has often resulted in a change in how, when, and where land management projects have been conducted, it has also forged a better understanding among researchers and managers. This information transfer from researchers to managers has been an evolving relationship cultured through understanding by both parties of needs, limitations, feasibility, and applicability. However, as a result of knowledge gained through some of these research projects, beneficial changes in forest management have resulted, including modifications to timber harvest methods directed by specific wildlife habitat management goals and objectives (for example, hard and soft mast production), better identification of appropriate sites for establishing desired tree species in forest regeneration operations through tree planting and natural regeneration, defined goals for forest restoration, detection and strategies for mitigating impacts to sensitive plant and animal species, and detection and strategies for mitigating forest health issues.

NCWRC RESEARCH PARTNERSHIPS

Through partnerships with researchers, cooperative projects, and management-hosted ventures, mutually beneficial outcomes have been accomplished that provide quantifiable data and applicable direction for both research and management professionals. Some examples of research projects on mountain region Game Lands in North Carolina that have directly influenced habitat management operations include studies of fire effects in table mountain-pitch pine on vegetation and wildlife habitat, fire and fire surrogate studies, regional oak regeneration studies, fire and ecosystem restoration monitoring, and regional oak savanna studies. NCWRC managers have worked with numerous research cooperators on these studies including the U.S. Forest Service Southern Research Station, Clemson University, North Carolina State University, Western Carolina University, University of Tennessee, The Nature Conservancy, North Carolina State Parks, and the Southern Blue Ridge Fire Learning Network. These researchers have provided well over 100 publications with results specific to NWWRC lands. The partnership with the Southern Blue Ridge Fire Learning Network researchers and managers in particular has also led to numerous cooperative projects and benefits to managers in the mountain region through Ecotype Modeling and Burn Project Prioritization, sharing of manpower and equipment resources through Memorandum of Understanding, partnership cooperative prescribed burning projects across landscapes on multiple land ownerships, and standardization of research monitoring plots among cooperators in mountain region landscapes for tracking forest restoration efforts. In most cases, research projects on mountain region Game Lands in North Carolina have been funded primarily by the researchers. In some cases, the NCWRC has provided relatively minor funding for these research projects; however, those costs have usually been mostly associated with implementing project treatments, which are often the same types of forestry and wildlife habitat management projects conducted routinely as part of regular Game Lands management. Additionally, many of the research projects hosted by NCWRC have included forestry treatments where timber is harvested and revenues are received by the NCWRC from these timber sales, more than covering any costs to NCWRC for their part in the research effort.

A challenge to both managers and researchers is to know what the right questions are to ask. Additionally, deciding this answer can often be complicated and involve a complexity of issues for managers hosting research, related to feasibility, logistics, costs, and revenues as well as study design, location, timing, and installation needs. On NCWRC Game Lands, there is also a Game Lands research approval process where ultimately applicability to management operations and benefits of the research to the State's natural resources are strongly considered and Memorandum of Understanding and contracts are the final step. Final research results and conclusions often require researchers to make an interpretation and translation to management action. This is where managers truly benefit from the modifications and tweaking of operational procedures and tools used, as per those recommendations, to more efficiently and effectively direct management efforts towards desired outcomes and results and at the same time, have a better understanding of management action impacts and effects. From a wildlife manager's standpoint, the wider the research "net is cast" or more parameters are measured for wildlife species and habitat components, the larger the data base for addressing impacts and effects. From salamanders to songbirds, bats to bog turtles, all data collected by researchers on these projects provides managers a data base of occurrence and potential changes associated with treatments. As stated early on, game species are a very important resource the NCWRC manages, and any research monitoring that includes these wildlife species is very valuable as well. Measures of forest vegetation and fuels accumulation data provided from researchers also add greatly to the information base that managers use in making management decisions.

Another benefit that managers have derived from management-research partnerships is exposure to new technology that they might not otherwise have opportunity to become familiar with. Advances in computer software, handheld devices, compact measuring tools, high-tech field equipment, and access to numerous other beneficial resources are often a result of establishing these partnerships. Additionally, the opportunity for networking with other researchers and managers, introduction to new sources of information, and even development of new contacts for sources of materials and equipment often results from the working relationships that develop among researchers and managers. The establishment of management-research partnerships provides opportunities for public information delivery, media day events, and educational outlets, especially on sites of manager-hosted research projects. This is a very beneficial and effective way to have management action results and effects explained and demonstrated through field review and on-site discussion.

CONCLUSION

In summary, management-research partnerships are a very valuable, beneficial, and important part of natural resource management and provide needed monitoring, evaluation, and quantifiable data for management actions, tools, and land management practices used. Research provides managers a measure of success for restoration efforts and results of implemented projects. Research can provide management direction for achieving State Wildlife Action Plan goals and Partners in Flight priorities more efficiently and effectively through a better understanding of wildlife habitat needs for providing and improving wildlife food resources (browse, plantings, mast, etc.), cover (for nesting, escape, etc.), and distribution (diversity on the landscape, habitat connectivity, etc.).

SILVAH: MANAGERS AND SCIENTISTS WORK TOGETHER TO IMPROVE RESEARCH AND MANAGEMENT

Susan L. Stout and Patrick H. Brose[1]

Abstract—SILVAH is a systematic approach to silvicultural prescription development based on inventory and analysis of stand data for Allegheny hardwood, northern hardwood, and mixed oak forests. SILVAH includes annual training sessions and decision support software, and it ensures a consistent, complete, and objective approach to prescriptions. SILVAH has created a community of practice with common vocabulary and framework for assessing forest stands. Lessons learned from thirty years of research-manager cooperation may be relevant to the work of the Consortium of Appalachian Fire Managers and Scientists. Managers benefit in at least three ways from participation in the SILVAH community of practice: their prescriptions are demonstrably based on data and science and are internally consistent; relationships with scientists help attract research attention to emerging problems; and they have access to lessons learned by other managers using SILVAH. Scientists also benefit: they have confidence that their work is on problems of high priority to managers; their impact is increased by early adoption of research by managers; the scale and scope of forest observation is increased by the community of observers sharing a common framework and vocabulary; and managers are often able and willing to help locate appropriate study sites and provide in-kind services, such as treatment applications.

INTRODUCTION

SILVAH, originally an acronym for Silviculture of Allegheny Hardwoods, is a systematic approach to silvicultural prescription development based on inventory and analysis of stand data for Allegheny hardwood, northern hardwood, and mixed oak forests of Pennsylvania and adjoining States. It is relevant to the Consortium of Appalachian Fire Managers and Scientists because of its success in creating a community of practice in which scientists and managers work together through the full cycle of research, from problem selection and hypothesis formation through study implementation, data collection, analysis, delivery of results, and organization of those results into guidelines useable by managers. Such a community increases the probability that problems of high priority to managers will receive appropriate research attention and that research results will actually influence practice. In this paper, we give a brief history of the development of SILVAH and the lessons learned about building a community of practice that improves research and management.

ORIGINS

In 1967, managers in northwestern Pennsylvania organized a Society of American Foresters (SAF) meeting around regeneration failures that were, in their opinion, too common in the local maturing second-growth Allegheny and northern hardwood forests, consisting of black cherry (*Prunus serotina)*, red and sugar maple (*Acer rubrum* and *saccharum)*, American beech *(Fagus grandifolia)*, black and yellow birch (*Betula lenta* and *allegheniensis)*, and other species. They invited Ben Roach (fig. 1), a research assistant director of the U.S. Department of Agriculture, Forest Service Northeastern Forest Experiment Station, headquartered near Philadelphia. Managers wondered about the relative importance of everything from seed production, soil and site factors, interplant competition and interference, to browsing by white-tailed deer (*Odocoileus virginianus)* and snowshoe hare (*Lepus americanus)* as possible reasons for the observed failures.

Roach assigned a protégée, David Marquis (fig. 1), to the Warren, PA, Forest Service Research Lab in northwestern Pennsylvania and helped him recruit scientists from around the region whose skills represented the possible explanations of regeneration failures. Ted Grisez (fig. 1), already in place, had a near-encyclopedic knowledge of local forest ecology and some familiarity with both natural and artificial regeneration methods (Grisez and Huntzinger 1965, Grisez and Peace 1973). John Bjorkbom (fig. 1) came from New England, where he had studied regeneration of the highly desirable birch species (*Betula* spp.) of those northern hardwood forests (Bjorkbom 1979, Bjorkbom and others 1979). Lew Auchmoody

---

[1]Susan L. Stout, Research Forester and Project Leader, USDA Forest Service, Northern Research Station, Irvine, PA 16365

Patrick H. Brose, Research Forester, USDA Forest Service, Northern Research Station, Irvine, PA 16329

Citation for proceedings: Waldrop, Thomas A., ed. 2014. Proceedings, Wildland Fire in the Appalachians: Discussions among Managers and Scientists. Gen. Tech. Rep. SRS-199. Asheville, NC: U.S. Department of Agriculture Forest Service, Southern Research Station. 208 p.

(fig. 1) came from West Virginia, where his research focused on soil nutrition and individual species responses to changes in nutrition (Auchmoody 1973, 1978). Steve Horsley (fig. 1) came from New Jersey, and his knowledge of ecophysiology was soon applied to understanding interference with regeneration from other native plants like ferns (Horsley 1977a, 1977b). Eventually, Roach himself became a scientist at the Warren Lab, where he focused on studies related to his long established expertise in quantifying relative density and growth responses to intermediate cuttings (Roach and Gingrich 1968, Roach 1977). Marquis himself took on additional studies on regeneration and the role of white-tailed deer browsing in regeneration failures (Marquis 1974, 1975).

As the scientists arrived in Warren, they prepared problem analyses and a plan of work focused on the regeneration problems. Figure 2 is from a flow chart in the problem analysis that organized the early research. First, the scientists adopted a definition of successful regeneration from earlier work that Roach and colleagues had conducted (Roach and Gingrich 1968). A stand was considered to have regenerated successfully if 70 percent of sample plots in the harvest area were stocked with desirable or commercial seedlings or saplings, with stocking criteria represented as numbers of seedlings taller than a certain height (Marquis and Bjorkbom 1982). The scientists thought about what decisions, data, and knowledge were essential to managers for making a successful regeneration prescription, and they organized their studies to provide the data and knowledge needed to make better decisions and achieve better outcomes. For example, they asked, "What constitutes adequate advance regeneration? Does abundant advance regeneration ensure success without fencing? What soil-site-stand factors are correlated with regeneration success?" And for each of these questions (and many more), they designed a study. The flow chart even prioritized the studies. Although we do not know this for certain, we suspect that in addition to the traditional scientific approach to choosing research questions, this flow chart was influenced by the ideas that had been expressed by managers at that 1967 SAF meeting, and by ideas that Marquis was hearing as he built relationships with managers of public and private forests across the region.

As the research began, collaboration between management and research deepened, as many of the new studies were done in partnership with management agencies. For example, Allegheny National Forest managers cooperated when researchers sought to erect fences within a subset of the harvest areas in which regeneration had failed to develop. Even though the fences were erected after the harvest had been declared a regeneration failure, full stocking of desirable seedlings developed inside fences on 87 percent of the study areas

(fig. 3). This result indicated that deer were a critically important barrier to regeneration success (Marquis 1974).

Another study on lands of the Allegheny National Forest showed that the presence of abundant advance regeneration was the most effective predictor of which final harvests would regenerate to desirable species composition and stocking (Grisez and Peace 1973, Marquis and Bjorkbom 1982). The news that advance regeneration mattered was delivered with recommendations for how to collect inventory data that would help managers recognize which stands met the advance regeneration requirements, and which would need some kind of silvicultural intervention to increase advance regeneration before a final harvest would lead to successful stand regeneration. Although understory inventory may seem obvious for hardwood silviculturists from a vantage point 40 years in the future, implementing such an inventory program demanded significant changes in forest management practice. Selecting appropriate stands to harvest had been something silviculturists could do based on overstory inventory data collected at any time of year. Now, they needed inventory data that were twice as expensive to gather, because both overstory and understory data were needed, and the effective season for such inventory was shortened to a few months in the growing season. Because the payoff was so high, and the guidelines for implementation were sensitive to managers' constraints, most agencies and industries on the Allegheny Plateau implemented the new inventory procedures. Managers implemented the inventory practices, but more important, they began to plan harvests in stands where advance regeneration was adequate. When those stands regenerated successfully, managers had real-world confirmation that the pre-harvest analysis was a sound basis for management.

BEGINNING A COMMUNITY OF PRACTICE

Another reason for widespread adoption of these early guidelines was the Allegheny Hardwood Silviculture training sessions (fig. 4). By 1976, research results had accumulated to the point that Roach and Marquis thought they were ready to give silviculturists something to aid with management decisions and improve outcomes from both regeneration harvests and intermediate treatments. Two people worked with the research staff to ensure that the content was useful and accessible to managers. One was the Penn State Extension forester of that era, Sandy Cochran, a partner from the very beginning. He had a special gift for asking the question everyone else was thinking, and he institutionalized post-session reviews of participant evaluations that led to progressive improvements in later sessions. The second person was Jim Redding (fig. 1), a forester from the Allegheny National Forest who joined the research staff and gave presentations at training sessions about how to use the SILVAH approach to inventory and marking and how the approach improved his practice. Cochran's role was later taken up by Dr. Tim Pierson.

In many ways, the training sessions shared the ideals of today's fire consortia: creating a forum for structured conversations about research needs, research results, and their application to management problems. The fundamental idea of the training sessions has not changed since the beginning; gathering high quality data about current conditions and analyzing those data using consistent and rigorous procedures gives professional resource managers an objective, research-based starting point in planning silvicultural prescriptions. This idea is the essence of what is now known as the SILVAH system. SILVAH guidelines were never intended as a substitute for professional judgment, but rather as a starting point, ensuring objective, consistent, and complete review of key factors.

When the first training sessions were given, the staff believed that in a few years they would have reached all the foresters on the Allegheny Plateau and the sessions would end. Very quickly, both managers and scientists realized that there were unforeseen benefits from annual training sessions. Organizers encouraged a diversity of participants, limiting any single agency or company to no more than 20 percent of the seats in any given class. They also encouraged full participation by the research staff, not "drop in, give a lecture, and depart." Marquis and his colleagues published a handbook of guidelines and a synthesis of their research basis, as well as the lectures from the training session (Marquis 1994; Marquis and others 1984, 1992). Organizers realized that the training sessions were creating relationships and a common vocabulary and framework for discussing emerging problems. In addition, as scientists regularly spent a week together listening to each other weave new research results into the SILVAH framework, they learned to resolve potential conflicts between results from different studies. Equally important, as agency heads and field foresters alike saw that research results could really help them do their jobs, the willingness—even eagerness—of management agencies to host research studies increased. Thus the cycle of research-management collaboration began to be self-perpetuating.

COMPUTERIZED DECISION SUPPORT

Even though the SILVAH approach to inventory, analysis, and prescription was always quantitative, it did not start out as a computer program. There were pages and pages of calculations, and in the early days, those were done with pen and pencil or a simple handheld calculator. Rich Ernst (fig. 1), a scientist at the Lab, began to program his handheld HP calculator to do the SILVAH calculations just to stay ahead of his crews in the training sessions. Over time, the software graduated to a Data General mainframe, then to early PCs, and continues to be updated as new scientific results are translated to management guidelines (Marquis and Ernst 1992; Knopp and Stout, in press). This happened just as PCs were beginning to be widely available, so we started to think that people might benefit from software to process their inventory data, producing both comprehensive analysis and the SILVAH recommendations. An early adopter was the Hammermill Paper Company, which used SILVAH to inventory all of its lands and develop a database of stand characteristics. In addition to helping with ownership-wide treatment plans —on how many acres will we plan to apply herbicide this year, and where are they?— the database also enabled them to have some market nimbleness: sugar maple (*Acer saccharum*) prices are up? We know exactly how to figure out which of our stands are stocked with a high proportion of sugar maple and which of those would benefit from a thinning.

EXPANDING SILVAH TO OTHER FOREST TYPES

When the Pennsylvania Bureau of Forestry sought third-party certification from the Forest Stewardship Council (FSC) in the 1990s, FSC commended the structured framework of SILVAH and recommended its expansion to mixed oak (*Quercus* spp.) forests. The Bureau of Forestry convened a committee of scientists and managers to address this recommendation. It included faculty from Penn State and Forest Service scientists from the Irvine, PA, (formerly Warren) Lab and from the Morgantown, WV, Lab. The process that emerged was quite remarkable. Participants worked to translate the important results from research elsewhere into the SILVAH framework. For example, using prescribed fire in combination with shelterwood harvests to regenerate oak forests in Pennsylvania was a novel approach, so research results from South Carolina (Barnes and Van Lear 1998) and Virginia (Brose and Van Lear 1998) were used to develop interim guidelines. Similarly, stump sprouting and dominance probabilities of oak reproduction in regenerating stands from Missouri (Sander and others 1976, 1984); and North Carolina (Loftis 1990) were used to develop interim criteria for inventorying oak seedlings. Equally important, the group identified research gaps and priorities to strengthen the recommended guidelines over time, and because the Bureau of Forestry has both regeneration and research funding available, they have been able to make a very substantial investment of dollars, lands, and in-kind support for silvicultural research to fill those gaps. The group also worked with field foresters to test the proposed new SILVAH procedures before full-scale adoption and to modify them as needed.

Once the SILVAH-Oak process had been validated and adapted to accommodate field forester observations and research studies had begun, Brose and others (2008) published a second SILVAH handbook for using SILVAH in mixed oak forests and launched a parallel series of training sessions focused on the SILVAH-Oak guidelines. The Bureau of Forestry is the primary partner in this effort. While there is considerable overlap of students within Pennsylvania for the SILVAH-Oak and Allegheny Hardwood Silviculture training sessions, the mixed oak sessions have also been in demand in several other States, and varying versions of the SILVAH-Oak training sessions have been offered in Indiana, Kentucky, Maryland, Ohio, and West Virginia.

MUTUAL BENEFITS ENSURE CONTINUED RESEARCH-MANAGEMENT COOPERATION

What has sustained SILVAH through 37 years since the first Allegheny Hardwood Silviculture training was offered in 1976? Why do foresters continue to use the software, attend the training sessions, and request specific research studies from the SILVAH team? Why do land management agencies, public and private, adopt SILVAH guidelines to support their silvicultural decision processes and provide sites and in-kind services for SILVAH-related studies? Why do scientists continue to work to ensure that research results are fit within the SILVAH system and reported at training sessions, and why do they continue to participate in the several weeks of preparation and participation that the training sessions demand each year? We believe that the success of the SILVAH system is due to the continued flow of benefits for both managers and scientists (table 1).

The benefits for managers include the obvious, consistent, and objective relationship between their decision-making criteria and scientific research. By using the SILVAH system, managers can show their stakeholders, from stockholders to members of the public, the link between research, the guidelines and data used for a specific decision, and the choices they make on the ground. For example, foresters in the Pennsylvania Bureau of Forestry must submit a SILVAH printout reporting both inventory results and SILVAH's recommended prescription when seeking approval of a timber sale. They are free to deviate from the SILVAH recommendation when working in a forest type SILVAH doesn't recognize, after mortality or wind events, in aesthetic road buffer zones, or on strip mine remediation. They are also encouraged to suggest deviations when local circumstances such as adjacency to a recently harvested stand, local evidence of a good seed crop of a seed-banking species, such as black cherry (*Prunus serotina*) or yellow-poplar (*Liriodendron tulipifera*), evidence of insect and disease impacts, or proximity to a stream suggest a modification, and they can

use the SILVAH vocabulary and framework to explain their deviation.[2] Similarly, the Allegheny National Forest plan cites SILVAH in its *Silvicultural Guides for ANF Forest Types*.(USDA Forest Service 2007, appendix A, page A-5).

An additional benefit for managers is the opportunity to interact with scientists and managers from other agencies on a regular basis, using a common vocabulary and framework. Many agencies and organizations encourage or even require new employees to participate in a SILVAH training session early in their tenure, and they allow more experienced employees to participate again after intervals of 5 to 10 years. A week-long shared experience with ample field time and informal engagement during breaks builds comfortable relationships among all participants in the sessions, making it easier for either a manager to phone a scientist with an observation, question, or concern or for a scientist to contact a land manager to confirm the range of a particular problem or situation or to seek a study site. It also creates relationships among those who work for different agencies, so that as one agency or institution develops new ways to apply or even modify SILVAH guidelines, the innovation is diffused to other agencies and to the research community more rapidly than it would diffuse between agency heads.

The third benefit for managers is the ability to participate in the scientific process. The SILVAH community of practice makes this happen in several ways. First, concerns and observations voiced by managers at training sessions or in followup conversations influence the choice of problem selection for scientists. Second, managers become aware of studies early in their development and have opportunities to see treatments as applied and view preliminary results in the field. Finally, managers and scientists in the community may be able to see and hear preliminary research results as they make their way through the sometimes long and arduous process of publication. Although there is some risk that peer review may result in re-interpretation of results, scientists can communicate these changes easily to those who have requested early results, and to agencies through the regular training sessions. The manager-scientist relationship also allows for immediate discussion of seemingly new or unique problems as they arise, as well as timely site visits to improve the effectiveness of consultations.

The SILVAH community of practice helps both scientists and managers better understand the different cultures of science and management (USDA Forest Service 1997),

---

[2]Personal communication. 2014. Scott A. Miller. Chief, Silviculture Section, Pennsylvania Department of Conservation and Natural Resources, Bureau of Forestry, P.O. Box 8552, Harrisburg, PA 17105-8552.

which in turn helps scientists design studies in ways that increase the probability that lessons learned will be relevant to management decisions and will help managers, over time, ask questions in ways that lend themselves to testable hypotheses and formal research studies. Such open communications also allow for adjustments in recommendations as information in older published results is superseded by new, yet-to-be-published findings.

A second benefit for scientists is a wide network of thoughtful observers. Managers who are increasingly comfortable with the culture of science are often able to classify their field observations into useful classes. Two examples from the SILVAH history illustrate this advantage. As scientists and managers began to share concerns about sugar maple health in the Allegheny Plateau ecoregion, it was the observations of astute managers across the ecoregion that helped scientists design a study to test slope position and glacial history as potential causes of variation in sugar maple health, growth, and regeneration. The resulting gradient study relied on cooperation with managers to identify 19 different locations, some glaciated and some unglaciated, all with sugar maple in plateau-top and lower landscape positions, where the study took place, leading to real breakthroughs in understanding the effects of site quality on sugar maple health (Horsley and others 1999, Long and others 2009). The second is a current study of oak regeneration problems in south-central Pennsylvania that was designed to test differences in soils resulting from different geological formations as observed by the forester on site.

A third major benefit for scientists is access to both research sites and in-kind services, such as treatments. The sugar maple example, where managers helped scientists find 19 different topographic gradients with sugar maple growing along the gradient, is also illustrative of this example. A more recent case involves a current test of the hypothesis that the impact of white-tailed deer on vegetation is a joint function of the actual density of deer and the heterogeneity of vegetative communities, age classes, and forage production in the landscape surrounding the subject stand. To test this hypothesis, which itself was generated by shared observations of scientists and managers, scientists needed to find more than 20 locations in which harvests were planned in a given year, and in which the prior treatments were essentially the same. The cooperation of managers, the use of similar silvicultural practices, and lots of scientific legwork later, the study moved forward with 25 sites representing 7 different ownerships. One land manager even agreed to plan a harvest specifically to create sites for the study, if needed. An example of in-kind services provided by cooperating managers involves another study of changing deer impact on vegetation, where landowners cooperating in the Kinzua Quality Deer Cooperative have completed more than 1,300 miles of transects to detect deer pellets and browse damage on seedlings over the last 12 years (Royo and others 2010, Stout and others 2013).

SUMMARY AND CONCLUSIONS: LINK TO CONSORTIUM OF APPALACHIAN FIRE MANAGERS AND SCIENTISTS

There are many parallels between the SILVAH community of practice and the Consortium of Appalachian Fire Managers and Scientists. These parallels include regular interactions dedicated to understanding each other's knowledge and observations, along with emerging problems and emerging solutions. The SILVAH experience suggests that a well-defined framework that integrates management challenges with research-based solutions and highlights and prioritizes research gaps using common vocabulary will strengthen research-management collaboration in the long run. The SILVAH example also confirms that there are benefits to all participants, including early access to emerging solutions, increased access to careful observations of natural phenomena, and increased access to research sites and in-kind services. The community of practice or consortium model provides a basis for sustained relationships between managers and scientists that allows for the orientation of new participants, the maturation of existing participants, and retention of collective memory as older participants retire.

ACKNOWLEDGMENTS

In addition to the many scientists who have contributed to SILVAH over the years, its research relies on contributions of an excellent team of forestry technicians, programmers, and data managers who share the team's commitment to research that engages managers and informs both policy and practice. These include Vonley Brown, John Crossley, Virgil Flick, Dave Saf, Harry Steele, Ernie Wiltsie, Eric Baxter, Josh Hanson, Greg Sanford, Julie Smithbauer, Corinne Weldon, Carl Bylin, Pete Knopp, and Scott Thomasma. This manuscript was substantially improved by comments from reviewers Lucy Burde, Tara Keyser, Gary Miller, Scott Miller, Chris Nowak, and Brian Salvato.

LITERATURE CITED

Auchmoody, L.R. 1973. Intensive culture of black cherry. Southern Lumberman. 227 (2824): 112-115.

Auchmoody, L.R. 1978. Response of young black cherry to fertilization. [Abstract] in Agronomy Abstracts: 70th Annual Meeting of the American Society of Agronomy. Madison, WI: American Society of Agronomy. 186 p.

Bjorkbom, J.C. 1979. Seed production and advance regeneration in Allegheny hardwood forests. Res. Pap. NE-435. Broomall, PA: U.S. Department of Agriculture Forest Service. Northeastern Forest Experiment Station. 10 p.

Bjorkbom, J.C.; Auchmoody, L.R.; Dorn, D.E. 1979. Influence of fertilizer on seed production in Allegheny hardwood stands. Res. Pap. NE-439. Broomall, PA: U.S. Department of Agriculture Forest Service. Northeastern Forest Experiment Station. 5 p.

Barnes, T.A.; Van Lear, D.H. 1998. Prescribed fire effects on advanced regeneration in mixed hardwood stands. Southern Journal of Applied Forestry. 22(3): 138-142.

Brose, P.H.; Van Lear, D.H. 1998. Responses of hardwood advance regeneration to seasonal prescribed fires in oak-dominated shelterwood stands. Canadian Journal of Forest Research. 28: 331-339.

Brose, P.H.; Gottschalk, K.W.; Horsley, S.B.; Knopp, P.; [and others]. 2008. Prescribing regeneration treatments for mixed-oak forests in the mid-Atlantic region. Gen. Tech. Rep. NRS-33. Newtown Square, PA: U.S. Department of Agriculture Forest Service, Northern Research Station. 100 p.

Grisez, T.J.; Huntzinger, H.J. 1965. Direct seeding studies with black cherry. In Abbott, H.G., ed. Proceedings of the symposium: direct seedling in the northeast - 1964. Amherst, MA: University of Massachusetts, College of Agriculture, Experiment Station: 41-43.

Grisez, T.J.; Peace, M.R. 1973. Requirements for advance reproduction in Allegheny hardwoods—an interim guide. Res. Note NE-180. Upper Darby, PA: U.S. Department of Agriculture Forest Service. Northeastern Forest Experiment Station. 5 p.

Horsley, S.B. 1977a. Allelopathic inhibition of black cherry by fern, grass, goldenrod, and aster. Canadian Journal of Forest Research. 7(2): 205-216.

Horsley, S.B. 1977b. Allelopathic inhibition of black cherry. II. Inhibition by woodland grass, ferns, and club moss. Canadian Journal of Forest Research. 7(3): 515-519.

Horsley, S.B.; Long, R.P.; Bailey, S.W. [and others]. 1999. Factors contributing to sugar maple decline along topographic gradients on the glaciated and unglaciated Allegheny Plateau. In: Horsley, S.B.; Long, R.P., eds. Sugar maple ecology and health: proceedings of an international symposium. Gen. Tech. Rep. NE-261. Radnor, PA: U.S. Department of Agriculture Forest Service, Northeastern Research Station: 60-62.

Knopp, P; Stout, S.L. [In press]. Users guide to SILVAH, a stand analysis, prescription, and management simulator program for hardwood stands of the Alleghenies. Gen. Tech. Rep. NRS-xx. Newtown Square, PA: U. S. Department of Agriculture Forest Service, Northern Research Station.

Loftis, David L. 1990. Predicting post-harvest performance of advance red oak reproduction in the southern Appalachians. Forest Science. 36(4): 908-916.

Long, R.P.; Horsley, S.B.; Hallett, R.A.; Bailey, S.W. 2009. Sugar maple growth in relation to nutrition and stress in the northeastern United States. Ecological Applications. 19(6): 1454-1466.

Marquis, D.A. 1974. The impact of deer browsing in the Allegheny hardwood regeneration. Res. Pap. NE-308. Upper Darby, PA: U.S. Department of Agriculture Forest Service, Northeastern Forest Experiment Station. 8 p.

Marquis, D.A. 1975. Seed storage and germination under northern hardwood forests. Canadian Journal of Forest Research. 5: 478-484.

Marquis, D.A., ed. 1994. Quantitative silviculture for hardwood stands of the Alleghenies. Gen. Tech. Rep. NE-183. Radnor, PA: U.S. Department of Agriculture Forest Service, Northeastern Forest Experiment Station. 376 p.

Marquis, D.A.; Bjorkbom, J.C. 1982. Guidelines for evaluating regeneration before and after clearcutting Allegheny hardwoods. Res. Note NE-307. Broomall, PA: U.S. Department of Agriculture Forest Service, Northeastern Forest Experiment Station. 4 p.

Marquis, D.A.; Ernst, R.L.; Stout, S.L. 1984. Prescribing silvicultural treatments in hardwood stands of the Alleghenies. Gen. Tech. Rep. NE-96. Radnor, PA: U.S. Department of Agriculture Forest Service, Northeastern Forest Experiment Station. 90 p.

Marquis, D.A.; Ernst, R.L. 1992. User's guide to SILVAH: stand analysis, prescription, and management simulator program for hardwood stands of the Alleghenies. Gen. Tech. Rep. NE-162. Radnor, PA: U.S. Department of Agriculture Forest Service. Northeastern Forest Experiment Station. 124 p.

Marquis, D.A.; Ernst, R.L.; Stout, S.L. 1992. Prescribing silvicultural treatments in hardwood stands of the Alleghenies (revised). Gen. Tech. Rep. NE-96. Radnor, PA: U.S. Department of Agriculture Forest Service, Northeastern Forest Experiment Station. 101 p.

Roach, B.A. 1977. A stocking guide for Allegheny hardwoods and its use in controlling intermediate cuttings. Res. Pap. NE-373. Upper Darby, PA: U. S. Department of Agriculture Forest Service, Northeastern Forest Experiment Station. 30 p.

Roach, B.A.; Gingrich, S.F. 1968. Even-aged silviculture for upland central hardwoods. Agric. Handbk. 355. Washington, DC: U.S. Department of Agriculture Forest Service, Washington Office. 39 p.

Royo, A.A.; Stout, S.L.; deCalesta, D.S.; Pierson, T.G. 2010. Restoring forest herb communities through landscape-level deer herd reductions: is recovery limited by legacy effects? Biological Conservation. 143: 2425-2434.

Sander, I.L.; Johnson, P.S.; Rogers, R. 1984. Evaluating oak advance reproduction in the Missouri Ozarks. Res. Pap. NC-251. St. Paul, MN: U.S. Department of Agriculture Forest Service, North Central Forest Experiment Station. 19 p.

Sander, I.L.; Johnson, P.S.; Watt, R.F. 1976. A guide for evaluating the adequacy of oak advance reproduction. Gen. Tech. Rep. NC-23. St. Paul, MN: U.S. Department of Agriculture Forest Service, North Central Forest Experiment Station. 7 p.

Stout, S.L.; Royo, A.A.; deCalesta, D.S. [and others]. 2013. The Kinzua Quality Deer Cooperative: can adaptive management and local stakeholder engagement sustain reduced impact of ungulate browsers in forest systems? Boreal Environment Research. 18 (suppl. A): 50-64.

U.S. Department of Agriculture (USDA) Forest Service. 1997. Integrating science and decisionmaking: guidelines for collaboration among managers and researchers in the Forest Service. FS-608. Washington, DC: U.S. Department of Agriculture Forest Service, Washington Office. 11 p.

U.S. Department of Agriculture (USDA) Forest Service. 2007. Allegheny National Forest Plan Record of Decision for Final Environmental Impact Statement and Land and Resource Management Plan. Warren, PA: U.S. Department of Agriculture Forest Service, Allegheny National Forest. 296 p.

Table 1—Attributes of the SILVAH system and the associated benefits to managers and scientists that have sustained the system through decades

Attribute of research/management cooperation	Benefit to managers	Benefit to scientists
SILVAH Decision Charts and Guidebooks provide objective, consistent, science-referenced basis for decisions	Demonstrably science-based decisions	Framework for resolving apparent conflicts as new research results emerge
Regular interactions provide scientists and managers with shared vocabulary and framework at training sessions	Access to emerging research results, relationships with scientists that provide timely consultations	Much wider network of systematic observations, relationships with managers that identify high-priority research needs
Managers are engaged in the full research cycle	Training sessions and resulting relationships allow users to participate in problem selection, research design, and science delivery	Scientists have increased confidence that research is relevant and that results will be adopted
Increased understanding of cultural differences between science & management	Managers develop increased understanding of scientific uncertainty	Scientists gain increased understanding of managers' timeframes and broader social context of decisions
Sharing of resources	Managers gain new tools for data collection, analysis, and interpretation	Scientists gain access to research sites and in-kind services.

Figure 1—Key members of the Forest Service team that launched the SILVAH system. Top row, left to right: Ben Roach, Dave Marquis, and Ted Grisez. Second row, left to right: John Bjorkbom, Lou Auchmoody, Steve Horsley, Rich Ernst, and Jim Redding.

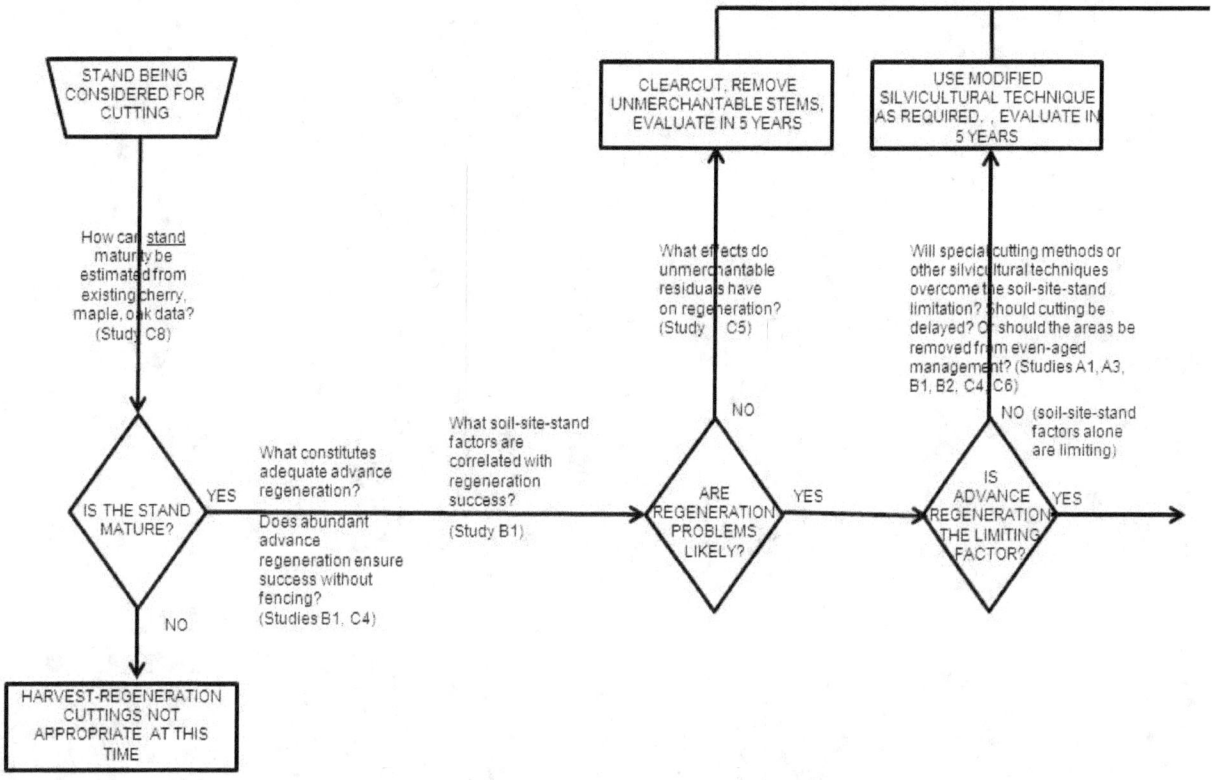

Figure 2—Excerpt from Research Problem Analysis, Research Work Unit NE-1108 (1971).

Figure 3—Regeneration on left is inside a deer-excluding fence and developed after the same harvest as the grasses on the right, which developed where deer eliminated seedling regeneration.

Figure 4—Participants in the first one-day SILVAH training session in 1976 and the most recent session in 2013.

THE SOUTHERN BLUE RIDGE FIRE LEARNING NETWORK: A COLLABORATIVE PARTNERSHIP TO RESTORE FIRE-ADAPTED ECOSYSTEMS AND BUILD RESILIENT FORESTS AND COMMUNITIES IN THE SOUTHERN BLUE RIDGE

Margit Bucher, Beth Buchanan, Wendy Fulks, Josh Kelly, Peter Bates,
Gary Kauffman, Steve Simon, and Helen Mohr[1]

ABSTRACT—The Southern Blue Ridge Fire Learning Network (SBR FLN) is a cooperative program between the Forest Service, the Department of the Interior agencies, and The Nature Conservancy. Its goal is to restore forests and grasslands and to make (human) communities safer from fire. Since 2007, the SBR FLN has engaged Federal, State, and private partners to integrate science and local knowledge. Eight landscape teams focus on restoring pine and pine oak forests, primarily through prescribed burning. Common vegetation maps/models are used to identify areas most in need of restoration, and to develop a common vision of restoration needs across the region. A burn prioritization tool ("ecomath") has been developed based on these maps in most landscapes. The modeling has enhanced our understanding of why and where fire is needed, focused planning, and begun to broaden support for burning and restoration through a systematic approach that can be explained. A network of monitoring plots tracks the effectiveness of restoration treatments. A partnership with the Consortium for Appalachian Fire Managers and Scientists (CAFMS) has accelerated transfer of knowledge through workshops, field trips, and webinars. The SBR FLN is currently expanding and integrating some of its activities with the Fire Adapted Communities Learning Network.

INTRODUCTION

The Fire Learning Network (FLN) is a national level cooperative program of the Forest Service, U.S. Department of Agriculture; agencies of the Department of the Interior; and The Nature Conservancy. Its goal is to restore forests and grasslands and to make (human) communities safer from fire working through regional networks. It provides a framework for land managers to collaborate with scientists in the planning and implementation of prescribed fire.

The Southern Blue Ridge Fire Learning Network (SBR FLN) was born out of the recognition by land managers, wildlife biologists, and ecologists that forests across the Southern Appalachian Mountains are changing due to a lack of fire. Recent studies of fire history (Delcourt and Delcourt 1997; Fesenmyer and Christensen 2010; Flatley and others 2012; Lafon and Grissino-Mayer 2007, 2011) show that thousands of years of frequent fires shaped pine and oak forest types across the region until the 19th century, when changes first in land use followed by fire policy led to fire suppression and exclusion (Pyne 1982).

Lack of fire is thought to be related to observed changes in forest structure and composition, leading—particularly in the eastern uplands—to "mesophication" (Nowacki and Abrams 2008). It has led to increased fuel loads and made both forests and human communities more vulnerable to catastrophic fire. In both situations, fire exclusion has worked to the detriment of fire-adapted species such as upland oaks and yellow pines. Reintroducing fire in the Southern Appalachians is expected to benefit pine and oak regeneration (Brose and others 2001, 2006; Elliott and others 2004, Kinkead and others 2013), wildlife (both game and nongame), and a number of rare animal and plant species such as golden-winged warbler (*Vermivora chrysoptera*) and mountain golden heather (*Hudsonia montana*). In some cases, prescribed fire will also reduce community wildfire risk. Hazardous fuels are an increasing concern in many

[1]Margit Bucher, Fire Manager, The Nature Conservancy, Durham, NC 27707

Beth Buchanan, Regional Fire Ecologist, USDA Forest Service Southern Region, Roanoke, VA 24019

Wendy Fulks, Associate Director, Fire Adapted Communities Network, The Nature Conservancy, Boulder, CO 80302

Josh Kelly, Botanist, Western North Carolina Alliance, Asheville, NC 28806

Peter Bates, Associate Professor, Western Carolina University, Cullowhee, NC 28723

Gary L. Kauffman, Botanist, USDA Forest Service, National Forests in North Carolina, Asheville, NC 28802

Steven A. Simon, Ecologist, Ecological Modeling and Fire Ecology Inc., Asheville, NC 28804

Helen Mohr, Forester, USDA Forest Service Southern Research Station, Clemson, SC 29634

Citation for proceedings: Waldrop, Thomas A., ed. 2014. Proceedings, Wildland Fire in the Appalachians: Discussions among Managers and Scientists. Gen. Tech. Rep. SRS-199. Asheville, NC: U.S. Department of Agriculture Forest Service, Southern Research Station. 208 p.

places, and some recent wildfires have been challenging and expensive to control (USDA Forest Service, Pisgah National Forest 2009).

The SBR FLN was formed in 2007 at a meeting of major public land managers (Forest Service, National Park Service, and State land management agencies) as well as nongovernmental organizations interested in forest health (such as The Nature Conservancy, Western North Carolina Alliance, and Land Trust for the Little Tennessee). The group collaboratively identified a project area (fig. 1) and five goals:

1. Enhance landscape-level fire planning to help restore and maintain fire-adapted ecosystems;
2. Transfer lessons learned about fire effects among SBR FLN partners;
3. Develop outreach tools to explain the benefits of fire to public and agency staff;
4. Find opportunities to increase and share resources for implementing prescribed fire; and
5. Exchange information about fire ecology and fire management using a variety of outlets.

The SBR FLN partners have since organized into place-based landscape teams formed by local stakeholders, and developed landscape goals appropriate for their areas and organizational missions (fig. 1). These teams selected focal areas to apply prescribed fire, developed annual work plans, and share ideas across the network through regular conference calls and an annual three-day workshop. The annual workshops provide opportunities for land managers and researchers to discuss lessons learned, network, and peer-review their ideas.

This paper uses examples for each of the goals to describe the methods and approaches used by SBR FLN partners to establish a science-informed restoration approach.

GOAL 1. ENHANCE LANDSCAPE-LEVEL FIRE PLANNING TO RESTORE AND MAINTAIN FIRE-ADAPTED ECOSYSTEMS

Ecological Zone Mapping

Based on the scientific literature and partner expertise, partners identified pine, oak pine, and oak-hickory as fire-influenced forest and woodland types. To identify areas that would potentially benefit most from re-introduction of fire, partners were looking for the best available map/model to show current and potential vegetation in the SBR. Partners settled on ecological zone (ecozone) mapping (Simon and others 2005). Ecological zones in the Southern Appalachian Mountains, identified from intensive field data that defined plant communities, were associated with unique environmental variables

characterized by digital models. In 2008, FLN and LANDFIRE provided funding to evaluate the usefulness of an updated ecological zone map to predict landscapes that support fire-adapted plant communities in the SBR. This map was completed by incorporating higher resolution digital elevation data and additional plot data from other areas within the Southern Appalachian Mountains and expanded ecological zone mapping to 5.9 million acres in the Southern Appalachians. Maximum entropy (Phillips and others 2006) was used in place of logistic regression as the statistical analysis tool in model creation, additional field data were collected, and more zones were mapped for a 3rd Approximation of Ecological Zones that expanded the model area to 8.2 million acres (Simon 2011).

Ecological zones are units of land that can support a specific plant community or plant community group based upon environmental factors such as temperature, moisture, and fertility that control vegetation distribution. They are equivalent to biophysical settings, which represent the vegetation that may have been dominant on the landscape prior to Euro-American settlement, and are based on both the current biophysical environment and an approximation of the historical disturbance regime (LANDFIRE 2009). Table 1 provides a snapshot of the distribution of ecozones in each landscape that could benefit from restoration. Each local landscape team has this information to inform management planning.

Network partners have found this common map/model very valuable as a consistent baseline and tool to assess fire needs across all lands. The ecozone map/model also served as a springboard for additional tools such as the burn prioritization referred to as "ecomath," and a forest structure assessment described below.

Ecomath

One of the landscape teams (Central Escarpment) sought a systematic way to identify burn priorities, and developed a computer-based scoring tool referred to as "ecomath" using ArcMap. The process required scoring various conservation assets in the landscape through a system of weighting and scaling. Factors considered included acreage of fire-adapted native vegetation, special biological areas, presence of rare species benefiting from fire, and anthropogenic early-successional habitat in wildlife openings.

In ArcMap, boundaries of potential burn units were intersected with ecozones, rare species occurrences, Significant Natural Heritage Areas (SNHAs) (North Carolina Natural Heritage Program) and wildlife openings. Ecozone modeling (Simon 2011) was used to delineate boundaries of ecosystem-scale forest types. Forest types were weighted by their historical fire return interval, with forest types where fire is not a significant disturbance weighted as zero (see table 2). The simplistic approach of assigning yellow pine-dominated forests a weight of three and oak dominated forests a weight of one was chosen, based on dendrochronology evidence that fire is two to three times more common in yellow pine forests than oak forests (Flatley and others 2012; Lafon and Grissino-Mayer 2007, 2011; McEwan and others 2013). Acreage of forest was scaled by dividing by 100 so as not to overwhelm other conservation targets such as maintaining important natural areas and management of fire-adapted rare species.

Rare species were weighted based on global and State rarity rankings (Gadd and Finnegan 2010). G1-G3 ranked species were given a weight of 10 points, and S1-S3 ranked species were given a weight of five points. Individual taxa were only counted once per unit, regardless of the number of occurrences. Special emphasis was given to mountain golden heather (*Hudsonia montana* Nutt.). *H. montana* is a restricted endemic whose entire range occurs on two ridges, covering less than 7 acres in total occupied habitat, in the study area. Without fire, this diminutive shrub is typically overtopped and displaced by other woody plants and does not regenerate due to absence of mineral soil (Frost 1990). Because of its affinity for fire and the conservation concern surrounding this plant, it was given a weight of 50 points.

High quality fire-adapted vegetation areas were scored using ratings provided by the North Carolina Natural Heritage Program (Gadd and Finnegan 2010). The top three rankings assigned to SNHAs were given a weight of 15, 10, and 5, respectively, if a SNHA with fire-adapted vegetation overlapped a burn unit. Open areas managed for wildlife were scored by assigning one point for every acre of wildlife opening present in a burn unit. Wildlife opening acreage by burn unit ranged from 0 acres to 16.6 acres.

In all, 42 potential prescribed fire areas totaling over 95,000 acres (38 445 ha) were evaluated, ranging in size from 5,163 acres (2089 ha) to 610 acres (247 ha). Scores ranged from a high of 175 to a low of 7, providing consistent separation in scores between units and giving a clear hierarchy of priorities for conservation-based prescribed fire.

Ecomath has helped managers and stakeholders understand and track which burn units will benefit most from fire. In addition, the process of developing the model, which involved experts from a variety of disciplines (e.g., timber management, fire management, wildlife management, conservation) and organizations, improved relationships and fostered the development

of a shared vision. Presentations on the development and use of the tool can be found at http://www.conservationgateway.org/Files/Pages/index-fln-webinar-recordi.aspx.

Forest Structure Assessment to Determine Restoration Goals

While recognizing the need for a restoration goal, we found defining reference or desired condition challenging. We know that ecosystems are naturally variable in their structure, and hence set as restoration goals not just the ecosystem type but also its natural range of variability (NRV). We estimate restoration needs by how far an ecozone's current structure and composition is departed from its NRV in the process summarized below. Accurately assessing ecosystem condition is dependent upon the quality of the data available, and we selected the study area based upon this requirement.

We used the ecozone approach described above to identify ecosystems on the landscape. Another national mapping approach called LANDFIRE' uses Biophysical Settings' to combine scientific research, historical information, and expert opinion to describe the disturbance probabilities of ecosystems. Biophysical Settings have fewer taxa and are mapped at a broader resolution than ecozones. Both approaches use computer models (Vegetation Dynamic Development Tool, or VDDT) to simulate a NRV. Light Detection and Ranging (LiDAR) data are recognized as one of the most comprehensive and accurate types of data for measuring vegetation structure. We used LiDAR to assess current conditions and then compared how current condition departed from NRV to inform restoration needs.

A study area was defined based on available data to include the overlap of the 2005 Phase III North Carolina LiDAR data and the proclamation boundary of Nantahala-Pisgah National Forest. In total, over 700 000 ha (1,760,000 acres) of forest were evaluated using LiDAR-measured height and Forest Service stand records to estimate forest age, and LiDAR measurements of canopy closure and shrub density to measure those physical characteristics.

In general, we found that ecosystems with a more frequent historical fire return interval were more departed from reference conditions than mesic forests. Of 11 forest ecosystems evaluated (see table 1), 5 were found to be highly departed from reference conditions. Both oak and pine ecosystems' canopies were much more closed than the reference models, while the canopies of cove ecosystems were more open than the reference models. For oak, cove, and spruce ecosystems, the NRV included a much higher proportion of old forests than the 2005 conditions, while the converse was true for shortleaf pine and pine-oak/heath ecosystems. Ecosystems with greater timber value (cove and northern hardwood forests) were found to be more disturbed than ecosystems with less economic value. This analysis indicates that increased fire management and the continued restoration of old-growth conditions would be ecologically beneficial. It will be provided to FLN and landscape partners as a tool to inform their restoration goals and plans.

GOAL 2. TRANSFER LESSONS LEARNED ABOUT FIRE EFFECTS AMONG PARTNERS

The ecozone mapping approach has been expanded across landscapes in the SBR FLN including North Carolina, Tennessee, Georgia, and South Carolina, and National Forest lands outside the boundary of the SBR FLN. Additionally, it has been used successfully for planning in our sister network, the Appalachian FLN, including both the George Washington and Jefferson (GWJeff) National Forests, and in the Coastal Plain of South Carolina on the Francis Marion National Forest.

Additionally, the systematic burn unit prioritization through ecomath has been adapted by other SBR FLN landscapes and across the National forests in North Carolina, and across portions of the Appalachian FLN including the GWJeff National Forests and Shenandoah National Park (Mahan and others 2012). All landscapes used ecozones as a base layer but modified criteria and weighting to meet their landscape needs and address the missions and goals of the agency.

The Cherokee National Forest pioneered ignitions along ridge lines allowing fire to back downhill. They also added burn days by adding a fall season. These practices have been shared during SBR FLN field trips and subsequently expanded to other landscapes.

Monitoring Program

In 2006, the SBR FLN began a monitoring program to assess the effects of operational prescribed fires on forest stand structure and fuels. Monitoring occurs in demonstration burn units established on properties owned or managed by SBR FLN partners including the Forest Service, North Carolina Wildlife Resources Commission, North Carolina State Parks, South Carolina Department of Natural Resources, The Nature Conservancy and the Land Trust for the Little Tennessee. Property managers have committed to restoring a historical fire regime on each demonstration unit, and beginning this effort an initial series of prescribed fires at 3- to 5-year intervals.

Fourteen burn units have been established that extend from eastern Tennessee through western North Carolina into north Georgia and the upstate of South Carolina (fig. 1). Seven units are dominated by oak-hickory

communities and seven are dominated by yellow pine communities. Twelve units have been burned once, one unit has been burned twice, and two units have not yet been burned. Nine of the completed burns have been spring burns, and the remaining three have been fall burns.

Our goal is to evaluate the overall effects of prescribed fire on forest structure and fuels and, where possible, tease out how these effects might vary with other factors, such as vegetative community, fire behavior, and season of burn. Fire effects are being monitored using a series of permanent, 0.1-acre plots established prior to each burn. Except for our first unit (where we installed more plots), we have installed 20 plots in or around each burn unit. Fifteen plots were established inside each burn unit and five plots were installed outside the burn unit and in areas where future burns are not planned, as control plots. Demonstration burn units vary in size from approximately 75 acres to over 2,000 acres, and plots are located using systematic randomization. Plot locations were predetermined in ArcGIS by randomly choosing intersections of UTM grid lines that fall within target vegetative communities (Simon 2005, 2011) in areas that are accessible.

All sampling is completed during the growing season. Pre-burn sampling is designed to occur during the summer prior to the first prescribed fire; however, in several cases burns have been delayed one or more years due to weather or other logistical constraints. Post-burn sampling is conducted during the second growing season following the prescribed fire. The following data are collected at each plot:

• A photograph taken from a permanent photopoint.

• Forest overstory: species, diameter at breast height (dbh), crown class, and condition (ranging from 1=healthy to 4=dead) for all trees ≥ 2 inches dbh.

• Tree regeneration (data collected in a 0.02-acre subplot): count of stems by species, height class (1 to 3 feet, 3 to 4.5 feet, and > 4.5 feet), and origin (single stem or stump sprout). All stump sprouts from the same origin are considered as a single plant.

• Ground cover and vegetative life forms (data collected in a 0.02-acre subplot): estimates of percent cover to the nearest 5 percent for bare ground, boulders, moss and lichens, grass and grass-like, herbs, vines, deciduous shrubs, coniferous shrubs (including mountain laurel and rhododendron), mountain laurel (separately), and rhododendron (separately). In addition, we estimated the average height of the top of the shrub layer.

- Fuels: litter depth; duff depth; and 1-hour, 10-hour, 100-hour, and 1,000-hour woody fuels were estimated along three, 50-foot transect lines following procedures outlined by Brown (1974).

- In addition, immediate post-burn sampling was completed in five units to assess fire severity in each plot based on bark char height, percent canopy scorch, and the percent of the plot characterized by each of five severity classes (1=unburned to 5=heavily burned).

The data from 10 demonstration units are currently being analyzed to assess the effects of the first prescribed burn. The results will inform managers of the degree to which forest structure and fuel loadings can be altered by a single burn. These results will also provide a tool to evaluate how well the results from research burns conducted under more tightly controlled conditions can be applied to larger, operational burns.

Collaboration with CAFMS

In 2010, the Joint Fire Science Program sought to connect researchers more closely with land managers to improve the transfer of science information into practice and to direct research more toward answering the questions land managers had. The SBR FLN has partnered with the Consortium of Appalachian Fire Managers and Scientists (CAFMS) since its inception. The partnership has brought mutual benefits by better connecting managers to researchers through workshop topics such as smoke management, and fire effects on bats and rattlesnakes. CAFMS also regularly solicits input from managers on needed research topics to be prioritized for funding through the Joint Fire Science Program.

GOAL 3. DEVELOP OUTREACH MATERIALS REGARDING THE BENEFITS OF FIRE FOR PUBLIC AND AGENCY STAFF

We recognized that we needed to explain to the public and a wider audience why the re-introduction of fire to the mountains was a beneficial change over fire suppression and exclusion practices in the past century. A brochure, *Bringing Fire Back to the Mountains*, was developed and distributed, and more informative press releases for controlled burns as well as wildfires have been shared among partners and with the North Carolina Prescribed Fire Council and distributed to a wider audience than in the past. We have conducted field trips inviting concerned neighbors, reached out to groups that might potentially oppose controlled burns, and shared reviews of lessons learned if burns did not go entirely as expected. It appears that improved outreach efforts are slowly building more public support based on responses and comments our partners receive.

GOAL 4. EXPLORE OPPORTUNITIES TO INCREASE AND SHARE RESOURCES FOR IMPLEMENTATION

The relationship-building that has occurred over the years through regular network activities (FLN meetings, conference calls, project meetings) has proven to be invaluable. Strengthened interpersonal and agency relations are facilitating cross-boundary prescribed burning across the region, allowing landscape teams to garner more resources, improving wildfire outcomes,[2] and creating better public relations outcomes.

The collaboration of a broad partnership in the development of the ecomath tool built trust and capacity that allowed the Central Escarpment landscape team to expand and successfully submit a grant proposal under the Collaborative Forest Landscape Restoration Act. This program has allowed the Forest Service to triple its acres treated through controlled burning in 2013 in this landscape (Kelly 2012).

Partners in North Carolina and Georgia have developed Memoranda of Understanding (with statewide or at least regional scope) that allow sharing of resources for all partners on cross-boundary burns. This allows for larger burns with safer fire lines and less impact, and it provides training opportunities. Multi-jurisdictional burning demonstrates consistency and unity among partnering agencies. Given these partnerships, the Southern Blue Ridge Escarpment landscape team, for example, has boosted their burn acreage by approximately 1,000-2,000 acres per year.

GOAL 5. SHARE FIRE ECOLOGY (E.G., FIRE HISTORY, FIRE EFFECTS) RESOURCES USING A VARIETY OF OUTLETS

SBR FLN partners have given presentations about FLN-related work at international, national, and regional conferences. Webinars hosted through the national FLN provided further opportunities for sharing lessons learned, new tools and ideas developed in other networks, and additional avenues for scientists to share pertinent information. A list of webinars is available on the FLN website (www.conservationgateway.org/fln).

A monthly newsletter (the *FLN Networker*) is published by the national FLN team and shared electronically with partners and interested parties to keep everybody informed on recent findings and training opportunities. This newsletter is mailed to more than 500 people and is regularly forwarded to others across the country. SBR FLN partners are regular contributors. The CAFMS

---

[2]Personal Communication. 2013. Nicholas Larson, 109 Lawing Drive, Nebo NC 28761.

newsletter is another vehicle for SBR FLN participants to share fire ecology findings.

CONCLUSIONS

We consider our landscape-level assessments and tools such as 'ecomath' as works in progress, designed to further systematic, science-informed restoration planning. We intend to evaluate the effectiveness of restoration actions through our monitoring network as well as research collaborations with CAFMS. The tools developed collaboratively by our partners have been exported to many interested partners and other regional FLN networks. We believe that we are on track and making good progress toward restoring fire-adapted ecosystems that will hopefully be resistant to climate change. Our success is demonstrated by the fact that our network is growing, from five landscapes in 2007 to eight in 2014.

ACKNOWLEDGMENTS

This work would not have been possible without the generous support by Promoting Ecosystem Resiliency through Collaboration: Landscapes, Learning and Restoration, a cooperative agreement between The Nature Conservancy, U.S. Forest Service, and agencies of the Department of the Interior (for more information, contact Lynn Decker at ldecker@tnc.org or (801) 320-0524), LANDFIRE, and U.S. Forest Service Southern Research Station. Special thanks go to Dean Simon, Ryan Jacobs, Mike Brod, Nathan Klaus, Jim Wentworth, Malcolm Hodges, Kristen Austin, Greg Salansky, Robert Klein, Robert Cherry, David Ray, John Crockett, Marek Smith, Greg Philipp, Bob Gale, Hugh Irwin, Greg Lowe, Katherine Medlock, Jim Smith, Megan Sutton, Gordon Warburton, Riva Duncan, Marek Smith, Sam Lindblom, Tom Dooley, Judy Dunscomb, Debbie Crane, and many others for inspiration and assistance with this work.

REFERENCES

Abrams, M.D., Nowacki G.J. 2008. Native Americans as active and passive promoters of mast and fruit trees in the Eastern USA. Holocene 18: 1123-1137.

Aldrich, S.R.; Lafon, C.W.; Grissino-Mayer, H.D. [and others]. 2010. Three centuries of fire in montane pine-oak stands on a temperate forest landscape. Applied Vegetation Science. 13: 36-46.

Brose, P.H.; Schuler, T.M; Van Lear, D.H.; Berst, J. 2001. Bringing fire back: the changing regimes of the Appalachian mixed-oak forests. Journal of Forestry. 99(11): 30-35.

Brose, P.H.; Schuler, T.M.; Ward, J.S. 2006. Responses of oak and other hardwood regeneration to prescribed fire: what we know as of 2005. In: Dickinson, M.E., ed. Fire in eastern oak forests: delivering science to managers. Gen. Tech. Rep. NRS-P-1. Newtown Square, PA: U.S. Department of Agriculture Forest Service, Pacific Southwest Research Station: 123-135.

Brown, J. K. 1974. Handbook for inventorying downed woody material. Gen. Tech. Rep. INT-016. Washington, DC: U.S. Department of Agriculture Forest Service, Intermountain Forest and Range Experiment Station. 24 p.

Delcourt, H.R.; Delcourt, P.A. 1997. Pre-Columbian Native American use of fire on southern Appalachian landscapes. Conservation Biology 11: 1010-1014.

Elliott, K.J.; Vose, J.M.; Clinton, B.D.; Knoepp, J.D. 2004. Effects of understory burning in a mesic mixed-oak forest of the Southern Appalachians. In: Engstrom, R.T.; Galley, K.E.M.; de Groot, W.J., eds. Proceedings of the 22nd Tall Timbers fire ecology conference. Tall Timbers Research Station, Tallahassee, FL: 272-283.

Fesenmyer, K.A.; Christensen, N.L. 2010. Reconstructing Holocene fire history in a southern Appalachian forest using soil charcoal. Ecology 91(3): 662-670.

Flatley, W.T.; Lafon, C.W.; Grissino-Mayer, H.D. 2011. Climatic and topographic controls on patterns of fire in the southern and central Appalachian Mountains, USA. Landscape Ecology. (2011) 26: 195-209.

Frost, C.C. 1990. *Hudsonia montana* final report. Effects of fire, trampling, and interspecies competition. 1985-1989. Parts I (Final Report) and II (Appendices). Submitted to the U.S. Fish & Wildlife Service, Asheville Ecological Services Field Office. 93 p.

Gadd, L.; Finnegan, J. 2010. Natural Heritage Program list of rare plant species of North Carolina 2010. North Carolina Natural Heritage Program Office of Conservation, Planning, and Community Affairs, NC Department of Environment and Natural Resources. 1601 Mail Service Center, Raleigh, NC 27699-1601. 136 p.

Kelly, J. 2012. An assessment of the ecosystems of Nantahala-Pisgah National Forest & surrounding lands: a synthesis of the eCAP methodology and LiDAR vegetation analysis. Report to the Fire Learning Network. 21 p. http://www.conservationgateway.org/ConservationPractices/FireLandscapes/FireLearningNetwork/NetworkProducts/Pages/Final-Report-SBR-Assessment-Kelly-2013.aspx. [Date accessed: 12/7/2013]

Kinkead, C.O.; Kabrick, J.M.; Stambaugh, M.C.; Grabner, K.W. 2013. Changes to oak woodland stand structure and ground flora composition caused by thinning and burning. In: Miller, G.W.; Schuler, T.M.; Gottschalk, K.W. [and others], eds. Proceedings, 18th Central Hardwood Forest Conference; 2012 March 26-28; Morgantown, WV. Gen. Tech. Rep. NRS-P-117. Newtown Square, PA: U.S. Department of Agriculture Forest Service, Northern Research Station. 373-383 p. CD-ROM.

LANDFIRE. [N.d.] Vegetation data products: Biophysical Settings. [Online]. Available: http://www.landfire.gov/NationalProductDescriptions20.php. [Date accessed: 29 Jan 2009].

Lafon C.W.; Grissino-Mayer, H.D. 2007. Spatial patterns of fire occurrence in the central Appalachian Mountains and implications for wildland fire management. Physical Geography. 28: 1-20.

Lafon, C.W.; Grissino-Mayer, H.D. 2011. Fire regimes and successional dynamics of yellow pine (*Pinus*) stands in the central Appalachian Mountains. College Station, TX: Texas A&M University. Final Report of Project 01C-3-3-09 to the Joint Fire Science Program. 24 p.

Mahan, C.G.; Young, J.A.; Forder, M. 2012. Prioritizing forest communities and areas for the use of prescribed fire at Shenandoah National Park. Natural Resource Technical Report. NPS/SHEN/NRTR-2012/625. Fort Collins, CO: National Park Service. Published Report-2191666.

McEwan, R.W.; Pederson, N.; Cooper, A. [and others]. 2013. Fire and gap dynamics over 300 years in an old-growth temperate forest. Applied Vegetation Science. 17: 312-322.

Nowacki, G.J.; Abrams, M.D. 2008. The demise of fire and the mesophication of forests in the Eastern United States. BioScience. 58(2): 123-138.

Phillips, S.J.; Anderson, R.P.; Shapire, R.E. 2006. Maximum entropy modeling of species geographic distribution. Ecological Modeling. 190: 231-259.

Pyne, S.J. 1982. Fire in America. Princeton, NJ: Princeton University Press. 654 p.

Simon, S.A.; Collins, T.K.; Kauffman, G. [and others]. 2005. Ecological zones in the Southern Appalachians: first approximation. Res. Pap. SRS-41. Asheville, NC: U.S. Department of Agriculture Forest Service, Southern Research Station. 41 p.

Simon, S.A. 2011. Ecological zones in the Southern Blue Ridge: 3rd approximation. U.S. Department of Agriculture Forest Service, National Forests in North Carolina. Unpublished report available through Gary Kauffman, 160 Zillicoa St., Suite A, Asheville, NC 28801.

U.S. Department of Agriculture (USDA) Forest Service, Pisgah National Forest. 2009. Grandfather Ranger District, Linville Gorge Wilderness Fire Management Plan. 26 p. Unpublished report for the National Forests in NC, 160 Zillicoa St., Suite A, Asheville, NC 28801.

U.S. Department of Agriculture (USDA) Forest Service, Pisgah National Forest, 2011. Grandfather Restoration Project: a collaborative forest landscape restoration proposal. February 9, 2011. 39 p. Submitted to U.S. Department of Agriculture Forest Service, Washington Office from the National Forests in North Carolina. On file with: 160 Zillicoa St., Suite A, Asheville, NC 28801.

Table 1—Fire mediated ecozones in each of the original SBR FLN landscapes (ecozone mapping is not yet available for the Georgia Blue Ridge Mountains Landscape)

Landscape	Pine-oak heath	Shortleaf pine[a]	High-elevation red oak	Dry-mesic oak	Dry oak[b]	Mesic oak[c]	Fire mediated ecozones	Non-fire ecozones[d]	Total acres	Percent fire adapted
Southern Blue Ridge Escarpment	14,261	81,207	1,044	109,674	37,493	19,593	263,272	64,091	327,363	80%
Unaka/ Great Smokies	116,009	20,451	19,917	78,357	44,714	180,158	459,606	401,268	860,874	53%
Central Escarpment	41,403	15,136	1,336	17,627	17,022	30,451	122,975	87,907	211,152	58%
South Mountains	3,527	478	0	4,976	10,403	5,656	25,040	8,950	33,990	74%
Northern Escarpment	3,743	0	2,060	4,570	2,466	10,807	23,646	20,844	44,490	53%
New River Headwaters	413	0	1,631	37	89	3,084	5,254	7,470	12,724	41%
Nantahala/ Balsam Mountains	60,497	62,885	39,940	89,826	42,003	166,274	461,425	407,802	869,227	53%

[a]Short eaf P ne = ow e evat on p ne and short eaf p ne-oak/heath.
[b]Dry Oak = dry oak evergreen heath and dry oak deciduous heath.
[c]Mesic Oak = montane oak-hickory shortleaf pine, montane oak-hickory cove, and montane oak-hickory rich.
[d]Non-fire adapted ecozones include: spruce-fir, northern hardwood slope, northern hardwood cove, rich cove, acidic cove.

Table 2—Ecological departure of ecosystems in the North Carolina Southern Blue Ridge

Ecosystem	Percentage of departure	Historic fire return intervals	Drivers of departure
Dry Oak Forest	80%	10	Too much closed canopy, lacks old-growth
Pine-Oak/Heath[a]	79%	5	Too much closed canopy, too much late-seral
Shortleaf Pine-Oak[a]	71%	3	Too much closed canopy, too much late-seral, lacks early-seral
Dry Mesic Oak-Hickory	71%	14	Too much closed canopy, lacks old-growth
Mesic Oak-Hickory	72%	18	Too much closed canopy, lacks old-growth
High Elevation Red Oak Forest	65%	18	Too much closed canopy, lacks old-growth
Rich Cove Forest	55%	70	Lacks old-growth
Acid Cove Forest	56%	70	Lacks old-growth
Spruce-Fir Forest[a]	39%	500	Too much mid-seral, too little late-seral; questions about species composition
Northern Hardwoods Cove[a]	10%	250	No significant departure, but old-growth not modeled
Northern Hardwoods Slope[a]	4%	250	No significant departure, but old-growth not modeled

[a]Old-growth S-classes are not included in these models.

Note: severely departed ecosystems are indicated in red, moderately departed in yellow, and other in green. Historic fire return intervals are based on LANDFIRE 2009.

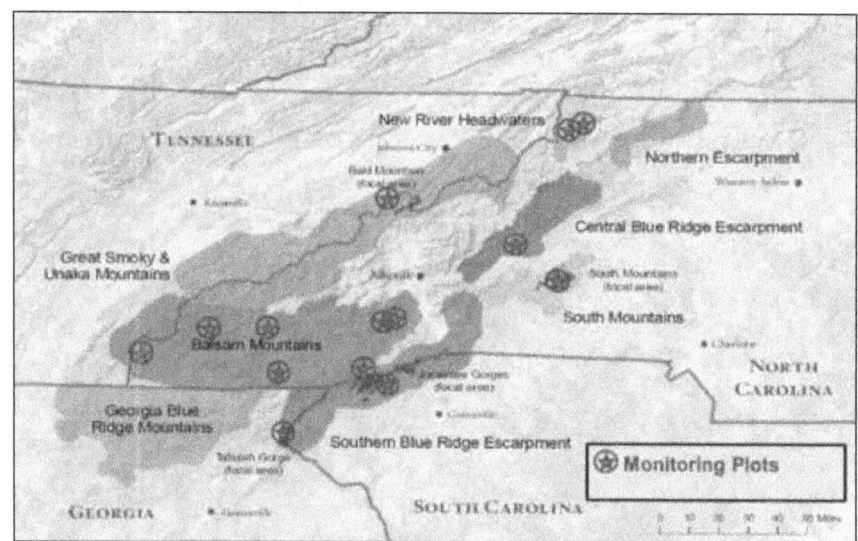

Figure 1—The map shows the eight landscapes and location of monitoring plots in the SBR FLN. Note: The Northern Escarpment and New River Headwaters joined the FLN in 2011, the Georgia Blue Ridge Mountains and Jocassee Gorges Focal area in summer 2013.

TECHNOLOGY TRANSFER: TAKING SCIENCE FROM THE BOOKS TO THE GROUND AT BENT CREEK EXPERIMENTAL FOREST

Julia E. Kirschman[1]

Abstract—Technology transfer has been an important part of the research program at Bent Creek Experimental Forest (Bent Creek) since its establishment in 1925. Our stated mission is to develop and disseminate knowledge and strategies for restoring, managing, sustaining, and enhancing the vegetation and wildlife of upland hardwood-dominated forest ecosystems of the Southern Appalachian Mountains.

Over the years, disseminating knowledge has taken many forms to address the needs of many different user groups. The diversity of user groups make disseminating knowledge challenging. Groups range from professors and scientists, graduate and undergraduate students, resource managers and foresters, to garden clubs, and Boy Scout troops. Bent Creek communicates research findings interpersonally—through tours of the demonstration forest, workshops, and presentations— and visually—through websites, publications, interpretive signs, and other written and electronic material.

Since the 1980s, Bent Creek has included a technology transfer specialist on staff. As a technology transfer specialist, there are many rewards and challenges. Some of the challenges are internal, and some are external. But the rewards are great when study results connect with individuals who understand, support, and are excited about the work being conducted by U.S. Forest Service Research and Development scientists.

INTRODUCTION

Congress established the Bent Creek Experimental Forest (Bent Creek) in 1925 originally on 1,100 acres of National Forest land set aside to conduct research on a variety of topics. Bent Creek is located on the Pisgah National Forest near Asheville, North Carolina, and is operated by the U.S. Forest Service, Southern Research Station (SRS). It is part of a network of experimental forests and ranges across the United States. Experimental forests were created to conduct scientific research in-house, apply research findings on National Forest System lands, continue long-term research, and demonstrate research results to cooperators and resource managers.

Each experimental forest is located strategically within ecosystems that represent the area. Bent Creek represents the Southern Appalachian Mountain region. The experimental forest is located within a watershed that reaches elevations from 2,100 to 4,000 feet and contains a rich diversity of flora and fauna. An additional 5,200 acres were added in 1935 bringing the total area to 6,300 acres. The research conducted at Bent Creek changes over time to address ecological issues affecting forests. Early 1920s work focused on fire control, surveying and mapping, creating 50-acre compartments for research on degraded stands, and reforestation planting. Our focus changed in the 1950s to large scale studies of hardwood stand management, even-aged versus uneven-aged forest management, long versus short rotations, tree grades, soil moisture, seed sources, managing woodlots, reclaiming land with laurel thickets, and white pine (*Pinus strobus*) plantations.

Today research includes replicated small plot research, long-term growth and yield, hardwood regeneration, site classification, mast and forest fruit production, restoration of American chestnut (*Castanea dentata*), effects of climate change on forests and wildlife, sustainability, and carbon sequestration. The research unit also added a wildlife component to examine bird, bat, small mammal, reptile, and amphibian community response to both silvicultural treatments and natural disturbances.

Though research topics at Bent Creek Experimental Forest have changed over the years with the emergence of new challenges and issues, the end products are still the same: valuable long-term data and research findings. A major challenge is to take the 90 years of research findings and make them accessible and relevant for today's resource managers. This paper discusses technology transfer and how it has become successful at the Bent Creek Experimental Forest.

---

[1]Julia E. Kirschman, Technology Transfer Specialist, USDA Forest Service, Southern Research Station, Asheville, NC 28806

Citation for proceedings: Waldrop, Thomas A., ed. 2014. Proceedings, Wildland Fire in the Appalachians: Discussions among Managers and Scientists. Gen. Tech. Rep. SRS-199. Asheville, NC: U.S. Department of Agriculture Forest Service, Southern Research Station. 208 p.

TECHNOLOGY TRANSFER

Technology transfer can be seen as science unto itself. Dr. Everett M. Rogers (2003), in *Diffusion of Innovations* defines technology transfer as the process of communicating a technology from a source organization to a receptor organization." There are three components in this process: knowledge, use, and commercialization.

For example, the U.S. Forest Service Research and Development branch that includes the Southern Research Station is a source organization, world leaders in producing scientific research. The source can be the whole organization, or specific units within an organization. Receptor organizations are the groups that receive the information from the source organization. We call these receptor organizations our user groups. Scientists who create knowledge through research comprise the knowledge component in the technology transfer process, while the second component is the "use" component that is made up of methods and formats that facilitate the use of that knowledge. The last is the commercialization component which is the process of how the knowledge is packaged and "sold" to the receptors. "Sold" in this use refers to persuading the use of an idea, not making a monetary exchange.

A technology transfer specialist can help organizations move their science from the knowledge stage to the use and commercialization stages. The job of the technology transfer specialist is to transfer this knowledge to different user groups through a variety of methods and formats. Over the years, technology transfer has evolved to become not just an art and skill, but a science as well.

METHODS

Technology transfer has evolved over the years at Bent Creek, and throughout the scientific community, in the way research results are disseminated to user groups. The knowledge component is still the same in that scientists still conduct research to obtain knowledge, but the way knowledge is transferred has radically changed over the years. Early transfer methods included interpersonal communication such as face-to-face contact between scientists and groups who participated in field trips to view and discuss research results. Nonverbal communication was in the form of written research papers published in peer-reviewed scientific journals and in-house publications (Muth and Hendee 1980).

In the 1980s, Forest Service project leaders began to see the importance of having a technology transfer specialist on staff, though the title "technology transfer specialist" was not yet an official job title. Technology transfer

specialists were listed mostly as research foresters performing technology transfer tasks. The specialist at Bent Creek served as the go-between for scientists and user groups. Their duties included promoting Bent Creek science by creating partnerships and outreaches, developing materials such as brochures and booklets, and organizing tours and events. The specialist also helped develop a hiking trail system that included metal signs on a variety of natural resources subjects and a demonstration forest installed in 1991 to show forest management treatments side-by-side.

Today, technology transfer Specialist is recognized as an official job description and title. SRS administration includes a Science Delivery Group that is responsible for the commercialization or the conversion of an idea from research into a product or service, a process that includes the packaging, production, manufacturing, marketing, and distribution. Technology fransfer specialists work with the Science Delivery Group to produce materials and design marketing strategies.

The advancements and use of mass media technology since the 1990s has allowed technology transfer methods to expand even further. A Web site, an online forest encyclopedia, modeling simulators, webinars, and an introductory film on Bent Creek were created over the past 15 years. The adoption of social media such as, Facebook, blogs (CompassLive!), and Twitter are now common formats for instantly posting events, new research findings, and other information, making it available to anyone.

The Bent Creek Research Work Unit created a week-long *Upland Hardwood Silviculture Workshop* in 1991as a result of numerous requests from State forest agencies for application of research results to the forest. Participants working in upland hardwood ecosystems came to learn from experts how to manage forests using the most up-to-date research available through indoor lectures and field trips (fig. 1). The workshop covers 16 topics under 7 modules by 10 or more experts in their respective fields of study. The topics ranged from management objectives, stand management on existing stands, stand management for regenerating new stands, forest health, site classification, restoration of American chestnut and other species, and wildlife. The first class was so successful that the week-long workshop became an annual event adding topics over the years to meet the needs of land managers. In 2007, the workshop was filmed to create an online course (available on DVD) that gives continuing learning credits.

Technology transfer duties still include tours on the demonstration forest and publications but also community events, information panels on the forest, research notes, brochures, fact sheets, educational programs, and interpretive signs. Scientists and technology transfer staff participate in speaking engagements at symposia, meetings, and other events such as the North Carolina Science Expo and the Forest Festival Day to promote science.

In earlier years, user groups (receptors) were mostly forestry students and professors, scientists, land managers, and an occasional visiting government official who contacted us for information and tours. The early user groups represented just a small percentage of the population from universities and professional forestry agencies that used our research. Because of the specialty of the research, just a small percentage of the public was being reached.

One goal of Bent Creek's technology transfer program was to expand the user groups and make this knowledge available to more people. With the experimental forest located within 10 miles of the city of Asheville, it has become a popular site for recreationists. Most people in the local area did not know the purpose of the experimental forest or about the research being conducted. If they did know, they did not know how to take the information and apply it on their own land. A new goal became reaching recreationists and local user groups. This required "selling the idea" or promoting our research by actively letting people know about the research, why the research is important, and how it affects them. The challenge was how to convey this knowledge to these new users groups.

With the nature of user groups changing, the technology transfer specialist must study and know the audience and use appropriate language to help people understand the information presented. Making contacts and gathering information on potential user groups and using different media to show research results expands the user groups.

A two-year Visitor Use survey conducted on the forest in 2005 and 2007 helped us assess who visits our forest and why. The survey collected data on education levels and also other demographic information, which helped us determine the education level to use for preparation of materials.

One method used was the installation of 33 interpretive signs (fig. 2). The signs have catchy titles and pictures with captions to pull the visitor in. Each sign has a "Research Shows" section with quick bullets, a "Did you know?" question and answer section, and a longer piece describing the research being done at that location. To have the most visual impact, the signs are strategically placed at trailheads where people congregate. The objective is to familiarize general public user groups with ongoing research at Bent Creek and why it is important to support this research. Educating the public about our research promotes good relationships and support.

Educational programs for children were added in 2000, with outreach to local schools offering classroom and field trip experiences to explore forests; teach forestry concepts; and learn about tree identification, forest ecosystems, tree growth, and other natural resource subjects.

Today we are reaching out not only to professional foresters and forestry students, but also State agencies, nonprofit organizations, international visitors, college students within other disciplines, along with recreationists, children, clubs, the media, and the general public.

CHALLENGES

My job is to take research results and disseminate (share/package) the information in useable and understandable formats—a challenging task. Some of the challenges are internal, such as budget constraints, breakdown in communications within departments, changes in priorities, and limited personnel. Leadership changes can change the support for technology transfer services. Another leader might not necessarily share the same view. Some challenges are external, such as not knowing your audience or how to get information on the audience. One of the biggest challenges is writing clearly about complex issues for all levels of communication.

Another challenge is forming partnerships and exchanging information within the organization and to outside user groups. This requires a lot of outreach and sitting down with resource managers to see what formats work best for their organization and finding out what they need from the scientific community.

A technology transfer specialist needs to understand the scientific community and also the audience. There is a gap between the two. Scientists create their own community subcultural language made up of scientific jargon and terminology that is not used by other community groups within their organization and the outside user groups. Creating materials in other languages to reach ethnic and specific user groups is important if you want to effectively diffuse the information.

Another challenge is the fact that scientists are sometimes thrown into technology transfer tasks and do not have the skills to format and commercialize their products in the most effective way to meet diverse audiences. Scientists and technology transfer specialists need to work together.

CONCLUSION

There are new avenues to explore in the area of technology transfer. Communication technology changes almost daily. The good news is that new formats can create new paths to disseminate knowledge to a wider and more diverse community. Being creative and understanding audiences and technology transfer principles are key to taking science from journal articles and getting it into the hands of managers to use on the ground.

LITERATURE CITED

Muth, R.M.; Hendee, J.C. 1980. Technology transfer and human behavior. Journal of Forestry. 78(3): 141-144.

Rogers, E.M. 2003. Diffusion of innovations, ed. 5. New York: Free Press. 576 p.

Figure 1—Managers and students interact with scientists in field trips showing ongoing research.

Figure 2—Interpretive signs are an important means of communicating with recreationists on the Bent Creek Experimental Forest.

FACILITATING KNOWLEDGE EXCHANGE ABOUT WILDLAND FIRE SCIENCE

Alan Long[1]

Abstract—The Joint Fire Science Program's Knowledge Exchange Consortia Network is actively working to accelerate the awareness, understanding, and adoption of wildland fire science information by Federal, tribal, State, local and private stakeholders within ecologically similar regions. Our network of 14 regional consortia provides timely, accurate, and regionally relevant science-based information to assist with fire management challenges. Regional activities, through which we engage fire managers, scientists, and private landowners, include online newsletters and announcements, social media, regionally-focused web-based clearinghouses of relevant science, field trips and demonstration sites, workshops and conferences, webinars and online training, and syntheses and fact sheets.

INTRODUCTION

Wildland fire research has been conducted by government and nongovernment organizations for over 80 years. Results have been available through research notes, conference proceedings, and refereed papers, and translated into a variety of training manuals and guides for fire manager use. With formation of the Joint Fire Science Program (JFSP) in 1998, federally-funded fire research ramped up across the United States to levels well above historical efforts. This increase in research funding has produced thousands of papers, reports and presentations, at a rate that is far greater than fire managers can follow; they do not have time to sift through and apply the plethora of research to their particular geographic and ecosystem conditions. Recognizing the opportunity to substantially improve the application of the immense body of new fire science information (as well as older research), in 2009, JFSP began developing regional consortia to facilitate communication about fire science and management.

Each consortium evolved from an intensive regional needs assessment that sought the experience and input of fire managers and scientists to identify mechanisms that would be most helpful to them for accessing and applying fire research results. JFSP provided sideboards for the consortia in terms of general goals and principles (http://www.firescience.gov/JFSP_consortia_vision. cfm), but they allowed each consortium to develop an implementation plan based on ecologically similar conditions, existing regional resources, and stakeholder input. Through this process, a network of 14 regional consortia evolved over a three-year period, covering all parts of the country except the Northeast (fig. 1). All consortia are now in full operation, working to accelerate the awareness, understanding, and adoption of wildland fire science information by Federal, tribal, State, local, and private stakeholders. This paper describes how the consortia are operating to provide timely, accurate, and regionally relevant science-based information to assist with fire management activities and challenges.

CONSORTIA PROGRAMS AND ACTIVITIES

The consortia use a variety of outreach methods: newsletters, fact sheets, research briefs, working papers, reports, websites, webinars, demonstration sites, field days, workshops, presentations at regional meetings, and conferences (LeQuire 2011). Each of these is strengthened through collaboration and partnerships.

Each consortium distributes regular electronic and/or printed newsletters that contain new research highlights, information on upcoming training/learning opportunities, applications of new and old fire science information, descriptions of various information resources, and a number of other types of information that may help fire managers in their particular operations. Fact sheets, research briefs, working papers, research syntheses, and reports may provide: a short summary of new research or a research publication, a broader synthesis of published research results relevant to a particular topic, or a detailed evaluation of a body of literature that addresses specific needs such as fuel reduction techniques.

Each consortium has also developed a website with varying functionalities, ranging from calendars of professional development and training opportunities

[1]Alan Long, Tall Timbers Research Station, Tallahassee, FL 32312-0918

Citation for proceedings: Waldrop, Thomas A., ed. 2014. Proceedings, Wildland Fire in the Appalachians: Discussions among Managers and Scientists. Gen. Tech. Rep. SRS-199. Asheville, NC: U.S. Department of Agriculture Forest Service, Southern Research Station. 208 p.

to lists of key research papers, to links to a variety of other wildland fire information resources. These websites have been developed to serve as a 'first stop' for locating region-specific fire science information without duplicating existing Web sites that provide a large amount of other fire information such as those maintained by the Geographic Area Coordination Centers and the National Wildfire Coordinating Group. A phenomenon experienced by some of the consortia was the keen interest in on-line forums expressed by fire managers and other stakeholders during the needs assessment, but to date there has been very limited use of forums that have been developed.

Written and Web-based products are effective for conveying new information, facilitating access to both new and old information, and increasing end user awareness and comprehension of fire science. However, science delivery is generally enhanced through webinars, presentations, and in-the-field interchange between researchers and managers. Although webinars are largely a one-way flow of information, they do provide opportunities for participants to ask questions. Thus, they represent a great opportunity for field personnel to increase awareness of research results and field applications, similar to conference presentations. All webinars have been archived so people can access them at a convenient time. Webinar use by consortia has rapidly increased during the last two years and provides an opportunity to reach fire science users when travel budgets are limited.

Research summaries and applications are frequently described in presentations at local and regional fire meetings. For example, Prescribed Fire Councils meet regularly in each State in the South and the Southern Fire Exchange has been able to give short presentations at most of those annual or biannual meetings that include highlights of recent published research. Scientists also frequently describe their work at these and other fire meetings. The best and most direct active science delivery occurs when scientists, managers, and landowners meet in the field (workshops, field days, demonstration areas) to discuss particular issues and topics and how research results have been, or might be, applied in different situations. Several of the consortia (Southwest, Great Basin, Northern Rockies, Northwest) have conducted very successful field workshops in the last two years. Most of the other consortia have assisted with at least one of these types of events, but all consortia will be doing more of these in the future. Unfortunately, participation in these is increasingly threatened by travel constraints for Federal agency employees, but the consortia at least partially overcome this challenge by utilizing the many collaborative partnerships they have developed.

COLLABORATION IS VITAL

Although programs in each consortium are built on a variety of collaborations and partnerships, perhaps the most valuable collaboration for the consortia has been with each other. Upon initiating the first round of consortia, JFSP made it clear that the consortia should not consider themselves in competition with one another. Consequently, the 14 consortia across the country have demonstrated a remarkable interest in working together, learning from each other, and building a community representing dozens of organizations with a commitment to cross pollination and mutually improving knowledge exchange about fire science and management. From annual meetings to regular conference calls to 'steady talk' via email, the consortia share ideas, describe pitfalls that others might want to avoid, cross-post information, and promote each other's programs. This is especially significant with consortia that share geographic boundaries, but widely-separated consortia also benefit from interacting with each other.

Collaboration is also vital within each consortium. Most of the consortia involve two or more organizations and agencies as principal partners. Each consortium also has an advisory group composed of representatives from many other organizations, including universities, Federal agencies, research stations, not-for-profit organizations, rural communities, State agencies, Prescribed Fire Councils, Fire Learning Network, and others. Many of these groups are also key partners in conducting programs.

WILL THEY MAKE A DIFFERENCE?

The regional consortia are becoming established mechanisms of fire science delivery, with strong continuing support from JFSP. 'Subscriber' lists to each consortium are growing. Web sites are maturing and regularly adding new information and features. Webinar and other research summary products are increasing. Annual evaluations indicate that the consortia are becoming recognized as major resources within each region for getting fire science 'on the ground.' Yet, the challenge remains to move increased awareness to application and adoption of scientific products. This will happen as we increase the opportunities for scientists and fire managers to interact more frequently regarding research applications and needs.

LITERATURE CITED

LeQuire, E. 2011. Knowledge exchange: a two-way street. Joint Fire Science Program Fire Science Digest 11. Boise, ID: National Interagency Fire Center: 15 p. http://www.firescience.gov/Digest/FSdigest11.pdf. [Date accessed: 4-22-13].

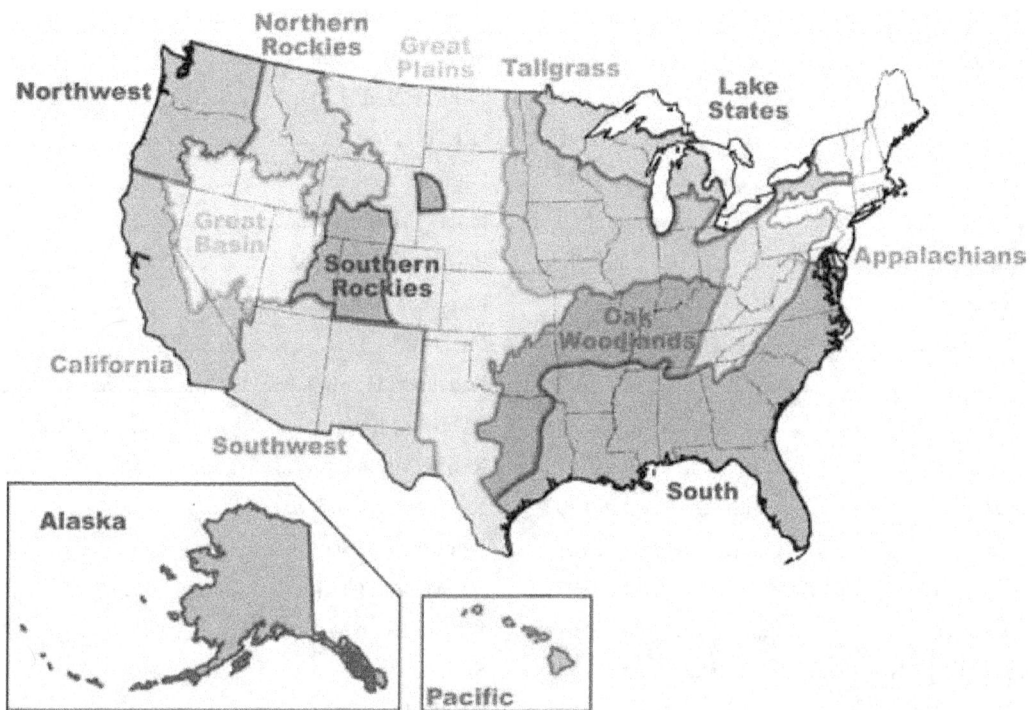

Figure 1—Map of the Joint Fire Science Program regional consortia.

Index of Authors

Waldrop, Thomas A., ed. 2014. Proceedings, Wildland fire in the Appalachians: discussions among fire managers and scientists. Gen. Tech. Rep. SRS-199. Asheville, NC: U.S. Department of Agriculture Forest Service, Southern Research Station. 208 p.

Many challenges face fire managers and scientists in the Appalachian Mountains because of the region's diverse topography and limited research supporting prescribed burning. This conference was designed to promote communication among managers, researchers, and other interested parties. These proceedings contain 30 papers and abstracts that describe ongoing research, successful technology transfer, and management tools for planning prescribed fires. Five categories of papers include ecology of plants and plant communities, wildlife ecology, fire history and fire effects, tools for forest management, and manager-scientist success stories.

How do you rate this publication?

Scan this code to submit your feedback or go to
www.srs.fs.usda.gov/pubeval